Communications
in Computer and Information Science   2123

Editorial Board Members

Joaquim Filipe⬤, *Polytechnic Institute of Setúbal, Setúbal, Portugal*
Ashish Ghosh⬤, *Indian Statistical Institute, Kolkata, India*
Lizhu Zhou, *Tsinghua University, Beijing, China*

Rationale

The CCIS series is devoted to the publication of proceedings of computer science conferences. Its aim is to efficiently disseminate original research results in informatics in printed and electronic form. While the focus is on publication of peer-reviewed full papers presenting mature work, inclusion of reviewed short papers reporting on work in progress is welcome, too. Besides globally relevant meetings with internationally representative program committees guaranteeing a strict peer-reviewing and paper selection process, conferences run by societies or of high regional or national relevance are also considered for publication.

Topics

The topical scope of CCIS spans the entire spectrum of informatics ranging from foundational topics in the theory of computing to information and communications science and technology and a broad variety of interdisciplinary application fields.

Information for Volume Editors and Authors

Publication in CCIS is free of charge. No royalties are paid, however, we offer registered conference participants temporary free access to the online version of the conference proceedings on SpringerLink (http://link.springer.com) by means of an http referrer from the conference website and/or a number of complimentary printed copies, as specified in the official acceptance email of the event.

CCIS proceedings can be published in time for distribution at conferences or as postproceedings, and delivered in the form of printed books and/or electronically as USBs and/or e-content licenses for accessing proceedings at SpringerLink. Furthermore, CCIS proceedings are included in the CCIS electronic book series hosted in the SpringerLink digital library at http://link.springer.com/bookseries/7899. Conferences publishing in CCIS are allowed to use Online Conference Service (OCS) for managing the whole proceedings lifecycle (from submission and reviewing to preparing for publication) free of charge.

Publication process

The language of publication is exclusively English. Authors publishing in CCIS have to sign the Springer CCIS copyright transfer form, however, they are free to use their material published in CCIS for substantially changed, more elaborate subsequent publications elsewhere. For the preparation of the camera-ready papers/files, authors have to strictly adhere to the Springer CCIS Authors' Instructions and are strongly encouraged to use the CCIS LaTeX style files or templates.

Abstracting/Indexing

CCIS is abstracted/indexed in DBLP, Google Scholar, EI-Compendex, Mathematical Reviews, SCImago, Scopus. CCIS volumes are also submitted for the inclusion in ISI Proceedings.

How to start

To start the evaluation of your proposal for inclusion in the CCIS series, please send an e-mail to ccis@springer.com.

Patricia Pesado · Walter Panessi ·
Juan Manuel Fernández

Editors

Computer Science – CACIC 2023

29th Argentine Congress of Computer Science
Lujan, Argentina, October 9–12, 2023
Revised Selected Papers

 Springer

Editors
Patricia Pesado
National University of La Plata
La Plata, Buenos Aires, Argentina

Walter Panessi ⓘ
National University of Luján
Luján, Buenos Aires, Argentina

Juan Manuel Fernández ⓘ
National University of Luján
Luján, Buenos Aires, Argentina

ISSN 1865-0929   ISSN 1865-0937 (electronic)
Communications in Computer and Information Science
ISBN 978-3-031-62244-1   ISBN 978-3-031-62245-8 (eBook)
https://doi.org/10.1007/978-3-031-62245-8

This Springer imprint is published by the registered company Springer Nature Switzerland AG
The registered company address is: Gewerbestrasse 11, 6330 Cham, Switzerland

If disposing of this product, please recycle the paper.

Preface

Welcome to the selected papers of the XXIX Argentina Congress of Computer Science (CACIC 2023), held in Lujan, Buenos Aires, Argentina, during October 9–12, 2023. CACIC 2023 was organized by the National University of Lujan on behalf of the Network of National Universities with Computer Science Degrees (RedUNCI).

CACIC is an annual congress dedicated to the promotion and advancement of all aspects of computer science. Its aim is to provide a forum within which the development of computer science as an academic discipline with industrial applications is promoted, trying to extend the frontier of both the state of the art and the state of the practice. The main audience for and participants of CACIC are seen as researchers in academic departments, laboratories, and industrial software organizations.

CACIC 2023 covered the following topics: intelligent agents and systems; software engineering; hardware architecture; networks and operating systems; graphic computation, visualization, and image processing; computer technology applied to education; databases and data mining; innovation in software systems; innovation in computer science education; signal processing and real-time systems; digital governance and smart cities.

This year, the congress received 142 submissions. Each submission was reviewed by at least 3, and on average 3.2 Program Committee members and/or external reviewers, following a single-blind, peer-review scheme. A total of 69 full papers, involving 239 different authors from 44 universities, were accepted. According to the recommendations of the reviewers, 27 of them were selected for this book.

During CACIC 2023, special activities were also carried out, including one plenary lecture, six discussion panels, a special track on Digital Governance and Smart Cities, and an International School with five courses.

Special thanks go to the members of the different committees for their support and collaboration. Also, we would like to thank the local Organizing Committee, reviewers, lecturers, speakers, authors, and all conference attendees. Finally, we want to thank Springer for their support of this publication.

April 2024

Patricia Pesado
Walter Panessi
Juan Manuel Fernández

Organization

Editors

Patricia Pesado   National University of La Plata[1], Argentina
Walter Panessi   National University of Lujan, Argentina
Juan Manuel Fernández   National University of Lujan, Argentina

Editorial Assistant

Pablo Thomas   National University of La Plata, Argentina

Program Committee

Maria Jose Abásolo	National University of La Plata, Argentina
Claudio Aciti	National University of Buenos Aires Center, Argentina
Hugo Alfonso	National University of La Pampa, Argentina
Jorge Ardenghi	National University of the South, Argentina
Marcelo Arroyo	National University of Río Cuarto, Argentina
Hernan Astudillo	Technical University Federico Santa María, Chile
Sandra Baldasarri	University of Zaragoza, Spain
Javier Balladini	National University of Comahue, Argentina
Luis Soares Barbosa	University of Minho, Portugal
Rodolfo Bertone	National University of La Plata, Argentina
Oscar Bria	National University of La Plata, Argentina
Nieves R. Brisaboa	University of La Coruña, Spain
Carlos Buckle	National University of Patagonia San Juan Bosco, Argentina
Alberto Cañas	University of West Florida, USA
Ana Casali	National University of Rosario, Argentina
Silvia Castro	National University of the South, Argentina
Alejandra Cechich	National University of Comahue, Argentina
Edgar Chávez	Michoacana University of San Nicolás de Hidalgo, Mexico
Carlos Coello Coello	CINVESTAV, Mexico

---

[1] RedUNCI Chair.

Sponsors

Network of Universities with Careers in Computer Science (RedUNCI)

National University of Lujan

I+D+I Agency

Invap

Scientific Research Commission (CIC)

Contents

Hardware Architectures, Networks, and Operating Systems

Innovation in Software Systems

Signal Processing and Real-Time Systems

Innovation in Computer Science Education

Computer Security

Digital Governance and Smart Cities

Agents and Systems

Nonlinear Models in Optimal Instrumentation. A Fast Technique for Precision Evaluation

José Hernández[1] , Silvia Simón[1], Gabriela Minetti[2] , Carolina Salto[2,3] ,
and Mercedes Carnero[1(✉)]

[1] Facultad de Ingeniería, Universidad Nacional de Río Cuarto, Río Cuarto, Argentina
mcarnero@ing.unrc.edu.ar
[2] LISI - Facultad de Ingeniería, Universidad Nacional de La Pampa, General Pico, Argentina
[3] CONICET, Buenos Aires, Argentina

Abstract. The aim of this work is to provide a tool for evaluating the precision of process variable estimates in the context of the optimal design of a sensor network in chemical plants. One of the possible formulations for the optimal design of an instrumentation system for monitoring tasks is the solution of nonlinear optimization problems with constraints, where the objective function is the cost of the instrument and the constraints are the observability and global precision associated with a sensor placement. When a metaheuristic approach is used to solve this problem, a methodology for computing the constraints is needed to evaluate the quality of a proposed solution. A simulation technique has been selected to solve the precision associated with a set of measurements. The simulator requires a variable classification methodology and a data reconciliation function that consists of solving another non-linear optimization. The proposed strategies have been applied to a continuous stirred tank reactor, a nonlinear problem including flows, compositions, and temperatures related by mass and energy balances. Results demonstrating the performance of the proposed metaheuristics are presented.

Keywords: Sensor Network Design · optimization · Monte Carlo approach · variable estimates

1 Introduction

The availability of a reliable knowledge of the actual chemical plant state has a significant impact on its energetic efficiency and the fulfillment of environmental and safety regulations. This knowledge can be obtained by installing an adequate sensor network at the design stage of the plant and applying data treatment procedures during its operation. Thus, data provided by sensors is transformed in consistent information to be used as input of monitoring, control and on line optimization methodologies. The number of sensors to be installed on the plant depends on the set of process variables that should be reliably known to execute the aforementioned procedures.

The optimal selection of chemical plant instrumentation is defined as the Sensor Network Design Problem (SNDP). Because the estimation of the required variables can be attained by locating diverse types of sensors to measure different process variables, a

P. Pesado et al. (Eds.): CACIC 2023, CCIS 2123, pp. 3–14, 2024.
https://doi.org/10.1007/978-3-031-62245-8_1

huge combinatorial optimization problem arises even for small scale plants. Its solution determines the set of process variables to be measured that optimizes the selected criteria and fulfills a set of constraints. In general, the number of variables that are involved in these problems for a real work scenario is quite large and the formulation can be more or less complex depending on the performance criteria and the restrictions set used.

In this paper, the SNDP for process performance monitoring proposal is considered. Plant operation is represented by a nonlinear system of algebraic equations. The design minimizes the instrumentation cost, and also satisfies the observability of a required set of process variables and the precision of some of them. Precision is evaluated in terms of the standard deviation of variable estimates calculated using two approach. First, a Monte Carlo simulation tool is used. Then a simulation methodology is applied using the concept of Taylor series.

First, a Monte Carlo simulation tool presented in a previous work [1] is used. Given the limitations encountered when trying to scale up this technique, a second approach is proposed: a simulation methodology using the concept of Taylor series.

The rest of this article is organized as follows. In Sect. 2 the SNDP is briefly reviewed, and the approach proposed for solving this problem is described. Section 3 presents one chemical process extracted from chemical engineering literature. An analysis of the results obtained using the two proposed methodology is included in Sect. 3. Finally, the main conclusions and future lines of research are drawn in Sect. 4.

2 Problem Formulation

Let us assume R is a set of nonlinear algebraic equations that represents the operation of a process under steady state conditions

$$\mathbf{R}(\mathbf{z}) = \mathbf{R}(\mathbf{x}, \mathbf{u}) = \mathbf{0} \qquad (1)$$

where $\mathbf{z}$ is the n dimensional vector of process variables, and $\mathbf{x}$ and $\mathbf{u}$ are the vectors of measured and unmeasured variables, respectively. The optimal selection of instruments for process monitoring consists in determining the partition of vector $\mathbf{z}$ in vectors $\mathbf{x}$ and $\mathbf{u}$ that optimizes a given criterion and satisfies a set of constraints. In general, restrictions are imposed on the degree of estimability of key process variables and also on the quality of their estimates. One particular selection problem obtains the minimum cost sensor network that satisfies a degree of estimability greater or equal to 1 and estimates precision constraints for a given set of required variables. This problem is stated by the following equation

$$
\begin{aligned}
&\min \quad \mathbf{c}^{\mathrm{T}}\mathbf{q} \\
&\text{s.t.} \\
&\qquad E_l(\mathbf{q}) \geq 1 \qquad \forall\, l \in S_E \qquad (2) \\
&\qquad \hat{\sigma}_k(\mathbf{q}) \leq \sigma_k^*(\mathbf{q}) \qquad \forall\, k \in S_\sigma \\
&\qquad \mathbf{q} \in \{0, 1\}^n
\end{aligned}
$$

where $\mathbf{q}$ is an n-dimensional vector of binary variables such that $q_i = 1$ if variable i is measured, and $q_i = 0$ otherwise, $\mathbf{c}^{\mathrm{T}}$ is the cost vector; E_l stands for the degree of estimability of the l-th variable included in S_E and $\hat{\sigma}_k$ is the estimate standard deviation of the

k-th variable contained in S_σ after a data reconciliation procedure is applied. Furthermore, S_σ and S_E are the set of key process variables with requirements on estimability and precision, respectively.

In this formulation, measurements are subject to non correlated random errors; there is only one potential measuring device for each variable, and there are no restrictions for the localization of instruments. Furthermore, the feasibility of the constraints can be checked by executing variable classification and data reconciliation procedures [1].

Tree-search algorithms, nonlinear mixed-integer programming techniques, and heuristic techniques have been used to solve the SNDP [2–5]. When a metaheuristic approach is used to solve this problem, a methodology for computing the constraints is needed to evaluate the quality of a proposed solution.

The precision constraint associated with the estimation of a required variable can be evaluated explicitly in linear systems. In [2], an SNDP is solved using linear algebra to determine a value for precision. For nonlinear systems, however, the evaluation of precision is not straightforward. Bagajewicz [6] has proposed to perform a linearization of the balance equations governing the plant model around a known operating point. In this case, it is possible to have an explicit expression for the error calculation with expressions that involve the computing the matrices inverse, which may have high condition numbers and could lead to non-valid solutions. A more realistic approach is to implement a Monte Carlo method, which has the advantage of flexibility and simplicity, but whose accuracy depends on the size of the sample with which the simulation is performed. The goal of this paper is to propose a methodology based on the second option for precision estimation that can be implemented in the optimal sensor placement methodology.

The feasibility of the solutions determined by a simulation procedure involves the resolution of non-linear optimization problems at a second level. The optimization strategy is dedicated to solve the following non-linear data reconciliation problem

$$\underset{\mathbf{x},\mathbf{u}}{Min}\ (\mathbf{y}-\mathbf{x})^T \Sigma^{-1}\ (\mathbf{y}-\mathbf{x})$$

$$subjet\ to$$
$$\mathbf{f}(\mathbf{x},\mathbf{u}) = \mathbf{0}$$
$$\mathbf{g}(\mathbf{x},\mathbf{u}) \leq \mathbf{0}$$

(3)

where $\mathbf{f}$ and $\mathbf{g}$ are the vectors of equality and inequality constraints, respectively, Σ stands for the variance-covariance matrix, and $\mathbf{y}$ represents the measurement vector.

For a given set of measured variables, the estimates vector attained solving problem (3), $\hat{\mathbf{z}}$, is a vector of random variables of certain joint probability distribution. The population standard deviation vector of $\hat{\mathbf{z}}$ can be estimated by a simulation procedure that generates a set of $\mathbf{y}$ vectors, obtains the corresponding $\hat{\mathbf{z}}$ vector for each $\mathbf{y}$ vector, and then calculates the sample standard deviation vector of $\hat{\mathbf{z}}$. The application of a variable classification technique and the data reconciliation methodology allows evaluating the estimate precision of each variable included in S_σ as it will be explained next. Each solution must be evaluated to determine the fitness of the proposal. An approach based on penalty functions is used to handle the constraints of the optimization problem given by Eq. (1). The working hypothesis is that the critical stage, in terms of computational effort, is the feasibility check of a solution associated with the precision calculation and, consequently the scaling of the SNDP for nonlinear systems needs the implementation of an additional strategy to manage the verification of precision constraints in a more bounded way. The Fig. 1 shows an outline of the procedure for the calculation of fitness.

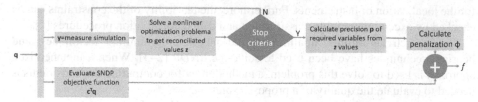

Fig. 1. Fitness calculation scheme with estimability constraints

2.1 Proposed Solution Approach: Estimating the Precision of Required Variables

This subsection addresses the estimate variance calculation for a required variable at the instrumentation design stage of a non-linear process. For a potential solution $\mathbf{q}$, this calculation depends on the results of the variable classification procedure, therefore let us revise some concepts related to this technique.

Process variables can be measured or unmeasured. A measured variable is classified as redundant if the measurement value can be adjusted by a data reconciliation procedure. If it is not the case, the measured variable is non-redundant. Regarding unmeasured variables, they are categorized as observable or unobservable. The first ones can be calculated using the measurements and the process model, while the second ones cannot be estimated.

Estimate variance calculation is straightforward for non-redundant measured variables. In this case the estimate variance is equal to the measurement variance, because the measurement value cannot be adjusted. Regarding non-observable unmeasured variables, their estimate variances are also calculated directly. They are infinite because those variables cannot be calculated.

The data reconciliation procedure allows estimating the redundant measured variable using $\mathbf{y}$ and the process model. In general form, the reconciled or adjusted value of the i-th redundant measured variable can be expressed as shown in Eq. 4.

$$\hat{X}_i = h_i(Y_1, Y_2, ..., Y_m) \tag{4}$$

where $(Y_1, Y_2, ..., Y_m)$ represents the random vector of measurements associated to a particular SN configuration. Given a realization of that vector, $\hat{X}_i$ is also a random variable. For specific functions h_i, the probability density function of $\hat{X}_i$ can be determined using variable transformation techniques. Therefore, its parameters (mean value and variance of $\hat{X}_i$) are known. A particular case arises if plant model is linear because analytical expressions of the reconciled variable value and its standard deviation is available.

In contrast, for non-linear process models the point estimate of the redundant measured variable is obtained by applying a numerical method, this is a non-linear optimization strategy. In this work, the weighted least square technique subject to non-linear process constraints is applied to obtain the point estimate, and a methodology is devised to calculate estimate variance from point estimates.

The treatment of unmeasured observable variables, U_j is similar to the one proposed for the redundant measured ones, except that in general they are expressed as a function of r reconciled variable values as Eq. 5 shows. Variable U_j is also a random variable. If function g_j satisfies specific conditions, the probability density function of U_j can be determined using variable transformation techniques to know its parameters (mean value and variance of U_j).

$$U_j = g_j(\hat{X}_1, \hat{X}_2, ..., \hat{X}_r) \tag{5}$$

In the rest of the subsection alternative methodologies to calculate the estimate variance of redundant measured variables and observable unmeasured ones from point estimates is analyzed. One of these methodologies is Monte Carlo Simulation and the other one is based on Taylor Series. Furthermore, it is considered from this point below that the expected value of $\hat{X}_i$ is equal to the nominal value of the variable used at the design stage of the plant, measurements are independent and the probability density function of each measurement is normal (nominal value, sensor standard deviation).

Monte Carlo Simulation

The Monte Carlo Simulation (MC) is a stochastic numerical procedure widely used in Engineering to simulate the behavior of a phenomenon or a real process that involves random variables such that their probability density functions are known. Its implementation is quite simple but it may require huge computational resources. The scheme proposed to calculate the precision of measured variables for a solution vector **q** is presented in Algorithm 1.

Algorithm 1. Pseudocode of MC

```
:input solution vector q
required process variables vector req
:output
vector of standard deviations of required variables std
N=0
/* run variable classification procedure */
cla=variable_classification(q,req)
if all req variables are measured and non redundant
    std= vector of standard deviation of instruments
elseif all req variables are measured or observable
    while not(stop_criteria)
        yob=sample of the random vector of measurements
        z0=Data_reconciliation(yob)  /*Get estimation*/
        N=N+1
    end_while
    std=Calculate_deviation_of_sample_reconciled_values
else
    std=Inf      /*no feasible solution*/
end_if
```

The sampling of the random measurement vector is performed considering the probability density function of each measurement. The stopping criterion used ensure that the estimated deviation value is bounded, within a small tolerance range ε, for a preset number of iterations, n_ε.

Simulation results are more precise increasing N, which is the number of calls to the non-linear data reconciliation function. This turns unpracticable the use of MC simulation even for medium scale design problems. Next and alternative approximated procedure to calculate estimates variance is presented.

Taylor Series Based Simulation (VAT)

Given a random vector of independent measurements $(Y_1, Y_2, ..., Y_m)$, the vector of their expected values $(\mu_{y_1}, \mu_{y_2}, ..., \mu_{y_m})$ and the estimator function h_i (see Eq. 2), a Taylor Series expansion of h_i around $(\mu_{y_1}, \mu_{y_2}, ..., \mu_{y_m})$ is expressed as follows:

$$
\hat{X}_i = h_i(\mu_{Y_1}, \mu_{Y_2}, ..., \mu_{Ym}) + (Y_1 - \mu_{Y_1}) \left. \frac{\delta h_i}{\delta y_1} \right|_{(\mu_{Y_1}..,\mu_{Ym})} + ... + (Y_m - \mu_{Ym}) \left. \frac{\delta h_i}{\delta ym} \right|_{(\mu_{Y_1},...,\mu_{Ym})} +
$$

$$
+ \frac{1}{2}(Y_1 - \mu_{Y_1})^2 \left. \frac{\delta^2 h_i}{\delta y_1^2} \right|_{(\mu_{Y_1},...,\mu_{Ym})} + ... + \frac{1}{2}(Y_m - \mu_{Ym})^2 \left. \frac{\delta^2 h_i}{\delta ym^2} \right|_{(\mu_{Y_1},...,\mu_{Ym})} + \tag{6}
$$

$$
+ \sum_{i=1,k>i}^{m} 2(Y_i - \mu_{X_i})....(Y_k - \mu_{X_k}) \left. \frac{\delta^2 h_i}{\delta y_i \delta y_k} \right|_{(\mu_{Y_1},...,\mu_{Ym})} + R_1
$$

$$
Var(\hat{X}_i) = \left[\left. \frac{\delta h_i}{\delta y_1} \right|_{(\mu_{Y_1}, \mu_{Y_2},...,\mu_{Ym})} \right]^2 \sigma_{Y_1}^2 + \left[\left. \frac{\delta h_i}{\delta y_2} \right|_{(\mu_{Y_1}, \mu_{Y_2},...,\mu_{Ym})} \right]^2 \sigma_{Y_2}^2 + ...
$$

$$
... + \left[\left. \frac{\delta h_i}{\delta y_n} \right|_{(\mu_{Y_1}, \mu_{Y_2},...,\mu_{Ym})} \right]^2 \sigma_{Ym}^2 \tag{7}
$$

where $\sigma_{Y_1}^2, \sigma_{Y_2}^2, ..., \sigma_{Ym}^2$ represent the variances of each measurement.

Because the relationship between the reconciled variable value and the measurements is only known for particular cases, i.e. a linear process model, the numerical method proposed in [8] is extended in this work to calculate the partial derivative of function h_i with respect to each measurement as follows:

$$
\left. \frac{\delta h_i}{\delta y_k} \right|_{(\mu_{Y_1}, \mu_{Y_2},...,\mu_{Ym})} \approx \frac{\hat{x}_{i,\delta_k} - \hat{x}_i}{\delta_k} \quad \text{for } k = 1 : m \tag{8}
$$

where $\hat{x}_{i,\delta_1}$ represents the reconciled variable value $\hat{x}_i$ obtained when the k-th measurement differs from the true value μ_{Y_k} in a small magnitude δ_k.

Thus the standard deviation of the reconciled value of the k-th measured variable is:

$$
\sigma_{\hat{X}_i} = \sqrt{ \left[\frac{\hat{x}_{i,\delta_1} - \hat{x}_i}{\delta_1} \right]^2 \sigma_{Y_1}^2 + \left[\frac{\hat{x}_{i,\delta_2} - \hat{x}_i}{\delta_2} \right]^2 \sigma_{Y_2}^2 + ... + \left[\frac{\hat{x}_{i,\delta_n} - \hat{x}_i}{\delta_m} \right]^2 \sigma_{Ym}^2 } \tag{9}
$$

For an unmeasured observable variable, U_j the methodology is similar. Its estimate is a function g_j of the reconciled measured values and its variance is calculated as follows:

$$Var(U_j) = \left[\frac{\delta g_j}{\delta \hat{x}_1} \bigg|_{(\mu_{Y_1}, \mu_{Y_2}, \ldots, \mu_{Y_m})} \right]^2 \sigma_{\hat{X}_1}^2 + \left[\frac{\delta g_j}{\delta \hat{x}_2} \bigg|_{(\mu_{Y_1}, \mu_{Y_2}, \ldots, \mu_{Y_m})} \right]^2 \sigma_{\hat{X}_2}^2 + \cdots$$

$$\cdots + \left[\frac{\delta g_j}{\delta x_m} \bigg|_{(\mu_{Y_1}, \mu_{Y_2}, \ldots, \mu_{Y_m})} \right]^2 \sigma_{\hat{X}_m}^2 \tag{10}$$

In general g_j functions are unknown, therefore the same numerical method is used to calculate the partial derivative of g_j with respect to each $\hat{x}_i$.

$$\frac{\delta g_j}{\delta \hat{x}_i} \bigg|_{(\mu_{x_1}, \mu_{x_2}, \ldots, \mu_{x_m})} \approx \frac{u_{j, \delta_i} - u_j}{\delta_i} \tag{11}$$

where now, δ_i is a very small perturbation around the expected value of $\hat{X}_i$, u_j is the value of the unmeasured variable calculated using the nominal values vector as the vector of reconciled variables and u_{j,δ_i} the corresponding value of u assuming the perturbation δ_i.

3   Results

This section presents a nonlinear application example. The case study is a continuous stirred tank reactor (CSTR) [7] whose model comprises 13 variables (total flow rates, compositions, and temperatures), 5 mass and energy balances and the reaction rate equation given by Eq. 6 to 11. The process flowsheet is shown in Fig. 2.

$$\frac{dC_A}{dt} = \frac{F_i}{V}(C_{A_i} - C_A) - r_A \tag{12}$$

$$\frac{dV}{dt} = F_1 - F \tag{13}$$

$$\frac{dT}{dt} = \frac{F_i}{V}(T_i - T) + \frac{r_A(-\Delta H)}{\rho C_p} - \frac{UA(T - T_c)}{V \rho C_p} \tag{14}$$

$$\frac{dT_c}{dt} = \frac{F_c}{V}(T_{ci} - T_c) + \frac{UA(T - T_c)}{V_j \rho_j C_{pj}} \tag{15}$$

$$\frac{dn}{dt} = r_A V - F_{vg} \tag{16}$$

$$r_A = C_d C_A k_0 \exp(-E/RT) \tag{17}$$

To evaluate the performance of the proposed methodology, a design problem which comprises three required variables is considered; these are C_A, T and F. The precision constraints are $\sigma_3^* = 2.227 \; 10^{-3}$, $\sigma_4^* = 5.700$ and $\sigma_{10}^* = 3.800 \; 10^{-1}$ (Table 1).

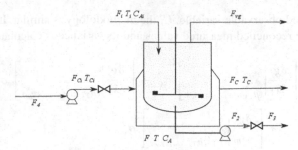

Fig. 2. Process Flowsheet – CSTR

Table 1. True variable values - CSTR

#	Variable	Nominal value	Cost of instrument	#	Variable	Nominal value	Cost of instrument
1	F_i	40.04	100	8	T_{ci}	530.64	35
2	C_{Ai}	0.5	270	9	F_{vg}	10.61	85
3	C_A	0.23	300	10	F	40.04	90
4	T	600.03	50	11	F_2	40.04	95
5	T_i	529.01	55	12	F_3	40.04	80
6	T_c	590.61	60	13	F_4	56.69	82
7	F_c	56.69	105				

Results obtained for three particular solutions, denoted as q^1, q^2 and q^3, are examined next. All the process variables are measured in q^1. Therefore, all variables are redundant and the reconciliation procedure is called to calculate the precision of the required variables. The same happens for q^2, where the proposal is to measure C_{Ai}, F_{Vg}, F_3 variables. In this case, the required variables are unmeasured and observable, then they are evaluated in terms of the measurements. Regarding q^3, it corresponds to the solution of the SNDP for the CSTR, that is $q^3 = q^*$. In this case the measured variables are C_{Ai}, C_A, T_{ci} y F_3. Figures 3, 4 and 5 display the reconciliated values of the required variables and the deviation of the sample mean of these values with respect to the true values for an increasing number of simulation trials.

The convergence of the sample mean of the reconciled values to the true ones is attained faster than the stabilization of the sample standard deviation around a certain value. Furthermore, the number of MC simulation trials required to achieve the convergence of the sample standard deviation depends on the analyzed solution.

The same analysis is performed using the VAT method, and results are shown in Figs. 6, 7 and 8. That technique achieves sample standard deviation values very similar to the ones obtained using MC simulation.

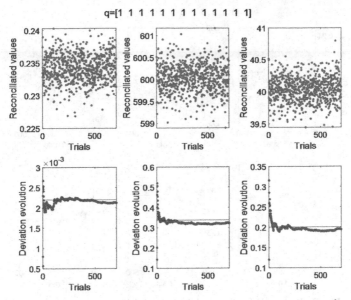

Fig. 3. Reconciled values and deviation of the sample mean for q^1

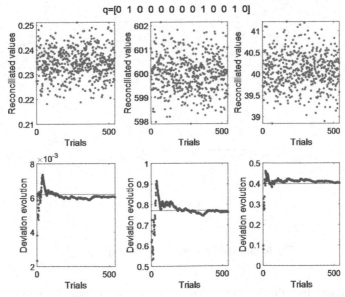

Fig. 4. Reconciled values and deviation of the sample mean for q^2

The simulation study performed allows inferring that MC method requires $N = 1000$ trials, in average, to provide a reliable estimate of the precision for a required variable. Therefore, an upper bound of the total computational effort necessary to verify the feasibility of precision constraints for a potential solution is N x #(required variables).

q=[0 1 1 0 0 0 0 0 1 0 0 1 0]

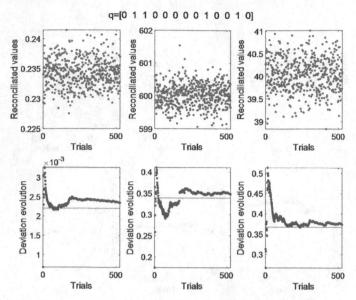

Fig. 5. Reconciled values and deviation of the sample mean for q*

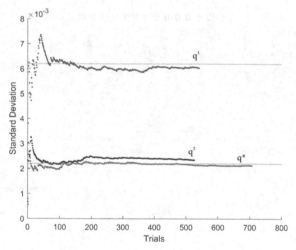

Fig. 6. Standard deviation of C_A for q^1, q^2, q^*

For the CSTR problem, the maximum number of calls to the data reconciliation function for each solution to be evaluated is 3000. To solve problems of larger size, MC simulation is unpracticable and others architectures should be used.

For the deterministic numerical method VAT, the maximum number of calls to the optimization procedure can be calculated assuming that all the required variables are reconciled and all the process variables are measured. In this case the upper bound

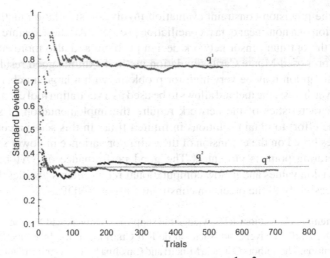

Fig. 7. Standard deviation of T for $\mathbf{q}^1$, $\mathbf{q}^2$, $\mathbf{q}^*$

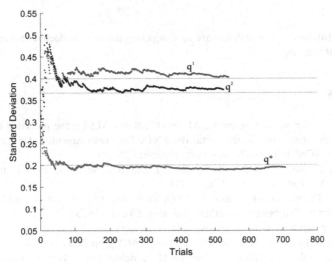

Fig. 8. Standard deviation of F for $\mathbf{q}^1$, $\mathbf{q}^2$, $\mathbf{q}^*$

of the computational effort is #required variables *n. For the CSTR problem, the data reconciliation procedure should be run 39 times at maximum.

4 Conclusions

In this work, a strategy has been developed for the precision evaluation associated with the estimation of a required variable in the optimal instrumentation schemes resolution framework for chemical plants. It is assumed that the plant model is represented by a set of global mass balances, by component and energy balances in steady state, which implies that the precision constraint evaluation involves a simulation method together with the solution of a nonlinear data reconciliation problem. All these features bring more generality to the optimal sensor network design problem and also more complexity to solve it. The proposed Monte Carlo simulation method exhibits good results, although the time consumption may be very high for problems with a large number of required variables. Nevertheless, the method allows to be used as a validation tool even in scenarios where the characteristics of the network require the implementation of strategies to rationalize the effort to obtain solutions in limited time. In this sense a computational methodologies based on the expansion of the estimator variance in power series around a known operating point is presented. The good performance of VAT regarding the achieved precision values and its low computational requirements justifies the testing to analyze the feasibility of the precision constraint for real SNDPs.

Acknowledgments. The authors acknowledge the support of Universidad Nacional de La Pampa (Project FI-CD-107/20), Universidad Nacional de Río Cuarto, and the Incentive Program from MINCyT, Argentina. The authors Gabriela Minetti and Carolina Salto are grateful for the support of the HUMAN-CENTERED SMART MOBILITY (HUMOVE) project, PID2020-116727RB-I00, Spain. Carolina Salto is also funded by CONICET, Argentina.

Disclosure of Interests. The authors have no competing interests to declare that are relevant to the content of this article.

References

1. Hernández, J., Simón, S., Carnero C., Minetti G., Salto, M.: On the precision evaluation in non-linear sensor network design; Actas del XXIX Congreso Argentino De Ciencias De La Computación (CACIC), pp. 48–56. Luján, Argentina (2023)
2. Romagnoli, J., Sánchez, M.: Data Processing and Reconciliation for Chemical Process Operations. Academic Press, San Diego (2000)
3. Carnero, M., Hernández, J.L., Sánchez, M.: Optimal sensor location in chemical plants using the estimation of distribution algorithms. Ind. Eng. Chem. Res. 57(36), 12149–12164 (2018)
4. Zhang, J., Chmielewski, D.J.: Profit-based sensor network design using the generalized benders decomposition. In: American Control Conference, (ACC), pp. 3894–3899 (2017)
5. Hernandez, J., Salto, C., Minetti, G., Carnero, M., Sanchez, M.C.: Hybrid simulated annealing for optimal cost instrumentation in chemical plants. Chem. Eng. Trans. 74, 709–714 (2019)
6. He, Y.J., Ma, Z.F.: Optimal design of linear sensor networks for process plants: a multi-objective ant colony optimization approach. Chemom. Intell. Lab. Syst. 135, 37–47 (2014)
7. Nguyen, D.Q., Bagajewicz, M.: Design of nonlinear sensor networks for process plants. Ind. Eng. Chem. Res. 47, 5529–5542 (2008)
8. Bhushan, M., Rengaswamy, R.: Design of sensor network based on the signed directed graph of the process for efficient fault diagnosis. Ind. Eng. Chem. Res. 39, 999 (2000)
9. Rameh, H.: Instrumentation optimale pour le suivi des performances énergétiques d'un procédé industriel. Energie électrique. Thèse de Doctorat de l'Université de recherche Paris Sciences et Lettres, PSL Research Universityes (2018)

Determination of Hyperparameters in the Development of a Frost Predictive Model with Data Science

María Isabel Masanet$^{(\boxtimes)}$ and Raúl Oscar Klenzi

Facultad de Ciencias Exactas, Físicas y Naturales, Universidad Nacional de San Juan, San Juan, Argentina
mimasanet@unsj.edu.ar, rauloscarklenzi@unsj-cuim.edu.ar

Abstract. The damages caused by the meteorological phenomenon of frost on crops result in significant economic losses. Farmers consistently seek assistance from experts or technological tools to forecast the occurrence of the phenomenon and protect crops. Following the Data Science process, the values of climate variables recorded by two weather stations have been preprocessed. Various techniques were necessary to generate datasets suitable for the developed predictive models. Sliding window was used for the data. The window size required a particular experiment. The models are based on an LSTM neural network. The learning rate for the network was obtained from a set of tests, in which metrics and graphical representations were analyzed. The models predict the temperature for a horizon of three hours. The best model operates with a three-hour sliding window, achieves a precision of 92% and 73% for recall for frost cases.

Keywords: Data Science · Machine Learning · LSTM Network · Sliding Window · Frost

1 Introduction

Agricultural production is impacted by the phenomenon of meteorological frost, resulting in significant losses in harvest. This affects exports, the employment of seasonal workers, and the overall economy of the affected region [1, 2]. In some cases, particularly due to late frosts, crop losses have exceeded 80% of production [3, 4].

Producers are interested in frost forecasting to implement actions that protect crops from the damages of the phenomenon. For forecasting, the producer relies on personal experience or expert opinion. It is based on the values of meteorological variables in the area where the crop is located. These variables exhibit variations between areas, even if they are close together; for example, the sunlight reaching the area influences the amount of energy it receives [5].

Meteorological data is of nonlinear nature, making forecasting a challenging task [6]. It involves a combination of computer models, on-site observations, and the understanding of trends and weather patterns through advanced methodology.

P. Pesado et al. (Eds.): CACIC 2023, CCIS 2123, pp. 15–29, 2024.
https://doi.org/10.1007/978-3-031-62245-8_2

Through Data Science, knowledge can be extracted from data, aiming to utilize that knowledge for predicting events, understanding the past and present, creating new products, among other applications [7]. The Data Science process involves several phases. Firstly, understanding the problem and defining the objective of data analysis. Then, the data exploration stage, to extract significant features that are used by modeling and analysis tools, ultimately obtaining and presenting the results [8]. At this point, there is a feedback loop; the new knowledge available allows for generating new questions, new issues that must be contextualized, and a new process begins [9].

The data exploration phase is highly significant, as it involves selecting and structuring the dataset for the model. In this study, the data were structured using a three-hour sliding window. To determine the window size, experimentation was conducted with sizes of 2, 3, and 4 h. Models typically employ a Machine Learning (ML) algorithm [8], learning through training with data specific to the problem being addressed.

Another relevant aspect concerns the hyperparameters of ML algorithms. While programming languages provide default values for them, these values may not be suitable for the problem at hand. So far, the only technique to determine an acceptable value is trial and error. In this study, a Long Short-Term Memory recurrent neural network (LSTM RNN) was used, which has hyperparameters such as the number of neurons in each layer, the learning rate, optimization algorithm, activation functions, among others. Different learning rates (lr) were analyzed through empirical experimentation.

The paper presents the development of the Data Science process to achieve a model that predicts temperature three hours in advance through an LSTM RNN. It details the tasks carried out to prepare the data and to establish one of the most important hyperparameters. The evaluation of the models as regression was performed through the mean squared error (MSE), root mean squared error (RMSE), and the R^2 coefficient. And as binary classification with recall and F1-Score for frost cases.

This article is an expanded and fully revised version of [9]. The work has been expanded to include:

- Experimentation conducted to select the size of the sliding window used to structure the data.
- Experimentation conducted to determine the learning rate for the neural network.
- The comparative analysis of models using only the temperature variable and with two variables, temperature and humidity.

The remaining sections of this article are organized as follows: in Sect. 2, It presents concepts of interest for the work. Next, in Sect. 3, the methodology used are described, and in Sect. 4, the experimental work carried out is detailed and the results obtained are analyzed. Finally, in Sect. 5, conclusions and possible lines of future work are presented.

2 Background

2.1 Data Science Process

In the execution of the Data Science process (Fig. 1), each phase requires analyzing, evaluating, and deciding on the techniques to apply. The sequence of phases is not strict; at any point in the process, it is feasible to regress to a previous phase with the aim of improving the solution to the stated problem.

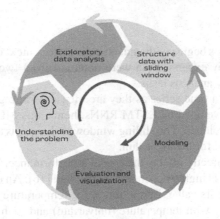

Fig. 1. Data Science Process applied in research. Source: Author

2.2 Time Series

The data measured at regular time intervals represent the temporal variations of an entity at fixed time points within a finite time interval and collectively describe a time series.

Prediction in a time series is highly useful and widely applicable in the real world. Data Science addresses issues related to weather, population growth, gross domestic product, and similar domains, using appropriate neural network algorithms to learn the dynamic behavior of a time series [10].

2.3 Imbalanced Data Sets

When modeling unusual or temporal events such as frosts in meteorology, it is highly probable that the real dataset will be unbalanced. That is, the number of non-frost records is notably higher than frost records. This bias in the training dataset affects the model's performance, resulting in the model being more accurate for majority cases than for minority ones.

An approach to addressing data imbalance issues involves applying some resampling method, some of which include SMOTE, ADASYN, SMOTEtomek, and SMO-TEENN [11, 12]. Balancing in data for applications dealing with time series should be applied in such a way that there is no loss in time correlation and dependencies between measurements [13].

2.4 Frost

Technically, the term "frost" refers to the formation of ice crystals on surfaces, either through the freezing of dew or by a phase change from water vapor to ice [14]. It occurs when the earth's surface and the air above it reach a temperature below 0 °C [15].

3 Methodology

The Data Science process begins with understanding the context of the problem through information provided by experts. Data were obtained from two weather stations and subjected to exploratory analysis tasks.

The data constitute a time series as they are measured at regular intervals of time. This characteristic is leveraged by LSTM RNNs, hence this ML algorithm is selected for the models to be developed. The sliding window technique is applied to give the data the appropriate structure for the algorithm.

The learning rate directly affects the model's performance. The appropriate value for this hyperparameter is highly dependent on the data [16]. An empirical test has been conducted to determine its value. Furthermore, for temperature prediction, the results of models trained solely with temperature (univariate) and with both temperature and relative humidity variables (bivariate) were analyzed.

In all cases, the models have a hidden layer with a number of neurons equal to the number of inputs. That is, 18 neurons for the univariate model and 36 for the bivariate model. Temperature prediction is made with a 3-h lead time.

Based on the results observed in [12], the analysis begins with a bivariate model with a 3-h window to analyze the learning rate. The determined value is then applied in the development of univariate and bivariate models for the three proposed window sizes. Figure 2 illustrates the flow of experiments conducted. Finally, model evaluation is performed using metrics (R^2, RMSE, accuracy, and recall, F1-Score for frosts) and graphical representations.

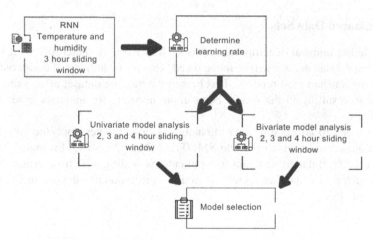

Fig. 2. Analysis flow to select the model. Source: Author

In the tasks of the process, the Python programming language has been utilized, employing various open-source libraries such as NumPy for different numerical operations for data preprocessing and structuring. The scikit-learn library provides classification, clustering, and regression algorithms, which are complemented by TensorFlow for the development of machine learning models. Additionally, the Matplotlib library enables the creation of various types of visualizations.

3.1 Understand the Context of the Problem

To understand the context of the problem, information was requested from experts. The data used originate from two meteorological stations installed in the province of San Juan, Argentina, separated by approximately 37 km. Both stations measure and record every 10 min the values of variables such as temperature, humidity, wind speed and direction, atmospheric pressure, solar radiation, dew point, among others.

One of the stations is installed at the San Francisco S.A. Establishment (private operation), in the locality of Cañada Honda, Sarmiento. These data were provided by the Institute of Automation (INAUT) of the Faculty of Engineering of the National University of San Juan.

Another station is located at the Agricultural Experimental Station (EEA) San Juan, part of the National Institute of Agricultural Technology (INTA) in the Pocito department. The data were shared by the Agrometeorology Service of this EEA.

3.2 Exploratory Data Analysis

From the INTA station, data from the year 2016 until July 2021 were considered, and from the San Francisco Establishment from April 2013 to 2018. A total of 299,671 records were available from San Francisco, of which 13,872 correspond to frosts (approximately 4.63%). For the INTA station, the total number of records is 301,899, which includes 3,854 cases of frost (around 1.28%).

The data recorded by the stations present a tabular structure and have required various preprocessing tasks on the data (Fig. 3).

- To unify. Both stations measure at equal time intervals and the same variables, but it was necessary to standardize column names and date and time format.
- Handling missing values. Records where the value of any of the variables of interest for the study was missing were identified and removed.
- Selecting records. For each year, the data corresponding to the period between the date of the first frost and the date of the last frost were selected. Additionally, only the hours within the occurrence range of the phenomenon (between 00:00 h and 08:00 h) were considered for each day [17].
- Feature selection. To analyze the characteristics, a linear correlation matrix was constructed with the meteorological variables: temperature, humidity, dew point, wind speed, atmospheric pressure, and solar radiation. It was observed that there is a correlation between temperature and humidity [12].

Table 1 shows the number of records contained in the original dataset and the number of records resulting from the selection tasks, discriminating between the quantity of frosts and non-frosts.

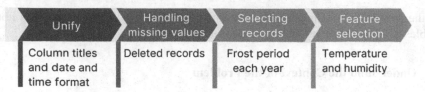

Fig. 3. Preprocessing tasks of the data. Source: Author

Table 1. Total quantity, frosts, and non-frosts from the original dataset and the resulting dataset from the case selection for each station.

Station	Record	Original	Selected
San Francisco	Total	299671	82975
	Heladas	13872	13814
	No Heladas	285799	69161
INTA	Total	301899	49973
	Heladas	3854	3830
	No Heladas	298045	46143

3.3 Data Structure

The sliding window technique has been employed to structure the data. In this technique, an important decision is the window size. For this purpose, empirical experimentation was conducted with window sizes of 2, 3, and 4 h of records of the selected meteorological variables. Since the station records every 10 min, 6 values of the per variable have been considered for each hour.

Datasets were generated solely with the temperature variable, as it is the most related to the frost phenomenon, but also with temperature and humidity. In all cases, the horizon was set to 3 h, which is the appropriate time for the producer to deploy damage mitigation mechanisms. Figure 4 shows part of the dataset of a variable with a window size of 3.

Meteorological stations measure temperature in degrees Celsius and humidity in percentage. Providing a neural network with data that takes large values or heterogeneous data can prevent the network from converging. To facilitate the learning of a neural network, the data should be homogeneous and have small values, preferably varying in the range of 0 to 1 or −1 to 1 [18]. To ensure that the data acquires these characteristics, a normalization task is performed for each value in the dataset.

Both the training and testing datasets must be representative of the available data. In models that aim to predict the future based on the past, data should not be randomly mixed before splitting them, as doing so will create temporal leakage [18]. The strategy employed to form these datasets involved using data from the San Francisco station for training and validation due to its higher number of frost records. The data from the INTA station were reserved for testing purposes.

	T18	T17	T16	T15	T14	T13	T12	T11	T10	T9	T8	T7	T6	T5	T4	T3	T2	T1	Y	DateTime
0	8.3	8.4	8.5	8.6	8.6	8.6	8.6	8.6	8.5	8.3	8.2	8.1	8.0	7.7	7.5	7.3	7.1	7.0	3.4	2016-04-25 23:50:00
1	8.4	8.5	8.6	8.6	8.6	8.6	8.6	8.5	8.3	8.2	8.1	8.0	7.7	7.5	7.3	7.1	7.0	6.8	3.2	2016-04-26 00:00:00
2	8.5	8.6	8.6	8.6	8.6	8.6	8.5	8.3	8.2	8.1	8.0	7.7	7.5	7.3	7.1	7.0	6.8	6.7	2.9	2016-04-26 00:10:00
15	7.3	7.1	7.0	6.8	6.7	6.6	6.5	6.3	5.9	5.6	5.1	4.6	4.3	4.1	3.9	3.8	3.8	3.7	1.7	2016-04-26 02:20:00
16	7.1	7.0	6.8	6.7	6.6	6.5	6.3	5.9	5.6	5.1	4.6	4.3	4.1	3.9	3.8	3.8	3.7	3.6	2.1	2016-04-26 02:30:00
17	7.0	6.8	6.7	6.6	6.5	6.3	5.9	5.6	5.1	4.6	4.3	4.1	3.9	3.8	3.8	3.7	3.6	3.6	2.4	2016-04-26 02:40:00
18	6.8	6.7	6.6	6.5	6.3	5.9	5.6	5.1	4.6	4.3	4.1	3.9	3.8	3.8	3.7	3.6	3.6	3.4	2.2	2016-04-26 02:50:00

Fig. 4. Sliding window of size 3 h with the temperature variable for a 3-h horizon.

The training and validation sets exhibited imbalance between frost and non-frost cases [9, 19], which were balanced by applying the SMOTEEN method [12]. The number of records in the training, validation, and test sets used for each window size is detailed in Table 2. These values are consistent for both univariate and bivariate datasets.

Table 2. Number of records for the training, validation, and test sets.

		Total	Frost	No Frost
2 h	Train	106858	55039	51819
	Validation	36936	18740	18196
	Test	37988	2587	35401
3 h	Train	65643	34000	31643
	Validation	21868	10810	11058
	Test	31613	3760	27853
4 h	Train	57844	30073	27771
	Validation	19203	9679	9524
	Test	29930	3729	26201

It can be observed that the number of records decreases as the window size increases.

3.4 Modeling

The developed models are based on LSTM RNNs, suitable for handling time series data. In all cases, the number of neurons in the hidden layer is equal to the number of neurons in the input layer. That is, for single-variable models, there are 12, 18, and 24 neurons for the 2, 3, and 4-h windows respectively. For two-variable models, there are 24, 36, and 48 neurons.

The following hyperparameters are common to all models: the RELU activation function in the hidden layer [20]; the loss function is MSE due to being a regression problem, and the optimization algorithm is Adam. Regarding the learning rate, an empirical experiment was conducted with different rates, and the best result was achieved with a learning rate of 8e−7. The output layer has one neuron with a linear activation function. The network was trained for 80 epochs.

3.5 Evaluation and Visualization

Each model provides as output the temperature forecast for a 3-h horizon. Subsequently, each record in the test set is labeled with 0 or 1, depending on whether the forecasted temperature corresponds to frost (Less than 0°) or non-frost, respectively. Thus, the results are transformed into a binary classification.

The evaluation of the models as a regression problem was done through the values of MSE, RMSE, and the R^2 coefficient. As binary classification, accuracy was considered, the correlation matrix was constructed, and the recall value and F1-Score were analyzed only for frost cases.

4 Experimental Results

4.1 Learning Rate

The analysis of the learning rate has been conducted using an LSTM RNN model that processes temperature and humidity data in a 3-h window with a 3-h horizon. In an initial experimentation, the values used for the learning rate were 1e−3, 1e−4, 1e−5, 1e−6, and 1e−7.

Comparing the metric values (Table 3) for learning rates of 1e−3, 1e−4, 1e−5, and 1e−6, no significant difference is observed between them. When observing the learning curves of the models, learning rates of 1e−3 (Fig. 5(a)) and 1e−4 (Fig. 5(b)) lead to overfitting and a learning curve with rebounds, indicating that they are high values.

Table 3. Results of training the models with each learning rate.

Metric	1e−3	1e−4	1e−5	1e−6	1e−7
Train R^2	0.87	0.83	0.82	0.80	0.52
Test R^2	0.55	0.66	0.70	0.67	0.34
Train RMSE	1.99	2.29	2.39	2.50	3.86
Test RMSE	3.30	2.89	2.72	2.85	4.03
Recall (Frost)	0.73	0.79	0.77	0.71	0.01
F1-Score (Frost)	0.62	0.64	0.67	0.66	0.01
Recall (No Frost)	0.95	0.95	0.96	0.97	1.00
F1-Score (No Frost)	0.97	0.97	0.97	0.97	0.96
Accuracy (test)	0.94	0.94	0.95	0.95	0.93

The value of 1e−7 is very low, and the algorithm converges slowly (Fig. 5(e)). The value of 1e−5, although it does not exhibit oscillations, drops abruptly in the initial epochs and then remains stable (Fig. 5(c)); the rate value is high. The value 1e−6 (Fig. 5(d)) is the most suitable among the analyzed set of rates [16].

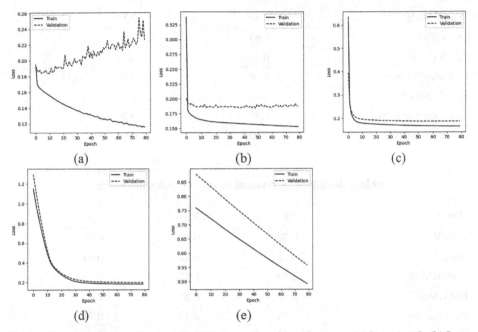

Fig. 5. Learning curves of the models with the analyzed learning rates. (a) Lr = 1e−3, (b) Lr = 1e−4, (c) Lr = 1e−5 (d), Lr = 1e−6, (e) Lr = 1e−7.

Given the previous results, attempts have been made to improve the learning rate by training the models with a rate between the values of 1e−6 and 1e−7. An experiment was conducted with the value of 8e−7. This learning rate shows a slight improvement in test RMSE and frost recall and F1-Score compared to 1e−6 (the best value from the initial experimentation) (Table 4).

After this comparative analysis, it has been decided to use the learning rate of 8e−7 due to the mentioned improvements.

4.2 Sliding Window Size

The analysis of the sliding window size was conducted for 2, 3, and 4 h for bivariate models (temperature and humidity). With the intention of reducing the amount of data to process, experiments were conducted with univariate models. These models only process temperature, the variable most related to the frost phenomenon.

Bivariate Model. The results for each window size with the bivariate model are presented in Table 5.

Table 4. Results of training the models with the rate 1e−6 and 8e−7.

Metric	1e−6	8e−7
Train R^2	0.80	0.80
Test R^2	0.67	0.66
Train RMSE	2.50	2.52
Test RMSE	2.85	2.59
Recall (Frost)	0.71	0.73
F1-Score (Frost)	0.66	0.69
Recall (No Frost)	0.97	0.95
F1-Score (No Frost)	0.97	0.95
Accuracy (test)	0.95	0.92

Table 5. Results of the bivariate model for each window size

Metric	2 h	3 h	4 h
Train R^2	0.78	0.80	0.79
Test R^2	0.58	0.66	0.64
Train RMSE	2.89	2.52	2.53
Test RMSE	3.19	2.60	2.67
Recall (Frost)	0.76	0.73	0.71
F1-Score (Frost)	0.67	0.69	0.67
Recall (No Frost)	0.96	0.95	0.94
F1-Score (No Frost)	0.97	0.95	0.95
Accuracy (test)	0.95	0.92	0.91

The regression metrics (R^2 and RMSE) do not show significant differences in any of the cases when comparing different window sizes. In this initial analysis, the 3-h window performs better in terms of regression metrics. However, for classification, the 2-h window exhibits higher precision and recall for frost cases.

The graphical representation of the prediction shows notable differences between the predictions made by the model with a 2-h window (Fig. 6) compared to the models with 3-h (Fig. 7) and 4-h (Fig. 8) windows. The three figures display the real value and the prediction for a subset of records from the test set. The months of May, June, and July are represented, which are the months with the highest number of frosts in the area where the data originated.

In the 2-h sliding window model (Fig. 6), the prediction values are notably lower than the actual values. Comparing with the 3-h (Fig. 7) and 4-h (Fig. 8) window models, it is observed that in the latter, the prediction is closer to the actual value.

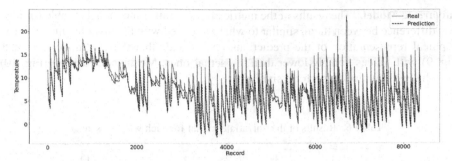

Fig. 6. Temperature prediction from the bivariate model with 2 h sliding window

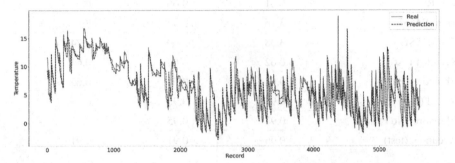

Fig. 7. Temperature prediction from the bivariate model with 3 h sliding window

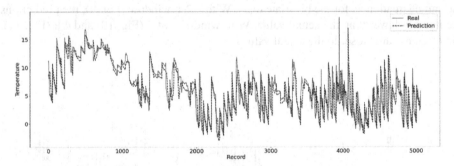

Fig. 8. Temperature prediction from the bivariate model with 4 h sliding window

Of the three models analyzed, the 2-h sliding window model achieved the highest accuracy, but the graphical representation of the prediction reveals that the forecasted values are not adequate compared to the other two models. Discarding this 2-h model, the remaining options (3 and 4 h) do not show significant differences in the analyzed metrics or in the graphs of the predicted values. With these results, the 3-h sliding window model has been selected because it has higher recall for frosts, and also, the amount of data to process for each record is lower.

Univariate Model. The results of the metrics for the univariate models (Table 6) show little difference between them, similar to what happened with the bivariate models. The graphical representation of the predictions also reveals that the 2-h model forecasts (Fig. 9) with values notably lower than the actual ones. Meanwhile, the 3-h (Fig. 10) and 4-h (Fig. 11) models perform similarly.

Table 6. Results of the univariate model for each window size.

Metric	2 h	3 h	4 h
Train R^2	0.74	0.80	0.79
Test R^2	0.61	0.66	0.62
Train RMSE	3.16	2.52	2.58
Test RMSE	3.08	2.60	2.74
Recall (Frost)	0.62	0.62	0.61
F1-Score (Frost)	0.62	0.64	0.63
Recall (No Frost)	0.97	0.96	0.95
F1-Score (No Frost)	0.97	0.95	0.95
Accuracy (test)	0.95	0.91	0.91

The graphical representation of predictions made by the univariate models exhibits the same situation as for the bivariate ones. With a 2-h window (Fig. 9), the predictions are notably lower than the actual value. With windows of 3 (Fig. 10) and 4 h (Fig. 11), the forecasts are closer to the actual values.

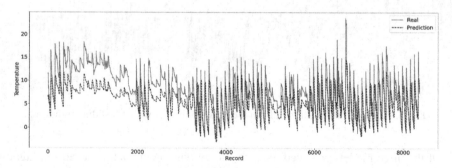

Fig. 9. Temperature prediction from the univariate model with 2 h sliding window

From this set of models, the 3-h window was also selected.

Finally, comparing the selected bivariate and univariate models, the regression metrics are very similar, but it can be observed that the bivariate model yields better recall. This metric is crucial as it denotes the fraction of frost cases predicted correctly out of

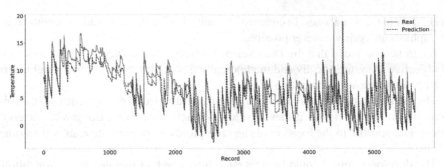

Fig. 10. Temperature prediction from the univariate model with 3 h sliding window

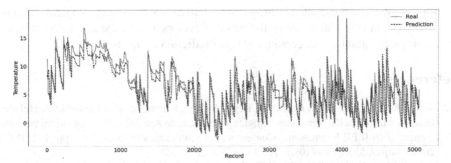

Fig. 11. Temperature prediction from the univariate model with 4 h sliding window

the total real frost cases. In summary, it is concluded that, among the analyzed sets of models, the bivariate model with a 3-h window produces the best result.

5 Conclusion and Future Work

Applying the Data Science process, a model based on an LSTM RNN has been developed to forecast the temperature over a 3-h horizon. Using meteorological variables such as temperature and relative humidity recorded at 10-min intervals over a period of 3 h. The model exhibits an accuracy of 92% and the capability to predict 73% of frost cases for a region in the southern province of San Juan, Argentina.

The applied process led to an intense preprocessing task for the data. By structuring the data with a sliding window, it was observed that the number of records decreases as the window size increases, thereby reducing the training and validation datasets. It was also concluded that increasing the window size does not necessarily improve the model's performance.

The graphical visualizations were decisive in establishing parameters for the models. A clear example was in determining the learning rate, where metrics were similar, but the graphs revealed overfitting and lack of convergence. Similarly, for the window size, the metrics of the models with a 2-h window did not differ significantly from those of 3 and 4 h, but the prediction graph highlighted that the predicted values significantly deviated from the actual ones. In conclusion, numerical analysis should be accompanied by graphical analysis whenever possible.

It can be concluded that the Data Science process has enabled the achievement of the objective of systematically and methodically developing a prediction model for the frost phenomenon with acceptable results.

The meteorological data is specific to a particular area (local phenomena) and exhibits variations among them even if they are close to each other. Forecasting with meteorological data specific to the location of the crop yields more accurate results than other forecasts.

The developed model could be integrated into a web or mobile application, allowing farmers to consult forecasts for specific areas and receive alerts of potential frost occurrences to take mitigation actions.

In future work, it is expected to incorporate data from other meteorological stations, improve the accuracy and recall of the model developed in this study, forecast other meteorological variables, and consider longer prediction horizons.

References

1. Möller-Acuña, P., Ahumada-García, R., Reyes-Suárez, J.: Predicción de Episodios de Heladas Basado en Información Agrometeorológica y Técnicas de Aprendizaje Automático. In: Conference: 2016 IEEE International Conference on Automatica (ICA-ACCA), pp. 1–7. IEEE (2016). https://doi.org/10.1109/ICA-ACCA.2016.7778386
2. Latif, R.M.A., Brahim, S.B., Saeed, S., Imran, L.B., Sadiq, M., Farhan, M.: Integration of google play content and frost prediction using CNN: scalable IoT framework for big data. IEEE Access **8**, 6890–6900. IEEE (2020). https://doi.org/10.1109/ACCESS.2019.2963590
3. Inforcampo. https://www.infocampo.com.ar/los-danos-por-heladas-tardias-alcanzaron-las-30-mil-hectareas-de-vid-y-16-mil-de-frutales-en-mendoza-en-2020/. Accessed 14 Apr 2022
4. Revista InterNos, Alerta entre los productores de Cuyo por las heladas tardías (2021)
5. Ángel, M., Chong, O., De Gobernación, S., Felipe, L., Espinosa, P.: SERIE Fascículos – Heladas. Mexico (2014)
6. Fuentes, M., Campos, C., García-Loyola, S.: Application of artificial neural networks to frost detection in central Chile using the next day minimum air temperature forecast. Chil. J. Agric. Res. **78**(3), 327–338 (2018). https://doi.org/10.4067/S0718-58392018000300327
7. Ozdemir, S.: Principles of Data Science: Learn the Techniques and Math You Need to Start Making Sense of Your Data. Packt Publishing Ltd., UK (2016)
8. Cady, F.: The Data Science Handbook, 1st edn. United States of America (2017)
9. Masanet, M.I., Klenzi, R.: Ciencia de Datos para el Desarrollo de un Modelo Predictivo de Heladas. In: XXIX Congreso Argentino de Ciencias de la Computación - CACIC 2023, 1a ed., pp. 38–47. U. N. de Luján (2024)
10. Konar, A., Bhattacharya, D.: Time-Series Prediction and Applications, vol. 127. Springer, Cham (2017). https://doi.org/10.1007/978-3-319-54597-4
11. Mohammed, R., Rawashdeh, J., Abdullah, M.: Machine learning with oversampling and undersampling techniques: overview study and experimental results. In: 2020 11th International Conference on Information Communication System ICICS 2020, pp. 243–248 (2020). https://doi.org/10.1109/ICICS49469.2020.239556
12. Masanet, M.I., Klenzi, R., Capraro, F.: Técnicas de balanceo de datos para predecir la ocurrencia del fenómeno meteorológico de la helada. Actas la XIX Reun. Trab. en Proces. la Inf. y Control. RPIC'2021, pp. 511–516 (2021). https://drive.google.com/file/d/1byaIS-ssvJP-SMH tKP9ahu8LQuoshyq6/view

13. Pisa, I., Santín, I., Vicario, J.L., Morell, A., Vilanova, R.: Data preprocessing for ANN-based industrial time-series forecasting with imbalanced data. European Signal Processing Conference, vol. 2019 (2019). https://doi.org/10.23919/EUSIPCO.2019.8902682
14. Snyder, R.L., de Melo-Abreu, J.P., Villar-Mir, J.M.: Protección contra las heladas: fundamentos, práctica y economía. Ser. FAO Sobre el Medioambiente y la Gestión los Recur. Nat. **1**, 257 (2010)
15. Yagüe, J.L.F.: Iniciación a la meteorología y climatología. España (2012)
16. Géron, A.: Hands-On Machine Learning with Scikit-Learn, Keras, and TensorFlow, 2nd edn. O'Reilly Media, Inc., United States of America (2019)
17. Cortez, J., Masanet, M.I., Klenzi, R., Ortega, M.O.: Procesamiento de datos meteorológicos para determinar la ocurrencia, intensidad y duración de heladas. Memorias de las JAIIO **9**, 7–20 (2023)
18. Chollet, F.: Deep Learning with Python, 1st edn. Manning Publications Co., USA (2017)
19. Kaur, H., Pannu, H.S., Malhi, A.K.: A systematic review on imbalanced data challenges in machine learning: Applications and solutions. ACM Comput. Surv. **52**(4) (2019). https://doi.org/10.1145/3343440
20. Aggarwal, C.C.: Neural Networks and Deep Learning: A Textbook, 1st edn. Springer, Cham (2018). https://doi.org/10.1007/978-3-031-29642-0_5

Distributed and Parallel Processing

Evaluation of Programming Languages for Memory Usage, Scalability, and Cold Start, on AWS Lambda Serverless Platform as a Case Study

Nelson Rodríguez[✉] [iD], María Murazzo [iD], Adriana Martín, and Matías Rodríguez

Departamento de Informática, Facultad de Ciencias Exactas Físicas y Naturales, Universidad Nacional de San Juan, San Juan, Argentina
nelson@iinfo.unsj.edu.ar

Abstract. Serverless Computing is a Cloud architecture, an alternative to the traditional model. It offers numerous advantages over the monolithic model, such as providing agility, innovation, automatic scaling, flexibility in development and better evaluation and control of costs. It emerged as an evolution of microservices running in containers and implementing functions, which is why it is sometimes called function as a service. Although it has the aforementioned advantages, there are also many challenges and problems to solve. Among them the initialization or startup of said functions, this problem known as cold start. Most scientific publications do not take programming languages into account for this analysis. In this work, the behavior of different programming languages in initialization, cold start, memory use and scalability is evaluated, under a serverless approach on the Amazon Web Services platform. Because the comparison of languages can be carried out in different aspects or taking different types of metrics, it was considered appropriate to perform the tests using CRUD operations. This also allows us to analyze their behavior when initializing the database. Therefore, a series of questions arise, such as: Are the initialization of the programming languages all the same? Is the initialization of the database with the programming languages independent of the language used? Is the cold start equivalent in the different languages? Is its impact relevant when the number of requirements is high? Does memory usage and scalability behave the same, regardless of the programming language?

Through the tests carried out, it was possible to evaluate the behavior of programming languages and answer some of the questions mentioned above.

Keywords: Serverless Computing · FaaS · Programming Language · Cloud Computing

1 Introduction

Cloud computing became essential for users and businesses primarily from the COVID-19 pandemic, accelerating the adoption of cloud services as organizations turned to online services and infrastructure to accommodate remote employees and customer demand for meetings, events, and e-commerce.

© The Author(s), under exclusive license to Springer Nature Switzerland AG 2024
P. Pesado et al. (Eds.): CACIC 2023, CCIS 2123, pp. 33–45, 2024.
https://doi.org/10.1007/978-3-031-62245-8_3

The term cloud computing came into popular use in 2008, although the practice of providing remote access to computing functions over networks dates back to the mainframe time-sharing systems of the 1960s and 1970s. Virtualization, created by IBM, allowed multiple virtual systems to run on top of a single physical system [1]. Subsequently, the Internet emerged globally and its expansion began when in 2002, Amazon introduced its web-based retail services. It was the first major company to think about using only 10% of its capacity as a problem to be solved [2, 3].

Following the evolution seen in the history of containerization, cloud services have adapted to offer better-fit containers that require less time to load (boot) and provide greater automation in the handling (orchestration) of containers on behalf of the customer [4]. Serverless computing promises to achieve complete automation in container management.

The serverless computing model is event-driven in which compute resources are provided as scalable services. In the traditional model, a fixed, recurring cost is charged for the server's computing resources, regardless of the amount of work performed by the server. However, the Serverless implementation has overcome this shortcoming, as you pay only for the use of the service and do not charge for downtime.

In this emerging paradigm, software applications are decomposed into multiple independent stateless functions [5, 6]. Functions only run in response to triggering actions (such as user interactions, messaging events, or database changes), and can scale independently and can be ephemeral (can last one invocation) and are fully managed by the cloud provider.

Different serverless computing platforms have been proposed by major cloud providers such as AWS Lambda, Microsoft Azure Functions, Google Functions, IBM Cloud Functions, Cloudflare Worker, Alibaba Function Compute. Such platforms make it easier and allow developers to focus more on business logic, without the overhead of scaling and provisioning infrastructure [7].

Castro et al. [8], offer a feature-based definition: Developers don't need to worry about the low-level details of server management and scaling, and they only pay when they process requests or events. He further adds that: serverless computing is a platform that hides server usage from developers and runs code on-demand automatically scaled and billed only for the time the code is running.

In most cases, you can write functions in whatever language the programmer deems most appropriate (Node.js, Python, Go, Java, and more) and use container and serverless tools, such as AWS SAM or the Docker CLI, to build, test, and deploy the functions [9].

On the other hand, specialists from Expert Market Research forecast that the global serverless computing market will grow in the period of 2022–2027 at a CAGR of 22.2% [10].

A function based model is suitable for bursts, intensive CPU usage, and granular workloads. Currently, FaaS use cases vary widely, including data processing, stream processing, edge computing (IoT), and scientific computing [3].

Serverless covers a wide range of technologies, which can be grouped into two categories: Backend-as-a-Service (BaaS) and Functions-as-a-Service (FaaS).

There are several challenges, opportunities, and problems to be solved, including developer experience [8], interoperability, testing, function composition, security, life-cycle management, non-functional requirements management, performance, overhead optimization, cost-performance engineering, among others [7].

Ideally, it would be desirable to have minimal overhead when invoking functions. However, when the platform needs to activate the first instance, the underlying resources still need time for initialization. This boot also occurs when the autoscaler provisions additional instances to handle traffic. The initialization time for each function instance introduces a delay until the instance can respond to requests. This problem is very common on serverless platforms and is known as the cold start problem. Although the FaaS offering typically suffers from cold boots, the overhead each platform incurs varies depending on the underlying implementation of the functions [11].

2 Related Work

In cloud-based software development, rented resources can always be kept activated to serve application execution, which has no cold boot issues for application executions. In addition, developers can flexibly select resource capacity and configure resource uptime.

In contrast, in serverless-based software development, the vendor is responsible for managing the runtime environment.

The advantage of this type of unified resource management is that it responds to any burst workload. These runtime environments are activated when applications are activated. When the required environments are not active, applications can face the issue of cold starting, which introduces a long preparation time. There have been many efforts to alleviate this problem [12–17]. However, none of these studies analyze the behavior of programming languages in this area.

A paper published by Pawel Zuk and Krzysztof Rzadca [18] is very clear in explaining the problem, stating the following: Serverless Computing is the latest model of cloud computing. In this model, the serverless platform offers instant elasticity on a per-request basis. Such elasticity usually comes at the expense of the "cold start" problem. This phenomenon is associated with a delay that occurs due to the provision of a runtime container to execute the functions.

Shortly after Amazon introduced this computing model with the AWS Lambda platform in 2014, several commercial and open-source platforms began adopting and offering this technology.

Each platform has its own solution for dealing with cold starts. Evaluating the performance of each platform under load and the factors influencing the cold start problem has received a lot of attention in recent years.

A recent article by Tam n. Nguyen, published in Future Generation Computer Systems (Elsevier), proposes a novel cold-start management policy that enables feedback loops with other higher-management policies and organizes lower-level cold-start optimization policies. It tries to predict the arrival of functions from 5 to 15 min in the future and also proposes evaluation strategies for both the TCN model and the Management Policy. The results of the assessment show that the TCN model works reliably on two tracking datasets from the major serverless platform vendors [20]. The author concludes that: communication between programmers and policy administrators is essential to manage different policies, including those for cold boot management.

Another paper published in 2024 by Daniel Fireman et al. [21], describes a practical technique, prebaking, to reduce function startup time based on restoring snapshots of previously executed processes. The basis of the technique is critical to deciding when to create a snapshot of a function. According to the authors, building a good snapshot function is not complicated.

In summary, it can be said that Serverless is an attractive cloud service model because it offers companies the same advantages of the Cloud at a fraction of the prices of other cloud service models. One of the biggest problems with serverless computing is the paradox of shutting down idle cloud resources to keep costs low versus keeping idle resources available for prompt execution of customer requests. In this case, there is a problem of conflicts, which can be common within complex cloud computing systems [20].

For this publication, we are based on the article approved at CACIC 2023 [22], which analyzes the programming languages used in AWS and adds other comparisons at the level of memory usage and scalability.

3　Methodology

The addressed problematic is the evaluation of programming languages´ behavior for initialization and cold start on a Serverless platform, taking Amazon Web Services as a case study.

In order to carry out the relevant laboratory studies on various variables in the execution and commissioning of Serverless Functions (FaaS), the following activities will be carried out:

- Analysis and study of the AWS Lambda service or platform
- Study and detailed operation of available databases in AWS.
- Determination of the languages to be compared by making use of functions.
- Determination of the scenarios to be used so as to compare the resulting values.
- Comparative study of the different parameters and values obtained.

To develop the research, we proceeded as shown in Fig. 1, consisting of a diagram summarizing the work carried out.

For the research we made the decision to develop Forms API, by using AWS services that allow a serverless development. We considered an API allowing the handling of different dynamic forms and that, in turn, preserve their relevant information along with their responses. A Form API was prepared for the comparison of the different programming languages in a serverless environment.

This was considered appropriate to reproduce a real-world problem in which scalable software resources are needed to support large volumes of users without affecting system performance.

The function of this API is to create dynamic Forms and store all the information required by them, including user responses.

Only one Form was needed to carry out the language evaluation in this context.

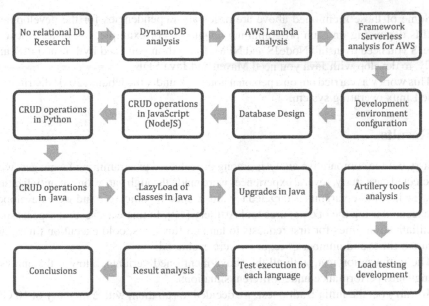

Fig. 1. Research process procedure outline

For the evaluation, a Form extract was implemented for the 2022 National Population, Households and Housing Census, since it has many fields and data of various types.

4 Database and Development Environment

In order to store the necessary data for the representation of forms and their responses, it was decided to use the AWS DynamoDB service as it allows to carry out the research under the serverless approach because this service is fully managed and it avoids the administrative burdens of having to use and scale databases.

This service also has the necessary power to create tables that allow thousands and even millions of data and requests to be stored and retrieved.

In this research, we set out to imitate in the best possible way the traffic of a real and constantly used application, so this service becomes essential to be able to replicate the desired context in which the chosen programming languages will be evaluated.

For the development of the forms APIs in the different languages on the AWS platform, several tools were used that allow and facilitate this development. They are:

- Github
- Serverless Framework
- AWS CLI
- NodeJS y NPM
- Python y PIP
- Maven
- Java SDK

Some of those mentioned above are necessary dependencies for the development of APIs depending on each programming language. For example, for JavaScript with NodeJS you need to install NodeJS and NPM; for Python you need Python and PIP; and finally, to develop with Java you need Maven and Java SDK.

This work was carried out on a personal notebook under the Ubuntu 20.04 distribution of the Linux operating system.

5 Results

To carry out the comparative analysis among the selected programming languages, with the selected case study, several experiences were made through variations of initialization tests. Each of these variants is targeted towards a specific objective and were developed and executed using the open-source tool Artillery [19]. In this way, several aspects such as: initialization times for first requests to lambda functions, cold execution times, hot execution times and number of requests were evaluated.

The initialization test, with all the above-mentioned variants, allowed the analysis of languages performance under different situations.

To carry out the initialization test, we decided to run them with a memory of 10 GB.

This is the maximum size memory offered by AWS in the Lambda service, which makes it possible to utilize the highest CPU power allowed by this service.

5.1 Initialization Test

The initialization test aims at testing CRUD operations in such a way that each lambda´s initialization execution context always occurs. When this situation takes place, AWS provides us an initialization time variable in its metrics indicating how long it took the platform to prepare the infrastructure and necessary dependencies to allow the code execution within the lambda that was written by the service consumer.

Five cold runs for each language and CRUD operation were performed, this was done by running the test flow already mentioned above.

It is worth noting that these executions were carried out every single hour to ensure that AWS deactivated the FaaS infrastructure, returning each function to a cold state.

Each time a cold run was done, a second run was also immediately performed to take the hot run time, allowing to compare cold and hot run times.

5.1.1 Initialization Times

Table 1 shows averages obtained from initialization times related to CRUD operations for each programming language.

Taking into account all CRUD operations, it can be seen a clear difference where Java read operation is the one with the longest initialization time with 1630.52 ms.

As for NodeJS and Python the most deficient operation is delete, with times of 442.15 ms. And 411.2 ms, respectively. These differences, though not significant, can be seen in Fig. 2. Following the same reasoning, the update operation is the one with the best performance when initializing the execution context for a lambda, regardless of the language.

Table 1. Average initialization times for each CRUD operation and programming language

Language	Create	Read	Update	Delete
JavaScript (NodeJS)	418,232	431,04	413,586	442,15
Python	384,902	400,43	361,624	411,2
Java	1623,528	1630,52	1526,12	1577,302

As mentioned above, results were also obtained regarding cold run times and a second hot run. Tables 2, 3, and 4 show the differences between cold and hot execution times for each CRUD operations and for each language.

Shaded cells correspond to the CRUD operation that achieves the greatest improvement. It can be seen that differences are greater in Java. For example, with delete, execution goes from 581,494 ms. in cold to 84,654 ms. in hot. That is, Java is the language with the greatest discrepancy between those execution times, obtaining an 84% average improvement. In other words, Java is the one that reduces times most abruptly.

Table 2. Execution Time in NodeJS for each CRUD operation

Execution Time Status	Create	Read	Update	Delete
Cold	76.698	74.592	84.04	77.768
Hot	51.238	39.248	45.536	41.066
Difference	25.46	35.294	38.504	36.702
Percentage of Improvement	33.195112	47.347803	45.816278	47.194218

Also, NodeJS and Python improve when running hot, finding the highest gains in Read and Delete, about 48% on average respectively.

Table 3 below shows Python cold and hot execution times values.

Table 3. Execution Time in Python for each CRUD operation

Execution time Status	Create	Read	Update	Delete
Cold	60.734	49.752	65.738	43.97
Hot	32.582	27.388	38.472	22.566
Difference	28.152	22.364	27.266	21.404
Percentage of Improvement	46.352948	44.950956	41.476771	48.6786445

Finally, results obtained after running the tests in Java programming language are shown.

Finally, Fig. 2 shows a summary of the results of all the executions carried out, even though some differences are not significant.

Table 4. Runtime in Java for each CRUD operation

Execution time Status	Create	Read	Update	Delete
Cold	701.192	664.628	644.328	581.494
Hot	116.638	98.102	116.89	84.654
Difference	584.554	566.526	527.438	496.84
Percentage of Improvement	83.365754	85.239562	81.858618	85.441982

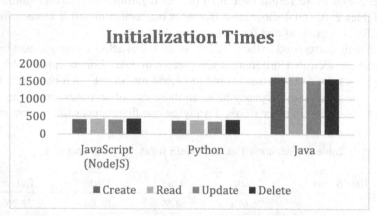

Fig. 2. Initialization times comparison of CRUD operations of different programming languages.

5.2 Scalability Test

Unlike the initialization test, this test seeks that different APIs undergo different loads of concurrent requests made in 1 s.

The purpose is to observe how the AWS Lambda service scales for each different programming language and how this affects lambdas´ execution times.

It is vitally important to observe those executions that suffered from initialization times, since this provides an explanation for some increases in the execution times obtained.

This test differs from the initialization test in defining its loading phases.

For this case, six phases that show the number of requests to be made in a second are shown. This number of requests is the load we will put on the developed APIs. Each of these loading phases, except for the last one, will be followed by a 1-min pause phase that will give rise to the next defined load The number of requests begins just with one, which allows to heat the infrastructure and then it increases to 10, 25, 50, 100 and 200 quantities.

Previously, in the initialization test it resulted that Java had the worst performance when preparing the infrastructure in charge of executing the code of a lambda function; however, it was also noted that it was the language with the widest range of improvement when the execution was done in hot.

The results shown in Fig. 3 correspond to the CRUD read operation for each language and allow us to validate those obtained in the previous test.

5.2.1 Execution Times

Java starts with a very bad time in the first runtime due to initialization delays; but then when increasing the number of concurrent executions we observe that times drastically improve to 20 ms. For 10 executions, having a better performance than NodeJS and Python whose times were 30 and 31 ms., respectively.

This superior Java performance is also due to the fact that no initialization took place in all 10 runs, while NodeJS and Python each suffered from 1 initialization which affected their runtimes.

Also, it can be observed that in the 25 executions Java gets worse because it goes through 6 initializations, undergoing a time of 158 ms while NodeJS and Python obtained times of 40 ms and 17 ms, respectively.

Finally, from 50 executions onwards, runtimes stabilize in all three languages, being Java the one that gets again the best times in the 200 executions, with a time of 14 ms against 27 ms and 15 ms of NodeJS and Python respectively (see table 5).

Table 5. Runtime for Read in milliseconds

Number of concurrent executions	NodeJS	Python	Java
1	70.32	58.11	652.72
10	30.359	31.658	20.001
25	39.9252	16.6476	58.3124
50	29.7432	17.994	24.3094
100	26.2374	16.5708	19.7675
200	26.6532	15.444	13.9122

5.3 Memory Test

One of the features to configure when deploying a Lambda function has to do with its memory size. This test was implemented in order to check if memory size affects functions performance in any way. The configuration file coincides with the initialization one; that is, a first cold execution is performed and then another one is carried out after a minute to force a hot execution. The first request provided information about how memory size affects functions initialization in different languages.

With the second call, data about runtimes and how these are altered by lambdas memory size was acquired.

This test was executed by modifying memory size, that is, we started by configuring lambdas with a 10 GB size and memory was decreasing as follows: 8, 6, 4, 2, 1 GB values. Finally, it was run with 512 MB lambdas.

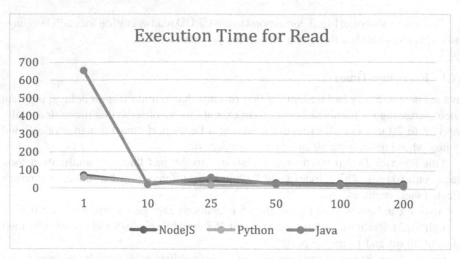

Fig. 3. Execution times for Read operation in each language

5.3.1 Execution Times According to Memory

The results obtained in this memory test can be seen in Fig. 4. As regards runtime, it can be seen that the less memory has a lambda function assigned, the greater the runtimes of each language are. This is the expected behaviour since AWS supplies less CPU as the allocated memory decreases; therefore, the container in charge of executing the function will increasingly have fewer resources. It is worth noting that a common point of languages for the CRUD create operation was found in the 4096 MB where runtimes of each language are very similar, being NodeJS the one with the best performance with 42 ms., while Python and Java obtained a time of 50 ms. And 48 ms. Respectively.

A very important aspect to take into account is Java performance when memory is less than 4096 MB. In this case you can see how runtimes increase, and once they are below 1024 MB runtime increases considerably.

With this test it also becomes interesting to note about initialization times that, although they are not important when talking about billing, they are of utmost importance for the response time of lambda functions. It is already known that when a lambda function is executed in a cold state, the final response time of the function will be given by the sum of its initialization time plus the execution time itself. According to the application in which the function is, these times may or may not be critical. In a CRUD function they are not really very critical, but even if functions take a couple of seconds, they can affect an end user experience when using a system or application. Proper memory provisioning of a lambda function can be vital to achieve a balance of both the execution time as seen above and also function initialization times. Furthermore, the shorter the execution times, the lower the amount billed by AWS, and the larger the allocated memory, the higher the cost to pay.

For these reasons, finding the right memory settings can provide a benefit in terms of cost and runtime lambda service.

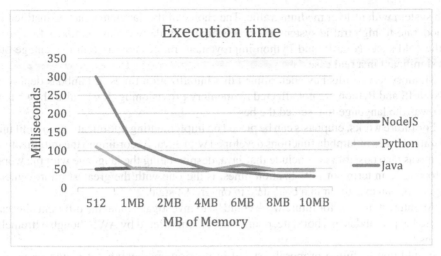

Fig. 4. Execution times for create, for each language and according to memory size

In Fig. 4 you can clearly observe that for NodeJS and Python memory provisioning does not affect lambda initialization times at all, but it is important to keep in mind that it does affect runtimes as previously seen. We finally have Java as the big loser when considering the initialization of a lambda.

As memory decreases from 10 GB to 6 GB you can see an irregular performance in Java since; for example, it is seen how times decrease from 1652 ms. in 8 GB to 1346 ms. in 6 GB, but from this point initialization times increase reaching a maximum time of 4000 ms. For a 512 MB memory size which is a very bad performance for a CRUD operation.

6   Conclusions and Future Work

In this work, a Rest API was developed with the goal of performing CRUD operations for loading a form and its responses. This API was developed in three different languages: Javascript with NodeJS, Python and Java. With these operations, performance variation, initialization time's latency, scalability and implications of memory size configured in the functions were broadly investigated. We investigated how the selection of programming languages affects when performing CRUD operations of a Rest API with a series of automatic tests. Python is the programming language with the best times when it comes to raising the execution context of a lambda function, obtaining the best times for any of the CRUD operations.

Similarly, differences between either Python or NodeJS are really insignificant. The choice between any of these two languages, considering lambdas initialization, won´t be very conflictive.

The most deficient language was Java, having very large initialization times compared to the others. Java, unlike NodeJS and Python, must lift a virtual machine and load the application code into memory, which causes its first execution to take longer. Choosing Java for a serverless Rest API with Lambda can cause slow response times if used on a system with little or medium traffic. The choice of this language may be justified in a moderate-to-high traffic system where it is highly unlikely to have lambdas functions in the cold state. NodeJS and Python improvement ranges are large in percentage but not significant in a real case.

Memory test results have determined that initialization times of lambdas deployed in NodeJS and Python are not affected by memory provisioning. It was also shown that Java was the language that scaled the best.

For future works, emphasis can be placed on implementing optimizations to limit initialization times of lambda functions developed with Java. According to the initialization test it was also possible to conclude that Java, despite being the language with the worst performance in terms of initialization times, is the one with the greatest improvement range, from an execution in a cold state to one in hot state.

An interesting case for future work could be to investigate about the different alternatives to keep lambdas in a hot state, being one of them offered by AWS though extremely expensive.

In addition to future proposals, stated in previous paragraphs, it would be useful to evaluate the behaviour of other programming languages such as Go, C#, Ruby and PowerShell.

References

1. Cloud computing: A complete guide. IBM. https://www.ibm.com/cloud/learn/cloud-computing-gbl
2. Armbrust, M., et al.: Above the clouds: A Berkeley view of cloud computing, In: Tech. Rep. No. UCB/EECS-2009-28 (2009)
3. Foote, K.D.: A Brief History of Cloud Computing (Dec. 2021). https://www.dataversity.net/brief-history-cloud-computing/
4. van Eyk, E., Toader, L., Talluri, S., Versluis, L., Uta, A., Iosup, A.: Serverless is more: from PaaS to present cloud computing. IEEE Internet Comput. 22(5), 8–17 (2018). https://doi.org/10.1109/MIC.2018.053681358
5. Adzic, G., Chatley, R.: Serverless computing: economic and architectural impact. In: Proceedings of the 2017 11th Joint Meeting on Foundations of Software Engineering, pp. 884–889. ACM (2917)
6. AWS Lambda: aws.amazon.com/es/lambda/
7. Bermbach, D., Karakaya, A., Buchholz, S.: Using application knowledge to reduce cold starts in FaaS services. In: SAC 2020, March 30-April 3, 2020, Brno, Czech Republic (2020)
8. Castro, P., Ishakian, V., Muthusamy, V., Slominski, A.: The rise of serverless computing. Commun. ACM **62**(12), 44–54 (2019)
9. Rodríguez, N., Atencio, H., et al.: Interoperabilidad de funciones en el Modelo de Programación de Serverless Computing. In: IV CICCSI. Universidad Champagnat (2020)
10. EMR: Global Serverless Computing Market Outlook
11. https://www.expertmarketresearch.com/reports/serverless-computing-market (2021)
12. Lin, P.-M., Glikson, A.: Mitigating Cold Starts In Serverless Platforms A Pool-Based Approach. https://arxiv.org/pdf/1903.12221.pdf
13. SAND: Towards high-performance serverless computing. In: Proceedings of the 2018 USENIX Annual Technical Conference. 923ś935

14. Cadden, J., Unger, T., Awad, Y., Dong, H., Krieger, O., Appavoo, J.: SEUSS: skip redundant paths to make serverless fast. In: Proceedings of the 15th European Conference on Computer Systems, pp. 1–15 (2020)
15. Oakes, E., et al.: SOCK: Rapid task provisioning with serverless-optimized containers. In Proceedings of the 2018 USENIX Annual Technical Conference, pp. 57–70. USENIX Association (2018)
16. Wang, K.-T.A., Ho, R., Wu, P.: Replayable execution optimized for page sharing for a managed runtime environment. In Proceedings of the Fourteenth EuroSys Conference 2019, pp. 1–16 (2019)
17. Vahidinia, P., Farahani, B., Aliee, F.S.: Cold start in serverless computing: current trends and mitigation strategies. In: 2020 International Conference on Omni-layer Intelligent Systems (COINS), Barcelona, Spain, 2020, pp. 1–7 (2020). https://doi.org/10.1109/COINS49042.2020.9191377
18. Zuk, P., Rzadca, K.: Scheduling methods to reduce response latency of function as a service. In: Proceedings of the 2020 IEEE 32nd International Symposium on Computer Architecture and High Performance Computing, pp. 132–140 (2020)
19. Artillery (s.f.) Artillery Docs. https://www.artillery.io/docs/guides/getting-started/core-concepts
20. Nguyen, T.: Fut. Gener. Comput. Syst. **153**, 312–325 (2024). https://doi.org/10.1016/j.future.2023.12.011
21. Fireman, D., Silva, P., Pereira, T.E., Mafra, L., Valadares, D.: Prebaking runtime environments to improve the FaaS cold start latency. Fut. Gener. Comput. Syst. **155**, 287–299 (2024). https://doi.org/10.1016/j.future.2024.01.019
22. Rodríguez, M., Rodríguez, N., Murazzo, M.: Evaluación de la inicialización y el arranque en frio de los lenguajes de programación en una plataforma serverless. Amazon Web Services como caso de estudio. Libro de actas - XXIX Congreso Argentino de Ciencias de la Computación - CACIC (2023)

Enhanced OpenMP Algorithm
to Compute All-Pairs Shortest Path
on X86 Architectures

Sergio Calderón[1,2], Enzo Rucci[1,3(✉)] ⬤, and Franco Chichizola[1] ⬤

[1] III-LIDI, Facultad de Informática, UNLP - CIC, 1900 La Plata, Bs As, Argentina
{scalderon,erucci,francoch}@lidi.info.unlp.edu.ar
[2] Becario de Entrenamiento, CIC, La Plata, Argentina
[3] Comisión de Investigaciones Científicas (CIC), 1900 La Plata,
Bs As, Argentina

Abstract. Graphs have become a key tool when modeling and solving problems in different areas. The Floyd-Warshall (FW) algorithm computes the shortest path between all pairs of vertices in a graph and is employed in areas like communication networking, traffic routing, bioinformatics, among others. However, FW is computationally and spatially expensive since it requires $O(n^3)$ operations and $O(n^2)$ memory space. As the graph gets larger, parallel computing becomes necessary to provide a solution in an acceptable time range. In this paper, we studied a FW code developed for Xeon Phi KNL processors and adapted it to run on any Intel x86 processors, losing the specificity of the former. To do so, we verified one by one the optimizations proposed by the original code, making adjustments to the base code where necessary, and analyzing its performance on two Intel servers under different test scenarios. In addition, a new optimization was proposed to increase the concurrency degree of the parallel algorithm, which was implemented using two different synchronization mechanisms. The experimental results show that all optimizations were beneficial on the two x86 platforms selected. Last, the new optimization proposal improved performance by up to 23%.

Keywords: Floyd-Warshall · Multicore · APSP · Xeon · Xeon Phi
Knights Landing · Core · OpenMP

1 Introduction

The Floyd-Warshall (FW) [3,17] algorithm computes the shortest path between all pairs of vertices in a graph and is employed in areas like communication networking [8], traffic routing [7], bioinformatics [9], among others. However, FW is computationally and spatially expensive since it requires $O(n^3)$ operations and $O(n^2)$ memory space, where n is the number of vertices in a graph. As the graph gets larger, parallel computing becomes necessary to provide a solution in an acceptable time frame. This is why the scientific community has made multiple efforts for this purpose [4,5,10,13–16,18]. Focusing on Intel Xeon Phi

P. Pesado et al. (Eds.): CACIC 2023, CCIS 2123, pp. 46–61, 2024.
https://doi.org/10.1007/978-3-031-62245-8_4

platforms, Rucci *et al.* [12] explored its use to accelerate FW in the first generation (KNC, Knights Corner), while Costi *et al.* [2] extended it to the second (Knights Landing, KNL).

In [1], we studied the code developed by [2] and adapted it to run on Intel x86 processors, losing the specificity of the Xeon Phi KNL. To do so, we verified one by one the optimizations proposed by [2], making adjustments to the base code where necessary, and analyzing its performance on two Intel servers under different test scenarios. This paper is an extended and thoroughly revised version of [1]. The work has been extended by providing:

– The proposal of a new optimization for the parallel FW algorithm (*intra-round parallelism*) and its implementation using different synchronization mechanisms (semaphores vs. condition variables).
– A performance analysis of the proposed optimization on 2 different Intel x86 servers.
– The creation of a public git repository with the different codes developed for this paper[1].

The rest of the paper is organized as follows. Section 2 introduces the background of this work. Section 3 details the adaptation process and the new optimizacion proposal. In Sect. 4, performance results are presented and finally, in Sect. 5, conclusions and some ideas for future research are summarized.

2   Background

2.1   Intel Xeon Phi

Xeon Phi is the brand name that Intel used for a series of many-core, HPC-oriented processors. In 2012, Intel launched the first Phi generation (KNC) with 61×86 pentium cores (4 hardware threads per core) equipped with a 512-bit vector unit (VPU) each. In contrast to KNC co-processors connected via a PCI Express bus to the host, the second Phi generation (KNL) can act as self-boot processors. KNL processors feature a large number of cores with hyper-threading support, the incorporation of AVX-512's 512-bit vector instructions, and the integration of a high-bandwidth memory (HBM), among others [11]. The latest generation (Knight Mills, KNM) was released in late 2017, being a KNL variant with specific instructions for deep machine learning. Finally, Intel announced that it would discontinue the Xeon Phi series in 2018 to focus on the development of graphics boards (GPUs)[2].

---

[1] https://bit.ly/cacic23-fw.
[2] https://hardzone.es/2018/07/25/intel-adios-xeon-phi-reemplazados-tarjetas-graficas/.

2.2 Intel Xeon and Core

Currently, Intel offers two processor segments in the x86 family: Xeon and Core. Intel Xeon processors are designed for enterprise and server tasks that require high-performance computing and reliability, while Intel Core processors are ideal for general-purpose use, including gaming, office applications and multimedia entertainment.

In terms of architectural features, Xeon processors tend to have more cores, specific technologies for virtualization and security, support for multi-socket configuration, among other advanced features. In opposite sense, Core processors tend to have higher frequencies, lower power consumption and lower price.

The choice between Xeon and Core will depend on the specific application needs, budget and user preferences.

2.3 FW Algorithm

The pseudocode of FW is shown in Fig. 1. Given a graph G of N vertexes, FW receives as input a dense $N \times N$ matrix D that contains the distances between all pairs of vertexes from G, where $D_{i,j}$ represents the distance from node i to node j[3]. FW computes N iterations, evaluating in the k-th iteration all possible paths between vertexes i and j that have k as the intermediate vertex. As a result, it produces an updated matrix D, where $D_{i,j}$ now contains the shortest distance between nodes i and j up to that step. Also, FW builds an additional matrix P that records the paths associated with the shortest distances.

```
for k ← 0 to N − 1 do
  for i ← 0 to N − 1 do
    for j ← 0 to N − 1 do
      if D_{i,j} ≥ D_{i,k} + D_{k,j} then
        D_{i,j} ← D_{i,k} + D_{k,j}
        P_{i,j} ← k
      end if
    end for
  end for
end for
```

Fig. 1. Pseudocode of the FW algorithm

Blocked FW Algorithm. At first glance, the nested triple loop structure of this algorithm is similar to that of dense matrix multiplication (MM). However, since read and write operations are performed on the same matrix, the three loops cannot be freely exchanged, as is the case with MM. Despite this, the FW algorithm can be computed by blocks under certain conditions [16].

The blocked FW algorithm (BFW) divides matrix D into blocks of size $BS \times BS$, totaling $(N/BS)^2$ blocks. Computation is organized in $R = N/BS$ rounds, where each round consists of 4 phases ordered according to the data dependencies between the blocks:

---

[3] If there is no path between nodes i and j, their distance is considered to be infinite (usually represented as the largest positive value).

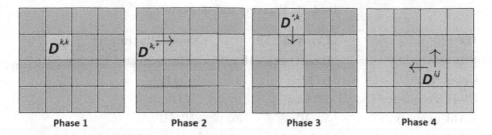

Fig. 2. BFW computation phases and block dependencies (Color figure online)

1. Phase 1: Update the $D^{k,k}$ block because it only depends on itself.
2. Phase 2: Update the blocks in row k of blocks ($D^{k,*}$) because each of these depends on itself and on $D^{k,k}$.
3. Phase 3: Update the blocks in column k of blocks ($D^{*,k}$) because each of these depends on itself and on $D^{k,k}$.
4. Phase 4: Update the remaining $D^{i,j}$ blocks of the matrix because each of these depends on blocks $D^{i,k}$ and $D^{k,j}$ on its row and column of blocks, respectively.

Figure 2 shows each of the computation phases and the dependencies between blocks. The pink squares represent blocks that are being computed, gray squares are those that have already been processed, and sky-blue squares are the ones that have not been computed yet. Last, arrows show the dependencies between blocks for each phase.

2.4 Base Code

As base code, we used the one from [2], which is a FWB algorithm specifically developed for Intel's Xeon Phi KNL processors. The following is a description of the different optimizations considered in the previous work:

– **Opt-0: Multi-threading**. A multi-threaded version is obtained using OpenMP. In Phases 2 to 4, the blocks are distributed among the different threads utilizing the `for` directive with `dynamic` scheduling. In the case of Phase 1, since it consists of a single block, the iterations within it are distributed among the threads.
– **Opt-1: MCDRAM**. Since this is a bandwidth-limited application, using this special memory is greatly beneficial. Executions are done using the `numactl` `-p` command to use the DDR memory as an auxiliary one.
– **Opt-2: SSE vectorization**. Using the OpenMP `simd` directive, the operations of the innermost loop are vectorized when computing each block. Typically, compilers use the 128-bit SSE instruction set by default, which allows the CPU to pack 2 double-precision multiply-add operations (4 flops) or 4 single-precision multiply-add operations (8 flops).

Table 1. Experimental platforms

ID	Core i5	Xeon Platinum
Processor	Intel Core i5-10400F	2×Intel Xeon Platinum 8276 L
Cores (ht)	6 (12)	56 (112)
Clock Frequency (base)	2.9 Ghz	2.2 Ghz
RAM memory	32 GB	250 GB
OS	Debian 11	Ubuntu 20.04 LTS

- **Opt-3: AVX2 vectorization**. AVX2 doubles the number of simultaneous operations concerning SSE. Thus, the CPU is guided to use 256-bit AVX instructions by adding the *-xAVX2* flag to the compilation process (if supported).
- **Opt-4: AVX-512 vectorization**. As the previous case, the *-xMIC-AVX512* flag is included to use 512-bit AVX512 extensions. In this way, the CPU can compute 8 double-precision multiply-add operations (16 flops) or 32 single-precision multiply-add operations (64 flops).
- **Opt-5: Data alignment**. _mm_malloc() allocates aligned blocks of memory, i.e., data is stored aligned to the beginning of each cache line. In this way, subsequent read and write operations are optimized.
- **Opt-6: Branch prediction**. The distance comparison is a hotspot of FW. By including the built-in __builtin_expect compiler macro, if statement branches can be better predicted. The more the scheduler gets right, the more instruction-level parallelism the processor can exploit.
- **Opt-7: Loop unrolling**. By fully unrolling the innermost loop and loop i only once.
- **Opt-8: Thread affinity**. Threads are distributed among cores according to the variable KMP_AFFINITY. Different affinity types (*balanced*, *compact* or *scatter*) and granularities (*fine*, *core* or *tile*) can be specified.

3 Implementation

3.1 Code Adaptation to X86 Architectures

The code base from Sect. 2 was adapted for its execution on the two x86 servers (see Table 1). In both cases, the Intel ICC compiler was used, which is part of the oneAPI suite (v2021.7.1).

The adjustments carried out to the different code versions are detailed below:

- **Opt-0:** No changes are required in this version.
- **Opt-1:** None of the platforms has MCDRAM memory, so the command *numactl* is ruled out.
- **Opt-2 / Opt-3:** No changes are required in these version.

- **Opt-4:** The associated flag is replaced by the one recommended for the Xeon Platinum (from *-xMIC-AVX512* to *-xCORE-AVX512*); at the same time, it is discarded on Intel Core i5 because that extension set is not available on that processor.
- **Opt-5:** The Xeon Platinum keeps SIMD_WIDTH = 512; while Core i5 reduces to 256 because AVX2 is the widest vectorization set available.
- **Opt-6 / Opt-7:** No changes are required in these versions.
- **Opt-8:** No changes are required in this version. The best affinity and granularity configuration is empirically selected.

3.2 Opt-9: Intra-round Concurrency

This section describes a new optimization proposal, which seeks to increase the concurrency in block computation. In the FWB algorithm, phase 4 of each round must wait for the end of phases 2 and 3 above. However, as phases 2 and 3 progress, some blocks of phase 4 could already be computed (those whose dependencies have already been resolved), without waiting for the end of phases 2 and 3. Figure 3 illustrates this improvement opportunity, where the computed blocks are shown in gray (five blocks of phase 2–3), and those in processing are shown in pink (six blocks of phase 4). This possible optimization becomes more relevant when T is *large* and BS is *small*.

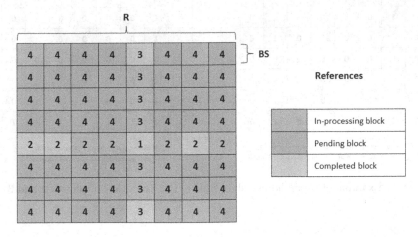

Fig. 3. Example of optimization opportunity when $R = 8$ and $k = 4$ (Color figure online)

From a coding perspective, this proposal requires finer-grained synchronization than OpenMP directives can provide; thus, it must work at the Pthreads level. In this sense, two possible implementations for this idea are described below, differing in the synchronization mechanism that it is used.

Semaphores. The first version employs semaphores to synchronize threads, through the POSIX library (`semaphore.h`). A semaphore matrix of dimension $R \times R$ is added and initialized to zero. Each cell represents a block of the D matrix. The computation of a phase 4 block is conditioned by d `sem_wait` operations, where d is the number of dependencies it possesses (in this case $d = 2$). The threads that compute the dependent blocks of phases 2 and 3 are responsible for performing the corresponding `sem_post` operations.

After a phase 2 block is computed, a `sem_post` is performed on each semaphore of its same column j (except on its own position). Similarly, after processing a phase 3 block, a `sem_post` is performed on each semaphore of its same row i (except on its own position). To compute a $D_{i,j}$ block of phase 4, two `sem_wait` operations are performed on its own position (i, j). In this way, the dependencies of phase 4 are respected at the block level.

When a round ends, all semaphores are set to zero again. The Fig. 4 shows the value of the semaphores before `sem_wait` operations by phase 4.

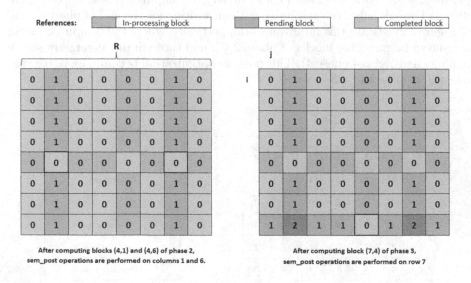

Fig. 4. Example of semaphores values during the execution of phases 2 and 3

Condition Variables. The second version employs condition variables (cv) to synchronize threads, which are included in Pthreads library. Three additional data structures are required for this version: a cv matrix (CV), a `mutex` matrix (M), and an integer matrix (F); all containing $R \times R$ elements. M is necessary to operate over CV while each cell $F_{i,j}$ indicates the number of pending dependencies to enable the computation of a block $D_{i,j}$, located in phase 4.

As in the previous case, $d = 2$ in phase 4. Therefore, F is initialized with this value for all its cells in each round. A thread will only continue when $F_{i,j} = 0$;

otherwise, it will remain suspended. After computing a phase 2 block, the remaining $R-1$ positions of the F matrix in the same j column are first decremented by one (ensuring mutual exclusion). Then, a `cond_signal` operation is performed on the associated condition variables. Analogously, after processing a phase 3 block, one unit is subtracted from the positions of the same column i in F (again, ensuring mutual exclusion). Then, a `cond_signal` is performed on the corresponding condition variables. Figure 5 illustrates F for the same case analyzed in Fig. 4.

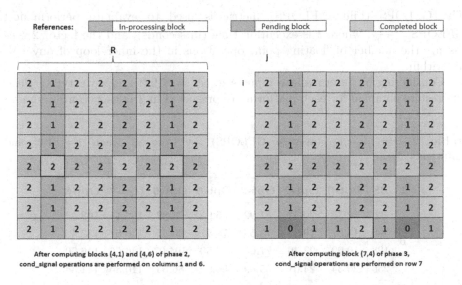

Fig. 5. Example of F values during the execution of phases 2 and 3 (Color figure online)

The matrix F must necessarily be included in this solution. When a `cond_signal` is performed on a cv, it will wake up the first thread in the queue (if any); otherwise, it will have no effect. Since the `cond_wait` operation always suspends a thread, it should only be called when pending dependencies exist. Additionally, each F update must be placed in a critical section, due to modification conflicts between phase 2 and 3 blocks (different threads could update the same cell).

4   Experimental Results

4.1   Experimental Design

The experiments were carried out on the experimental platforms described in Table 1. The tests considered the variation of workload ($N = \{4096, 8192, 16384\}$), data type (*float*, *double*), number of threads ($T_{Core} = \{6,12\}$, $T_{Xeon} = \{56,112\}$) and block size ($BS = \{32, 64, 128, 256\}$), where necessary.

All code versions work with the same input data, considering 30% of null values in the distance matrix. Each particular test was executed 8 times to minimize fluctuation, and the performance was computed based on the average of these multiple runs. Last, all code versions are available in a public web repository: https://bit.ly/cacic23-fw.

4.2 Experimental Results of x86 Adaptation

The GFLOPS (billion FLOPS) metric is used to evaluate performance: $GFLOPS = \frac{2 \times N^3}{t \times 10^9}$, where t is execution time (in seconds), and the factor 2 represents the number of floating point operations in the inner loop of any FW algorithm.

Considering an intermediate input size ($N = 8192$) and data type $= float$, the results obtained for each platform are presented in Tables 2 (Core i5) and 3

Table 2. Performance (average GFLOPS) on Core i5 when N = 8192 and datatype = float

T	BS	Opt-0	Opt-2	Opt-3	Opt-5	Opt-6	Opt-7	Opt-8
6	32	12.35	20.62	61.92	65.95	78.89	103.11	103.44
	64	14.37	19.38	73.58	78.41	95.47	136.61	137.42
	128	19.99	23.40	77.06	83.50	104.07	146.66	146.70
	256	20.34	24.61	55.09	56.99	86.83	110.86	111.34
12	32	16.24	28.15	66.85	70.26	87.15	112.24	112.65
	64	19.99	25.52	78.29	81.36	101.56	146.24	147.05
	128	21.09	29.92	78.41	82.82	107.65	154.22	154.29
	256	21.22	32.13	60.51	62.12	94.19	110.68	110.80

Table 3. Performance (average GFLOPS) on Xeon Platinum when N = 8192 and datatype = float

T	BS	Opt-0	Opt-2	Opt-3	Opt-4	Opt-5	Opt-6	Opt-7	Opt-8
56	32	62.03	111.06	116.07	185.12	222.85	346.40	374.78	494.90
	64	62.95	81.35	111.03	189.76	230.82	472.82	480.55	710.57
	128	87.15	110.83	132.55	215.53	334.13	507.52	559.67	831.70
	256	87.90	111.65	112.06	185.94	232.88	441.03	444.93	641.24
112	32	79.23	157.39	224.92	261.30	273.38	422.60	440.06	463.17
	64	78.10	101.26	402.67	447.31	491.73	587.05	611.58	664.20
	128	124.09	163.40	425.86	489.67	593.25	700.64	766.82	866.31
	256	124.47	169.32	336.85	354.80	372.23	432.98	456.85	470.91

Table 4. Incremental improvement for each x86 platform when N=8192

x86 platform	Opt-1	Opt-2	Opt-3	Opt-4	Opt-5	Opt-6	Opt-7	Opt-8
Core i5	–	1.42	2.62	–	1.06	1.30	1.43	<1.01
Xeon Platinum	–	1.32	2.61	1.15	1.21	1.18	1.09	1.13
Xeon Phi KNL	1.03	1.57	2.19	2.10	1.05	2.63	1.40	<1.01

(Xeon Platinum). It can be seen that the best performance for both servers is achieved using one thread per logical core and $BS = 128$ from *Opt-3* onwards.

Table 4 presents the improvement factor for each version over its predecessor, including their comparison with [2]. Figure 6 and 7 show the performance achieved using the aforementioned optimal configuration on the Core i5 and Xeon Platinum machines, respectively. It can be seen that each optimization proposal effectively leads to an increase in the GFLOPS obtained on both machines. The largest improvement is achieved in the *Opt-3* version by vectorizing with *AVX-2* (approximately 2.6×). Then, when comparing the widest vectorization option versus the one that does not vectorize (*Opt-0*), a total improvement of 3.96× and 3.72× are obtained on the Xeon Platinum and the Core i5 platforms, respectively. On its behalf, branch prediction leads to a remarkable performance improvement (*Opt-6*), reaching 1.30× for Core i5, and 1.18× for Xeon Platinum. In the same line, loop unrolling provides good acceleration rates, especially for Core i5 (1.43×).

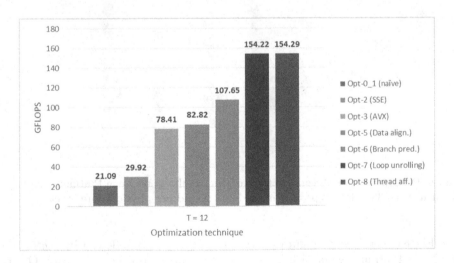

Fig. 6. Performance on Core i5 when N8192 and data type = *float* (optimal configuration for each version)

For the implementation *Opt-8*, six combinations of granularity (*core, fine*) and affinity (*balanced, compact and scatter*) were tested on both platforms [6]

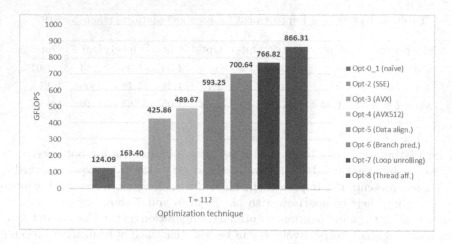

Fig. 7. Performance on Xeon Platinum when N = 8192 and data type = *float* (optimal configuration for each version)

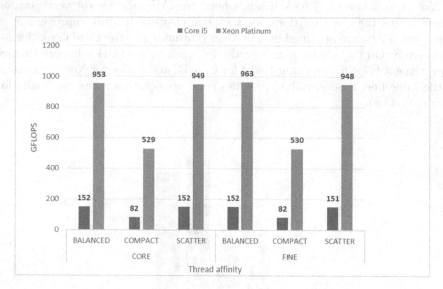

Fig. 8. Performance for all combinations of thread affinity on Xeon Platinum and Core i5 when N=16384, data type = *float*, and one thread per physical core is set

(see Fig. 8). The best configuration was *balanced* closely followed by *scatter* on the Xeon Platinum when using one OpenMP thread per physical core. On its behalf, no significant differences are observed between *balanced* and *scatter* on the Core i5, probably due to the small number of available cores. Last, the granularity option does not seem to affect the performance of both machines while the *compact* affinity, on the contrary, affects it negatively.

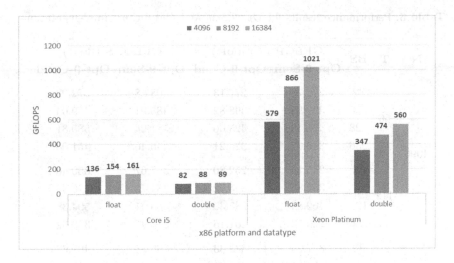

Fig. 9. Performance of optimal implementation on Xeon Platinum and Core i5 varying N and data type

When comparing *Opt-8* to *Opt-0*, an overall improvement of 7.31× and 6.98× are reached for Core i5 and Xeon Platinum, respectively. Like the Xeon Phi KNL case, it can be noted that all optimizations were beneficial, although not all of them impacted in the same way.

Finally, Fig. 9 shows performance achieved with the best implementation for each platform, data type, and input size tested, using the optimal configuration of T and BS. First, higher GFLOPS are obtained in the Xeon server than in the Core i5, considering its computational power. Second, it is observed that performance improves as N increases, given the higher ratio of compute versus synchronization. In particular, the magnitude of this difference is more noticeable when more threads are available (Xeon Platinum case). Third, using a wider precision data type such as *double* can lead to a more reliable result; however, it should be noted that it will come at a cost in response time, as performance drops by as much as 45%.

4.3 Experimental Results of Opt-9

Table 5 shows the performance for the *Opt-9-Sem* and *Opt-9-Cond* versions on the Xeon Platinum machine. It can be seen that the optimal block size is stabilized at $BS = 128$, regardless of the data type, number of threads, or problem size used. This represents an advantage over previous versions with variable optimal BS since it requires adjustment for each situation.

Figure 10 summarizes the performances obtained for both versions on the Xeon Platinum (T=112), when varying N and data type. First, it can be seen that both versions of *Opt-9* outperform *Opt-8*. From the synchronization mechanism perspective, no significant performance difference can be appreci-

Table 5. Performance results for *Opt-9-Sem* and *Opt-9-Cond* implementations

N	T	BS	GFLOPS (double)		GFLOPS (float)	
			Opt-9-Sem	Opt-9-Cond	Opt-9-Sem	Opt-9-Cond
4096	56	32	272.76	277.13	408.88	372.02
		64	397.35	398.82	485.91	479.04
		128	423.49	423.66	581.04	585.81
		256	326.07	326.21	446.40	451.08
	112	32	245.19	252.80	357.67	350.46
		64	352.83	353.72	484.72	476.35
		128	402.84	387.35	586.41	594.38
		256	220.53	201.16	315.45	319.62
8192	56	32	317.65	333.33	469.88	497.63
		64	494.51	499.41	639.82	738.00
		128	550.83	554.76	855.15	857.87
		256	424.43	427.21	657.77	657.24
	112	32	315.18	326.49	436.02	483.08
		64	466.42	468.68	623.87	688.01
		128	585.31	549.29	905.83	909.03
		256	316.91	297.33	480.62	499.98
16384	56	32	409.05	426.83	582.79	631.27
		64	584.32	583.84	717.50	904.71
		128	593.36	590.39	976.98	978.05
		256	456.67	455.32	750.52	754.21
	112	32	414.55	429.33	534.50	627.63
		64	556.36	541.68	706.58	828.90
		128	629.38	589.54	1034.44	1038.15
		256	339.68	316.24	797.82	561.74

ated between using semaphores or condition variables. Finally, the improvement achieved with *double* data type is significantly larger than with *float*. In particular, performance improves up to 5% and 23% when *float* and *double* are used, respectively. The improvement factor is higher with *double* because idle time is (proportionally) shorter than with *float*, since operations with the former are more expensive than with the latter.

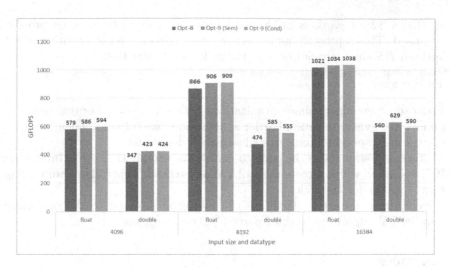

Fig. 10. Performance of implementation *Opt-9* on the Xeon Platinum when varying N and data type

5   Conclusions and Future Work

In this paper, we studied the code developed by [2] and adapted it to run on Intel x86 processors, losing the specificity of the Xeon Phi KNL. To do so, we verified one by one the optimizations proposed by [2], making adjustments to the base code where necessary, and analyzing its performance on two Intel servers under different test scenarios. In addition, a new optimization was proposed to increase the concurrency degree of the parallel algorithm, which was implemented using two different synchronization mechanisms. From the results obtained and their subsequent analysis, the following conclusions can be mentioned:

- *Opt-1* was discarded because of the absence of MDCDRAM memory on the x86 platforms used. In addition, the vectorization flags were modified to the corresponding SIMD sets.
- Like the Xeon Phi KNL case, all optimizations were beneficial on the two x86 platforms selected. Particularly, the use of SIMD instructions provided the greatest performance improvement.
- The performance improves as N increases, given the higher ratio of compute versus synchronization. Besides, using wider precision data can lead to a more reliable result although at the cost of a significant increase in response time.
- Both versions of *Opt-9* outperform *Opt-8*. From the synchronization mechanism perspective, no significant performance difference can be appreciated between using semaphores or condition variables. In the opposite sense, the improvement achieved with *double* data type is significantly larger than with *float*.
- Beyond the reduction in execution time, an indirect benefit of *Opt-9* results in no variation of optimal BS. Using *Opt-9* the optimal block size is stabilized

at $BS = 128$, regardless of the data type, number of threads, or problem size used. This represents an advantage over previous versions with variable optimal BS since it requires adjustment for each situation.

Future work will focus on:

- Proposing new algorithmic optimizations as an inter-round optimization, to remove the synchronization barrier at the end of each round. Then, performing the corresponding tests to evaluate their feasibility.
- Making adjustments to the code to enable its compilation using Intel's new ICX compiler, which incorporates LLVM as *backend*. This will guarantee long-term support for the code.
- Developing a library to facilitate the inclusion and use of the optimized, parallel FW algorithm in third-party C/C++ programs.

References

1. Calderon, S., Rucci, E., Chichizola, F.: Adaptación de algoritmo openmp para computar caminos mínimos en grafos en arquitecturas x86. In: Actas del XXIX Congreso Argentino de Ciencias de la Computación (CACIC 2023), pp. 489–500 (2023)
2. Costi, U.: Aceleración del Algoritmo Floyd-Warshall sobre Intel Xeon Phi KNL. Tesina de Licenciatura en Informática, Universidad Nacional de La Plata (2020)
3. Floyd, R.W.: Algorithm 97: hortest path. Commun. ACM **5**(6), 345 (J962). https://doi.org/10.1145/367766.368168
4. Han, S.C., Franchetti, F., Püschel, M.: Program generation for the all-pairs shortest path problem. In: Proceedings of the 15th International Conference on Parallel Architectures and Compilation Techniques, PACT 2006, New York, NY, USA, pp. 222–232. ACM (2006).https://doi.org/10.1145/1152154.1152189
5. Han, S., Kang, S.: Optimizing all-pairs shortest-path algorithm using vector instructions. Technical report, Carnegie Mellon University, USA (2006)
6. Intel Corporation: Thread Affinity Interface. https://www.intel.com/content/www/us/en/develop/documentation/cpp-compiler-developer-guide-and-reference/top/optimization-and-programming/openmp-support/openmp-library-support/thread-affinity-interface.html
7. Jalali, S., Noroozi, M.: Determination of the optimal escape routes of underground mine networks in emergency cases. Saf. Sci. **47**(8), 1077–1082 (2009). https://doi.org/10.1016/j.ssci.2009.01.001
8. Khan, P., Konar, G., Chakraborty, N.: Modification of floyd-warshall's algorithm for shortest path routing in wireless sensor networks. In: 2014 Annual IEEE India Conference (INDICON), pp. 1–6 (2014).https://doi.org/10.1109/INDICON.2014.7030504
9. Nakaya, A., Goto, S., Kanehisa, M.: Extraction of correlated gene clusters by multiple graph comparison. Genome Inform. **12**, 44–53 (2001)
10. Penner, M., Prasanna, V.: Cache-friendly implementations of transitive closure. In: Proceedings 2001 International Conference on Parallel Architectures and Compilation Techniques, pp. 185–196 (2001). https://doi.org/10.1109/PACT.2001.953299
11. Reinders, J., Jeffers, J., Sodani, A.: Intel Xeon Phi Processor High Performance Programming Knights, Landing Morgan Kaufmann Publishers Inc., Boston (2016)

12. Rucci, E., De Giusti, A., Naiouf, M.: Blocked all-pairs shortest paths algorithm on Intel Xeon Phi KNL processor: a case study. In: De Giusti, A.E. (ed.) CACIC 2017. CCIS, vol. 790, pp. 47–57. Springer, Cham (2018). https://doi.org/10.1007/978-3-319-75214-3_5
13. Schoeneman, F., Zola, J.: Solving all-pairs shortest-paths problem in large graphs using apache spark. In: Proceedings of the 48th International Conference on Parallel Processing. ICPP '19, ACM (2019).https://doi.org/10.1145/3337821.3337852
14. Solomonik, E., Buluç, A., Demmel, J.: Minimizing communication in all-pairs shortest paths. In: 2013 IEEE 27th International Symposium on Parallel and Distributed Processing, pp. 548–559. IEEE (2013).https://doi.org/10.1109/IPDPS.2013.111
15. Srinivasan, T., Balakrishnan, R., Gangadharan, S., Hayawardh, V.: A scalable parallelization of all-pairs shortest path algorithm for a high performance cluster environment. In: 2007 International Conference on Parallel and Distributed Systems, pp. 1–8 (2007). https://doi.org/10.1109/ICPADS.2007.4447721
16. Venkataraman, G., Sahni, S., Mukhopadhyaya, S.: A blocked all-pairs shortest-paths algorithm. In: SWAT 2000. LNCS, vol. 1851, pp. 419–432. Springer, Heidelberg (2000). https://doi.org/10.1007/3-540-44985-X_36
17. Warshall, S.: A theorem on Boolean matrices. J. ACM **9**(1), 11–12 (1962). https://doi.org/10.1145/321105.321107
18. Zhang, L.Y., Jian, M., Li, K.P.: A parallel Floyd-Warshall algorithm based on TBB. In: 2010 2nd IEEE International Conference on Information Management and Engineering, pp. 429–433 (2010). https://doi.org/10.1109/ICIME.2010.5477752

Technology Applied to Education

Embedded Systems Programming Through *eUCCvm*, an Integrated Educational Tool

Cristian F. Perez-Monte[1]([✉]) [ID], Gustavo Mercado[1] [ID], Carlos Taffernaberry[1] [ID], Ana Laura Diedrichs[1] [ID], Fabiana Piccoli[2,3] [ID], Mario Sebastian Tobar[1] [ID], Marcelo Ledda[1] [ID], Raúl Moralejo[1] [ID], and Rodrigo Gonzalez[1] [ID]

[1] GridTICs, Universidad Tecnológica Nacional, Facultad Regional Mendoza, Mendoza, Argentina
{cristian.perez,gustavo.mercado,carlos.taffernaberry,sebastian.tobar, rodrigo.gonzalez}@gridtics.frm.utn.edu.ar,
{cristian.perez,ana.diedrichs,marcelo.ledda, raul.moralejo}@docentes.frm.utn.edu.ar
[2] Universidad Nacional de San Luis, Ejército de los Andes 950, San Luis, Argentina
mpiccoli@unsl.edu.ar
[3] Universidad Autónoma de Entre Ríos, 25 de Mayo 385, Concepción del Uruguay, Entre Ríos, Argentina
http://www.gridtics.frm.utn.edu.ar

Abstract. Rethinking our teaching practices and forms, whether due to world events such as the pandemic or the particularities of our reality, such as social and economic conditions, is necessary. This work presents an open-source and universal cross-compilation tool for programming Embedded Systems: *eUCCvm*. It is possible to develop application programming activities for Embedded Systems on multiple architectures through its use. *eUCCvm* can be used in academic and work fields and any modality, whether virtual or in-person. Finally, we will present a brief survey about its inclusion in some University subjects at the Universidad Tecnológica Nacional, Regional Mendoza.

Keywords: Embedded Systems · Architecture Programming · Educational Software · Open Source

1 Introduction

eUCCvm (*Educational/Embedded/Electronic/Entertainment use Universal Cross Compiler Virtual Machine*) is a system based on a virtual machine for development, compilation, and programming of embedded systems free of charge, used as a tool for the development of practical classes in different subjects of the National Technological University, Mendoza Regional Faculty. It was initially developed in 2017 for the specific programming of EDU-CIAA [4,8]. In 2018 and 2019, its use was extended to other microcontroller and microprocessor

P. Pesado et al. (Eds.): CACIC 2023, CCIS 2123, pp. 65–77, 2024.
https://doi.org/10.1007/978-3-031-62245-8_5

architectures [28], those used mainly in the Digital Techniques II [25] and III [26] classes. A process began to adapt the entire educational system and the curriculum to virtuality in March 2020 with the start of the pandemic. Likewise, in this same sense, a series of improvements were made to *eUCCvm* in order to adapt it, taking into account the new needs of students and professors to carry out activities derived from the ASPO (Preventive Social Isolation and Mandatory provided by Decree of the Argentine Republic 297/2020). In the following years, we added microcontroller and microprocessor architectures, including those used in home computers and video game consoles. Finally, starting this year, microcontrollers with open hardware architecture RISC-V [22] were added, which are central to the future of teaching digital techniques classes. In addition to the above, as *eUCCvm* is a public tool for educational use, it is possible to download it from [24].

This work is an extended version of the previous work [27] and is organized as follows: in the Sect. 2, we describe its impact on the academic field. The Sects. 3 and 4 respectively detail the general and specific features of *eUCCvm*. In Sect. 5, we present different types of application cases for conducting activities in the educational environment. The Sect. 6 shows results regarding the impact of your application. Finally, we present the conclusions and future work in the Sect. 7. We organized the work as follows: in the Sect. 2, we describe its impact on the academic field. The Sects. 3 and 4 respectively detail the general and specific features of *eUCCvm*. The Sect. 6 shows results regarding the impact of your application. Finally, we present the conclusions and future work in the Sect. 7.

This extended version of the work [27] includes updated information on the latest improvements made to *eUCCvm* up to December 2023, advantages of using entertainment-oriented architectures when applied to education, and a taxonomy of the types of examples used for conducting activities in the educational environment.

2   *eUCCvm* and Its Application in the Academic Field

eUCCvm is developed to teach you how to program embedded systems in a safe and controlled environment without worrying about damaging your operating system.

For the design and development, we incorporate the STS (Science, Technology, and Society) perspective [6,20,21], which consists of taking into account the ideological, cultural aspects and personal experience (values, feelings, motivations, among others), in addition to the technical and operational aspects.

eUCCvm allows the use of computers that do not necessarily have many resources since it demands few requirements for its use by students, which is why it is ideal for implementation in underdeveloped or developing countries. In addition, it allows for solving problems imposed during virtuality, such as intermittent, poor, or no access to the Internet, constituting an essential barrier to carrying out activities. In this context, *eUCCvm* provides a comprehensive tool where everything is included and is ready to be used without the need for permanent access to the Internet in carrying out virtual activities for students. Thus, it is possible to carry out activities indistinctly in virtuality from home without the need to resort to advanced computing resources or Internet access, as well as from the academic environment, maximizing, in this case, the class time dedicated to programming and developing projects with microcontrollers.

To adapt it to the conditions imposed by virtuality, *eUCCvm* has not only the ability to program, compile, and flashing on the hardware of many architectures but also has support documentation and challenging activities for the individual or group competition.

Additionally, as another advantage it offers is its open-source nature. Using a tool with this source code allows students to modify the tool to enhance it for their development and for teachers to adapt their practices. Also added is the possibility of using open hardware, such as the RISC-V architecture, and the benefits of its use [12].

eUCCvm provides a wide range of microcontroller hardware platforms, not only to enhance programming skills on each of them but also to strengthen the learning capabilities of new architectures that may emerge in the future. In other words, it reinforces the abilities to 'learn to learn' new architectures and/or programming languages for them.

Furthermore, having architectures of different levels of complexity allows students to learn at their own pace and apply their knowledge as they progress through the course. This allows them to develop complete projects on real hardware either individually or in groups.

Another of its characteristics, and which we consider an additional incentive, is the inclusion of architectures used in the video game industry; in order to know them and be able to program them, not only to expand knowledge regarding new architectures but also to focus on those that students are familiar from previous use. It is already widely known and debated that integrating video games into the educational environment is very beneficial [7,11].

The potential skills and benefits of using *eUCCvm* in students who take subjects related to Embedded Systems programming are:

- Promote programming in assembly and C languages for different microcontrollers.
- By allowing programming and the compilation and flashing of the program on real hardware, complete practical exercises are possible, allowing students to see how theoretical concepts are applied in real-world situations.
- By offering the possibility of working on various microcontroller hardware architectures, it not only strengthens programming skills in each of them but also enhances skills in learning new architectures that may emerge.
- Promote skills in microcontroller programming for managing storage, visualization, communications, sensing, and actuator systems.
- Enhance skills in designing and programming communications interfaces for the interconnection between microcontrollers or between microcontrollers and other devices such as sensors, actuators, or input-output devices.

– Promote collaborative work by carrying out challenge activities to enhance the development of group or individual projects.
– Reinforce skills in the use of hardware description languages.
– Discern the most appropriate architecture for the project.
– Discern which programming language is most suitable for certain architectures and developed projects.
– Reinforce skills in using the command line for advanced use of a Linux operating system.
– Reinforce skills in programming, compiling, versioning, and using repositories using Linux with the command line.
– Strengthen advanced theoretical and programming knowledge in architectures used for entertainment, which the student is already familiar with due to its use in video games.

For all the above, we can determine that *eUCCvm* has many properties that make it a good candidate when considering software for developing programming practices in Embedded Systems, whatever its modality, and without significant resource requirements.

3 General Features of *eUCCvm*

eUCCvm is developed on a [10] virtual machine based on the Linux Ubuntu 18.04 LTS operating system. It can be used on different operating systems of real machines thanks to VirtualBox [17].

We selected a 32-bit version for installation to allow virtualization even on computers without hardware virtualization features or AMD64/EMT64 instructions. In addition, we chose a server configuration to obtain a lightweight operating system without a graphical environment for virtualization on machines with only 256 MB of RAM, such as the netbooks available from the Conectar Igualdad Plan [18].

The virtual machine has various compilers installed from the official Ubuntu repositories. It also includes others compiled from the developers' official source code and several development SDKs for different architectures.

eUCCvm includes essential documentation to support each architecture's hardware development and programming.

Below are specified in greater detail some of the characteristics of *eUCCvm*.

4 Specific Characteristics

The developed system adds the following capabilities to the operating system:

– Code writing. It allows the generation of code in different programming languages, especially assembly language [13] and C [30].
– Modification of existing codes. Interpret the operation of existing example codes and their modification to adapt them to solve new proposed problems.

- Compilation. Generation of machine code for different hardware architectures.
- Flashing of compiled programs on real embedded devices.
- Simulation of microcontrollers described in Verilog (NEORV32, RISC-V RV32 architecture).
- Secure remote access (SSH) to allow multiple consoles and access to the entire file system for editing inside or outside the virtual machine.
- Supporting documentation.
- Development environments with multiple teaching examples.
- Practical challenge activities to solve individually or in groups.

The system is limited to using command line environment (CLI) tools to allow a lightweight and transportable environment, preventing the execution of tools that require a graphical mode (GUI). Standard editors available for Linux are used to write and modify code.

4.1 Architectures, Modules and Other Technologies

Currently, several architectures are supported, allowing easy updating and inclusion of future ones.

The embedded system architectures considered for compilation, both in *bare metal* execution and for execution in GNU/Linux (in the case of the most powerful ones), are:

- Microchip PIC [31].
- AVR (used in Arduino. [9] NANO, UNO and MEGA).
- Xtensa LX106 (used by ESP8266 [29] and ESP32).
- ARM Cortex M3 [5] [33] (used in Bluepill and Arduino DUE).
- ARM Cortex M4 (used in Black Pill and EDU CIAA) [33]
- RISC-V RV32IMC (used in modules such as ESP32-CX and ESP32-H2) [15]
- ARM 11 32-bit [1] (used in Raspberry PI 1).
- ARM Cortex A, A7 32-bit [2] [32] (used in Raspberry PI 2) and A53 64-bit [3] [14] (used in Raspberry PI 3).

In addition to the most advanced architectures for execution on Linux, such as:

- x86 estándar and x86 (amd64/emt64).
- MIPS.
- SPARC.
- ALPHA.
- 68k.
- POWERPC.
- RISC-V RV64

Finally, and in the case of home computers and video game consoles, the architectures included are:

- Ricoh 2A03 (Nintendo Entertainment System)
- 6507 (ATARI 2600)
- 68K (ATARI ST - AMIGA OCS - SEGA GENESIS)
- ARM (GameBoy Advance)
- Ricoh 5A22 (Super Nintendo)
- Zilog Z80 (Sega Master System)
- MOS 6502 (Atari400/800)
- Sharp LR35902 (GameBoy)
- MIPS I R3000 (Playstation)
- MIPS III NEC VR 4300i + GPU RCP de 64 bits (Nintendo 64)
- 68K+Z80 (Sega MegaDrive)
- MIPS-IV R5900 (Playstation II)
- PowerPC CELL (Playstation III)
- Hitachi SH-2 (Sega Saturn)

Furthermore, it adds examples for the use of modules, which offer function-alities to the architectures mentioned above, such as:

- GPIO modules, analog variable sensing, and 7-segment numerical display.
- High-resolution LCD and OLED screens.
- Connectivity modules: Ethernet, GPRS radio, WiFi or Bluetooth.
- CCD modules.
- Storage with microSD.
- Global positioning modules.

The system also has simple examples for the implementation of different electronic input-output and communications technologies, such as:

- Use of general purpose digital inputs and outputs.
- Use of analog inputs and outputs.
- SPI [16] and I2C communications protocol.
- Parallel communications protocols.

Among the integrated tools, there are those corresponding to flashing the compilation in various architectures for embedded systems, such as:

- Flashing via USB port of AVR Arduino Uno and Mega.
- ARM BluePill, ARM Black Pill, Arduino Due, and EDU-CIAA.
- ESP8266 and ESP32.
- Microchip PIC with PICkit 2 [19].

All examples are available within the system and organized into folders, archi-tecture, and modules used.

4.2   Advantages of Using Architectures Dedicated to Entertainment

eUCCvm has been developed with the ability to program virtually all hardware architectures used for video game consoles or entertainment-oriented computers. This type of architecture has been explored in depth due to the following advantages:

- Wide variety of architectures that allows, from an educational point of view, a tour of a wide variety of architectures, giving the student a broad vision to adapt to programming them and prepare them for new ones that may appear in the future.
- Availability of hardware at low cost due to the widespread production of these architectures.
- If the student does not have the hardware, high-quality emulators are available to test the compilation of the developed codes.
- Architectures with limitations in hardware capacity that allow the student to strengthen skills for code optimizations and better use of hardware resources in programming.
- Video game consoles, especially the old ones, allow the expansion of their features through the development of accessory hardware and the software necessary for their use.
- Video game consoles generally do not have an operating system, which allows training in bare-metal programming for very diverse architectures.
- Linking programming with video games can be an essential incentive at an educational level.

Virtually all the specific architectures applied to the entertainment market until 2013 have been incorporated. After 2013, hardware architectures exceptionally dedicated to entertainment ceased to exist, unifying the market in applying the x86-64 architecture with support in *eUCCvm*.

5   Types of Application Cases

It is important to include a number of examples that serve to master all the key aspects of each architecture when working with different architectures at an educational level. From them, we present the two types of examples that must exist when characterizing and allowing the mastery of each architecture. These are:

- Characteristic Examples: This example type aims to master a specific feature, such as managing a GPIO pin, a communications port, or a graphical interface.
- Performance Examples: This example seeks to demonstrate not a specific characteristic of an architecture but its performance, such as mathematical or graphical processing.

Table 1. Applied example types

Characteristic	Examples of Feature	Examples of Performance
GPIO Pin as output	Turn on and off a pin	Turn a pin on and off at its maximum frequency
Analog Converter to Digital	Read an analog value	Convert in burst to maximum frequency AD conversion
Digital Converter to Analog	Set an analog value	Convert in burst to maximum frequency DA conversion
GPIO Pin as input	Read a state of a pin	Read states at its maximum frequency
Graphical interface	Hello world or simple drawing	Generate pixel at maximum speed of graphical interface
Device storage	Write a small file	Write data to the maximum interface or device speed
Port communications	Send a character per port	Send data to the maximum port speed

For every feature example, there is usually a performance example for the feature for a given architecture. In Table 1, we will show, in the case of *eUCCvm*, different examples of characteristics and their performance counterpart.

In this way, for each *eUCCvm* architecture, all the characteristics are identified, presenting qualitative use examples. Finally, *eUCCvm* includes examples of performance, which determine the speed or any other quantitative aspect that said characteristic has for the architecture under analysis.

6   Results

The system has been used in Digital Techniques III since 2017 and in Digital Techniques II from 2018 to the present year. Table 2 shows the topics developed using *eUCCvm* in the practical area of Digital Techniques II, year by year. On the one hand, through guided activities during the development of the subject, the hardware (modules, consoles, or computer systems) with their respective architectures applied to the indicated subject.

On the other hand, in addition, specific activities for integrating technologies or functionality modules into different architectures are also shown through the application of unique activities for group or individual challenges. We can observe how the number of activities integrated into the subject carried out with *eUCCvm* increased year by year, becoming much more growing starting in 2020 and its adaptation to virtuality.

In terms of academic use, in Table 3, we outline the number of students who used *eUCCvm* in each year of study, the number of downloads from the server of the UTN Regional Mendoza, and the number of versions released for improvement incorporation. As can be observed, the number of downloads is correlated with the number of students and versions released.

Table 2. Applied Thematic Areas

Year	Architectures	Funcionality	# Activ
2018	EDU-CIAA (ARM CORTEX M4)	Example of firmware_v2 usage	1
2019	Microcontroladores PIC with pickit 2 Módulo PIC DM164140(16F18855) Arduino UNO(AVR Atmega328) Arduino MEGA(AVR Atmega2560) Arduino DUE (ARM CORTEX M3) Bluepill (ARM CORTEX M3) ESP8266 (Tensilica Xtensa L106) ESP32 (Tensilica Xtensa LX6) CIAA-Z3R0 (ARM CORTEX M0+)	Example of firmware_v3 usage Challenge activity of communications port usage with ARM	12
2020	Blackpill (ARM CORTEX M4) Nintendo (MOS 6502 /2A03) Super Nintendo(MOS 65C816/5A22) Sega Genesis (68K + Z80) Nintendo64 (MIPS III +GPU RCP)	-	23
2021	-	Challenge activity of communication port and storage systems application with AVR systems	25
2022	-	Challenge Activity of communication and Analog-to-Digital Converter usage Application with ARM"	27
2023	NEORV32 and ESP32-C3 (RISC-V) Playstation I (MIPS I R3000) Playstation II (MIPS III/IV R5900) Playstation III (CELL POWER PC) Sega Saturn (Hitachi SH-2)	Challenge activity of LCD Screen Application comunicación paralela	33

Table 3. Academic Impact

Year	Number of students	Number of downloads	Number of versions of *eUCCvm*
2019	44	440	31
2020	43	400	9
2021	43	405	2
2022	33	187	2
2023	16	131	6

The project is being used, not only within the university academic environment but also in other contexts. Since 2019, it has been publicly shared through various channels, one of which is [23], independent of UTN's courses. From this platform, hundreds of downloads indicate the growing interest, beyond academic use.

To develop an analysis of the impact of *eUCCvm* on students, a survey was conducted among students who used the tool in various capacities during the study of certain subjects, and among others who did not use it because it was not available at that time. The sample used consisted of 40 students from the years 2018 to 2023 out of an approximate population of 220, and another 20 students who attended before 2018 and did not use it. For the latter group, we only described the general characteristics of *eUCCvm* for the survey.

The survey consisted of the following two types of inquiries:

- General inquiries about the software tools used in the course.
- Specific inquiries about *eUCCvm*.

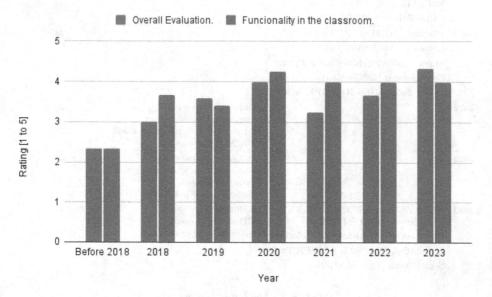

Fig. 1. General inquiries about *eUCCvm*

Regarding the general inquiries, it allowed students to evaluate tools used in the course such as *eUCCvm* among others. This allowed us to conduct a comprehensive assessment, including years of study in which *eUCCVm* was not yet implemented.

The results of the general inquiries can be observed in Fig. 1.

The specific inquiries about *eUCCvm* could only be conducted in a limited manner and with restrictions starting from students of 2018, with most functionalities available in the year 2019. The results of these specific inquiries can be observed in Fig. 2.

The initial version, in 2018, only considered one board: the edu-ciaa. Starting from 2019, all those detailed in Table 2 were added. Figure 2 shows how the students from 2018 had a lower assessment compared to subsequent years regarding architectures. With constant updates, all other parameters also increased.

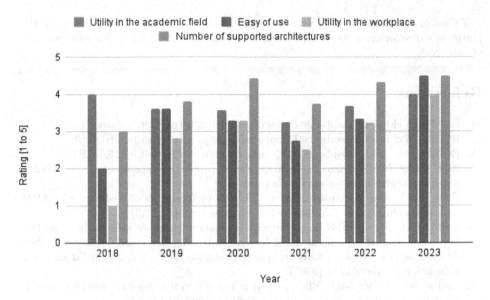

Fig. 2. Specific inquiries about *eUCCvm*.

7 Conclusions and Future Work

With the development and integration of *eUCCvm* in various courses at UTN Regional Mendoza since 2018, the tool has shown satisfactory results both in face-to-face and virtual settings. The outcomes extended beyond the academic realm and practical problem-solving, also enabling its application in work and research environments, highlighting its ease of use and range of supported architectures. It's worth noting the pivotal role it acquired during the year 2020, with its utilization in the virtual setting.

It's important to highlight that with *eUCCvm*, students have a 'ready-to-use' tool, allowing them to optimize class time by carrying out activities without the need to download or install additional programs. Additionally, as an open-source software tool, it's noteworthy for its continuous evolution, with numerous improvements being added year by year, including the inclusion of new architectures and implemented activities.

As a line of future work, there are several aspects to consider. One of them is to carry out different improvements, among which stands out the update of the virtual machine to the latest LTS version of Ubuntu, as well as the native integration of support for 64-bit systems and the use of Docker. Additionally, it is planned to incorporate the possibility of carrying out activities directly on the platform through its web integration, which will offer a smoother and more accessible experience for users.

Acknowledgments. We appreciate the support of the GridTICs group belonging to UTN - FRM and the professors of the Digital Techniques II and III courses for including *eUCCvm* or collaborating in its development. The rest of the hardware necessary for the platform's development has been obtained through private funding from the authors of this work.

References

1. BCM2835 chipset, Raspberry Pi documentation. http://bit.ly/2woaRKW
2. BCM2836 chipset, Raspberry Pi documentation. http://bit.ly/2HDmLH9
3. BCM2837 chipset, Raspberry Pi documentation. http://bit.ly/2K76gET
4. EDU-CIAA-NXP (Marzo 2017). http://www.proyecto-ciaa.com.ar/devwiki/doku.php?id=desarrollo:edu-ciaa:edu-ciaa-nxp
5. Blem, E., Menon, J., Sankaralingam, K.: A detailed analysis of contemporary ARM and x86 architectures. UW-Madison Technical Report (2013)
6. Cabo, J.M., Moralejo, R.O.: Desarrollo de instrumentos de evaluación educativa hacia tecnologías específicas desde la perspectiva ciencia, tecnología y sociedad: El caso de la calidad del software. In: II Congreso de Tecnología en Educación y Educación en Tecnología (2007)
7. Coller, B.D., Scott, M.J.: Effectiveness of using a video game to teach a course in mechanical engineering. Comput. Educ. **53**(3), 900–912 (2009)
8. Dell'Oso, M., Lanzarini, L.C., Ridolfi, P.: Prototipo funcional de un sistema de detección de caídas basado en la plataforma CIAA. In: XXII Congreso Argentino de Ciencias de la Computación (CACIC 2016) (2016)
9. D'Ausilio, A.: Arduino: a low-cost multipurpose lab equipment. Behav. Res. Methods **44**(2), 305–313 (2012)
10. Goldberg, R.P.: Survey of virtual machine research. Computer **7**(6), 34–45 (1974). https://doi.org/10.1109/MC.1974.6323581
11. Griffiths, M.D.: The educational benefits of videogames. Educ. Health **20**(3), 47–51 (2002)
12. Hannig, F., Teich, J.: Open source hardware. Computer **54**(10), 111–115 (2021). https://doi.org/10.1109/MC.2021.3099046
13. Hyde, R.: The art of assembly language. No Starch Press (2003)
14. Ivković, J., Radulović, B.: The advantages of using Raspberry Pi 3 compared to Raspberry Pi 2. SoC computers for sensor system support. In: International Conference on Applied Internet and Information Technologies, pp. 88–94 (2016)
15. Kuo, Y.M., Garcia-Herrero, F., de la Cuerda, J.A.M.: Design, implementation, and characterization of custom risc-v soft-core processors for future communication networks
16. Leens, F.: An introduction to I2C and SPI protocols. IEEE Instrument. Measur. Mag. **12**(1), 8–13 (2009)
17. Li, P.: Selecting and using virtualization solutions: our experiences with VMware and VirtualBox. J. Comput. Sci. Coll. **25**(3), 11–17 (2010)
18. Martínez, S.L., Marotias, A., Amado, S.: Inclusión digital en la educación pública argentina. el programa conectar igualdad. Revista Educación y Pedagogía **24**(62), 205–218 (2013). http://bit.ly/2wm5Ke3
19. Meriac, M.: Heart of darkness-exploring the uncharted backwaters of hid iclass (tm) security. In: 27th Chaos Communication Congress (2010)
20. Moralejo, R.O., Cabo, J.M.: Visión de la tecnología en estudiantes de ingeniería en sistemas de información en mendoza-argentina. In: IX Workshop de Investigadores en Ciencias de la Computación (2007)

21. Pacey, A.: La cultura de la tecnología, méxico, fce. Enfoques sobre la Tecnología en: http://www.cneq.unam.mx/[Consulta: 21 de octubre de 2014] (1990)
22. Patterson, D., Waterman, A.: The RISC-V Reader: an open architecture Atlas. Strawberry Canyon (2017)
23. Perez-Monte, C.F., Diedrichs, A.L.: eUCCvm: Plataforma educativa de programación y compilacioón cruzada universal de sistemas embebidos (May 2019). https://doi.org/10.6084/m9.figshare.8185169.v1. https://doi.org/10.6084/m9.figshare.8185169.v1
24. Perez-Monte, C.F., Diedrichs, A.L.: eUCCvm: Plataforma educativa de programación y compilación cruzada universal de sistemas embebidos (2023). https://doi.org/10.6084/m9.figshare.8185169.v10, https://doi.org/10.6084/m9.figshare.8185169
25. Perez Monte, C.F., Diedrichs, A.L.: Programatecnicasdigitalesii-2023.pdf (2023). https://doi.org/10.6084/m9.figshare.23895969, https://figshare.com/articles/preprint/ProgramaTecnicasDigitalesII-2023_pdf/23895969/1
26. Perez Monte, C.F., Diedrichs, A.L.: Programatecnicasdigitalesiii-2023.pdf (2023). https://doi.org/10.6084/m9.figshare.23895963, https://figshare.com/articles/book/ProgramaTecnicasDigitalesIII-2023_pdf/23895963/1
27. Perez-Monte, C.F., et al.: EUCCVM: Una herramienta educativa integral para la programación de sistemas embebidos. In: XXIX Congreso Argentino de Ciencias de la Computación (CACIC 2023) (2023)
28. Perez-Monte, C.F., et al.: EUCCVM: Plataforma educativa de programación y compilación cruzada universal de sistemas embebidos. CASE 2019 (2019)
29. Prachchhak, G., Bhatt, C., Thik, J.: Data logging and visualization using bolt IoT. In: Kamal, R., Henshaw, M., Nair, P.S. (eds.) International Conference on Advanced Computing Networking and Informatics. AISC, vol. 870, pp. 155–164. Springer, Singapore (2019). https://doi.org/10.1007/978-981-13-2673-8_18
30. Ritchie, D.M.: The development of the C language. ACM SIGPLAN Notices **28**(3), 201–208 (1993)
31. Sanchez, J., Canton, M.P.: Microcontroller Programming: The Microchip PIC. CRC press (2006)
32. Soper, M.E.: Raspberry Pi System Anatomy. In: Expanding Your Raspberry Pi, pp. 1–15. Apress, Berkeley (2017). https://doi.org/10.1007/978-1-4842-2922-4_1
33. Yiu, J.: The Definitive Guide to ARM® Cortex®-M3 and Cortex®-M4 Processors. Newnes (2013)

Assessing Participation and Academic Performance in Discussion Forums: A Systematic Review

Paula Dieser[1](✉) (iD), Cecilia Sanz[2,3] (iD), and Alejandra Zangara[2] (iD)

[1] School of Exact and Natural Sciences, UNLPam, La Pampa, Argentina
`pauladieser@exactas.unlpam.edu.ar`
[2] Institute of Research in Computer Sciences, III – LIDI, School of Computer Sciences, UNLP, Buenos Aires, Argentina
`csanz@lidi.info.unlp.edu.ar`
[3] Scientific Research Commission from the Province of Buenos Aires, Buenos Aires, Argentina

Abstract. The discussion forum format is usually used to promote interaction in digital technology-mediated distance education proposals. The activities carried out in these forums could help students become cognitively engaged during their learning process. Assessing how they participate in these spaces requires protocols that allow capturing various characteristics of this type of interaction. Some of these protocols are often used to evaluate students' academic performance. This work offers a systematic review of the literature that addresses these issues in the field of Higher Education. Based on 54 research works carried out between 2015 and 2020, four methodologies are identified (simple statistics, content analysis, social media analysis, and processes analysis) that evaluate different aspects (quantity, quality, temporality, and relationships) of participation. Five of these articles also assess student performance in these interactive spaces. The results are analyzed and discussed with special focus on the possibilities offered by these methodologies to promote constructive learning in collaborative contexts.

Keywords: Forums · Participation · Academic Performance · Assessment Methodologies

1 Introduction

Interaction is a defining element in education, and it involves a communication process [1]. In distance education and, by extension, in any mediated educational relationship, its approach has been the subject of continued research [1].

A common tool to promote academic interaction and learning in mediated educational proposals is the discussion forum [2, 3], which is recognized as a space for interaction that promotes critical thinking, problem-solving skills and knowledge building [3, 4].

The potential uses of these spaces have generated multiple investigations around the topic. Part of these works have focused on the application and development of methodologies that allow analyzing aspects such as forum user participation and interaction [2,

P. Pesado et al. (Eds.): CACIC 2023, CCIS 2123, pp. 78–90, 2024.
https://doi.org/10.1007/978-3-031-62245-8_6

5] and their relationship or impact on other variables such as academic performance [2]. Studying these topics helps identify variables to consider in the design, implementation and framework for this type of activities that foster good student performance. It should be noted that, even though active participation is required in forums [6], this does not necessarily translate to deeper and more collaborative learning, or to better contributions [5].

This article presents a review of the methodologies used in articles that have been published or accepted for publication between 2015 and 2020 dealing with these processes in digital technology-mediated proposals for Higher Education Institutions (HEIs). Specifically, the protocols that have been used to assess participation in forum activities and the aspects or dimensions they assess are considered. This is an extension of previous work [7]. As such, previously obtained results are further analyzed and expanded by considering useful methodologies to assess academic performance in activities characterized by written and asynchronous exchanges.

Some supporting theoretical concepts will be presented before delving into the review itself, specifically, pertaining to some aspects of the technological micro-context of interest, *i.e.*, a discussion forum, and the constructs to be evaluated in this space. Then, the review methodology used is explained, including details of the search process and inclusion and exclusion criteria. After this, the articles in the review *corpus* are described and the results obtained are analyzed in relation to the methodologies used to evaluate various aspects of participation, as well as academic performance. Finally, some conclusions are presented and lines of future work are outlined, in the context of a master's thesis, based on the results obtained with this review.

2 Academic Discussion Forums

A forum is a communicative and collaborative virtual space in which a group of individuals discuss a topic of common interest [8]. It is conceived as a place for expressing oneself, giving opinions and consulting with other members [8] that encourages the exchange, coordination and consensus of ideas [9].

It is a tool based on asynchronous communication through written text [8, 9] that takes place in a web space and can be moderated [3, 8]. Its minimum condition for openness and sustainability is participation, which may be restricted to some members of the community (private forum) or not (public forum). In turn, participation may or may not be anonymous, depending on whether the author of each contribution is identified [8].

Forum-mediated discussion has the potential to cognitively engage students during their learning process [4]. In forums, students are at the center of the training process, and they are guided towards the development of critical thinking, problem solving, and the collaborative construction of knowledge [3]. Additionally, forums can be used to promote communication, social and collaboration skills, metacognition, time management skills, and self-paced learning [10]. Despite this, the lack of student participation in these spaces is common [11], even though it is necessary for successful performance [6]. Consequently, studying methodologies aimed at identifying participation patterns that could lead to better student results and performance, as well as ways to assess this performance in forum activities, is a field of interest. These constructs are defined below, followed by a review of relevant background information on their evaluation in Higher Education.

2.1 Participation

In education, forums have gained popularity as a tool for participation and communication in virtual teaching and learning environments (VTLEs). They allow users to access previous contributions and make new ones. Consequently, participation cannot be identified just through the messages posted in this space. According to [6], participation is "the process by which interventions interrelate and produce meaning that goes beyond the simple succession of messages" (p. 3). This process is generated by connecting messages, texts, emoticons, context, audience, and so forth.

Forum users participate through interventions that interrelate and produce meaning (active participation) or by viewing previously posted contributions (passive participation) [6]. In this sense, [12] speaks of vicarious interaction. This is referred to in terms of a student actively processing the interactions of others without leaving visible traces on the mediating tool. This form of interaction, as opposed to the direct one, together with the actor and non-actor categories, offers a classification of students that can interact in mediated educational processes [12]. A student is an actor if he or she makes unilateral contributions without considering the reactions or comments of others; and a non-actor if he/she does not participate in any way [12]. These ideas are summarized in Fig. 1.

Fig. 1. Correspondence between types of participation [6, 12]. Own elaboration.

2.2 Academic Performance

Academic performance is a construct with a complex definition and of multidimensional nature [13]. It can be understood as the result of the learning process mediated by the teacher's didactic activity that impacts on the student [13]. Other authors expand this idea and state that it works as an amorphous construction that incorporates a wide range of educational outcomes [14] that are functions of three sets of elements:

1. The elements (inputs) that students bring to the institution (*e.g.*, demographic and family background, academic and social experiences),
2. The context (environment), given by the institution, inside or outside the building (*e.g.*, people, programs, policies, cultures and experiences), and
3. The results (outcomes) after the learning experience (*e.g.*, knowledge, skills, attitudes, values, beliefs and behaviors).

These authors [14] link academic performance to this third set and build a model based on a series of concepts discussed in the literature. They define this model in terms of six dimensions: academic achievement, attainment of learning objectives, acquisition of skills and competencies, satisfaction, persistence, and career success (Fig. 2).

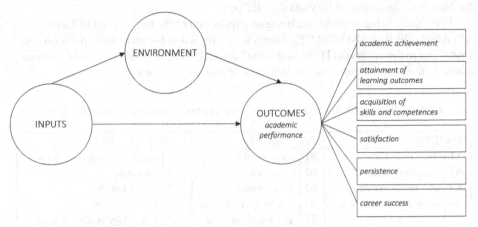

Fig. 2. Model of academic performance. Adapted from [14].

However, digital technology includes tools that can help optimize the assessment of learning and academic performance in general [15]. They allow keeping a flexible and comprehensive record of performance data. Based on the trace left by students when interacting with these technologies, their cognitive development, knowledge construction and skill acquisition processes can be tracked. In forums, this is achieved through access logs, contribution transcriptions, and metadata.

3   Methodology

For this work, a systematic review [16] of empirical studies was carried out following the guidelines outlined in [17] updated based on the contributions in [18]. The search strategy for retrieving the initial studies and the selection criteria for inclusion in the *corpus* are described below.

3.1   Search Strategy

An automatic search was performed using EBSCOhost's advanced search tools on the following databases, digital libraries, and journal portals: Academic Search Premier, Scopus, Education Resources Information Center (ERIC), Education Full Text, Directory of Open Access Journals (DOAJ), IEEE Xplore Digital Library, Scientific Electronic Library Online (SciELO), ScienceDirect, JSTOR Journals, and publishers included in the Complementary Index (Elsevier, Wiley, Springer, Taylor & Francis, Sage, ACM Digital Library). Snowballing techniques were also used [19], and studies were added based on expert suggestion or identified through manual search on the tables of contents in American Journal of Distance Education, Journal of New Approaches in Educational Research (NAER), Revista Iberoamericana de Tecnología en Educación y Educación en Tecnología (TE&ET), and minutes of conferences and congresses on topics related to the pedagogical use of digital technologies available in the Institutional Repository of the National University of La Plata (SEDICI).

The search string resulted in a Boolean expression of the terms listed in Table 1 (OR A*) AND (OR B*) AND (OR C*). Filters were applied to the identified articles so as to limit them to the context of HEIs; to this end, the terms *higher education*, *postsecondary education*, *undergraduates* and *undergraduate student* were used.

Table 1. Search terms according to topics and context of interest. Own elaboration.

DISCUSSION FORUMS		ASSESSMENT		MEDIATED EDUCATION	
A1	discussion forum	B1	assessment	C1	digital learning environment
A2	discussion board	B2	evaluation	C2	e-learning
A3	online discussion	B3	achievement	C3	online learning
A4	asynchronous commu-	B4	quantitative method	C4	virtual learning
	nications	B5	qualitative method	C5	technology enhanced learn-
A5	asynchronous discus-	B6	descriptive statistics		ing environment
	sion	B7	sequential analysis	C6	web-based learning environ-
A6	computer mediated	B8	content analysis		ment
	communication	B9	social network anal-	C7	learning management system
A7	virtual community of		ysis	C8	ICT mediated environment
	inquiry			C9	ICT mediated learning
				C10	ICT mediated education

3.2   Selection Criteria

Full-text, peer-reviewed articles, written in English or Spanish, published or accepted for publication between January 2015 and December 2020, and considering HEI students as the population of interest were included. Consequently, any articles that were non peer-reviewed, in a language other than English or Spanish, dealing with a different topic, or not about HEIs were excluded.

4   Results and Discussion

In the following paragraphs, the main characteristics of the articles included in the *corpus* and the results that answer the research questions are described.

4.1   Description of Selected Articles

As shown in Fig. 3, the initial search returned 401 documents. The digital object identifier (DOI) and bibliographic references allowed identifying 53 duplicates. After reviewing the title and abstract of the remaining 348 articles, 259 works were discarded for not complying with inclusion criteria. Then, the 89 potentially eligible articles were read in full. After this, 35 additional articles were discarded for not fully meeting the defined inclusion criteria, resulting in a final selection of 54 articles for review and synthesis. Five of these papers also consider student academic performance in forum spaces. The table, accessible through the QR code in Fig. 3, includes the references and a summary of the main characteristics of these papers.

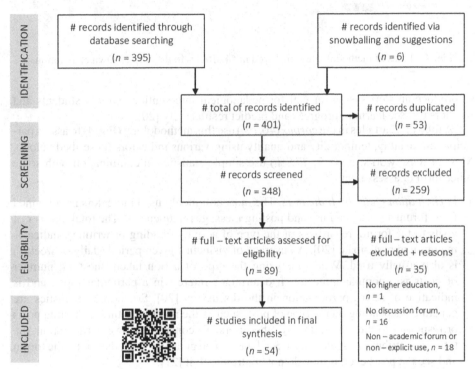

Fig. 3. Flow diagram of papers included in review. Characteristics of the 54 articles of the review *corpus* available at https://acortar.link/IOsLql. Own elaboration.

4.2 Methodologies for Assessing Participation

The bibliographic review surfaced four methodologies (simple statistics, content analysis, social network analysis, and process analysis) that evaluate different aspects (quantity, quality, temporality, and relationships) of participation (Fig. 4). Many research works (n = 24; 44.4%) combine protocols. The remaining articles (n = 30, 55.6%) use a single form of evaluation. The four methodologies are described in the following paragraphs.

Analysis Using Simple Statistics. The web systems used to host forums allow tracking user interaction. Analyzing these data is an efficient tool for data mining and learning analytics to understand participation [20]. Based on these data, statistics can be generated

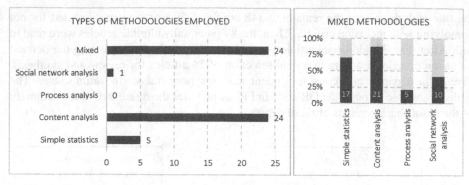

Fig. 4. Types of methodologies employed in 54 articles in the *corpus*. Own elaboration.

to produce an alert system or call for pedagogical interventions so that students and teachers can see learning progress and predict results early [20].

A total of 22 articles in the *corpus* (40.7%) use this methodology (Fig. 4) to assess participation quantity, temporality and quality using various indicators (described below). Most of these works (n = 17; 77.2%) use simple statistics in combination with some other form of assessment.

1. *Participation Quantity Indicators*. The most commonly used indicators are obtained from forum access, reading, and posting messages frequencies. The total number of visits to the forum, regardless of the type of activity (reading or writing), indicates intention to participate [20]. An average of visits in a given period (daily or weekly) is also usually used. When analyzing the type of action taken, the total number of posts is a popular indicator. It determines interest in a particular topic, and is indicative of active participation in the discussion [20]. Sometimes, statistics are generated depending on the type of post, such as the number of thread-starting posts or responses to threads started by other users. To consider passive participation, the total of contributions seen is used. Students can be great listeners; they enter the forum and see the posts even if they do not contribute to it [21].

2. *Participation Temporal Indicators*. These indicators work as a complement to quantitative indicators. They are obtained from event timestamps (date and time). A simple metric is the total time spent on the forum reading other user's posts or writing posts. In the case of students who do not contribute actively to the forum, they allow assessing passive participation [21]. Forum access interval. mean is a metric pointing to self-paced learning regularity [21]. Finally, punctuality by role can be assessed using a binary index depending on whether or not the assigned task was completed within the scheduled time.

3. *Participation Quality Indicators*. These indicators assess active and quality participation. The average number of views and contributors on threads started by a student and the total number of responses to a post are ways to reward those who initiated important threads that also engaged many members [21]. Votes and endorsements articulate human judgment and prevent the forum from being flooded with meaningless threads in order to increase contribution count [21]. Based on these records, the number of student posts assessed or supported is considered. Other possible metrics are post

depth (level within a thread) and thread depth (maximum response level within the thread). These allow obtaining thread growth patterns based on a taxonomy (short, extended, split) [11].

Content Analysis. Student contribution transcriptions can be used for studying learning mechanisms [22] from a cognitive, metacognitive, affective and motivational viewpoint [23]. Therefore, multiple authors have used this protocol to assess participation quality.

In fact, a total of 45 articles in the *corpus* use this methodology (Fig. 4). Almost half (n = 21; 46.7%) use it in combination with another form of assessment to analyze student participation and interactions dynamics [20].

All these articles discuss the quantitative dimension of the methodology, *i.e.*, they calculate frequencies for the events of interest through transcript qualitative analysis. This allows recording and categorizing communications content, and then comparing and contrasting the results obtained [20]. The qualitative dimension is characterized by the method (manual or automatic) and the coding approach (*a priori* or emergent) for the item analysis (post, topic or syntactic unit). In the following sub-section, the manual and automatic frameworks used in *corpus* investigations are reviewed.

1. *Manual Frameworks.* The most frequent ones are widely used and usually combined with each other. These frameworks have similar behaviors in relation to cognition depth and intensity [24]. In particular, learning is analyzed with a cognitive approach using the method discussed in [22], evidence of critical thinking is reviewed using the framework presented in [25], and knowledge construction is considered using the Interaction Analysis Model presented in [26]. Based on the Inquiry Community Model [27], frameworks are developed to assess cognitive, social and teaching presences. To reveal cognitive processes, Bloom's revised taxonomy [28] is used. Other frameworks are used in a single article to interpret speech acts, assess post quality, and so forth.

2. *Automatic Frameworks.* Manual coding cannot successfully handle the large volume of data generated on forums. Therefore, automatic coding procedures are necessary. Only five papers in the *corpus* (11.1%) have developed these automatic methods and show the potential of data mining techniques and natural language processing to assess different aspects of the learning process in these spaces. In particular, knowledge construction, cognitive presence, feelings, speech acts and prominent topics. One of the challenges of automating content analysis is that important constructs in education are latent and not explicitly present in the transcripts [23]. However, they open the doors to the development of real-time automated feedback systems on areas that require intervention [23].

Sequential Process Analysis. This analysis examines the significance of the sequential occurrence of behaviors, and shows these behaviors in transition diagrams [29]. This is relevant because interaction processes in forums are cumulative, and the sequence in which behaviors occur affects what is learned and how it is learned [30].

These behaviors are usually identified by analyzing forum contributions content. Both methodologies are used in combination in five articles (11.1%) in the *corpus* (Fig. 3). In these, the sequential analysis has been used to identify sequences of knowledge construction, cognitive processing, and speech acts.

Social Network Analysis. This analysis examines the structural attributes of the relationships that are established [31] and is used to identify central, prominent or prestigious individuals in the forum. These attributes also reflect aspects of group cohesion, as well as interaction quantity and quality.

However, this methodology has received little attention from researchers [32] and, by itself, it is not enough to fully understand interaction patterns in a given learning environment [23]. To achieve this comprehensive understanding, it should be applied as a complementary approach to content analysis and used together with other indicators such as simple statistics [23]. This is the case in 10 out of 11 articles in the review *corpus* (20.4%) that use social network analysis to assess various aspects of the networks generated in educational forums (Fig. 4).

In these research works, a diaspora of metrics has been used to assess multiple aspects based on directional and non-directional relationships.

1. *Actor and Network Centrality.* The metrics that are most frequently used are degree, closeness and betweenness.
2. *Group Cohesion.* Group cohesion is characterized by network density and network centrality.

Other useful instruments are the sociogram and matrix representations [31]. These allow understanding the social construction of learning and class dynamics, and facilitate the identification of students at risk. Consequently, they are tools that support planning and decision-making [20, 32].

4.3 Methodologies for Assessing Academic Performance

Sometimes, participation in discussion forums is evaluated as a contributing aspect to the final grade of a course. This is demonstrated by a set of five articles in the *corpus* that use these exchange spaces for discussing topics linked to the content [4, 21, 33, 34] or for solving problems [35]. To assess academic achievements in these initiatives, researchers develop different instruments such as rubrics and specific metrics. These protocols are described in the following paragraphs. However, regardless of the assessment instrument chosen, making expectations explicit regarding the depth of contributions, exploration or problem solving, and collaboration or reflection allows students to value and use these processes to expand their thinking and improve their standards of participation in tasks mediated by discussion forums [4, 21].

Rubrics. Four of the research works use rubrics to assess student individual or group achievements in terms of contribution quality or participation standard compliance based on a set of criteria. Namely:

1. Some authors [33] consider a group rating based on the level achieved (0–5) in four criteria: analysis depth, topic clarification, information collection, and conclusions drawn.
2. The second article [34] uses forums' formative evaluation to provide feedback to students on the quality of their weekly posts. The tool allows using a custom scale (objective, meets standard, needs improvement, missing or absent) to grade student posts using a drop-down menu.

3. Another author [4] reviewed and assessed previous frameworks and designed a set of participation rules, which then underwent multiple design, implementation, research, and redesign cycles. Compliance with these rules is used as a way of evaluation through comparison. A set of nine rules was obtained, which are: contributes new ideas or insights to the discussion; expands the idea or insight mentioned in the previous post; assesses the previous post and presents his/her own point of view; provides an evidence-based contribution; answers questions; asks questions that lead to deeper discussions on the topic or that bring out different perspectives; references course materials; provides constructive criticism on previous posts; and summarizes and relates previous posts on the topic.

4. In a fourth and final article [35], students' achievements in the forum are assessed using an analytical rubric that includes four criteria: coherence with the topic, providing explanations and ideas to support ideas, thinking and writing as experts in the discipline, and using culturally receptive communication behavior. These are evaluated on a numerical scale (0–3) according to the development level achieved (initial, developing, completed). The final score (0–10) is obtained by adding the individual scores for each criterion.

Metrics. In the remaining work [21], a series of metrics are considered that allow obtaining weighted scores for various indicators corresponding to participation quantity, quality and temporality, as well as to the relationships established between members or participants.

5   Conclusions and Future Work

A discussion forum is a virtual space that fosters interaction and promotes critical thinking, knowledge construction and problem solving. These potential uses require student participation. Studying the way in which students interact in these spaces is a topic of constant interest in the academic and scientific field.

This work reviews ways to assess participation in forums as covered by 54 research works carried out at HEIs and published between 2015 and 2020. These efforts describe four methodologies that can be used non-exclusively and allow assessing different aspects of the construct. Later works [36, 37] move forward along the same lines and demonstrate similar perspectives.

Among these, the most popular method is content manual analysis to assess contribution quality. Due to the difficulties and time required by this way of processing content, some automatic protocols have been developed that take into account the possibilities of machine learning and natural language processing to assess the learning process and collaboration in discussion forums.

Content analysis is usually accompanied by a sequential analysis of the interventions to describe temporality and interventions sequence. The latter is used less frequently among the research works reviewed in the *corpus*.

As a complement to these two methodologies, the calculation of simple statistics based on recorded data is recognized as an efficient way to carry out educational data mining and learning analytics, in particular because these statistics are easy to obtain and interpret. Therefore, this is the second most widely used methodology in the *corpus*, and it also provides information on participation quantity.

Finally, social network analysis allows identifying patterns and displaying member interaction. This allows teachers to grasp implicit aspects from the raw data and support their awareness of the underlying collaborative process. Thus, timely and flexible educational interventions are promoted.

When considering the benefits and limitations of each methodology, the integration of various protocols is a research trend that can contribute to a better understanding of student participation in discussion forums.

Sometimes, participation in discussion forums is evaluated as a form of academic achievement. This is demonstrated by five works in the *corpus*. To assess academic achievements in these initiatives, researchers develop different strategies. Rubrics stand out because they allow assessing contribution quality or compliance with the standards established for participation through a set of criteria. In another case, a series of metrics is used based on a set of indicators for participation quantity, quality and temporality, as well as participation relational aspects.

The results of this review that expands a previous one [7], together with those of a previous review [38], lead to the development of a comprehensive methodology that studies participation actions and academic performance in a group of postgraduate students during a forum activity [39], as well as self-regulated learning strategies [40] and relationships between the aforementioned constructs. This methodology is one of the main contributions of a master's thesis.

Disclosure of Interests. The authors have no competing interests to declare that are relevant to the content of this article.

References

1. García Aretio, L.: Fundamento y componentes de la educación a distancia. Revista Iberoamericana de Educación a Distancia 2(2), 28–39 (1999)
2. Almatrafi, O., Johri, A.: Systematic review of discussion forums in Massive Open Online Courses (MOOCs). IEEE Trans. Learn. Technol. 12(3), 413–428 (2019)
3. Roig, R., Rosales, S.: Assessing participation in online discussion forums: a proposal for multidimensional analysis. Píxel-Bit 40, 137–149 (2012)
4. Wang, Y.: Enhancing the quality of online discussion: assessment matters. J. Educ. Technol. Syst. 48(1), 112–129 (2019)
5. Gros Salvat, B., Silva, J.: El problema del análisis de las discusiones asincrónicas en el aprendizaje colaborativo mediado. Revista de Educación a Distancia 16 (2006)
6. Núñez Mosteo, F., Gálvez Mozo, A., Vayreda, A.: La participación en un foro electrónico: motivos, auditorios y posicionamientos. REDcientífica 47, 1–14 (2003)
7. Dieser, P., Sanz, C., Zangara, A.: Metodologías de evaluación de la participación en foros de debate académicos: Una revisión sistemática. In: Libro de Actas XXIX Congreso Argentino en Ciencias de la Computación – CACIC 2023, Luján, Buenos Aires, pp. 652–661 (2024)
8. Sanz, C., Zangara, A.: Los foros como espacios comunicacionales – didácticos en un curso a distancia. Una propuesta metodológica para aprovechar sus potencialidades. In: Actas XII CACIC, Potrero de los Funes, San Luis, pp. 1021–1033 (2006)

9. Arango, M.: Foros virtuales como estrategia de aprendizaje. Debates latinoamericanos **2**, 85–105 (2004)
10. Gašević, D., Adesope, O., Joksimović, S., Kovanović, V.: Externally facilitated regulation scaffolding and role assignment to develop cognitive presence in asynchronous online discussions. Internet Higher Educ. **24**, 53–65 (2015)
11. Ghadirian, H., Ayub, A., Bakar, K., Hassanzadeh, M.: Growth patterns and e-moderating supports in asynchronous online discussions in an undergraduate blended course. Int. Rev. Res. Open Distrib. Learn. **17**(3), 189–208 (2016)
12. Sutton, L.: The principles of vicarious interaction in computer-mediated communication. J. Interact. Educ. Commun. **7**(3), 223–242 (2001)
13. Lamas, H.: Sobre el rendimiento escolar. Propósitos y Representaciones **3**(1), 351–386 (2015)
14. York, T., Gibson, C., Rankin, S.: Defining and measuring academic success. Pract. Assess. Res. Eval. **20**(5), 1–20 (2015)
15. Barberà, E.: Aportaciones de la tecnología a la e-Evaluación. Revista de Educación a Distancia (2006)
16. Sánchez Meca, J.: Cómo realizar una revisión sistemática y un meta-análisis. Aula Abierta **38**(2), 53–63 (2010)
17. Petticrew, M., Roberts, H.: Systematic Reviews in the Social Sciences: A Practical Guide. Blackwell Publishing, Oxford (2006)
18. Lavallée, M., Robillard, P.N., Mirsalari, R.: Performing systematic literature reviews with novices: an iterative approach. IEEE Trans. Educ. **57**(3), 175–181 (2014)
19. Greenhalgh, T., Peacock, R.: Effectiveness and efficiency of search methods in systematic reviews of complex evidence: audit of primary sources. BMJ **331**(7524), 1064–1065 (2005)
20. Jo, I., Park, Y., Lee, H.: Three interaction patterns on asynchronous online discussion behaviours: a methodological comparison. J. Comput. Assist. Learn. **33**(2), 106–122 (2017)
21. Bihani, A., Paepcke, A.: QuanTyler: Apportioning credit for student forum participation. In: International Conference on Educational Data Mining, Raleigh (2018)
22. Henri, F.: Computer conferencing and content analysis. In: Kaye, A. (ed.) Collaborative Learning Through Computer Conferencing, pp. 117–136. Springer, London (1992)
23. Joksimović, S., et al.: Comprehensive analysis of discussion forum participation: from speech acts to discussion dynamics and course outcomes. IEEE Trans. Learn. Technol. **13**(1), 38–51 (2019)
24. O'Riordan, T., Millard, D.E., Schulz, J.: How should we measure online learning activity? Res. Learn. Technol. **24**, 30088 (2016)
25. Newman, D.R., Webb, B., Cochrane, C.: A content analysis method to measure critical thinking in face-to-face and computer supported group learning. Interpersonal Comput. Technol. **3**(2), 56–77 (1995)
26. Gunawardena, C., Lowe, C., Anderson, T.: Analysis of a global online debate and the development of an interaction analysis model for examining social construction of knowledge in computer conferencing. J. Tech. Writ. Commun. **17**(4), 397–431 (1997)
27. Garrison, D., Anderson, T., Archer, W.: Critical inquiry in a text-based environment: computer conferencing in Higher Education. Internet Higher Educ. **2**(2–3), 87–105 (2000)
28. Anderson, L., Krathwohl, D.: A Taxonomy for Learning, Teaching, and Assessing. A Revision of Bloom's Taxonomy of Educational Objectives. Addison Wesley, New York (2001)
29. Wu, S.Y., Hou, H.T.: How cognitive styles affect the learning behaviors of online problem-solving based discussion activity: a lag sequential analysis. J. Educ. Comput. Res. **52**(2), 277–298 (2015)
30. Reimann, P.: Time is precious: variable -and event- centred approaches to process analysis in CSCL research. Comput. Supp. Collab. Learn. **4**, 239–257 (2009)

31. Wasserman, S., Faust, K.: El análisis de las redes sociales en las ciencias sociales y del comportamiento. In Análisis de redes sociales: Métodos y Aplicaciones, pp. 35–58. Centro de Investigaciones Sociales, Madrid (2013)
32. Ghadirian, H., Salehi, K., Ayub, A.: Analyzing the social networks of high and low performing students in online discussion forums. Am. J. Distan. Educ. **32**(1), 27–42 (2018)
33. Ghadirian, H., Salehi, K., Ayub, A.F.M.: Exploring the behavioural patterns of knowledge dimensions and cognitive processes in peer-moderated asynchronous online discussions. Int. J. E-Learn. Distan. Educ. **33**(1) (2018)
34. Smith, T.W.: Making the most of online discussion: a retrospective analysis. Int. J. Teach. Learn. Higher Educ. **31**(1), 21–31 (2019)
35. Williams, S.S., Jaramillo, A., Pesko, J.C.: Improving depth of thinking in online discussion boards. Quart. Rev. Dist. Educ. **16**(3), 45–66 (2015)
36. Liu, Z., Zhang, N., Peng, X., Liu, S., Yang, Z.: Students' social-cognitive engagement in online discussions: an integrated analysis perspective. Educ. Technol. Soc. **26**(1), 1–15 (2023)
37. Norz, L., Dornauer, V., Hackl, W., Ammenwerth, E.: Measuring social presence in online based learning: An exploratory path analysis using log data and social network analysis. Internet Higher Educ. **56** (2023)
38. Dieser, P., Sanz, C., Zangara, A.: Metodologías para la evaluación de la autorregulación del aprendizaje en contextos educativos mediados por tecnología digital. Una revisión sistemática. In: Actas XVII Congreso TE&ET, pp. 26–35 (2022)
39. Dieser, P., Sanz, C., Zangara, A.: Propuesta metodológica para la evaluación de la participación y el rendimiento académico en foros de debate. Revista Iberoamericana de Tecnología en Educación y Educación en Tecnología, **36**(e2) (2023)
40. Dieser, P., Sanz, C., Zangara, A.: Hacia una comprensión dinámica y contextual de la autorregulación del aprendizaje: Propuesta metodológica para su evaluación en foros académicos. In: Actas XVIII Congreso TE&ET, pp. 42–51 (2023)

Basic Electronics Virtual Laboratory for University Students in an Extended Classroom

Leonardo Navarria[1,2]([envelope]) [iD], Alejandro González[3,4] [iD], and Alejandra Zangara[3] [iD]

[1] Facultad de Ciencias Astronómicas y Geofísicas (UNLP), Paseo del Bosque S/N,
La Plata, Argentina
leonardo.navarria@ing.unlp.edu.ar
[2] Facultad de Ingeniería (UNLP), 1 esq. 47, La Plata, Argentina
[3] Instituto de Investigación en Informática III-LIDI-Facultad de Informática (UNLP),
50 esq. 120, La Plata, Argentina
[4] Dirección General de Educación a Distancia y Tecnologías, UNLP Argentina Calle,
7 nro.776, La Plata, Argentina

Abstract. The objective of this work was to develop virtual basic electronics laboratories for university students within an extended classroom and evaluate their content using expert jury judgment. In the face-to-face teaching of careers that have practical content, it is essential to carry out practices to consolidate knowledge. The exercise in them involves the student's attendance at certain shifts with fixed schedules, in a place limited in equipment and space resources. With the use of virtual work methodologies, it is possible for many students to have access to practical content to become familiar with basic electronic instruments and components that are of fundamental importance for the acquisition of practical knowledge. At the end of the work, the results obtained globally by the stated methodology are shown.

Keywords: Laboratory · virtual · extended classroom

1 Introduction

1.1 A Subsection Sample

This work is derived from the Thesis work obtaining the master's degree in computer technology applied to education taught at the Faculty of Computer Science of the National University of La Plata [1].

The author is a professor at the Faculty of Engineering and the Faculty of Astronomical and Geophysical Sciences, both at UNLP. In the subjects in which the author exercises his teaching position, basic contents of electrical engineering are taught, such as fundamental laws, behavior of electrical and electronic components, analysis of different types of circuits such as direct and alternating current (DC/AC). As these are subjects with theoretical and practical content, the analyzes of the different types of circuits can be verified using circuit simulators and implemented in a practical way, where

P. Pesado et al. (Eds.): CACIC 2023, CCIS 2123, pp. 91–104, 2024.
https://doi.org/10.1007/978-3-031-62245-8_7

it is vitally important to know how to use the instruments that allow measuring electrical variables.

In the face-to-face teaching of careers that have practical content, it is essential to carry out practices to consolidate knowledge. The exercise in them involves the student's attendance at certain shifts with fixed schedules, in a place limited in equipment and space resources. With the use of virtual work methodologies, it is possible for many students to have access to practical content to become familiar with basic and advanced electronic instruments and components.

To evaluate whether the content of the laboratories improves the students' skills, the contents of each of the laboratories were validated using the expert jury judgment method. This sought to investigate the possibility of improving the content, verifying whether laboratory practices improved cognitive processes, using simulators in the teaching, and learning process, and evaluating informative material.

To evaluate the use of the laboratories by the student's, closed questionnaires were carried out for students before and after they used the laboratories.

2 Purpose

2.1 Laboratory Practice

Laboratory practice is a powerful pedagogical strategy for the construction of procedural competencies and for this reason it is used in a wide variety of academic programs, usually synchronized with its corresponding theoretical subject. The work of Infante Jiménez [2] addresses the importance of in-person laboratories in applied science careers, for example Engineering, Physiochemistry, Chemistry, etc., however, as educational models have become more flexible and focused on competencies, The inclusion of Information and Communication Technologies (ICT) has radically changed the concept of physical space; This has revealed a series of limitations because despite its enormous importance for learning, it cannot offer the ideal versatility that is currently needed. It is also a fact that laboratory practice has high response times, which tend to lower productivity.

Infante Jiménez highlights the cost of experiments with real plants in terms of time, money, energy, maintenance, conditions that are difficult to sustain if there are no suitable personnel with high availability to meet the demand of the practices. Along with the latter, there must be supervision by tutor teachers or laboratory managers. All this leads to a physical limitation of the number of students. Thinking about a time of the COVID-19 pandemic, the cost of sanitation would have to be added and that the laboratories should be for only one student since by protocol it is impossible to share elements and measuring instruments. Added to this is the negative impact of the carbon footprint since the transportation of the student and teacher, unless combustion vehicles are not used, generate greenhouse gas (GHG) emissions into the atmosphere.

The article by Contreras Gélvez [3] explores the habits related to the use of simulators to support knowledge transfer processes in basic sciences and programming. This work starts from the premise to investigate the contribution of simulators to the training of university engineering students. The study is contextualized in the development of physics, mathematics, and programming knowledge classes. There were physical laboratories equipped with sufficient workstations for the number of students.

The use of virtual laboratory tools is considered to generate student-tutor interaction through a formal virtual teaching environment.

The virtual laboratory as a learning object has the following attributes:

- Be reusable: they can be used again without losing any features.
- Be digital.
- Be a resource: it does not constitute knowledge, but rather promotes and strengthens it in an easier way.
- Serve as learning emphasizes the explicit and intentional characteristic that the person must learn through the learning object

As a result, "it can be said, in general, that the use of simulators as a teaching strategy, through which knowledge is transferred, does have an impact on the student´s learning process, since classes become more interesting, There is greater student participation, the explanations given are clearer, retention increases when content is presented, and motivation and pleasure in learning increases" [2]. It should be considered that the use of simulations as a teaching tool has multiple advantages; however, their integration into specific teaching designs requires that teachers know the characteristics, potential and limitations of these resources.

In the teaching of engineering and technical careers, it is desirable to carry out pedagogical activities that allow the student to put into practice previous knowledge and acquire new ones, corroborated in the field of real experience. This role is played by the practical laboratory, which, inexorably, requires the physical presence of the student to be able to manipulate the control systems and existing plants in a controlled environment, under the supervision of the teacher [4].

2.2 Problem-Based Learning

Problem-Based Learning (PBL) as a teaching and learning methodology is used in numerous higher education institutions in various areas of knowledge. The purpose of Problem-Based Learning is to train students capable of analyzing and facing problems in the same way they will do during their professional activity, that is, valuing and integrating the knowledge that will lead them to the acquisition of professional skills.

As they advance in their career, using PBL as a student-centered teaching-learning method will allow them to acquire knowledge, skills, and attitudes through real-life situations. Not teaching the application of PBL will mean that the student will not be able to build their knowledge based on real-life problems and situations and, furthermore, will not do so with the same reasoning process that they will use when they become a professional.

The most innovative characteristic of PBL is the use of problems as a starting point for the acquisition of new knowledge and the conception of the student as the protagonist of the management of their learning.

Improving the resolution of situations using PBL could benefit fundamental issues such as:

- Unification of criteria regarding problem resolution
- Language unification

- Resolution of situations
- Correct foundation
- Acquisition of criteria to practice as a future professional.

In the work subjects, the PBL methodology is used to solve practical work problems oriented to real situations that the student may encounter in their professional life. Problem-based learning.

2.3 Learning Based on Laboratory Work

According to López Rúa and Tamayo [6], simulations and practical laboratory work or experimental work constitute one of the most important activities in science teaching because they promote the acquisition of a series of scientific procedures and skills, from the most basic (use of multimeters, measurement of variables, data collection, data processing, etc.) to the most complex (investigating and solving problems using experimentation). This indicates the fundamental importance that practical work must have as a learning activity.

In the area of science, laboratory work favors and promotes learning, since the student confronts his previous knowledge with reality by verifying it through practices [7].

The experimental activity should not only be seen as a knowledge tool, but as an instrument that promotes the conceptual, procedural, and attitudinal objectives that any pedagogical proposal must include.

Following this line of thought, Andrés, Pesa and Meneses [8] propose that in the development of practical laboratory work, learning in the methodological domain should predominate and in an inseparable relationship with some theoretical framework associated with the proposed experience, the student learns in action in the face of the situation.

The permanent research, innovation, integration, and development of technological and computer systems in the field of education are allowing the implementation of new practices in the way of constructing the teaching and learning process. Such is the case of carrying out practical laboratory work whether on an object of virtual or real existence but carried out remotely, as an activity that is accessed through a virtual teaching-learning environment.

It can be stated that the laboratory work, depending on the degree of student participation, establishes that:

- The student is involved in the use of technical and scientific procedures
- A work methodology is established
- The use of specific material and instruments is required, and in some cases reconditioned and adapted so that the student can use them to carry out the practices.
- They are carried out in places other than the classroom where the classes are taught, these may be a laboratory, placing in the case of study, electronics or directly field, as is the case of geophysics, laboratory to measure the Earth's magnetic field.
- There are risks for the student regarding the manipulation of some components.
- There are risks of damage to measuring instruments
- Activities are carried out that have an organizational complexity greater than the resolution of an exercise in the study material.

- Motivation is generated on the part of the student.
- It helps to understand the theoretical content presented in the classroom.
- The development of scientific reasoning is encouraged.
- The understanding of real problems modeled for resolution in the study portfolio is facilitated.
- A base of content is established on which research attitudes are developed.
- They must be fundamental for the teaching and learning of technical knowledge.

3 Development

The phenomenon of digital technological advances in the field of communication and computing has enriched the instruments of educational technology with the incorporation of equipment for recording, reproduction and transmission of text, sound, and image. And let's not forget that a good part of these technologies is found today in the homes of many citizens.

Thus, students, through independent study, will learn at least as effectively as the student in a conventional center. More than the method itself, how well it is used is important, as numerous research shows.

Education in virtuality, that is, from non-presence in virtual learning environments, is not necessarily situated in any specific educational orientation. Just as in person there is coexistence between diverse orientations and didactics, if these act in a manner consistent with the educational purposes and with the purposes of education, the same happens in virtuality [9]. The learning process in virtual environments is the result of several stages in which the student constructs the learning process. Likewise, it can be the product of practice, such as the use of simulators. In this way, there is a critical analysis as there is also in person, giving rise to different perspectives of assessment.

The most important difference between in-person and virtual education is the change of medium and the treatment that must be done to optimize each of the mediums. The same actions should not and cannot be carried out in different media, even if our educational objectives are the same. You should know that the paths to follow are different. The medium of communication is of fundamental importance and can lead to the success or failure of the educational process.

Below is a list of some of the laboratories carried out along with their links:

Analysis of direct current circuits, Fig. 1:

The link of the first laboratory can be followed at https://lc.cx/ZvBX8x.

For this laboratory, the genial.ly tool was used for web design. Physical components of electrical circuits such as breadboards, resistors, cables, etc. were used. Several measurements were made with instruments for measuring electrical variables so that the student linked the real circuit with a schematic.

The objectives were: Experimentally verify Kirchhoff's laws of currents and voltages. Learn to perform and interpret measurements of currents and voltages in Direct Current. Understand the concepts of electrical circuits and power. Link a real circuit with a schematic. Perform calculations and check the results obtained.

The second laboratory, analysis of alternating current circuits can be followed at https://youtu.be/Z6-fXSLZ1Pc. Physical components of electrical circuits, resistors,

Del circuito real al protoboard

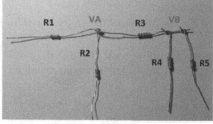

Circuito Soldado   Circuito en Protoboard

Fig. 1. Soldered circuit and protoboard mounted circuit

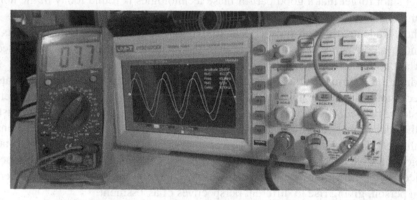

Fig. 2. Oscilloscope and multimeter used for AC measurement

cables, inductors, and capacitors were used. A multimeter, oscilloscope (Fig. 2) and a signal generator were used.

The objectives were: Interpret the use of signal generators. Understand the use of the multimeter. Set up use of an oscilloscope.

The Rectifier Laboratories (Fig. 3) can be found at the following links:

- https://youtu.be/k3vcU75SsUw
- https://youtu.be/0KVOVrWAToU
- https://youtu.be/SAEMP_zOwng

This laboratory had the following objectives: Self-assess the student's knowledge on the topic of rectifiers. Understand the operation of rectifiers by studying in real time with measurements from measuring instruments. Check the results obtained using the LTSPICE electrical circuit simulator. Obtain conclusions from the results obtained.

For this third laboratory, a Branching scenario (H5P) was used. This tool allows you to make decisions about the behavior of a certain circuit. Likewise, an LTspice circuit simulator was used, together with the real circuit, measurement instruments and

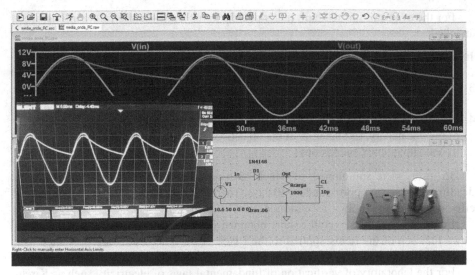

Fig. 3. The Rectifier Laboratories

the carrying out of the laboratories was filmed, comparing the results obtained with the simulated ones as shown in Fig. 3.

4 Evaluation of the Contents of the Laboratories by Juries

The general objective of the work carried out by the thesis student was to evaluate the effectiveness of carrying out basic electronics practices with virtual laboratories within an extended classroom. The evaluation was carried out by a jury of experts, which consists of asking a series of people to make a judgment about an object, an instrument, a teaching material, or their opinion regarding a specific aspect. Each of the laboratories carried out was designed so that the student improves the problem-solving skills of each of the subjects in question. To select the experts according to what was indicated in the previous paragraphs, the following were considered:

- Professional experience.
- Link to research.
- Expertise on the subject.
- Academic level.
- Participation in research projects

To carry out the expert judgment, the Individual Aggregates technique was used, which consists of each expert answering a series of questions on a Likert scale about the different dimensions of the laboratories. The individual aggregate method allows experts to be consulted individually and simultaneously using an electronic form. The authors Corral [10], Cabero [11] agree that the construction of the inquiry instrument becomes a key tool, since there would be no other interaction with the experts other than the sending and receiving of the complete instrument. The experts evaluate individually and cannot exchange their opinions, points of view and experience with the other selected experts.

For the evaluation of the built materials, the items shown in the following list were attacked:

1. Quality of content: Update, Quality, Sequence and structure, Clarity of explanations.
2. Technical aspects: Media quality, Graphic and letter sizes.
3. Motivation: Degree of attraction of the tool: Interest aroused, Duration, Scope of objectives
4. Didactic value: Adaptation to the Curriculum, Favors the learning process, Adequacy of the vocabulary, Explanation of the objectives, The problems presented correspond to real situations, Conclusions.

15 jurors were summoned, of which 13 responded to the questionnaire after the deadline, which was approximately 30 days. Therefore, the degree of call shows an 87% effective call, losing only a 13% sample.

Figure 4 shows the overall results obtained in the Laboratory testing Kirchhoff's Laws for each of the items applied to the Likert scale. The results are presented as a percentage.

For the laboratory of verification of fundamental laws of electricity such as Kirchhoff's Laws, the acceptance value is 95% divided between Very Good and Good. However, notes are taken of the contributions indicated by some of the experts in the case of the conclusions obtained, the duration of the laboratory and the interest aroused by this first laboratory.

Item	Very Good	Good	Sufficient	Insufficient	Total
Goal reach	62%	38%	0%	0%	100%
Adaptation to the curriculum	62%	38%	0%	0%	100%
Favoring the learning process	69%	23%	8%	0%	100%
Vocabulary adequacy	54%	38%	8%	0%	100%
Explanation of objectives	77%	15%	8%	0%	100%
Correspondence between real situations	69%	31%	0%	0%	100%
Conclusions obtained	62%	31%	0%	8%	100%
Content update	54%	31%	15%	0%	100%
Design quality	46%	46%	8%	0%	100%
Sequence and structure	46%	46%	8%	0%	100%
Clarity of explanations	69%	31%	0%	0%	100%
Media quality	38%	62%	0%	0%	100%
Graphics and letters size	77%	23%	0%	0%	100%
Degree of tool attraction	69%	23%	8%	0%	100%
Piqued interest	62%	31%	8%	0%	100%
Duration	69%	23%	8%	0%	100%
Average	62%	33%	5%	0%	100%

Fig. 4. Results Obtained from the verification of Kirchhoff's Laws

Figure 5 shows the results obtained from the second laboratory, use of instruments for measuring electrical variables in alternating current.

For the laboratory of use of measuring instruments, it is observed that it has an acceptance of 93%. There are points to review regarding the conclusions obtained and the motivation, this must adjust the motivation for carrying out this laboratory by adding a more conceptual degree of justification.

Item	Very Good	Good	Sufficient	Insufficient	Total
Goal reach	62%	38%	0%	0%	100%
Adaptation to the curriculum	62%	38%	0%	0%	100%
Favoring the learning process	85%	8%	8%	0%	100%
Vocabulary adequacy	62%	38%	0%	0%	100%
Explanation of objectives	62%	38%	0%	0%	100%
Correspondence between real situations	62%	31%	8%	0%	100%
Conclusions obtained	69%	23%	8%	0%	100%
Content update	69%	23%	8%	0%	100%
Design quality	62%	31%	0%	8%	100%
Sequence and structure	69%	15%	15%	0%	100%
Clarity of explanations	69%	31%	0%	0%	100%
Media quality	69%	23%	8%	0%	100%
Graphics and letters size	69%	23%	8%	0%	100%
Degree of tool attraction	46%	46%	8%	0%	100%
Piqued interest	62%	23%	8%	8%	100%
Duration	69%	15%	15%	0%	100%
Average	65%	28%	6%	1%	100%

Fig. 5. Instruments for measuring electrical variables in alternating current

Figure 6 shows the results of the third laboratory, analysis of rectifiers, which obtained 100% acceptance by the juries.

Item	Very Good	Good	Sufficient	Insufficient	Total
Goal reach	92%	8%	0%	0%	100%
Adaptation to the curriculum	62%	38%	0%	0%	100%
Favoring the learning process	77%	23%	0%	0%	100%
Vocabulary adequacy	69%	31%	0%	0%	100%
Explanation of objectives	62%	38%	0%	0%	100%
Correspondence between real situations	85%	15%	0%	0%	100%
Conclusions obtained	77%	23%	0%	0%	100%
Content update	62%	38%	0%	0%	100%
Design quality	77%	23%	0%	0%	100%
Sequence and structure	62%	38%	0%	0%	100%
Clarity of explanations	69%	31%	0%	0%	100%
Media quality	46%	54%	0%	0%	100%
Graphics and letters size	62%	38%	0%	0%	100%
Degree of tool attraction	77%	23%	0%	0%	100%
Piqued interest	69%	31%	0%	0%	100%
Duration	54%	46%	0%	0%	100%
Average	69%	31%	0%	0%	100%

Fig. 6. Results of the third laboratory, analysis of rectifiers

5   Evaluation of the Laboratories by Students

As an extension of the additional work presented at CACIC 2023 [12], work has been carried out with the survey carried out on students about the use of laboratories in class.

To evaluate the use of the laboratories by the student's, closed questionnaires were carried out for students before they used the laboratories. After using the virtual laboratories, the same questionnaire was administered again prior to the completion of the subject. The student questionnaires were closed, with responses based on a Likert scale with five possible answers:

- Totally agree,
- Partially agree,
- Neither agree nor disagree,
- Partially disagree,
- Totally disagree.

The tool used to carry out the questionnaire was the Google form. The link to the forms was made via the Moodle of each chair, indicating that a deadline was available to resolve it. The indication was made through internal messaging and through synchronous videoconferences in the explanation classes.

The dimensions evaluated were about:

a. Expectations: Consultation was made regarding the increase in the student's skills, knowledge, and training. The questions asked were three:
   (1) Through these multimedia systems practices I hope to gain new skills and knowledge to understand electrical circuits.
   (2) Carrying out these multimedia systems practices will increase my knowledge
   (3) My motivation regarding these internships is based on the interest in improving my training
b. Usefulness: a survey was conducted on improving skills and abilities to solve electrical circuits. The questions asked were two:
   (1) I consider it very useful that carrying out these multimedia systems practices improves my skills.
   (2) I hope that through these practices I will be able to solve electrical circuit problems.
c. Content and method: questions were asked about the consolidation of basic knowledge, the expansion of the tools used and whether the teaching content was precise, understandable, and up to date. The questions asked were three:
   (1) Believe that the content of these practices will consolidate my basic knowledge and expand the use of the tools used in them.
   (2) Considers it necessary that the didactic content of the practices be precise, understandable, and updated
   (3) Carrying out remote practices on multimedia systems is an innovative and very practical methodology.
d. Tools: multimedia applications, computer resources, simulators, adequacy with respect to the contents shown were evaluated. The questions asked were three:
   (1) Do you expect that the multimedia applications offered in these practices will help me relate the practical part with the theory, so that the assimilation of content has been easier?
   (2) Do you think it is important that the computer tools used have been adjusted to the explanation of multimedia applications?
   (3) Do you think that there should be a real and effective adaptation between the multimedia content that is made available on the platform and its didactic uses?

The surveys prior to carrying out the laboratories were answered by 68 students. The subsequent surveys were answered by 60 students, with 8 students having a sample loss of 11.8%, achieving a call grade higher than 88%.

Figure 7 shows the results of the surveys obtained prior to carrying out the laboratories.

In the previous surveys, the expectations regarding the increase in the student's skills, knowledge, and training have a degree of acceptance of total agreement of 58% and 23% of partial agreement, registering around 80% as positive. On the other hand, in a negative way, only 10% think that expectations will not be good.

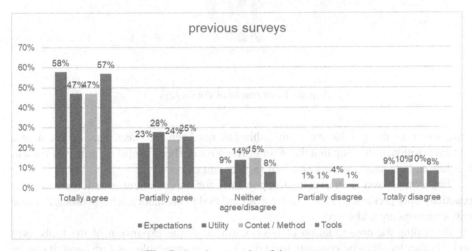

Fig. 7. Previous results of the surveys

Regarding the usefulness of improving skills and abilities to solve electrical circuits, 75% positively believe that it will improve their skills and, on the other hand, 11% do not.

Regarding the content and methodology for the consolidation of basic knowledge, the expansion of the tools used and whether the didactic contents were precise, understandable, and updated, 71% previously agreed, but 14% did not believe so.

The tools used such as multimedia applications, computer resources, simulators, adaptation to the content, 82% of those surveyed agree that they will be useful and only 10% believe otherwise.

Figure 8 shows the results of the surveys obtained after carrying out the laboratories.

Comparing the results (Fig. 7 and Fig. 8) in a positive way (agree) vs negative results (disagreement) positive expectations have decreased by 5% and negative expectations have been reduced by 3%. It can be considered that the laboratories have met what was expected by the students regarding the increase in the student's skills, knowledge, and training.

Performing the same analysis as in the previous stage, it is observed that prior to solving the laboratories, the students maintained that they would improve the skills and abilities to solve problems proposed by the classes about electrical circuits. The

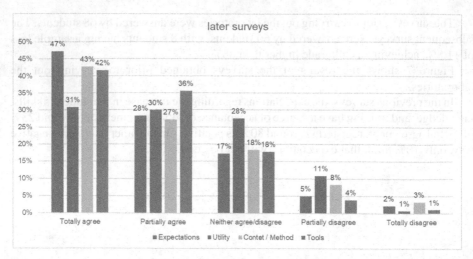

Fig. 8. Later results of the surveys

comparison of the graphs shows that this has not been the case, leaving them in a neutral position, indicating that the laboratories have not been useful to improve problem resolution, but there is no increase in disagreement either.

This comparison is an excellent opportunity for improvement to articulate that the practical work presented in the subject is articulated to the laboratories presented where real situations are addressed.

Regarding the consolidation of basic knowledge, the expansion of the tools used and whether the didactic contents were precise, understandable, and updated, it can be seen that there are no major changes with respect to what was expected and what was obtained. The negative aspects have been improved, but what was expected and what was obtained are unchanged.

Finally, in the item of multimedia applications, computer resources, simulators, and their adequacy with respect to the contents, acceptance and non-acceptance have decreased, indicating a neutral zone, but 77% of those surveyed continue to agree that the tools used are suitable for virtual laboratories, only 5% have indicated a neutral position regarding the tools.

6   Conclusions

Through the laboratories, it was proposed to improve skills in knowledge covered. The evaluation of competencies provides a change of approach with respect to traditional evaluation since it attempts to determine the knowledge and skills achieved in the learning process.

The pedagogical proposal for the inclusion of the virtual laboratory in a traditional course scheme contemplated the stage of real experience, virtual experience, simulation, comparison of results and drawing conclusions.

The teacher's criteria are decisive for the selection of the virtual laboratory that best suits the objectives consistent with competency-based training. The laboratory designs have required extra effort on the part of the teacher.

Regarding the results obtained from the surveys carried out on the students, the expectations meet the increase in the student's skills, knowledge and training; however, many students have considered that they have not increased their knowledge to improve problem solving, despite, they do not show disagreement in this item.

It is necessary to continue promoting studies that contribute to knowledge about the use of technologies in education and the transfer of knowledge.

Acknowledgments. First, to Mg. Alejandro H. González and Dr. Alejandra Zangara that without their directives this work would not have been possible.

To colleagues who have participated in the expert judgment.

References

1. Navarria, L.: Laboratorio virtual de electrónica básica para alumnos universitarios dentro de aula extendida. Comprobaciones de las leyes básicas de circuitos eléctricos y aplicaciones sobre semiconductores (2023). http://sedici.unlp.edu.ar/handle/10915/154689
2. Jiménez, C.I.: Propuesta pedagógica para el uso de laboratorios virtuales como actividad complementaria en las asignaturas teórico-prácticas. Revista mexicana de investigación educativa, 917–937 (2014). http://www.scielo.org.mx/scielo.php?script=sci_arttext&pid=S1405-66662014000300013&lng=es&tlng=es
3. Contreras, G., Gloria, A., García Torres, R., Ramírez, M., María, S.: Uso de simuladores como recurso digital para la transferencia de conocimiento. Apertura, 2 (2010). ISSN: 1665-6180. https://www.redalyc.org/articulo.oa?id=688/68820841008
4. Lorandi, A.P., Hermida, G., Hernández, J., Ladrón de Guevara, E.: Los Laboratorios Virtuales y Laboratorios Remotos en la Enseñanza de la Ingeniería. Revista Internacional de Educación en Ingeniería, **4**, 24–30 (2011). http://bibliografia.eovirtual.com/LorandiA_2011_Laboratorios.pdf
5. Dormido, S., Sanchez, J., Morilla, F.: Laboratorios virtuales y remotos para la práctica a distancia de la Automática (2007)
6. López, R., Ana, M., Tamayo, A., Óscar, E.: Las Prácticas De Laboratorio En La Enseñanza De Las Ciencias Naturales. Revista Latinoamericana de Estudios Educativos (Colombia), **8**(1), 145–166 (2012). ISSN: 1900-9895. https://www.redalyc.org/articulo.oa?id=134129256008
7. Osorio, Y.W.: El experimento como indicador de aprendizaje. Boletín PPDQ **43**, 7–10 (2004)
8. Andrés, M.M., Pesa, M.Y., Meneses, J.: Efectividad de un laboratorio guiado por el modelo de aprendizaje matlaf para el desarrollo conceptual asociado a tareas experimentales. Enseñanza de las Ciencias, **26**(3), 343–358 (2008)
9. Sangrà, A.: Enseñar y aprender en la virtualidad (2001). http://www.redined.mec.es/oai/indexg.php?registro=007200230138
10. Corral, Y.: Validez y confiabilidad de los instrumentos de investigación para la recolección de datos. Revista Ciencias de la Educación. 19 (2009)
11. Cabero Almenara, J. Llorente Cejudo, M.C.: La aplicación del juicio de experto como técnica de evaluación de las tecnologías de la información (TIC). EnEduweb. Revista de Tecnología de Información y Comunicación en Educación (2012). http://tecnologiaedu.us.es/tecnoedu/images/stories/jca107.pdf

12. Navarria, L., González, A., Zangara, A.: Laboratorio virtual de electrónica básica para alumnos universitarios dentro de aula extendida. Libro de Actas: XXIX Congreso Argentino de Ciencias de la Computación – CACIC 2023 Compilación de Juan Manuel Fernández. - 1a ed. - Luján : Universidad Nacional de Luján (2024). ISBN 978-987-9285-51-0
13. Navarria, L.J.: Laboratorio virtual de electrónica básica para alumnos universitarios dentro de aula extendida (Magister dissertation, Universidad Nacional de La Plata) (2023). http://sedici.unlp.edu.ar/handle/10915/154689

Graphic Computation, Images
and Visualization

Improving Cryptocurrency Visual Analysis
with *CryptoVisualizer+*

Mercedes Barrionuevo[1]([✉])[ID] and María Luján Ganuza[2][ID]

[1] Universidad Nacional de San Luis, San Luis, Argentina
mdbarrio@unsl.edu.ar
[2] Inst. for Computer Science and Engineering, ICIC (CONICET-UNS),
San Andrés 800, 8000 Bahía Blanca, Argentina
mlg@cs.uns.edu.ar

Abstract. With the rapid expansion of the cryptocurrency market, there is a growing need for tools that can effectively handle the complexity of cryptocurrency data. The temporal aspect of cryptocurrency data plays a crucial role in understanding market behavior and making informed decisions. Cryptocurrency prices are highly volatile and can change rapidly over short periods. Therefore, analyzing the temporal patterns and trends in cryptocurrency data is essential for predicting future price movements and identifying trading opportunities. In this paper, we present *CryptoVisualizer+*, an integral visual analysis tool for temporal data associated with cryptocurrencies. Our proposal integrates different visualization methods and interactions to empower users in exploring and understanding temporal patterns, trends, and relationships in cryptocurrency markets.

Keywords: Visualization · Temporal Data Visualization · Cryptocurrencies · Visual Data Analysis

1 Introduction

Visualizing temporal data involves using visual representations to explore and understand data that changes over time. This process includes analyzing patterns, trends, and relationships within the temporal data to gain insights and extract meaningful information. Understanding temporal patterns and trends is crucial in many academic disciplines for making informed decisions and extracting significant insights. Visualization techniques allow researchers to examine and compare data at different time scales, which helps in interpreting and analyzing information more effectively [1,2].

The visual analysis of temporal data also plays a key role in effectively communicating scientific findings. It can illustrate significant changes, show the evolution of variables over time, and reveal trends and patterns that emerge over time. This field has become increasingly important in recent years, driven by the growing availability of time-series data across various domains [3].

© The Author(s), under exclusive license to Springer Nature Switzerland AG 2024
P. Pesado et al. (Eds.): CACIC 2023, CCIS 2123, pp. 107–118, 2024.
https://doi.org/10.1007/978-3-031-62245-8_8

Several traditional visualization techniques have been applied to this kind of data, (like line charts, bar charts, and heat maps, among others) and dedicated techniques have been presented [4–6]. In this context, Andrienko and Andrienko [7] proposed a taxonomy of tasks for time-oriented data to help researchers and practitioners understand the diverse challenges and objectives of working with temporal data.

Visualizing cryptocurrencies is crucial for gaining insights into market trends and making informed investment decisions. Cryptocurrency markets are highly volatile and complex, with prices and trading volumes fluctuating rapidly. Visualizations, such as charts and graphs, help traders and investors understand these fluctuations by providing a visual representation of the data. They can reveal patterns, trends, and correlations that may not be apparent from raw data alone. For example, visualizations can show how the price of Bitcoin correlates with other cryptocurrencies, or how trading volume changes over time. By using visualizations, traders and investors can better understand market dynamics and make more informed decisions about buying, selling, or holding cryptocurrencies [8].

Cryptocurrency visualization encompasses a variety of methods [8–11]. In 2023, we presented *CryptoVisualizer* [12], a cryptocurrency visualization tool specifically focused on 4 cryptocurrencies of interest: Bitcoin (BTC), Ethereum (ETH), Cardano (ADA), and Dogecoin (DOGE). It was designed as a combination of two dashboards, one integrating several views related to prices and the other integrating views designed to analyze the transaction volume of the currencies. Although this study introduced two comprehensive dashboards featuring insightful views for cryptocurrency analysis, the inherently temporal nature of this data has prompted us to devise new views that facilitate more efficient temporal exploration. Therefore, in this article, we present *CryptoVisualizer+*, an extension of our previous work, with the main objective of designing new enhanced views and integrating them on a unique dashboard.

In the next section, we define the questions that will serve as the basis for defining the *CryptoVisualizer+*'s requirements. In Sect. 3, we describe our proposal, detailing the characteristics of the data, the designed dashboard, and the supported interactions. In Sect. 3.2, the results are presented, explaining how the developed tool addresses the questions defined in Sect. 2. Finally, in Sect. 4 we elaborate on the conclusions and future work.

2 Requirements

As an initial step in designing a tool for analyzing cryptocurrency data, we conducted a comprehensive analysis of the current state of the art based on Andrienko and Andrienko's taxonomy of tasks for time-oriented data [7]. This taxonomy provides a structured framework that helps in understanding the fundamental categories of tasks involved in analyzing time-oriented data effectively [13]. This structured approach aids in selecting appropriate visualization methods and tools that align with the complexity and requirements of the data being analyzed, ultimately enhancing the usability and effectiveness of visual analytics solutions for time-oriented data visualization.

Our primary goal was to identify relevant questions that could serve as the foundation for the tool's requirements. While our earlier work [12] tackled the four initial questions that sparked the inception of this investigation, the design process of the *Cryptovisualizer* and its subsequent usage led to the emergence of new questions. Some of these new questions raised the need to incorporate new views and redesign the dashboard.

In this context, the *Cryptovisualizer+* was developed, with the main objective of answering the following questions:

1. *Q1: Is there any relationship between the closing price of each cryptocurrency and its transaction volume?*
2. *Q2: Is there any daily seasonality regarding the transaction volume of cryptocurrencies?*
3. *Q3: Is there any month seasonality regarding the transaction volume of cryptocurrencies?*
4. *Q4: How does the variability of cryptocurrency prices change over different time intervals, and what patterns or trends can be observed?*
5. *Q5: In the current year, did any cryptocurrency reach a new all-time high price? or has it stayed at constant average values?*

3   CryptoVisualizer+

For this proposal, we have updated the dataset used in our previous work [12] by combining four datasets downloaded from the Yahoo! Finance repository [14]. These datasets contain information related to the prices and transaction volumes of BTC, ETH, ADA, and DOGE between 2014 and 2024.

3.1   Availability and Design

CryptoVisualizer+ is an extension of *CryptoVisualizer* [12]. It is a coordinated multi-view data visualization tool developed with Tableau [15] freely accessible from any browser[1].

Differing from our previous work, the main goal behind the design of *CryptoVisualizer+* was to integrate information related to transaction volumes and cryptocurrency prices into a single dashboard. In this context, our proposal consists of a single dashboard integrating enhanced views. The dashboard (see Fig. 1) integrates four views, each designed taking into account the defined requirements.

To analyze month seasonality regarding the transaction volume of cryptocurrencies (**Q3**), we included the "Volume Radar Chart" (see Fig. 1A). In this plot, each month of the year is mapped to a radial axis. The length of each spoke is proportional to the average transaction volume for each cryptocurrency in the corresponding month. Each cryptocurrency is overlapped and represented with a different color. The "Volume Radar Chart" is illustrated in Fig. 2(left). As it

---

[1] https://tinyurl.com/CriptoVisualizerPlus (English version).

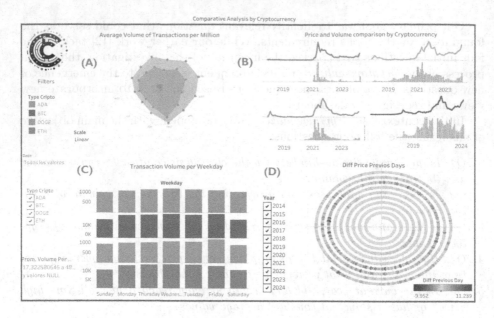

Fig. 1. *CryptoVisualizer+* Dashboard

can be observed, the transaction volumes of BTC and ETH over the month can be clearly appreciated but the behavior of ADA and DOGE are difficult to identify. This is because the data we are representing covers a wide range of values, and there are very large differences between the values (between ADA and BTC transaction volumes, for example). To solve this issue, this view supports a "scale selector" that allows the user to choose between linear and logarithmic scale (see Fig. 2(right)).

To explore the relationship between the closing price of each cryptocurrency and its transaction volume (**Q1**) we designed the "Price-Volume Small Multiples" (see Fig. 1B). This view consists of a series of small charts, with each chart representing a different cryptocurrency. Each chart includes a line graph depicting the price movement over time and a bar graph showing the transaction volume for that cryptocurrency (see Fig. 3(left)). This visualization allows for a quick comparison of price trends and transaction volumes across multiple cryptocurrencies.

For daily seasonality regarding the transaction volume (**Q2**) we integrated a "Weekdays Small Multiples" (see 1C). This view consists of a series of small bar charts, with each bar chart representing a different cryptocurrency. Each bar chart shows the average transaction volume for each weekday for that cryptocurrency. In Fig. 3(right) the "Weekdays Small Multiples" shows data from 2021 onwards expressing, in general, less transaction volume for weekends.

Finally, for the variability of prices over time (**Q4 and Q5**), we designed the "Spiral Difference"(see 1D). This is a visual representation where each loop represents one year. As you move along the spiral, you progress through time,

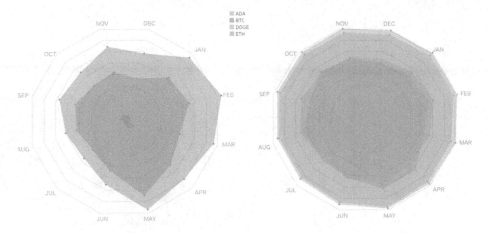

Fig. 2. The "Volume Radar Char". It depicts the average of transaction volume over the month for all the cryptocurrencies using a linear scale (left) and a logarithmic scale (right).

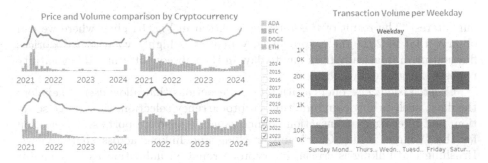

Fig. 3. Small Multiples in *CryptoVisualizer+*. The "Price-Volume Small Multiples" (left) and "Weekdays Small Multiples" (right). Both views are showing data from 2021 onwards.

with the innermost loop representing the earliest year and the outermost loop representing the most recent year. This design allows for a compact display of data over time, with each data point plotted at the corresponding position along the spiral based on its year. In our "Spiral Difference" chart each point represents one day, and its size is mapped to the magnitude of the difference in the price compared to the previous day. The color indicates whether the difference is positive or negative. The spiral chart provides a unique way to visualize trends and patterns over time, making it easier to interpret complex data sets and identify long-term patterns. Figure 4(left) shows the initial configuration of the "Spiral Difference" at the beginning of the analysis session. By default it integrates all the cryptocurrencies from 2014 onwards, showing smaller differences during the early years (from 2014 to 2017) and from 2018 to 2019, and more differences in the later years. Fortunately, we can filter to analyze in detail the period of

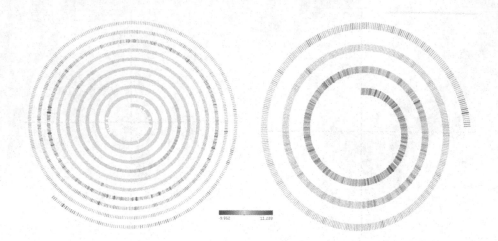

Fig. 4. "Spiral Difference" integrating all cryptocurrencies from 2014 onwards (left) and from 2021 (onwards).

our interest. The result of this filtering is shown in Fig. 4(right), where we can observe that in 2021 the cryptocurrency market is highly volatile, with prices fluctuating dramatically from day to day. In the subsequent years, this volatility persists but gradually subsides.

Crypto Visualizer+ offers a rich set of interactions that allow users to explore the data, such as single and multiple cryptocurrency selection, time range selection, and filtering by transaction volume range. It also supports scale selection for the "Volume Radar Char" and brushing and linking across all the views. Brushing and linking is crucial in cryptocurrency visualization as they enable interactive exploration of complex data. These techniques allow users to select and highlight data in one view, with corresponding points highlighted in linked views.

3.2   Results

As a starting point, we are interested in analyzing the relationship between the closing price of each cryptocurrency and its transaction volume (**Q1**), exploring the potential correlation between the closing price of a cryptocurrency and its transaction volume. Understanding this relationship can provide insights into market dynamics and investor behavior. For example, a strong positive correlation between price and volume may indicate that price movements are supported by high trading activity, suggesting a healthy market. On the other hand, a divergence between price and volume could signal potential market manipulation or a shift in market sentiment.

To perform this task we use the "price-volume small multiples" view, which allows the exploration of each cryptocurrency price along with the volume of transactions for each month. As shown in Fig. 5, with this representation there

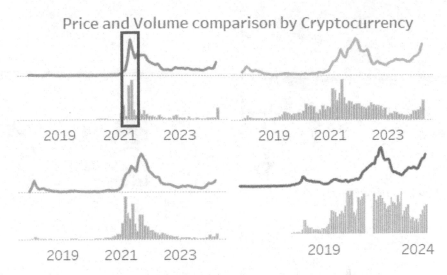

Fig. 5. The price-volume small multiples. For each currency, the price (as a line chart) and average transaction volumes (as a bar chart) are depicted over time.

appears to be a strong correlation between price and transaction volume for all the currencies, as shown on Doge coin, highlighted with a red rectangle. In general, when the price rises for a currency, its transaction volume increases, and when the price falls, the transaction volume decreases. In addition, as these small views are linked, it is also possible to analyze whether cryptocurrencies are related or exhibit similar price movements. When selecting a specific period in one view (a particular cryptocurrency in this case), the behavior of the other cryptocurrencies in that period is highlighted, allowing us to verify if they are exhibiting similar behaviour. Figure 6 shows some examples of this exploration and reveals that during the end of 2023 and the beginning of 2024, all currencies raise their prices (A). The figure also reveals that a drop in the price of ETH during the first half of 2022 (B), and a rise in BTC's price during 2021 (C), were also reflected in the other cryptocurrencies.

For daily seasonality regarding the transaction volume **(Q2)**, a similar question is posed in [16], seeking to answer whether the "Monday effect" or "January effect" exists in financial markets. These are phenomena in which certain days of the week or months of the year are significantly higher or lower compared to the rest of the periods. The concept of "Monday effect" in financial markets refers to the phenomenon where stock returns on Mondays are often lower compared to the rest of the week. This effect has been attributed to various factors, including investor sentiment over the weekend and the release of negative news on Mondays. When considering daily seasonality in cryptocurrency transaction volume, there might be a potential link to the "Monday effect" phenomenon if there is a significant increase or decrease in transaction volume on Mondays compared to other days of the week. For example, if cryptocurrency transaction volume

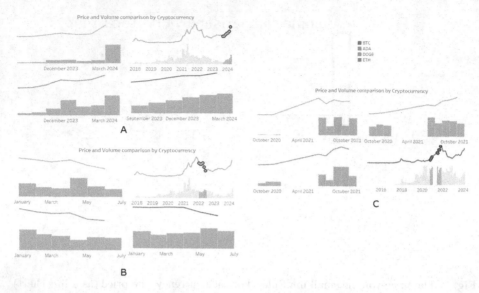

Fig. 6. Brushing and Linking in the price-volume small multiples. (A) All cryptocurrencies experienced a rise in prices during the end of 2023 and the beginning of 2024. (B) A drop in the price of ETH during the first half of 2022, and (c) a rise in BTC's price during 2021, were also reflected in the other cryptocurrencies.

tends to be higher on Mondays, this could be due to increased trading activity as investors react to news and developments over the weekend, potentially leading to higher price volatility. Understanding these patterns could provide insights into how market participants behave in response to weekly cycles and how this behavior impacts cryptocurrency prices.

Figure 7 illustrates the "Weekdays Small Multiples", iterating four bar charts corresponding to each cryptocurrency. In each of them, it can be observed that Saturdays and Sundays are the days with the fewest transactions, while Mondays present the smallest transaction volume during weekdays for BTC (blue bars), DOGE (green bars), and ADA (orange bars). For ETH (purple bars), and by a very small margin, Fridays show the smallest transaction volume.

Month seasonality in cryptocurrency is also interesting to explore **(Q3)**, as it may reveal patterns or trends that could impact trading strategies and market behavior. Understanding month seasonality in cryptocurrencies could provide insights into potential trading opportunities or risks associated with different times of the year. For example, certain months might historically experience higher or lower transaction volumes or price volatility, which could be attributed to factors such as market sentiment, regulatory changes, or macroeconomic events. The *Volume Radar Chart* integrated into *CryptoVisualizer+* allows the analysis of month seasonality of the transaction volume for all cryptocurrencies.

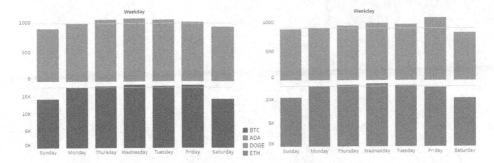

Fig. 7. Average transaction volume for each day of the week across various cryptocurrencies, depicted as small multiples of bar charts. (Color figure online)

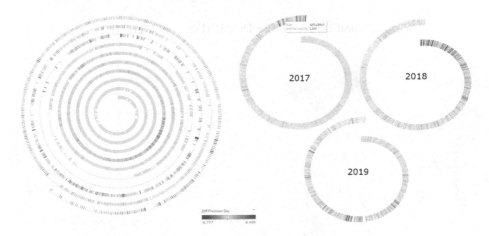

Fig. 8. "Spiral Difference" for BTC. Each loop represents one year, starting in the center in 2014. Each point represents one day and its size and color are mapped to the difference in price compared to the previous day. On the left all years are represented. On the right only one year (2017, 2018, and 2019) is represented.

In Fig. 2(left) it can be observed that for Bitcoin and ETH, the average transaction volume is higher from January to May, while for DOGE is higher from April to May. In this view, the behavior of ADA's transaction volume over the month is difficult to appreciate, as the magnitude of ADA's transactions is considerably smaller than the rest of the currencies. To solve this problem, *CryptoVisualizer+* supports a logarithmic scale for the *Volume Radar Chart*, which helps to deal with data that spans several orders of magnitude. The logarithmic scale compresses the data, making it easier to see patterns and trends in both small and large values. Figure 2 (right) shows the logarithmic scale for the radar chart. In this case, the currency ADA can be easily explored and compared.

Regarding variability of prices over time **(Q4)**, we chose to perform a daily price volatility study. In our previous work [12], we presented a custom-designed

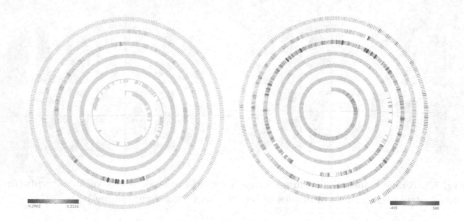

Fig. 9. "Spiral Difference" for DOGE (left) and ETH (right).

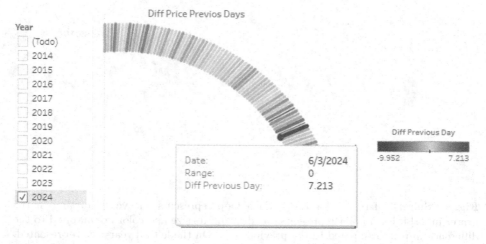

Fig. 10. New historical peak reached by BTC on March 6, 2024. (Color figure online)

view that allows analyzing losses and gains by representing the difference in closing price compared to its value from the previous day. For *Crypto Visualizer+* we improved that representation by presenting the "Spiral Difference", which allows us to represent in a single glance the complete time range and visualize for each day the difference in closing price compared to its value from the previous day's. Figure 8 shows the "Spiral Difference" for the BTC currency over the complete time range (left). It can be observed that until 2017 there was not much daily volatility in the prices. If we filter one year at a time, it is shown with more detail that there is more daily price volatility at the end of 2017, the beginning of 2018, and in 2019.

It is also possible to configure the "Spiral Difference" to visualize other currencies. Figure 9 (left) illustrates the daily price volatility for DOGE, showing more volatility in 2017. On the other hand, ETH shows more volatility from 2017 onwards (see Fig. 9 (right)).

To address question **(Q5)**, we must select the current year and analyze each cryptocurrency individually, examining their price behavior using the Spiral Difference diagram. In Fig. 10, we observe an intense green bar for BTC on March 6, 2024, indicating that it reached its historical peak on that date.

4 Conclusions and Future Work

In this paper, we introduce a visualization tool designed for analyzing financial data from the cryptocurrency market. A review of the existing literature highlights the wide range of visualization techniques available for studying financial markets, with a particular focus on cryptocurrencies. In 2023, we *CryptoVisualizer* [12], a cryptocurrency visualization tool specifically focused on 4 cryptocurrencies of interest: Bitcoin (BTC), Ethereum (ETH), Cardano (ADA), and Dogecoin (DOGE). It was designed as a combination of two dashboards, one integrating several views related to prices and the other integrating views designed to analyze the transaction volume of the currencies.

As we continued our work on this topic, we found it necessary to delve into the temporal aspect of the data. It is crucial to pay attention to the temporal aspect of cryptocurrency data due to the volatile and dynamic nature of this market. Temporal analysis helps identify trends, patterns, and cycles that can influence investment decisions. Additionally, the use of radar and spiral charts is particularly relevant in this context. Radar charts are useful for comparing multiple variables in a single graph, making it easier to visualize the evolution of cryptocurrencies across different aspects. On the other hand, spiral charts can show how prices change over time more clearly than other types of charts, making them ideal for visualizing price variation in the cryptocurrency market. Therefore, we decide to enhance our previous views including the mentioned techniques, and to integrate all these views on a single dashboard. In this context, we present *CryptoVisualizer+*, an extension of our previous work, with the main objective of designing new enhanced views and integrating them on a unique dashboard.

Future work includes collaboration with domain experts, implementing *CryptoVisualizer+* in a lower-level language, and automating pattern detection with intelligent interactions.

Acknowledgements. This work was partially supported by PGI 24/N048 and PGI 24/ZN38 research grants from the Secretaría General de Ciencia y Tecnología, Universidad Nacional del Sur (Argentina), and by 28720210100824CO (PIBAA) granted by National Council for Scientific and Technical Research (CONICET).

Disclosure of Interests. The authors have no competing interests to declare that are relevant to the content of this article.

References

1. Meirelles, I.: Design for information: an introduction to the histories, theories, and best practices behind effective information visualizations (2013)
2. Munzner, T., Maguire, E.: Visualization Analysis and Design. A K Peters visualization series. CRC Press, Boca Raton, FL (2015)
3. Aigner, W., Miksch, S., Schumann, H., Tominski, C.: Visualization of Time-Oriented Data, 1st edn. Springer Publishing Company, Incorporated (2011). https://doi.org/10.1007/978-1-4471-7527-8
4. Aigner, W., Miksch, S., Müller, W., Schumann, H., Tominski, C.: Visualizing time-oriented data-a systematic view. Comput. Graph. **31**(3), 401–409 (2007)
5. Weber, M., Alexa, M., Müller, W.: Visualizing time-series on spirals. In: Andrews, K., Roth, S.F., Wong, P.C. (eds.) IEEE Symposium on Information Visualization 2001 (INFOVIS 2001), San Diego, CA, USA, 22–23, October 2001, pp. 7–14. IEEE Computer Society (2001)
6. Tominski, C., Abello, J., Schumann, H.: Axes-based visualizations with radial layouts. In: ACM Symposium on Applied Computing (2004)
7. Andrienko, N.V., Andrienko, G.L.: Exploratory Analysis of Spatial and Temporal Data - A Systematic Approach. Springer, Heidelberg (2006). https://doi.org/10.1007/3-540-31190-4
8. Rodriguez, J., Kaczmarek, P.: Visualizing Financial Data. Wiley (2016)
9. Coinmarketcap (July 2023). https://coinmarketcap.com/es/
10. Coingecko (July 2023). https://www.coingecko.com/es
11. Sun, G., et al.: On visualization analysis of stock data. J. Big Data **1**(3), 135–144 (2019)
12. Mercedes, B., Ganuza, M.L.: Visual analysis of temporal data associated with cryptocurrencies. In: XXIX Congreso Argentino de Ciencias de la Computación (CACIC). Universidad Nacional de Luján, pp. 160–169 (2023)
13. Aigner, W.: Interactive visualization and data analysis: visual analytics with a focus on time. Ph.D. thesis (2013)
14. Kottarathil, P.: (July 2023). https://es.finance.yahoo.com/criptomonedas/
15. Tableau software. Consultado en Julio de (2023). https://www.tableau.com/
16. Bariviera, A.F., de Andrés Sánchez, J.: Existe estacionalidad diaria en el mercado de bonos y obligaciones del estado? evidencia empírica en el periodo 1998-2003. *Análisis Financiero*, **98**, 16–21 (2005)

Software Engineering

Formally Verifying Data Science Systems with a Sound an Correct Formalism

Fernando Asteasuain[1,2]([✉]) [iD]

[1] Universidad Nacional de Avellaneda, Avellaneda, Argentina
[2] Universidad Abierta Interamericana - Centro de Altos Estudios CAETI,
Buenos Aires, Argentina
fasteasuain@undav.edu.ar

Abstract. The state explosion problem arises as one of the most problematic issues to be faced against when trying to formally validate Data Science Software Systems. This challenge imposes the synergy and combination of tools. Taking this into consideration in this work we present a robust theoretical feature of our behavioral framework *VG-FVS*: we formally prove that our approach relies on a sound, complete and correct formalism. VG-FVS is a brand new new version of our framework FVS (Feather weight Visual Scenarios), which is specially developed to address the state explosion problem by integrating FVS with MaRDi-GraS, a generic library which eases the state space exploration using a MAP-REDUCE software architecture.

Keywords: Formal Verification · Data Science · State Explosion

1 Introduction

The emergence of new software paradigms pushes the Software Engineering community to adapt the current state of its tools mechanisms, procedures and methodologies to build modern software with the desired quality. For example, user interface design, validation and testing were overhauled to address the construction of systems to run in modern smart phones technologies [14, 19, 21]. The continuous growth of the so called Data Science Software Development [13, 17, 19] constitutes another important milestone for the evolution of software engineering. The vast and amorphous data and information to be explored and analyzed imposes the appearance of new ways to guarantee the quality of developed software. Some of approaches addressing this evolution by for example, optimizing resources and performance, are work like [5, 12, 15, 16, 22]. In particular, formal verification been flagged as one of the areas that more urgently need to be tackled. According to [11, 15], only two of nearly one hundred analyzed approaches addressing new software engineering methods for Data Science Software Systems were related to formal validation.

In [1] we took an important first step in the road to offer new contributions for the formal verification of Data Science Systems. We presented *VG-FVS*, a

P. Pesado et al. (Eds.): CACIC 2023, CCIS 2123, pp. 121–136, 2024.
https://doi.org/10.1007/978-3-031-62245-8_9

specially designed version of our behavioral framework FVS [2,3] to address formal verification in this domain. FVS, which stands for *Feather Weight Visual Scenarios*, is a very expressive declarative graphical language to express the desired behavior of systems. Due to its flexility it can be fully integrated with other model checking tools to expand its applicability [3]. For example, FVS specifications can be synthesized to automatically obtain a controller of the system. In [1] we combined FVS with the MaRDiGraS tool [4,5] given birth to a new flavour of our tool that we named *VG-FVS*. This version is specially suited to tackle a famous issue when formally verifying software systems: the state explosion problem [24]. Usually, the space to be explored by an automatic tool such as model checker is given as a set of states, and a mathematical function that given the occurrence of a new event indicates the next state. However, as the problem complexity increases the number of states grow exponentially and became a serious menace to formally verification tools. This problem exacerbates in the context of Data Science Software Systems. The mentioned MaRDiGraS tool employs an astute way of dealing with the explosion of states. It relies on a widely known technique used in distributed systems to optimize resources: Hadoop MapReduce architecture [10,25].

Since MaRDiGraS can be easily extended in [1] we integrated this tool with FVS. We now deepen that line of research by providing formal proofs demonstrating that this integration is *sound and complete*. To provide formal proofs of the soundness and correctness of any formalism or mechanism is a crucial and highly desirable feature, especially when dealing with formal verification techniques . For example, work like [6,18,20,26] provides formal assurance of their correct behavior in several domains such as robotic missions, probabilistic measures or temporal logics. *Besides providing the formal proof of VG-FVS soundness and correctness, in this work we also enrich the formal aspects of VG-VFS early introduced in [1] and also formal aspects of the integration of FVS and MaRDiGraS.*

The rest of this work is structured as follows. Section 2 briefly introduces FVS's main features whereas Sect. 3 describes FVS's formal characterization. This is needed in order to understand how FVS is integrated with MaRDiGraS, a procedure which is detailed in Sect. 4. Section 5 exhibits the formal proofs proving that VG-FVS is sound, correct and complete. Finally, Sects. 6 and 7 present future and related work and enumerates some final conclusions.

2   Feather Weight Visual Scenarios

In this section we will informally highlight the standing features of FVS. The reader is referred to [2] for a formal characterization of the language.

FVS is a graphical language based on scenarios. Scenarios are partial order of events, consisting of points, which are labeled with a logic formula expressing the possible events occurring at that point, and arrows connecting them. An arrow between two points indicates precedence. For instance, in Fig. 1-(a) is shows an scenarios where three events are occurring in a *Formula 1* simulator system:

two consecutive *Box* events and an *EntersPit* event. In this scenario, the *EntersPit* is preceded by the two *Box* events. We use an abbreviation for a frequent sub-pattern: a certain point represents the next occurrence of an event after another. The abbreviation is a second (open) arrow near the destination point. For example, in Fig. 1-b the scenario captures the very next *FlatEnabled* following an *DRSEnabled* event, and not any other *FlatEnabled* event. Conversely, to represent the previous occurrence of a (source) event, there is a symmetrical notation: an open arrow near the source extreme. This is also shown in Fig. 1-b, where the rightmost scenario handles the immediate previous occurrence of the *DRSEnabled* event given the occurrence of a *FlatEnabled* event. Finally, we provide a useful way to restrict behavior and denote prohibited situations. This is achieved by labelling arrows denoting the precedence events. For example, in Fig. 1-c the *Push* event is followed by an *Accelerate* event given that no *RedFlag* event occurs between them. This is because when a red flag is raised in Formula 1 races, all the cars must significatively reduce their speed.

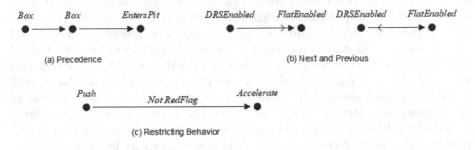

Fig. 1. Basic Elements in FVS

2.1   VG-FVS Rules

We now introduce the concept of FVS rules, a core concept in the language. The intuition is that whenever a trace "matches" a given antecedent scenario, then it must also match at least one of the consequents. In other words, rules take the form of an implication: an antecedent scenario and one or more consequent scenarios. Graphically, the antecedent is shown in black, and consequents in grey. Since a rule can feature more than one consequent, elements which do not belong to the antecedent scenario are numbered to identify the consequent they belong to.

Two simple examples taken from the Formula 1 simulation system are shown in Fig. 2. The first describes an overtake from a legendary *Ferrari* racing car given that the driver receives a push instruction to accelerate its car given that no red flag situation occurred. The second rule shows two possible alternative given the occurrence of a tyre degradation event. Consequent 1 reflects the behavior where a boxes call is made whereas Consequent2 shows the behavior when it is decided to maintain the car in the track.

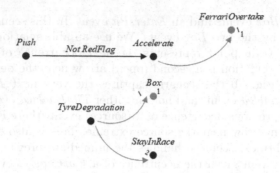

Fig. 2. Two VG-FVS rule examples

3 FVS Formal Definitions

Big journeys begin with small steps. Our final goal and main objective is to provide a formal proof that *VG-FVS*, the declarative and behavioral specification language oriented to diminish the state explosion problem, is sound and correct. In order to do so we must first provide formal definitions of VG-FVS building blocks. That is, we need to understand the theory behinds our graphical scenarios, the motion given by algebraic morphisms, the notion of what we call *situations*, which formally define a photo of our scheme in execution, how rules of our language are logically satisfied or not, and how our scenarios are translated into Büchi automata. This latter aspect involves the definition of FVS states, how the successors of states are built and how transitions between states are constructed and labeled. These formal definitions will be the first step of the ravishing journey to demonstrate that our approach is sound and complete.

Our graphical scenarios are defined first.

Definition 1 (VG-FVS Scenario). *An VG-FVS scenario is a tuple* $\langle \Sigma, P, \ell, \equiv, \not\equiv, <, \gamma \rangle$, *where:*
S1: Σ *is a finite set of propositional variables standing for types of events such that* $\Sigma = \Sigma_c \bigcup \Sigma_{uc}$ *where* Σ_c *represents controllable events and* Σ_{uc} *non controllable events*
S2: P *is a finite set of points;*
S3: $\ell : P \to \mathcal{PL}(\Sigma)$ *is a function that labels each point with a given formula;*
S4: $\equiv \; \subseteq P \times P$ *is an equivalence relation;*
S5: $\not\equiv \; \subseteq P \times P$ *is an asymmetric relation among points;*
S6: $< \subseteq (P \uplus \{0\} \times P \uplus \{\infty\}) \smallsetminus \{\langle 0, \infty \rangle\}$ *is a precedence relation between points, where* $\mathbf{0}$ *and* ∞ *represent the beginning and the end of execution, respectively;*
S7: $\gamma : (\not\equiv \cup <) \to \mathcal{PL}(\Sigma)$ *assigns to each pair of points, related by precedence or separation, a formula which constrains the set of events occurrences that may occur between the pair.*

Now we provide the notion of *morphisms*. A morphism can be seen as as mathematical function that relates two scenarios, indicating how an scenario can be embedded into another one, uniting points and labeling functions. This operation can be seen as a traditional "specialization" operation [8]. points exhibiting how a scenario "specializes" another one [8].

Definition 2 (Morphism). *Given two scenarios S_1, S_2 (assuming a common universe of event propositions), and f a total function between P_1 and P_2 we say that f is a morphism from S_1 to S_2 (denoted $f : S_1 \to S_2$) iff*
M1: $\ell_2(a) \Rightarrow \ell_1(\mathsf{p})$ *is a tautology for all* $\mathsf{p} \in P_1$ *and all* $a \in P_2$ *such that* $a \equiv_2 f(p)$;
M2: $\gamma_2(f(\mathsf{p}), f(\mathsf{q})) \Rightarrow \gamma_1(\mathsf{p}, \mathsf{q})$ *is a tautology for all* $\mathsf{p}, \mathsf{q} \in P_1$;
M3: if $\mathsf{p} \equiv_1 \mathsf{q}$ *then* $f(\mathsf{p}) \equiv_2 f(\mathsf{q})$ *for all* $\mathsf{p}, \mathsf{q} \in P_1$;
M4: if $\mathsf{p} \not\equiv_1 \mathsf{q}$ *then* $f(\mathsf{p}) \not\equiv_2 f(\mathsf{q})$ *for all* $\mathsf{p}, \mathsf{q} \in P_1$;
M5: if $\mathsf{p} <_1 \mathsf{q}$ *then* $f(\mathsf{p}) <_2 f(\mathsf{q})$ *for all* $\mathsf{p}, \mathsf{q} \in P_1$.

In particular, morphisms are important since they allow to properly define the concept of rules. Intuitively, a rule consist of an scenario playing the role of the antecedent, and one or more scenarios playing the role of the consequents. However, in order to build a rule morphisms must be provided to denote how the antecedent is connected to each consequents. This semantics "bureaucracy" is naturally hidden in our graphical flavour, but it is crucial to formally define our language. Rules formal definition is presented next.

Definition 3 (VG-FVS Rule). *Given a scenario S_0 (antecedent) and an indexed set of scenarios and morphisms from the antecedent $f_1 : S_0 \to S_1$, $f_2 : S_0 \to S_2$, ..., $f_k : S_0 \to S_k$ (consequents), we call* $R = \langle S_0, \{(S_i, f_i)\}_{i=1...k} \rangle$ *an FVS Rule.*

We now need to relate morphisms and events. We rely on the classical definition of traces as a linear sequence of events, and those traces accepted by the set of FVS rules defines the language of the system. The formal definitions are given below.

Definition 4 (Traces). *A trace* t *is seen as the sequence* $\{t_0, t_1, \ldots, t_k\}$.

Definition 5 (VG-FVS Semantics). *Given a rule R and a trace t $\{t_0, t_1, \ldots, t_k\}$, if $\forall\, t_i$, $0 <= i <= k$, $t_i \in t$ $\exists$ a morphism* m $t_i \xrightarrow{m_i} t_{i+1}$ *then* t $\models R$.

3.1 Tableau Algorithm: Translating FVS Scenarios into Büchi Automata

The next step in our picturesque formal journey is to establish how VG-FVS graphical scenarios are translated into Büchi Automata. This is a necessary step since it enables the possibility to combine our tool with model checkers and other verification formal tools such as MaRDiGraS [4,5] as it is currently done in this work.

The translation is given by a tableau procedure, which is fully detailed [2]. Nonetheless, we introduce in this section its main components and behavior so that this paper can be read in a stand-alone manner.

The tableau heavily relies on a semantic construction that we denominate as **situation**. In few words, a situation symbolizes all the possible combinations showing how a given sequence of events or trace can be embedded into a given rule. That is, a situation captures all partial possible matches from the antecedent to the consequent of a given rule. Consider the following example in Fig. 3. In this case, a rule with two consequents is shown. Furthermore, there are three partial matches for consequent one, and two for consequent two. Therefore, η_1 consists of the three morphisms in the first column (g_1^1, g_1^2, g_1^3), whereas η_2 consists of the two morphisms in the second column (g_2^1, g_2^2).

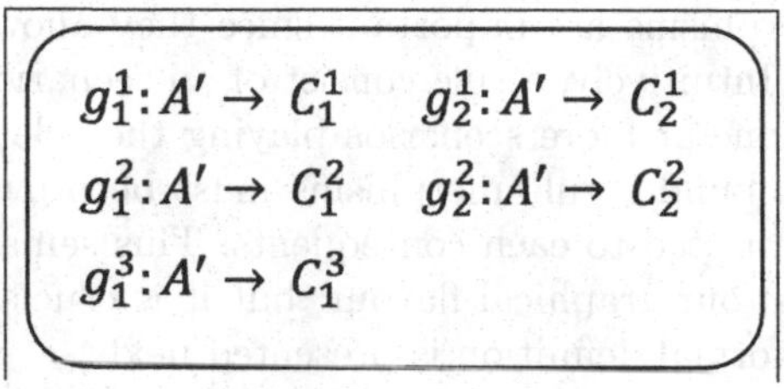

$$
\begin{aligned}
&g_1^1 \colon A' \to C_1^1 \qquad g_2^1 \colon A' \to C_2^1 \\
&g_1^2 \colon A' \to C_1^2 \qquad g_2^2 \colon A' \to C_2^2 \\
&g_1^3 \colon A' \to C_1^3
\end{aligned}
$$

Fig. 3. A situation example

In what follows we formally define the notion of **situation**.

Definition 6 (Situation). *Given*

- $f_j : A \to C_j$, $j \in [1..n]$, *standing for a rule with antecedent* A *and consequents* $C_1, C_2, ..., C_n$.
- $e : A' \to A$, *a morphism standing for the partial matching* A' *of the antecedent* A
- $: e_j^m : C_j^m \to C_j$, $m \in [1..k_j]$, *morphisms representing partial matches for each consequent* C_j

*a **situation** η is an indexed set of morphisms such that index η_i returns all the partial matches for consequent C_i. More formally, a **situation** η is an indexed set of morphisms $g_j^i : A' \to C_j^i$, $i \in [1..k_j]$ such that the following conditions holds:*

- *Condition 1: A' is a configuration for A and $e_j^i(C_j^i)$ is a configuration for $C_i \setminus \{f_j(e(A'))\}$. That is, A' and each $e_j^i(C_j^i)$ represent partial instantiations of the rule's antecedent and consequents.*
- *Condition 2: $f_i \circ e = e_j^i \circ g_j^i$. The morphisms g_j^i are consistent with the partial matches of the antecedent and consequents of the rule.*
- *Condition 3: $e_j^i(C_j^i) \cap f_j(A) = f_j(e(A'))$. The partial matches of the antecedent and consequents are complete. That is, no point has been "missed" by any of the partial matches.*

Given the occurrence of an event, all the possible advances of the antecedent and consequents is reflected in the current situations. What is more, the states of the built automaton will consist of a set of situations, representing the partial advances up to that point for a given trace or sequence of events. We now define the notion of FVS state, which constitute the state of the output automaton of the tableau algorithm.

Definition 7 (FVS State). *Given a rule R, the tableau builds a Büchi Automaton $\mathcal{B} = \langle \Sigma, S, S^0, \Delta, F \rangle$ such that Σ constitutes minterms over Σ_R and the set of states S are triples $(\Upsilon_R \times bool \times \mathcal{PL}(\Sigma_R))$, where $\mathcal{PL}(\Sigma)$ is a function that labels each point with a given formula. The set Υ_R associated to a state (a set of situations η), denoted situations(S), symbolically represents all the possible combination of partial matches obtained up to that state from the antecedent to each consequent. The second term of the triple identify accepting states. This boolean variable is set to* **true** *when the pattern is completely matched and will make the state transient. Finally, a third element is needed to maintain future obligations of the trace. These formulas are needed when rules predicate about conditions that must hold until the end of the trace. Initially, this element is initialized with { true }.*

The initial state S^0 is given by the empty configuration: $\Upsilon(i) = \{\emptyset\} \; \forall \; i \in [0..k]$. Starting from the initial state $(\langle \emptyset, false, true \rangle)$, the tableau procedure will aim to incrementally "construct" the pattern as events, represented by minterms, occurs. The algorithm takes into account the decision to match or not a given event by producing two different *situations*, one where the the new element is added (matched), and the other one remains unchanged (not matched). Recall that we simply define states as a set of situations, denoting all the possible matches from the trace to the rule.

The heart of the algorithm is those lines where the successor of a state is obtained. In what follows we simply delineate how this is achieved. This part of the tableau is called *Succ*. It receives as input a state S and a minterm representing the actual trace, and the output is the successors of S. This *Succ* routine is invoked until all the paths are covered, obtaining a fully well formed automaton, with a initial state, accepting states, accepting conditions, and trap states (error states). This algorithm rely on two auxiliary functions: *advanceAntecedent* and *advanceConsecuents*. A high-level description of both of them is given in Algorithm 1 and Algorithm 2 respectively.

---

1 *Algorithm advanceAntecedent(η : situation, m : minterm): η situation ;*
2 *return $\{z_j^i : A' \cup \mathcal{F}_j^i \to C_j^i \cup \{[f(\mathcal{F}_j^i)]_\equiv\}$ such that: $g_j^i : A' \to C_j^i \in \eta \land$*
   $A' \xrightarrow{m} A' \cup \mathcal{F}_j^i \land C_j^i \xrightarrow{m} C_j^i \cup \{[f(\mathcal{F}_j^i)]_\equiv\} \land g_j^i(A') = z_j^i(A') \land z_j^i(\mathcal{F}) = f(\mathcal{F}) \land$
   $m \in \mathcal{R}_{[f(\mathcal{F}_j^i)]_\equiv}(C_j^i)\} \cup \{g_j^i : A' \to C_j^i$ such that $m \in \mathcal{R}(A')\}$

Algorithm 1: Procedure advanceAntecedent

---

1 *Algorithm advanceConsequent*(η : *situation*, m : *minterm*): η situation;

2 *return*$\{z_j^i : A' \rightarrow C_j^i \cup \mathcal{F}_j^i$ such that: $g_j^i : A' \rightarrow C_j^i \in \eta \wedge C_j^i \xrightarrow{m} C_j^i \cup \mathcal{F}_j^i \wedge$
   $g_j^i(A') = z_j^i(A') \wedge m \in \mathcal{R}_{\mathcal{F}_j^i}(C_j^i)\} \cup \{g_i : A' \rightarrow C_j^i$ such that $m \in \mathcal{R}(C_j^i)\}$

Algorithm 2: Procedure advanceConsequent

These two auxiliary functions are invoked from the main algorithm *Succ*, which can be depicted in Algorithm 3. Lines 5 and 6 of 3 invoke the *advanceAntecedent* and *advanceConsecuents* routines. Line 7 deals with trap situations. A very common construction in the automata world is the error states: those states representing an unusual or error condition. In those cases, the system must remain in these states. In our case, a trap situation is given when an antecedent is found, but none of the consequents can be matched. Therefore, the rule can not be satisfied.

The next two lines (Lines 8 and 9 from Algorithm 3) raise a flag in case a consequent has been matched. This is, *goalmatched*[i] = *true* if and only if *consequent* C_i is matched. Accepting states are tagged in line 10. An accepting state contains a matched consequent and it is not a trap state. This concludes all the possible successors for a given state. The resulting set of states is returned in Line 11. If more than one consequent is matched, then all possible combinations of situations are considered. Specifically in the algorithm, non-determinism is introduced by the condition $GM \rightarrow goalMatched$ (line 11). When the latter holds the *true* value two states are added, one with $GM=true$ and the other with $GM=false$. In the first case a consequent is matched and obligations of the consequent are added as future restrictions of the trace. The second case represents the situation where the consequent achievement is omitted.

---

1 *Algorithm Succ*(S : *State*, m : *minterm*) : set of states;

2 *Precondition* : $m \wedge obligations(S)$ is satisfiable;

3 *newSits* := $\emptyset$;

4 **foreach** $\eta \in Situations(S)$ **do**

5   *newSits* := *add*(*newSits*, *advanceAntecedent*(η, m));

6   *newSits* := *add*(*newSits*, *advanceConsequent*(η, m));

7 *trapSituation* : $\exists \eta \in newSits \; \forall i \forall j \in [1..n] \; g_j^i : A' \rightarrow C_j^i \in \eta \wedge A' = A \wedge C_j^i$ it is not a configuration of C_j;

8 **foreach** $j \in [1..n]$ **do**

9   *goalmatched*[j] := $\exists \eta \in situations(S) \wedge$
       $g_j^i : A' \rightarrow C_j^i \in \eta \wedge C_j^i \xrightarrow{m} C_j \cup \mathcal{F}_j^i \wedge m \in (R_F(C_j^i)) \wedge C_j^i \cup \mathcal{F}_j^i = C_j$;

10 *goalMatched* := $(\exists j \; (goalmatched[j])) \wedge (\neg trapSituation)$;

11 return $\{ \langle newSits, GM, Obligations \rangle$ such that
   $GM \rightarrow goalMatched \wedge GM = true \rightarrow \exists j(goalmatched[j]) \wedge Obligations =$
   $Obligations(S) \wedge \bigwedge_{j \in I} \mathcal{R}(C_j) \wedge GM = false \rightarrow Obligations = Obligations(S)$

Algorithm 3: Successor states

4   VG-FVS: FVS Plus MaRDiGraS

In this section we show how FVS is connected to the MaRDiGraS tool. In order to achieve this, we first explain MaRDiGraS main concepts (Sect. 4.1) and latter on, how them are extended to cope with FVS definitions (Sect. 4.2).

4.1   MaRDiGraS

As explained in [4] MaRDiGraS is a distributed software tool aimed to built big states spaces for different kinds of formalisms. It is a very helpful tool since it is designed for simplifying the task of dealing with a large amount of reachable states by exploiting large clusters of machines. It was conceived as a generic library built on top of Hadoop MapReduce [10,25].

Map Reduce constitute a classical way of computation inherited from the functional paradigm, since a couple of operations are performed as mathematical function's composition. It captures a repetitive behavior, where the same group of activities is performed over a possible very large collection of items to generate a bunch of partial results. These results are, in turn, aggregated to compute the final outcome. The map function addresses the repetitive activities whereas the reduce functions deals with the aggregation aspect. In MaRDiGraS the map function is in charge of computing the new states and the reduce function computes equivalence and the inclusion relationship between states. As in all major frameworks, most of the technical aspects of this distributed oriented architecture are transparent to the final user. This is a notable feature of the MaRDiGraS tool. The final users must only concentrate in defining notions as states, edges, the transition relationship and functions to calculate equivalence and inclusion of states. Once these aspects are defined, the framework apply the mad reduce philosophy in a transparent way.

The main formalism employed to build all the definitions are the usual labeled state transition system. Labeled transitions systems ease the application of formal techniques to address the state explosion problem. This is achieved by constructing abstraction of the actual (concrete) states so that a group of concrete states (which are somehow related) can be mapped into the same abstract state. Computation starts by considering the initial state of the system under analysis and goes on with a sequential state-space building phase until the set of states not yet explored becomes large enough, where "large enough" is a threshold to be defined for each system [4]. The user must define the concept of state, how to build abstract states, how to link concrete to abstract states, how to obtain a successor of a state, and the notion of accepting and reachable states. The design implementation follows the Open Close principle. This application model can be easily extended to any other formalism. For example, in [4] it is shown how several kinds of Petri Nets can be adapted and used in the MaRDiGraS tool. By extending the application model definitions in order to match the desired formalism the tool will run under the expected modified constructions.

Architecturally, the MaRDiGraS contains two main artifacts: The Data component and the Core Component. The Data component consists of the "business" entities, such as the *State* or the *Edge* classes. This is the component to be addressed when trying to incorporate a given formalism into the tool. On the other hand, the Core components contains the implementation of all the algorithms that implements MaRDiGraS's main functioning. Figure 4 represents the basic functioning of the MaRDiGraS tool.

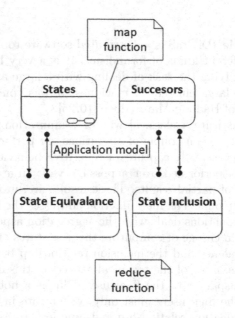

Fig. 4. MaRDiGraS architecture

In concrete, in order to adapt any formalism to this tool the following elements from the MaRDiGraS software must be extended:

- State: is an abstract class which should be extended to instantiate the state concept in a particular formalism.
- Successors: this method must return a list of new State objects representing the states directly reachable from the subject of the call. It must be defined for each formalism to be employed.
- IdentifyRelationship: this method must evaluate the actual relationship between (abstract) states sharing some specific features. The possible output values are: NONE, EQUALS, INCLUDED and INCLUDES.
- Edge: an abstract class which should be extended to represent the edge concept.
- GetFeatures: this functions analyses the equivalence between states.
- addLabel: a simply method to initialize an edge between two states.

4.2   VG-FVS: Combining FVS and MaRDiGraS

Given the formal definitions characterizing our FVS language given in Sect. 3 the combination of FVS with MaRDiGras is described as follows.

We represent MaRDiGraS **state class** employing the concept of Büchi state defined when translating our graphical scenarios into Büchi automata. Definition 7 in Sect. 3 defines the concept of state and Algorithm 3 describes how the automaton is built. Since both notions of states (MaRDiGrass and ours) rely on automata concepts, this part of the integration into MaRDiGraS was pretty straightforward.

The next challenge was to give a proper implementation of the *Succesors* method. Again, this was very smoothly done since we directly applied the *Succ* method detailed in Algorithm 3.

Regarding the **Edge** class , we simply take advantage of the morphism operation. A morphism can be seen as an edge between *situations*, and our states are no more that a set of *situations*. The labelling function which assigns occurring events into points in a scenario can be straightforward implemented as the *addLabel* MaRDIGrass method.

To complete the integration with the MaRDIGrass tool two additional functions must be defined: the **IdentifyRelationship** function and the **GetFeatures** function.

The **IdentifyRelationship** function deals with the necessary abstraction function in states, which is a crucial aspect when dealing with the state explosion problem. This function correlates abstract and concrete states. To achieve this goal, any pair states of interest must be analyzed to determine whereas one state includes the other one, and if the two of them can be logically connected. We implemented this function relying on the notion of FVS *situations* (see Definition 6 in Sect. 3). Given two situations S_1 and S_2 this function must return one of these possible outputs:

- NONE: if S_1 and S_2 do not match.
- EQUALS: if S_1 and S_2 are equivalent.
- INCLUDED: if S_1 includes S_2 but they are not equivalent.
- INCLUDES: if S_2 includes S_1 but they are not equivalent.

The main behavior of this procedure can be seen in Algorithm 4. Line 2 verifies if every morphism in S_1 is included in S_2 where Line 3 do the dual work: to verify if every morphism in S_2 is included in S_1. These results are stored in two boolean variables: *Condition1* and *Condition2*. Finally, lines 4 to 7 in Algorithm 4 calculate the demanded output.

The last item to be implemented to fully integrate FVS with MaRDiGraS is the **GetFeatures** function. This function analyzes equivalence between states. In our case this is reflected with the following behavior: given two states, S_1 and S_2, the function must calculate all the possible combinations of partial matches obtained up to that states from the antecedent to the consequents simultaneously. This output is returned as a set of FVS *situations*. Algorithm 5 exhibits our implementation for the **GetFeatures** function. In Line 2 it is verified that

---

1 *Algorithm IdentifyRelationship(S_1 : situation, S_2 : situation);*
2 *condition1 = if $\forall g_j^i : A' \rightarrow C_j^i \in S_1 \; \exists f_j^i : A' \rightarrow C_j^i \in S_2$;*
3 *condition2 = if $\forall f_j^i : A' \rightarrow C_j^i \in S_2 \; \exists g_j^i : A' \rightarrow C_j^i \in S_1$;*
4 *if condition1 and condition2 then return EQUALS ;*
5 *if !condition1 and !condition2 then return NONE ;*
6 *if condition1 and !condition2 then return INCLUDED ;*
7 *if !condition1 and condition2 then return INCLUDES ;*

Algorithm 4: Procedure IdentifyRelationship

both consequents and antecedents are matched simultaneously since morphisms must exits in the set of situations of both states. Finally, all the morphisms satisfying this conditions are returned.

---

1 *Algorithm GetFeatures(S_1 : State, S_2 : State);*
2 *return { all η such that exists $g_j^i : A' \rightarrow C_j^i \in S_1 \wedge g_j^i : A' \rightarrow C_j^i \in S_2$ };*

Algorithm 5: Procedure GetFeatures

This concludes the formal definitions needed to embed FVS mechanisms into the MaRDiGraS tool. Table 1 resumes the integration between FVS and MaRDiGraS. With the same objective, Fig. 5 exhibits this tools' combination in a graphical manner.

Table 1. FVS-MaRDiGraS Integration

MaRDiGraS Element	FVS Element
State	FVS Büchi State
Successors	FVS Succ Method
addLabel	Labeling Function
Edge	Morphisms
IdentifyRelationship	Configurations Equivalence
GetFeatures	Morphisms Fulfilment

5   VG-FVS: Sound and Complete

In this section we provide the formal proofs needed to assure that the integration between FVS and MaRDiGraS is sound and complete. FVS itself has been proved sound and correct [2]. Similarly, this has been done for the MaRDiGraS tool [4]. This indicates that we only need to prove that the FVS integration into MaRDiGraS is sound and complete. The rest of this section addresses this issue.

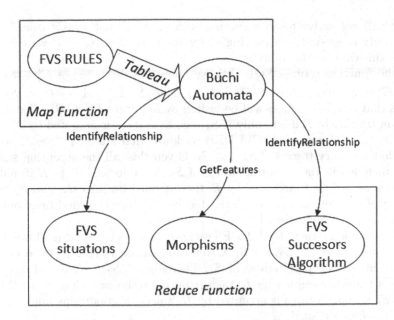

Fig. 5. VG-FVS and MaRDiGraS

Since FVS is sound and complete we know that the following condition holds: given a rule R, and a trace scenario $\mathcal{S}_\sigma$ $\mathcal{S}_\sigma \models R$ if and only if $\mathcal{S}_\sigma$ seen as a trace is accepted by B (i.e., $\mathcal{S}_\sigma \in \mathcal{L}(B)$), where B is the Büchi automaton built by by the tableau for rule R. In order to prove that VG-FVS is sound and complete we need to verify that this conditions holds for all the items shown in Table 1: *state, successors, addLabel, Edge* and functions *IdentifyRelationship* and *GetFeatures*. For the *state, successors, addLabel* and *Edge* constructions there is nothing to prove since they are implemented directly as FVS formal definitions, so the condition trivially holds. Therefore, to complete the sound and complete proof we need to prove the condition for the functions *IdentifyRelationship* and *GetFeatures*. This is addressed in the next two subsections.

5.1   IdentifyRelationship Function is Sound and Complete

We know that given a rule R, and a trace scenario $\mathcal{S}_\sigma$ $\mathcal{S}_\sigma \models R$ if and only if $\mathcal{S}_\sigma$ seen as a trace is accepted by B (i.e., $\mathcal{S}_\sigma \in \mathcal{L}(B)$), where B is the Büchi automaton built by by the tableau for rule R. In particular, for each situation $\eta \in States(R)$ given a trace $t = \{t_0, t_1, \ldots, t_k\}$ $\exists$ morphism m $t_i \xrightarrow{m_i} t_{i+1}$, $0 <= i <= k$.

The *IdentifyRelationship* functions returns one of four possible results: EQUALS, NONE, INCLUDES or INCLUDED. We need to prove that the mentioned conditions holds in every case.

If the function returns NONE, we know that $\forall g_j^i : A' \to C_j^i \in S_1$ $\nexists f_j^i : A' \to C_j^i \in S_2$ and also that $\forall f_j^i : A' \to C_j^i \in S_2$ $\nexists g_j^i : A' \to C_j^i \in S_1$. This implies that trace t will not arrive to an accepting state and will not satisfy rule R. Since we are only interested in accepting states to prove that $S_\sigma \models R$ we can safely discard this case for the analysis.

If the function returns EQUALS, we know that $\forall g_j^i : A' \to C_j^i \in S_1 \ \exists f_j^i : A' \to C_j^i \in S_2$ and also that $\forall f_j^i : A' \to C_j^i \in S_2 \ \exists g_j^i : A' \to C_j^i \in S_1$. This implies that accepting states will be visited by any trace $t \in \mathcal{L}(B)$. Then we can conclude that $S_\sigma \models R$ if and only if S_σ seen as a trace is accepted by B.

If the function returns INCLUDED we know that state $S_1 \subset S_2$. This indicates that for every trace $t \in S_1$, $t \in S_2$. Given this, all the accepting states in S_1 are included in the accepting states of S_2. Therefore, if $S_1 \models R$ if and only if S_σ seen as a trace is accepted by B. then it must be the case that $S_2 \models R$ if and only if S_σ seen as a trace is accepted by B. Since the conditions holds for both states it is fully satisfied.

If the function returns INCLUDES we know that state $S_2 \subset S_1$. This indicates that for every trace $t \in S_2$, $t \in S_1$. Given this, all the accepting states in S_2 are included in the accepting states of S_1. Therefore, if $S_2 \models R$ if and only if S_σ seen as a trace is accepted by B. then it must be the case that $S_1 \models R$ if and only if S_σ seen as a trace is accepted by B. Since the conditions holds for both states it is fully satisfied.

Since we can demonstrate that given a rule R, and a trace scenario S_σ $S_\sigma \models R$ if and only if S_σ seen as a trace is accepted by B holds in every case of the function, it can be established that the *IdentifyRelationship* function is sound and complete. $\Box$.

5.2   GetFeatures Function Is Sound and Complete

The *GetFatures* function, given two states S_1 and S_2, returns a set of situations S_3 containing all the possible matches from the antecedent to the consequents in both states. Since both S_1 and S_2 are states of the rule R, we know that for every trace $t \in S_1 \cup S_2$, $t \in \mathcal{L}(B)$), where B is the Büchi automaton built by by the tableau for rule R. Since S_3 contains all situations η such that morphisms $g_j^i : A' \to C_j^i \in S_1$ and $g_j^i : A' \to C_j^i \in S_2$ we can establish that for every trace $t = \{t_0, t_1, \ldots, t_k\}$, $t \in S_1 \cup S_2$, $\exists$ morphism m such that $t_i \xrightarrow{m_i} t_{i+1}, 0 <= i <= k$. This implies that trace t will always lead to an accepting state concluding that $t \in \mathcal{L}(B)$), which was the result we needed to prove. $\Box$.

5.3   Soundness and Completeness: Final Remarks

Since all the elements composing the integration between VG-FVS and MaRDi-GraS has been proved to be sound and complete we can affirm that VG-FVS is a sound and complete formalism. $\Box$.

6   Related and Future Work

Work in [9] brilliantly summarizes modern tools and techniques addressing the state explosion problem in formal methods. The common element behind all the described approaches is abstraction. Abstraction is intensively applied in all the described and proposed methods. Given this, we would like to further extend VG-FVS in this direction.

Interesting approaches like [23] or [7] somehow relates to our work. [23] proposes a complete and sound framework to specify behavioral models of spatially-distributed systems. Requirements are expressed in Spatio-Temporal Reach and Escape Logic (STREL), a domain specific logic formalism. We would definitely like to investigate the possibility to amalgamate VG-FVS with this technique, extending even further our horizons. This work also provides formal proofs of their correctness. On the other hand, [7] focuses on formal validation of distributed systems in the cloud introducing a framework denominated *Maude*. Our tool could benefit introducing some of the architectural patterns employed in *Maude*.

7   Conclusions

In this work we provide formal proofs to guarantee the soundness and correctness of VG-FVS, the framework that combines the super powers of FVS and MaRDiGraS. Demonstrating that a formalism is sound, complete and correct is a key feature when dealing with formal verification techniques. In this way, we can state that VG-FVS can be seen as a solid alternative to verify behavior in Data Science Software systems. Besides featuring powerful results to deal with the state explosion problem a robust theoretical aspect is added to our approach to provide further assurance.

References

1. Asteasuain, F.: A parallel tableau algorithm for big data verification. In: CACIC, pp. 275–287 (2023). ISBN 978-987-9285-51-0
2. Asteasuain, F., Braberman, V.: Declaratively building behavior by means of scenario clauses. Requirements Eng. **22**(2), 239–274 (2017). https://doi.org/10.1007/s00766-015-0242-2
3. Asteasuain, F., Calonge, F., Dubinsky, M., Gamboa, P.: Open and branching behavioral synthesis with scenario clauses. CLEI E-JOURNAL **24**(3), 1–20 (2021)
4. Bellettini, C., Camilli, M., Capra, L., Monga, M.: Mardigras: Simplified building of reachability graphs on large clusters. In: RP workshop. pp. 83–95 (2013)
5. Bellettini, C., Camilli, M., Capra, L., Monga, M.: Distributed CTL model checking using mapreduce: theory and practice. CCPE **28**(11), 3025–3041 (2016)
6. Blume, M., McAllester, D.: Sound and complete models of contracts. J. Funct. Program. **16**(4–5), 375–414 (2006)
7. Bobba, R., et al.: Survivability: design, formal modeling, and validation of cloud storage systems using Maude. In: Assured Cloud Computing, pp. 10–48 (2018)
8. Braberman, Víctor., Garbervestky, Diego, Kicillof, Nicolás, Monteverde, Daniel, Olivero, Alfredo: Speeding up model checking of timed-models by combining scenario specialization and live component analysis. In: Ouaknine, Joël., Vaandrager, Frits W.. (eds.) FORMATS 2009. LNCS, vol. 5813, pp. 58–72. Springer, Heidelberg (2009). https://doi.org/10.1007/978-3-642-04368-0_7

9. Camilli, M., et al.: Coping with the state explosion problem in formal methods: advanced abstraction techniques and big data approaches (2015)
10. Dean, J., Ghemawat, S.: Mapreduce: simplified data processing on large clusters. Commun. ACM **51**(1), 107–113 (2008)
11. Ding, J., Zhang, D., Hu, X.H.: A framework for ensuring the quality of a big data service. In: 2016 SCC, pp. 82–89. IEEE (2016)
12. Hummel, O., Eichelberger, H., Giloj, A., Werle, D., Schmid, K.: A collection of software engineering challenges for big data system development. In: SEAA, pp. 362–369. IEEE (2018)
13. Kim, M., Zimmermann, T., DeLine, R., Begel, A.: Data scientists in software teams: State of the art and challenges. IEEE Trans. Softw. Eng. **44**(11), 1024–1038 (2017)
14. Klein, A.M., Kölln, K., Deutschländer, J., Rauschenberger, M.: Design and evaluation of voice user interfaces: what should one consider? In: Salvendy, G., Wei, J. (eds.) International Conference on Human-Computer Interaction, pp. 167–190. Springer, Cham (2023). https://doi.org/10.1007/978-3-031-35921-7_12
15. Kumar, V.D., Alencar, P.: Software engineering for big data projects: domains, methodologies and gaps. In: IEEEBIGDATA, pp. 2886–2895. IEEE (2016)
16. Laigner, R., Kalinowski, M., Lifschitz, S., Monteiro, R.S., de Oliveira, D.: A systematic mapping of software engineering approaches to develop big data systems. In: SEAA, pp. 446–453. IEEE (2018)
17. Martínez-Fernández, S., et al.: Software engineering for AI-based systems: a survey. TOSEM **31**(2), 1–59 (2022)
18. Menghi, C., Tsigkanos, C., Pelliccione, P., Ghezzi, C., Berger, T.: Specification patterns for robotic missions. IEEE Trans. Software Eng. **47**(10), 2208–2224 (2019)
19. Salman, H.M., Wan Ahmad, W.F., Sulaiman, S.: A design framework of a smartphone user interface for elderly users. Univ. Access Inf. Soc. **22**(2), 489–509 (2023)
20. Schellhorn, G., Derrick, J., Wehrheim, H.: A sound and complete proof technique for linearizability of concurrent data structures. ACM Trans. Comput. Logic (TOCL) **15**(4), 1–37 (2014)
21. Soui, M., Haddad, Z.: Deep learning-based model using densnet201 for mobile user interface evaluation. Int. J. Hum.-Comput. Interact. **39**(9), 1981–1994 (2023)
22. Sri, P.A., Anusha, M.: Big data-survey. Indonesian J. Electr. Eng. Inform. (IJEEI) **4**(1), 74–80 (2016)
23. Tsigkanos, C., Nenzi, L., Loreti, M., Garriga, M., Dustdar, S., Ghezzi, C.: Inferring analyzable models from trajectories of spatially-distributed internet of things. In: SEAMS, pp. 100–106. IEEE (2019)
24. Clarke, E.M., Klieber, W., Nováček, M., Zuliani, P.: Model checking and the state explosion problem. In: Meyer, B., Nordio, M. (eds.) LASER 2011. LNCS, vol. 7682, pp. 1–30. Springer, Heidelberg (2012). https://doi.org/10.1007/978-3-642-35746-6_1
25. Zhang, J., Lin, M.: A comprehensive bibliometric analysis of Apache Hadoop from 2008 to 2020. IJICC **16**(1), 99–120 (2023)
26. Zhao, L., Wang, X., Shu, X., Zhang, N.: A sound and complete proof system for a unified temporal logic. Theoret. Comput. Sci. **838**, 25–44 (2020)

API Management and SQuaRE: A Comprehensive Overview from the Practitioners' Standpoint

Eder dos Santos[✉][iD] and Sandra Casas[iD]

Universidad Nacional de la Patagonia Austral, 9400 Río Gallegos, Argentina
{esantos,sicasas}@uarg.unpa.edu.ar
http://www.uarg.unpa.edu.ar

Abstract. In recent years, APIs have become fundamental components of software ecosystems, with organizations increasingly integrating software applications to exchange complex digital assets. Yet, the management of APIs presents considerable challenges, with companies facing numerous quality-related issues. Our objective is to understand how practitioners perceive the quality traits associated with API management requirements. To accomplish this, we conducted a methodical survey targeting professional developers, system administrators, and software functional analysts located in Rio Gallegos City, Argentina. We adopted the ISO/IEC 25010 standard as our framework. Survey questions were crafted around the fundamental API management capabilities outlined in contemporary literature, and their alignment with the ISO/IEC 25010 quality dimensions. A descriptive analysis of the 136 addressed topics unveiled Functional Suitability and Security as the key quality characteristics, providing valuable insights for future research.

Keywords: First keyword · Second keyword · Another keyword

1 Introduction

Over recent years, the distribution models for information systems have been moving towards XaaS [1] paradigms. This shift entails organizations providing their digital assets as services to customers [2]. In this context, microservices architectures are swiftly becoming the preferred choice, offering a flexible framework [3] that enables organizations to efficiently distribute their information systems into a highly scalable set of services.

In general, such services are supported by APIs. According the Postman annual survey [4], two-thirds of the 40,261 respondents from around the world said their APIs generate revenue. Revenue was judged the second-most important metric of public API success, just after usage. 1.29 billion requests were created in 2023 by over 25 million users. These APIs typically adhere to REST [5] principles.

Supported by Universidad Nacional de la Patagonia Austral.

P. Pesado et al. (Eds.): CACIC 2023, CCIS 2123, pp. 137–150, 2024.
https://doi.org/10.1007/978-3-031-62245-8_10

APIs present both a business side and a technical side [6]. The first one can be considered "a business enabler" as it determines how the organizations want to use their assets to deliver value not only across internal organizational units but also to external third parties, while the latter refers to "a technical answer to a business problem" and can be understood as a set of requirements that govern how applications can interact and exchange data. In this sense, the term "API Economy" reflects the ongoing trend across industries towards innovative approaches to enhancing their business frameworks. This involves developing and monetizing solutions that showcase their APIs as part of their service portfolios [4, 7].

The API Economy scenario exerts additional pressure in developing, deploying, and maintaining information systems. Since APIs have gained a critical aspect [8], organizations need to proactively address the risks of failure by enhancing API Management [6, 9] capabilities and managing their APIs through API Management platforms.

API Management Platforms provide the basic capabilities to create, analyze, and manage APIs in a secure and scalable environment such as providing helpful documentation, controlling access to the API, as well as monitoring and analyzing its usage. At the core of digital integration strategies, these platforms facilitate the creation, analysis, and governance of APIs within a secure and flexible framework. Equipped with features such as thorough documentation, access control, and usage analytics, these platforms streamline API management processes [9–11].

In spite of the above, API management activities pose numerous challenges in both internal [6, 12] and decentralized [13] software ecosystems. In this sense, many software quality models comprise a set of quality attributes or characteristics that establish the groundwork for evaluating the quality of software elements. This evaluation is a crucial step in offering practical solutions that can be easily adopted by professionals in the software industry, in order to improve the software ecosystems quality.

Quality models empower organizations to continuously monitor their software components' quality, enabling quick intervention in case of deviations, thereby maintaining high standards. Therefore, it becomes paramount to understand how practitioners in the software industry perceive quality characteristics related to common API management functions capabilities. This understanding aids in defining benchmarks and offering valuable insights into emerging trends at different phases of the software product's life cycle. In this direction, ISO/IEC 25000 - System and Software Quality Requirements and Evaluation -, also known as SQuaRE, is the de facto series of standards in the current industry. It includes the software product quality model as specified in the ISO/IEC 25010 standard. This paper presents the outcomes of the first survey focused on a group of professionals based in the Santa Cruz province, Argentina. In this preliminary exploratory instance, our focus lies in uncovering the correlation between the quality attributes outlined in the ISO/IEC 25010 standard and the core API management capabilities.

It is important to remark that this work is an extended version of [14]. As such, in this chapter, we introduce as main contributions: i. we present an in-depth description and analysis of the survey results, and ii. we discuss how upcoming definitions and trends from both academy and industry may be addressed in future work.

The structure of this paper is as follows: Section 2 delineates the methodology utilized for formulating and executing the survey, establishing its role as an initial exploration that will underpin forthcoming, more targeted research endeavors in subsequent studies. Then, we provide a comprehensive breakdown of the findings in Sect. 3. Finally, in Sect. 4, we encompass a succinct discussion on API surveys and analyze our findings from various points of view, namely: correlation between the survey results and current research main trends, potential threats to validity and limitations, reflections on the significance and impact of the study, concluding remarks, and insights into future research.

2 Materials and Methods

This section delineates the methodological approach taken to conduct a survey, serving as a preliminary study that will provide a foundation for more specialized research in the future. We've structured our survey around an exploratory methodology, utilizing the classification framework outlined by [15] for experimentation. The purpose of the survey was to collect valuable insights into the API management practices and its relation to the quality characteristics in API management platforms. Preliminary findings from this study will lay the groundwork for forthcoming research efforts focusing on various specific facets of API management.

2.1 Sampling Technique

The survey employed a non-probabilistic sampling method, specifically convenience sampling, based on recommendations by [15–17].

Rather than using random selection techniques, convenience sampling relies on choosing individuals who are convenient to reach based on their accessibility. The study recruited participants from computer science professionals located in Santa Cruz province, Argentina, with academic credentials in the discipline and ongoing employment in both public and private sectors. The selection of this sample was deliberate, chosen for its expertise and direct relevance to the studýs core objectives.

2.2 Survey Design

The survey questions were constructed by integrating the eight core quality characteristics delineated in ISO/IEC 25010 and a curated selection of 15 API management capabilities as outlined in current literature. The survey comprised of two principal categories of questions, as delineated below.

The first set of prompts included five open-ended questions intended to collect demographic data and gather information about the career paths of the respondents. These questions were designed to gather comprehensive census data and gain insights into the respondents' backgrounds, focusing on their experiences within the API management domain.

The second group comprised 15 closed-ended multiple-choice grid questions, each mapped to a key API management capability [9,10,18]. As suggested by [9], capabilities can be classified into four main groups of capabilities, namely: Developer Enablement for APIs; Secure, Reliable, and Flexible Communications; API Lifecycle Management; and API Auditing, Logging and Analytics. Within this framework, this study focused on the capabilities belonging to the "Secure Reliable and Flexible Communications" category, namely: 1. Authentication; 2. Authorization (Access Control); 3. Identity mediation; 4. Data privacy through encryption; 5. Data privacy through masking; 6. Key and certificate management; 7. DoS protection; 8. Threat detection; 9. Consumption quota; 10. Spike arrest; 11. Usage throttling; 12. Traffic prioritization; 13. Format translation; 14. Protocol translation; and 15. Service and data mapping. The definition of each capability was explicitly stated within the survey's graphical interface.

Each grid contained eight lines with Yes/No (Related / Not related) options, representing the main ISO/IEC 25010 quality characteristics, namely Functional Suitability, Performance Efficiency, Compatibility, Usability, Reliability, Security, Maintainability and Portability. This design permitted assessing the degree to which each API management capability aligned with each quality attribute. In order to mitigate validity threats, mandatory radio buttons were used. The designed scheme for the questions is presented in Table 1, and a sample question can be seen in Table 2.

Table 1. The question grid template.

#QuestionId. Capability name: A brief definition of the capability.		
ISO Characteristic	Related	Not related
1. Functional Suitability		
2. Performance Efficiency		
3. Compatibility		
4. Usability		
5. Reliability		
6. Security		
7. Maintainability		
8. Portability		

Each respondent was required to tackle 125 questions in total, comprising both open-ended and closed-ended inquiries. The survey remained active for a period of two weeks to ensure a sufficient response rate and gather a representative sample as respondents, who are professionals based in the province of Santa

Table 2. A survey's question sample format.

1. Authentication: Authentication is the process of uniquely determining and validating the identity of a client.

ISO Characteristic	Related	Not related
1. Functional Suitability		
2. Performance Efficiency		
3. Compatibility		
4. Usability		
5. Reliability		
6. Security		
7. Maintainability		
8. Portability		

Cruz, Argentina, with academic background in computer science and currently working in the field, both in private companies and government departments, had ample time to access the survey and complete the questionnaire at their convenience.

2.3 Data Collection

In order to optimize accessibility and streamline data collection procedures, we leveraged an online survey platform to execute the survey and gather data.

3 Results

The survey was conducted as a pilot study and involved a small cohort of professionals from the IT sector. In total, six participants took part in the study. The demographic and professional profiles of the participants are outlined as follows:

Age: The participants' ages spanned from 27 to 42, with a mean age of 31 years.

Experience: The professional experience of the participants ranged from 4 to 20, with an average experience of 9 years.

Regarding the labor sphere, it's worth mentioning that some participants provided multiple answers for both their labor sphere and their current role, which suggest their engagement across different domains or responsibilities within the IT-related industry. Detailed results are provided as follows:

Private Companies (28.57 %), Government Departments: (71.43 %).

Roles were self-described by the participants, and included Software Development (coding, full stack), Help and Technical Support, Functional Analysis, Project Management, and Research. Most of respondents identified themselves as Software Developers, as can be seen in Fig. 1.

As this study was a pilot experiment aimed at gathering preliminary insights, the findings emerged from the data collected can be seen as follows. In order to

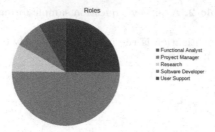

Fig. 1. Roles of the respondents.

provide a comprehensive overview of results, we followed guidelines proposed by [9] to group the capabilities into three categories: API Security, API Traffic Management and Interface Translation.

API Security grouping encompasses authentication, authorization, identity mediation, data privacy (through encryption and masking), key and certificate management, DoS protection, and threat detection capabilities. Responses related to Authentication capability are displayed in Fig. 2. A column-line graph is provided and displays positive responses as a count (% of total participants). The horizontal axis of the graph represents the quality characteristics described in the ISO/IEC 25010 standard, while the bars represent the responses. Additionally, the line represents the median value for each quality attribute over the eight API Security capabilities.

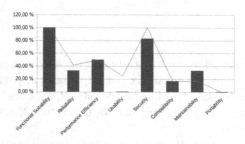

Fig. 2. "Authentication" and its relation with ISO/IEC 25010 characteristics.

Due to the extensive nature of the survey, which covered 15 capabilities in total and eight capabilities among API Security grouping, the data from all positive responses has been synthesized and presented in Fig. 3. To enhance the visualization and understanding of the results, a color scale was adopted, with the midpoint set at the 50th percentile. The figure includes the median values for reference.

As seen, respondents unanimously considered functional suitability and security as related traits, which indicates full compliance with functional requirements and security measures. Reliability and performance efficiency followed

		ISO/IEC 25010:2011 Capabilities							
		Functional Suitability	Reliability	Performance Efficiency	Usability	Security	Compatibility	Maintainability	Portability
API Security Capabilities	Authentication	100,00 %	33,00 %	50,00 %	0,00 %	83,00 %	17,00 %	33,00 %	0,00 %
	Authorization	100,00 %	33,00 %	67,00 %	33,00 %	100,00 %	17,00 %	17,00 %	0,00 %
	Keys and certificates	100,00 %	83,00 %	0,00 %	67,00 %	100,00 %	17,00 %	17,00 %	17,00 %
	Identity mediation	100,00 %	17,00 %	50,00 %	17,00 %	100,00 %	67,00 %	83,00 %	17,00 %
	Data encryption	100,00 %	17,00 %	67,00 %	50,00 %	83,00 %	17,00 %	17,00 %	0,00 %
	Data masking	100,00 %	50,00 %	17,00 %	33,00 %	100,00 %	17,00 %	0,00 %	0,00 %
	DoS protection	100,00 %	50,00 %	83,00 %	0,00 %	100,00 %	17,00 %	17,00 %	17,00 %
	Threat detection	100,00 %	50,00 %	50,00 %	0,00 %	100,00 %	17,00 %	17,00 %	0,00 %
	Mean Value	100,00 %	41,50 %	50,00 %	25,00 %	100,00 %	17,00 %	17,00 %	0,00 %

Fig. 3. API Security capabilities survey results.

with moderate associations to specified functional requirements, scoring at 41.50% and 50% respectively.

Within API Traffic Management grouping lie consumption quota, spike arrest, usage throttling, and traffic prioritization capabilities. Survey responses related to consumption quota capability are displayed in Fig. 4. The same scheme of Fig. 2 is adopted, and the line represents the median value for each quality attribute over the four API Traffic Management capabilities.

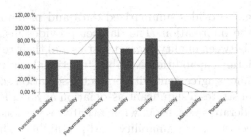

Fig. 4. "Consumption Quota" and its relation with ISO/IEC 25010 characteristics.

Additionally, summarized data and median values are displayed in Fig. 5. As we examine the data pertaining to quality characteristics, findings reveal a spectrum of performance across various attributes, with notable disparities warranting careful consideration. While performance efficiency and security demonstrate commendable median values of 100% and 83% respectively, lowest association rates emerge in usability, compatibility, and maintainability, each registering at 25%, 17%, and 0% respectively. Finally, reliability and functional suitability denote a moderate link with this grouping of capabilities.

Service and data mapping, format translation, and protocol translation capabilities fall under Interface Translation grouping. Figure 6 showcases survey responses concerning format translation capability. Layout is identical as illustrated in Fig. 2: the bars portray the data, while the line denotes the median value for every quality attribute among the three Interface Translation capabilities.

		ISO/IEC 25010:2011 Capabilities							
		Functional Suitability	Reliability	Performance Efficiency	Usability	Security	Compatibility	Maintainability	Portability
API Traffic Management Capabilities	Quotas	50,00 %	50,00 %	100,00 %	67,00 %	83,00 %	17,00 %	0,00 %	0,00 %
	Usage throttling	83,00 %	50,00 %	100,00 %	17,00 %	100,00 %	67,00 %	0,00 %	0,00 %
	Spike arrest	50,00 %	67,00 %	100,00 %	0,00 %	83,00 %	17,00 %	0,00 %	0,00 %
	Traffic prioritization	100,00 %	67,00 %	100,00 %	33,00 %	33,00 %	0,00 %	0,00 %	0,00 %
	Mean Value	66,50 %	58,50 %	100,00 %	25,00 %	83,00 %	17,00 %	0,00 %	0,00 %

Fig. 5. API Traffic Management capabilities survey results.

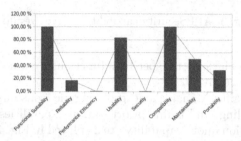

Fig. 6. "Format Translation" and its relation with ISO/IEC 25010 characteristics.

In addition, Fig. 7 provides summarized data and median values, offering a clear snapshot of the information. The dataset provides insights into the perceived associations between quality characteristics and their respective attributes for Interface Translation capabilities. Notably, functional suitability and compatibility garner unanimous agreement with perfect association scores of 100% each. Usability also demonstrates a significant association at 83%. However, maintainability gained a moderate association, while attributes such as reliability, performance efficiency, security, maintainability, and portability exhibited lower levels of association, ranging from 17% to 0%.

		ISO/IEC 25010:2011 Capabilities							
		Functional Suitability	Reliability	Performance Efficiency	Usability	Security	Compatibility	Maintainability	Portability
Interface Translation Capabilities	Format translation	100,00 %	17,00 %	0,00 %	83,00 %	0,00 %	100,00 %	50,00 %	33,00 %
	Protocol translation	100,00 %	17,00 %	100,00 %	50,00 %	0,00 %	100,00 %	50,00 %	17,00 %
	Service and data Mapping	83,00 %	0,00 %	0,00 %	100,00 %	0,00 %	67,00 %	17,00 %	0,00 %
	Mean Value	100,00 %	17,00 %	0,00 %	83,00 %	0,00 %	100,00 %	50,00 %	17,00 %

Fig. 7. Interface Translation capabilities survey results.

4   Discussion

The utilization of surveys directed towards API practitioners is a commonly employed initiative by industry-leading organizations. These surveys result in influential guiding documents for both the web API production and consumption sectors. In our study, we have incorporated select items from the RapidAPI survey to enrich our analysis.

On a global scale, the company Smartbear annually publishes their report titled "State of Software Quality - API" [19] with the goal of "Identifying the latest benchmarks and gaining insights into the trajectory of the API industry". This report collates information on "the latest methodologies, practices, and tools used by software teams across the world." The survey responses encompassed more than 1,100 API practitioners and customers, spanning various industries, and ranged from startups to large enterprises in terms of company size.

Furthermore, "The Rapid Developer Survey" [20] garnered 850 responses from over 100 different countries. A substantial majority of respondents identified as professional developers, with over 85% reporting active programming as part of their vocation or educational pursuits. The survey participants represented a diverse spectrum of organizational sizes, experience levels, and industries.

Moreover, 40,261 and anonymous developers from around the world have answered the Postman annual [4]. Regarding to API Management and quality, respondents reported significant improvements in many API Management capabilities such as Recovery Time and Security. Lack of documentation and difficulty in discovering APIs where those capabilities reported as main obstacles to consuming APIs, as Lack of documentation, managing too many APIs and difficulty in discovering supporting APIs where highlighted as main obstacles to producing APIs. Finally, overall quality (79%), reliability (64%) and security (53%) quality and were the most important priorities over cost optimization (35%).

Within an Argentinian perspective, [21] presented the outcomes of the first-ever survey specifically targeting developers in Argentina. The primary objective of this investigation was to comprehend the usage patterns and challenges faced by software developers when consuming web APIs within the Argentinean context.

Despite the existence of prior surveys, there is still a dearth of evidence pertaining to investigations specifically targeting the perceived quality of stakeholders in the industry, as proposed in this current work and our ongoing research agenda. Our focus is on characterizing quality aspects concerning API management requirements, capabilities, and best practices, utilizing the ISO/IEC 25010 standard as our quality reference model.

It is important to note that these findings should be interpreted with caution due to the small sample size and the exploratory nature of the pilot experiment. They provide initial insights that can guide further research in this area. In this study, our primary objective was to identify which quality characteristics were perceived as related to API Management capabilities, according to the opinions of the participants. The evaluation encompassed 15 API management capabilities, and participants were asked to indicate their relevance to the eight ISO 25010 quality characteristics.

The quality characteristic of Functional Suitability received the highest average percentage of related responses at 91.07%. This suggests that a significant portion of the evaluated API Management capabilities align well with meeting the intended functionality and user needs. The mean value of 100% further supports the strong association between the capabilities and the quality characteristic of functional suitability. We hypothesized that capabilities, serving as functional requirements of API Management software products, would exhibit a high rate of functional suitability. The results strongly support this hypothesis.

Security obtained a relatively high average percentage of related responses, at 71%. This indicates that a substantial number of the API Management capabilities included in this study contribute to ensuring security aspects within the platforms. The mean value of 83% further confirms the strong alignment with the security quality characteristic.

Reliability garnered an average percentage of related responses at 40.07%. Though lower than Functional Suitability, the results still indicate a moderate relationship between API Management capabilities and reliability. The mean value of 50% implies that half of the evaluated capabilities are considered relevant to ensuring the reliable performance of API management platforms.

Participants attributed an average percentage of 58.93% to Performance Efficiency, indicating that many API Management capabilities contribute to efficient performance. The mean value of 67% signifies that a significant portion of capabilities supports the quality characteristic of performance efficiency.

Usability received an average percentage of related responses at 36.67%. This suggests that some API Management capabilities are associated with the user-friendliness and ease of use of the platforms. The mean value of 33% indicates a moderate level of relevance between the capabilities and the usability quality characteristic.

Compatibility received an average percentage of related responses at 36.93%. This suggests that certain API Management capabilities contribute to compatibility with external systems and technologies. The mean value of 17% indicates a relatively lower level of relevance with the compatibility quality characteristic.

Maintainability garnered an average percentage of related responses of 21.2%. This implies that some API Management capabilities relate to the ease of maintenance and updates. The mean value of 17% reinforces the moderate level of alignment with the maintainability quality characteristic.

Portability obtained the lowest average percentage of related responses, with only 6.73%. This suggests that very few API Management capabilities are seen as related to portability. The mean value of 0% confirms the limited alignment with the portability quality characteristic.

These findings provide valuable insights into the perceived associations between API Management capabilities and the ISO 25010 quality characteristics. It is essential to consider these results when designing, developing, and enhancing API management platforms to better meet user needs and ensure high-quality performance.

4.1   Threats to Validity and Limitations

When conducting surveys, it is important to consider the potential threats to the validity of the results. In this sense, the sample and population size can be particularly considered as potential threats to the validity of survey results. Specifically, two types of threats related to sample and population size are worth considering: a) Sampling Bias [22,23] can limit the generalizability of the findings and lead to inaccurate conclusions about the broader population. b) Limited Statistical Power [24,25]: the study may lack sufficient statistical power to detect meaningful relationships or differences, which can increase the likelihood of Type II errors (false negatives) and limit the ability to draw accurate conclusions from the data.

To mitigate this threat, we have implemented various strategies as described in [26]. These strategies include utilizing personal networks, constructing a sample based on convenience, authority, and credibility. Given that our study is an academic research project conducted by a national university, we included all necessary research details in the questionnaire. Additionally, we designed a brief and concise survey, carefully considering the type and number of instructions provided. Moreover, it is worth noting that the sample size in our study is comparable to other surveys targeting software developers using APIs, as reported in the literature. For instance, in [27], the sample consisted of 6 participants.

Additionally, to mitigate the risk of false negatives and eliminate errors due to ambiguous responses, the survey questions were designed as mandatory radio button selections. This design choice aimed to ensure clear and unambiguous choices between "Related" and "Not Related" options, reducing the potential for misinterpretation or inaccurate responses.

While the study provides valuable contributions, it is not without limitations. Given the pilot nature of the experiment, it is essential to acknowledge the limitations inherent in the study design. These limitations include: a) Small sample size: The study involved only six participants, which may limit the generalizability of the findings. b) Lack of diversity: The sample consisted of a reduced group of participants, which may not be representative of the broader population of professionals in the IT-related industry. c) Preliminary nature: The study aimed to gather preliminary insights and may not provide definitive conclusions.

4.2   Impact and Significance

The findings of this study have significant implications for the field of API management and software development. Understanding the relationships between API Management capabilities and ISO 25010 quality characteristics provides valuable insights into the design, development, and enhancement of API management platforms as software products. The study's insights on the associations between capabilities and ISO 25010's quality characteristics can guide platform providers in making informed decisions to improve specific aspects of their API management offerings. By addressing the identified gaps and weaknesses, developers can work towards creating more robust, efficient, and user-friendly API management platforms that meet users' expectations and industry standards.

Additionally, the study's results can help API management platform users, developers, and decision-makers make informed choices when selecting or customizing platforms to align with their specific needs and quality requirements. The understanding of which capabilities contribute significantly to each quality characteristic empowers stakeholders to make data-driven decisions in their platform evaluation and adoption processes. In this sense, confirming the identified high rate of functional suitability and security among capabilities through wider surveys may indicate that developers and organizations can prioritize and invest in functionalities that align well with user needs and overall system functionality.

4.3   Concluding Remarks and Future Directions

In conclusion, this study successfully identified the quality characteristics that participants perceived as related to API Management capabilities. The high rate of functional suitability among capabilities confirms our hypothesis, emphasizing the platforms' strong alignment with meeting functional needs and user requirements.

The results of this study contribute to the existing body of knowledge in API management and software development. While the study has its limitations, such as the relatively small sample size, the findings lay the groundwork for future research in this domain. For instance, the high rate of security relatedness may establish new hypothesis in future work.

The moderate associations found between capabilities and ISO/IEC 25010 quality attributes present opportunities for improvement. Addressing the identified gaps can lead to enhanced API Management functional suitability, reliability, performance efficiency, usability, security, compatibility, maintainability, and portability.

Our recommendation is for future investigations to examine these connections using broader and more heterogeneous samples to improve the generalizability of the outcomes. Additionally, considering other factors that may influence participants' perceptions, such as their experience with API management platforms, could provide further insights into quality characteristic prioritization.

In conclusion, the findings derived from this study reveal valuable guidance to API management platform providers, developers, and users, promoting the continuous improvement and adoption of high-quality API management software products that meet the evolving needs of the software industry.

As previously suggested in [14], in view of the preliminary findings and the identified limitations, forthcoming studies in this area should ponder the following directions: a) Increase sample size: It is important to address the potential threats by carefully considering the sample size and ensuring that it is appropriate for the research objectives and the target population. Conducting the study with a larger and more diverse sample would enhance the generalizability of the results, as larger sample sizes can help improve the representativeness of the sample and enhance the statistical power of the study, reducing the risk of sampling bias and increasing the likelihood of detecting meaningful effects. b) Explore additional variables: Investigate other factors or variables that may influence the observed patterns to gain a more comprehensive understanding. c) Additional statistical analysis through multi-valued analysis and other techniques.

Also, as the limited nature of this study, we suggest future work can extend or adapt this survey, in order to incorporate other aspects of API Management such as caching, auditing, logging, API developer enablement and API life cycle management, among others. Finally, as the corpus in the area is recent and constantly evolving, we recommend to update this survey as new quality models and API Management characterizations arise.

References

1. Duan, Y., Fu, G., Zhou, N., Sun, X., Narendra, N.C., Hu, B.: Everything as a service (XaaS) on the cloud: Origins, current and future trends. In: 2015 IEEE 8th International Conference on Cloud Computing, pp. 621–628. IEEE (2015)
2. Fehling, Christoph, Leymann, Frank, Retter, Ralph, Schupeck, Walter, Arbitter, Peter: Cloud Computing Patterns. Springer, Vienna (2014). https://doi.org/10.1007/978-3-7091-1568-8
3. Gamez-Diaz, Antonio, Fernandez, Pablo, Ruiz-Cortes, Antonio: An analysis of RESTful APIs offerings in the industry. In: Maximilien, Michael, Vallecillo, Antonio, Wang, Jianmin, Oriol, Marc (eds.) ICSOC 2017. LNCS, vol. 10601, pp. 589–604. Springer, Cham (2017). https://doi.org/10.1007/978-3-319-69035-3_43
4. Postman Inc.: 2023 state of the API report (2023)
5. Fielding, R.T.: Architectural Styles and The Design of Network-based Software Architectures (2000)
6. Andreo, Sebastien, Bosch, Jan: API management challenges in ecosystems. In: Hyrynsalmi, Sami, Suoranta, Mari, Nguyen-Duc, Anh, Tyrväinen, Pasi, Abrahamsson, Pekka (eds.) ICSOB 2019. LNBIP, vol. 370, pp. 86–93. Springer, Cham (2019). https://doi.org/10.1007/978-3-030-33742-1_8
7. Brown, A., Fishenden, J., Thompson, M.: API Economy, Ecosystems and Engagement Models, pp. 225–236. Palgrave Macmillan UK (2014)
8. Bloch, J.: How to design a good API and why it matters. In: Companion to the 21st ACM SIGPLAN Symposium on Object-Oriented Programming Systems, Languages, and Applications, pp. 50–507. ACM (2006)
9. De, Brajesh: API Management. Apress, Berkeley, CA (2017). https://doi.org/10.1007/978-1-4842-1305-6
10. Preibisch, Sascha: API Development. Apress, Berkeley, CA (2018). https://doi.org/10.1007/978-1-4842-4140-0
11. Gamez-Diaz, A., Fernandez, P., Ruiz-Cortés, A.: Governify for APIs: SLA-driven ecosystem for API governance. In: Proceedings of the 2019 27th ACM Joint Meeting on European Software Engineering Conference and Symposium on the Foundations of Software Engineering, ESEC/FSE 2019, pp. 1120–1123. Association for Computing Machinery. event-place: Tallinn, Estonia (2019)
12. Schultis,K.-B., Elsner, C., Lohmann, D.: Architecture challenges for internal software ecosystems: a large-scale industry case study. In: Proceedings of the 22nd ACM SIGSOFT International Symposium on Foundations of Software Engineering, pp. 542–552. ACM (2014)

13. Wilde, E., Amundsen, M.: The challenge of API management: API strategies for decentralized API landscapes. In: Companion Proceedings of The 2019 World Wide Web Conference, pp. 1327–1328. ACM (2019)
14. Dos Santos, E., Casas, S.: An empirical study of API management and ISO/IEC SQuaRE: a practitioners' perspective. In: Libro de Actas del XXIX Congreso Argentino de Ciencias de la Computación (CACIC 2023), pp. 332–341. Universidad Nacional de Luján (2023)
15. Wohlin, C., Runeson, P., Höst, M., Ohlsson, M.C., Regnell, B., Wesslén, A.: Experimentation in Software Engineering. Springer, Heidelberg (2012). https://doi.org/10.1007/978-3-642-29044-2
16. Fowler, F.J.: Survey Research Methods. SAGE Publications, Inc., 5th edn. (2013). OCLC: 918559564
17. Kasunic, M.: Designing an Effective Survey, p. 2727665 Bytes (2005)
18. Mathijssen, M., Overeem, M., Jansen, S.: Identification of practices and capabilities in API management: a systematic literature review (2020)
19. SmartBear: State of software quality - API: Latest trends and insights for 2023 (2023)
20. RapidAPI: State of API report 2022 (2022)
21. Constanzo, M., Casas, S., Vidal, G., Cruz, D.: Usos y problemas de las APIs web en la república argentina. (44), 79–97 (2022)
22. Cochran, W.G.: Sampling Techniques, 3rd edn. Wiley (1977)
23. Kish, L.: Survey Sampling. Wiley (1995)
24. Cohen, J.: Statistical power analysis for the behavioral sciences, 2nd edn. L. Erlbaum Associates (2013)
25. Rosenthal, R., Rosnow, R.L.: Essentials of Behavioral Research: Methods and Data Analysis. McGraw-Hill, 3rd edn. (2008). OCLC: ocm69645797
26. Ghazi, A.N., Petersen, K., Reddy, S.S.V.R., Nekkanti, H.: Survey research in software engineering: problems and mitigation strategies. IEEE Access **7**, 24703–24718 (2018)
27. Espinha, T., Zaidman, A., Gross, H.G.: Web API growing pains: stories from client developers and their code. In: 2014 Software Evolution Week - IEEE Conference on Software Maintenance, Reengineering, and Reverse Engineering (CSMR-WCRE), pp. 84–93. IEEE (2014)

Towards Optimal Non-functional Requirements Elicitation and Documentation in Agile Software Development: A Case Study

Lourdes Romera, Jeremías González, Andrea Lezcano, Juan A. Carruthers, and Emanuel Irrazábal[✉]

Software Quality Research Group – FaCENA-UNNE, Corrientes, Argentina
{alezcano,jacaruthers,eirrazabal}@exa.unne.edu.ar

Abstract. In agile software development, non-functional requirements are often underspecified and improperly handled due to the focus on rapidly delivering functionality. Neglecting NFRs in early phases of development may compromise software quality and customer satisfaction. In our previous paper, we introduced a guideline for handling non-functional requirements in Agile. This guideline was evaluated in a case study, revealing that improved identification of non-functional requirements led to enhanced development stability and client communication, without losing agility in the process. In this paper, we propose an extension of the guideline aimed at improving the documentation of each stage and incorporating a NFR testing phase.

Keywords: non-functional requirements · agile software development · system stories

1 Introduction

Since the introduction of the Agile Manifesto in 2001, agile software development (ASD) has been experiencing vertical growth within organizations. Agile methodologies focus on the quick delivery of software in order to satisfy customer expectations [1]. An initial step in this process involves redefining customer needs as project requirements, which are categorized into two groups: functional requirements (FR) and non-functional requirements (NFR). Functional requirements refer to the operations that the software must perform, and non-functional requirements, also known as quality requirements (QR) [2], represent software requirements that describe how the software should operate and the desired quality of the software. They can also be development constraints, such as project time, cost, the resources available, the processes to be used, or the construction technology. NFRs are important because even if the promised functionality is delivered, users will not perceive the system favorably if it lacks, for instance, adequate performance or reliability.

NFR analysis and integration into the developed software is critical for the success of the project. Customers may not have a comprehensive understanding of all NFRs in the initial stages of the project. Instead, they prioritize developing functional requirements [2]. Furthermore, the agile methodology lacks a clear approach for managing NFRs and allows minimal documentation, which leads to traceability issues of NFRs resulting in increased maintenance costs, accumulated technical debt, and occasionally, project failures.

According to the findings of the systematic mapping study (SMS) by Woubshet Behutiye [3], there is not a large number of procedures, guidelines, or best practices to support the documentation of NFRs, and the few that have been found tend to address specific types of NFRs, such as usability or security. Based on the results obtained in the SMS, it is evident the need to create a set of practices for managing NFRs, considering the perspectives of the different roles and artifacts involved in ASD.These practices should be evaluated to effectively support professionals aiming to maintain the agility of the software development process in terms of speed and simplicity.

This study is an extension of [4] that proposes the evaluation through a case study of a first approach to a guide for the management of NFR in agile software development teams, as a prior step to the construction of a set of procedures. As an addition to the previously published work, new tasks and detailed diagrams based on software process modeling languages have been added. The resulting guide facilitates the core activities of requirements engineering, including requirements elicitation, documentation, validation, and testing.

This paper is organized as follows: Section one provides an introduction, Sect. 2 presents the case study conducted in a small software development company, Sect. 3 outlines the results of the case study, and Sect. 4 discusses the research questions. Finally, Sect. 5 concludes the paper.

2   Study Design

This study aims to evaluate the impact of a guideline for managing non-functional requirements on the workflow of an agile team in a small software development company. To this end, the following research questions (RQs) were formulated:

- RQ1: How did the guideline impact the early identification of non-functional requirements?
- RQ2: What is the effect of using the guideline on customer satisfaction in the non-functional requirements management process?
- RQ3: How did the inclusion of new practices and work artifacts impact the agility level of the work teams?

We chose a case study approach to address the research questions. Following the methodology proposed by Yin [5], we performed the following steps: case study design, data collection, analysis of the collected data, and presentation of the results. We describe each of these steps in detail in the following subsections.

2.1 System Under Study

The case under study centered around a small software development company situated in the northeast region of Argentina, comprising 12 employees divided into four teams. Of these, we selected for analysis two teams that employed the Agile Scrum development methodology, and that lacked prior experience in handling NFR.

We chose this research method to assess the real impact of the guideline and observe how its implementation affects the process of eliciting and managing NFRs. To achieve this, we conducted a study consisting of four phases described below:

Phase 1: Development and utilization of the guideline for non-functional requirements management within the development teams.

Phase 2: Analysis of the quantity and quality of non-functional requirements between projects prior to and following the implementation of the guideline.

Phase 3: Analysis of delivered results and subsequent maintenance.

Phase 4: Measurement of the agility level of the development teams before and after applying the guideline using the survey proposed in [6].

2.2 Guideline and Data Extraction

In this section, we describe the specific activities carried out for each phase defined in Sect. 2.1. The participating company played an active role in both the formulation and validation processes of the guideline. Every activity was conducted in close collaboration with the development team and NFR analyst involved in the selected projects, ensuring a coherent and complete collection of information relevant to the study.

Additionally, Figs. 2 and 3 showcase, from the behavioral and organizational perspectives, the process proposed by the guideline modeling with SPEM [7].

Phase 1. Figure 1 illustrates the project life cycle developed with Scrum, as described by Van den Broek [8], including aspects of testing. Red captions denote the elements integrated into the flow, encompassing the management of NFRs across the stages of project initiation, initial Sprint, Sprint planning, and Sprint execution. Following this, the elements incorporated at each step will be described.

Project Initiation stage. Traditional Scrum roles that lead the projects such as product owner and project manager may not always have the required skills for defining RNFs [3].

The guideline recommends assigning roles to professionals with expertise on NFRs management who deal exclusively with the exhaustive analysis of RNFs, evaluating their impact on the system, identifying dependencies with functional requirements and performing tests to validate their compliance [9]. In this case, we included a project leader with more than two decades of experience in maintaining a high-performance system. This professional contributed to the development of the guideline while assuming the role of NFR Analyst during the Sprints.

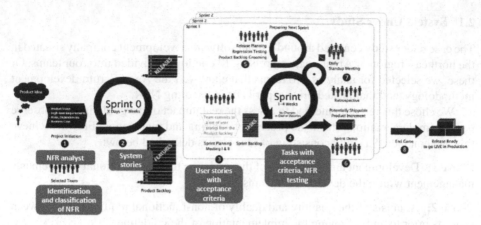

Fig. 1. Scrum life cycle with modifications.

Initial Sprint stage. At this stage, we tackled the identification and classification of NFRs, involving the following activities:

Eliciting preliminary requirements: Requirements are gathered through interviews with the product owner. This step is focused only on collecting the FRs from the customer. The outcome of this process is a set of epics detailing the major functionalities.

Identification of software type: Considering the initial requirements, the software is aimed to be classified into one of the categories shown in Table 1 [10, 11]. Subsequently, an initial list of NFRs to be considered is generated.

Table 1. Classification of systems and their relevant NFRs, taken from [10, 11].

ID	System Type	Recommended NFRS
1	Real-time systems	Compatibility, completeness, conformance, extensibility, installability, portability, dependability, maintainability, integrity, accuracy, confidentiality, verifiability, availability, performance, security, usability, reliability, safety
2	Safety Critical systems	Communicativeness, dependability, safety, reliability, performance, security, usability, integrity
3	Web systems	Interoperability, privacy, scalability, performance, security, usability, integrity
4	Information systems	Provability, reusability, standardizability, reliability, accuracy, confidentiality, verifiability, availability, performance, security, usability, interoperability, privacy, traceability, viability
5	Process-controlled systems	Maintainability, safety, reliability, availability, performance, security, usability

Classification of NFRs: Using the initial list of NFRs and the initial requirements, a categorization is conducted based on the classification scheme proposed by Chung and do Prado Leite [12].

Identification of conflicts: To examine conflicts between internal and external quality attributes [13, 14], developers should construct a mapping matrix of these attributes (see Table 2) to pinpoint potential conflicts. The aim is to identify the most critical attributes and strike a balance between them. Then, these matrices are negotiated with the client until agreement is reached on the final attributes, which will serve as the baseline for NFRs.

Table 2. Mapping between external and internal attribute [13, 14]

Internal quality attributes	External quality attributes			
	Usability	Reliability	Performance	Accuracy
Maintainability			x	
Flexibility	X			
Portability		x		
...				

Construction and refinement of system stories: After the estimation of candidate NFRs, the NFR Analyst constructs the system stories [15], as described later.

Presentation and refinement with the customer: Through a meeting, system stories are validated with the client, resulting in the final list of NFRs to be implemented.

Construction of testable NFR specification: The NFR Analyst is responsible for drafting testability NFR cards as outlined in Table 3 for the development team to utilize during Sprint execution.

Table 3. Testable NFR specification

Field	Description
Issue type	Story
Story	Add test cases to reach test coverage of 90%
DoD	With additional test cases the test coverage should reach 90%

After completing all the steps, the team obtained the NFRs for future use alongside the FRs. The system stories [15], serve as complementary artifacts to user stories, encapsulating and managing the non-functional behavior characteristics analyzed previously. Their structure is explained in Table 4.

The user story ID and the NFR ID link both types of requirements, for example, the NFR: "Every transaction must be completed in less than one second" is associated with all user stories whose functionality is fulfilled through a transaction.

Table 4. Components of a System Story.

Component	Description
ID NFR	Non-functional requirement identifier
ID HU	Identifier of the FR User Story to which this NFR is associated
NFR	Description of the NFR
Sub-NFR	Description of the NFR subclassification
Priority	NFR priority assigned by the client
Dependence	NFR that depends on the current NFR

The description of the NFR and sub-NFR includes the property name, property type, and value, for example: "The response time in the search registration must not exceed 5 s." In this case, the structured description would be:

- NFR = Response time,
- Sub-NFR = Performance, Time, Behavior,
- Type = Time in seconds, Value = 5.

The priority of the NFRs is of relative importance considering their relevance to the overall success of the project. The model proposed by Muhammad et al. [16] was utilized to define this score.

Sprint Execution Stage. User stories, along with system stories, constitute the Product Backlog and are utilized as inputs to detail the stories to be addressed in the Sprint. At this stage, clear and quantifiable acceptance criteria were included in the user stories as part of the "definition of done," as described by Behutiye in [17]. Moreover, it is necessary to designate a team member responsible for reviewing the completion of the user story [17], using the NFR test card. Additionally, this individual can employ the UNITE framework [18] to evaluate the NFRs addressed in the sprint via the following steps:

- Utilize log messages to capture metrics of interest, such as the timing of events or the values of elements within an event.
- Identify relevant metrics within the log messages using message constructs, such as: {STRING ident} sent message {INT eventId} at {INT time}.
- Formulate unit tests to analyze non-functional concerns (such as end-to-end response time, overall latency, or system reliability) by crafting equations utilizing the identified metrics, which may encompass multiple log messages

Phase 2. ASD teams participated in general RNF training to develop RNF documentation and management skills. In July and August of 2022, they started two projects using.Net and PHP technologies, respectively. The company used Jira as a task management tool, categorizing tasks by type and criticality. One of the task types in the tool is "requirements," preceding user stories. We selected the requirements, user stories, and Sprint tasks from the last two completed projects by each team. The content was

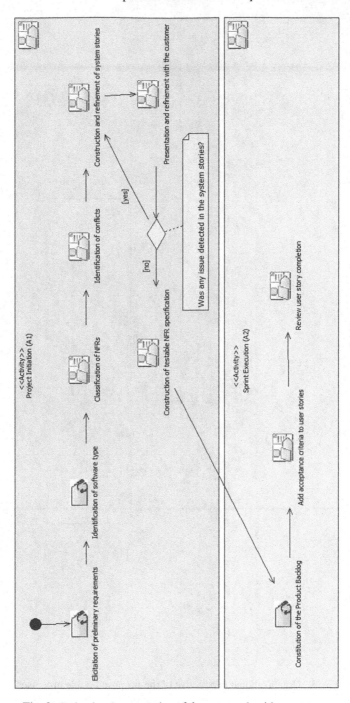

Fig. 2. Behavioral perspective of the proposed guide processes.

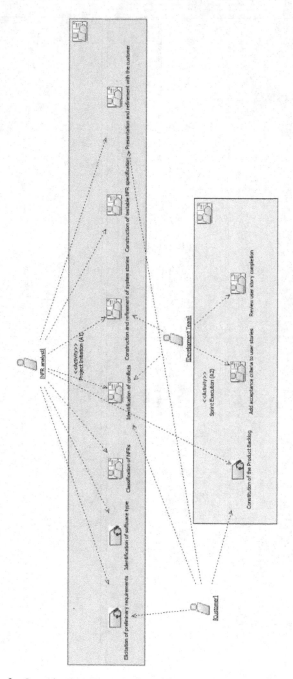

Fig. 3. Organizational perspective of the proposed guide processes

analyzed to describe the identified NFRs based on the guideline, quantifying the amount by type, determining if it contained sufficient details to verify NFR compliance, and its testability. This analysis was independently conducted by two authors of the study, with results compared and discussed in the event of divergent conclusions.

Phase 3. Upon completion of each project, the company conducted a satisfaction survey following best practices and standards for quality management in the workflow process, such as ISO 9001. In this case, we collected survey results from projects before and after the implementation of the guideline. Once the first version of each project was delivered, maintenance tasks commenced, which were also managed using the Jira tool. Developers associated these tasks with user stories and related systems during their creation. Based on this information we were able to evaluate the quantity and criticality of system incidents caused by RNF management.

Phase 4. Team's agility level was analyzed by answering the "essential" questions from the questionnaire [6]. This was conducted at two points in time: before the introduction of the NFR guideline at the project's outset and once the projects were completed. This allowed for a comparison of results, in addition to a qualitative analysis of respondents' opinions.

Additionally, one of the authors of the study participated in project retrospective meetings, posing questions to the work team and the NFR analyst to identify the usefulness of the guideline. The results of these interactions are discussed in Sect. 4.

3 Results

Below, Table 5 describes the results obtained from the analysis of the identified NFRs before and after the inclusion of the activities outlined in Phase 1 of the case study. In addition to the column containing the teams (#E) and projects (#P), there is a column indicating the final story point count for each project (PI), the number of identified NFRs (#NFR), the density of story points per identified NFR (DPR), the number of quantified NFRs (Quant.), and the number of tested NFRs (Test.); in the latter two cases, the percentage is also provided relative to the total number of NFRs.

Table 5. NFR analysis

#E	#P	PI	#NFR	DPR	Quant.	% Quant.	Test.	% Test
1	1	122	13	9,4	8	62%	6	46%
1	2	87	10	8,7	5	50%	4	40%
2	3	99	15	6,6	9	60%	8	53%
2	4	135	12	11,3	10	83%	9	75%
1	5	130	27	4,8	24	89%	22	81%
2	6	117	31	3,8	29	94%	26	84%

In Fig. 4, the data summarizing the first four projects conducted without the guideline and the two most recent projects with the guideline are presented. Both teams enhanced their ability to detect and describe NFRs, both in quantity and quality. Similarly, the data obtained in Phase 3 when analyzing customer surveys are as follows: Table 6 summarizes the satisfaction level, and Table 7 summarizes the quantity and quality of incidents related to NFR aspects.

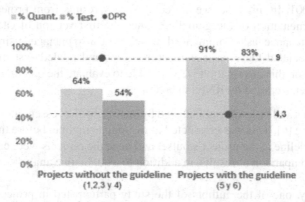

Fig. 4. Analysis of the RNF before and after incorporating the guide.

Table 6 shows 7 of the items requested in the customer satisfaction survey and the responses on a 5-point Likert scale of the six projects evaluated (from P1 to P6). In the PSG column the first four projects carried out without the RNF guide are averaged and in the PCG column the two projects developed with the guide are averaged. Customer satisfaction was similar with small variations in the items related to meetings, speed of delivery and the customer's perceived quality of what was delivered.

Table 6. Degree of customer satisfaction.

Item	P1	P2	P3	P4	P5	P6	PSG	PCG
The initial meetings	4	4	4	4	5	4	4	4,5
Planning meetings	4	4	4	4	4	5	4	4,5
Demo meetings	5	5	5	5	5	5	5	5
The speed of delivery of developments	4	4	5	4	4	4	4,25	4
The quality of the developments delivered	4	4	4	4	4	5	4	4,5
Confidence in the company for future developments	5	5	5	5	5	5	5	5
General company service	5	5	5	5	5	5	5	5

Table 7 summarizes the information obtained from maintenance tasks entered in the task management tool: the number of maintenance incidents per project (#Incidents), the average severity ranging from 1: very low severity to 5: very high severity (Avg. Severity), and the total hours invested in the incidents (#Hours).

Table 7. Timing and criticality of NFR-related incidents.

#P	PI	#NFR	#Incidents	Avg. Severity	# Hours	D_IPI	D_HI
1	122	13	8	3,8	58	15,3	7,3
2	87	10	9	3,8	55	9,7	6,1
3	99	15	7	4,9	74	14,1	10,6
4	135	12	4	3,3	23	33,8	5,8
5	130	27	5	2,6	28	26,0	5,6
6	117	31	3	2,7	18	39,0	6,0

The last two columns represent the density of incidents per story point (D_IPI) and the density of work hours per incident (D_HI). A clear decrease in the number of hours invested per incident, lower severity, and higher density of functionality delivered per incident can be observed. This is evident by aggregating the data before and after the implementation of the guideline, as depicted in Fig. 5. Finally, during Phase 4, Table 8 was completed as described in the previous section. The table only includes items with some variation before (column B) and after (column A) implementing the guideline. These two columns were filled out with three closed options: YES, NO, and Partially (Part.). Also included is an item with no apparent variation but where some discussed differences were found qualitatively.

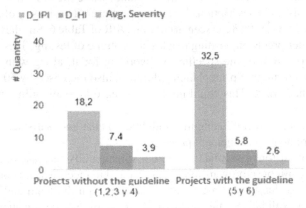

Fig. 5. Summary of the incidents before and after the implementation of the NFR work guide.

The incorporation of the NFR Analyst has shifted the focus away from the Product Owner, particularly due to the initial and synchronization work required between user stories and system stories to organize the Product Backlog. Regarding daily meetings, the approach remains the same, but issues and impediments now also encompass those related to NFRs. The Sprint duration saw an increase, with the inclusion of NFRs resulting in more testing tasks and a slight decrease in team velocity. Ultimately, the product at the end of each Sprint was not always fully functional, but this was already occurring before the adoption of the NFR guideline.

Table 8. Internal Agility Questionnaire.

Items	B	A
The Product Owner (PO) is empowered to order	Yes	Partial
PO has the knowledge to organize the Product Backlog	Yes	Partial
Problems and impediments are mentioned in the daily meeting	Yes	Yes
Iteration time is 4 weeks or less	Yes	Partial
Muestra producto funcionando y probado	Partial	Partial

4 Discussion

This section discusses the obtained results and addresses the research questions.

RQ1: How did the guideline impact the early identification of non-functional requirements?

Upon analyzing the detected NFRs, we found a clear difference in quantity and quality. On one hand, new NFR types were included, while the system stories template improved the precision in descriptions for testing purposes. The density of NFRs regarding story points was over 100%, as seen in column DPR of Table 6. Similarly, NFRs were crafted with greater precision, leading to a higher volume of testing. This was expected due to the incorporation of the specific role working for it, along with the guideline and previous team training. Sprint planning duration also increased by 50%, from 60 to 90 min per planned week. This could imply a decrease in team agility, not evident in subsequent studies.

RQ2: What is the effect of using the guideline on customer satisfaction in the non-functional requirements management process?

The degree of customer satisfaction did not substantially increase due to guideline use. We observe a minor improvement in items related to meetings and communication, we infer that this is due to increased interactions between the team and the customer during system story validation. Maintenance tasks did show a change in quantity, severity, and hours invested. This heightened the customer's perception of final software product quality, though not fully reflected in the satisfaction survey as it was administered only at the project's end. Similarly, the work team expressed increased stability in maintenance tasks, particularly due to the decrease in critical incidents, almost halved as observed in Tables 7 and 8.

RQ3: How did the inclusion of new practices and work artifacts impact the agility level of the work teams?

The team's agility was not altered according to the survey results or the teams' perceptions in retrospective meetings. A qualitative analysis of tasks after guideline inclusion showed an increase in system story-related tasks and associated testing. In response, teams chose to extend Sprint duration to maintain a stable number of story points delivered per iteration. This team decision may be viewed as a decrease in agility.

5 Conclusions

This paper presents the results of a case study evaluating the inclusion of a guideline for managing non-functional requirements in a small agile software development company.

The data for the evaluation of the research questions were obtained through the analysis of the company's task management tool, participation in retrospective meetings of each Sprint, and the application of data collection instruments such as customer satisfaction surveys or the questionnaire for measuring team agility.

Our findings revealed that there was an increase in the quantity and accuracy in the identification of non-functional requirements and that their explicit inclusion in planning discussions with the client and the team led to a greater number of tasks in each Sprint for verification. Consequently, there was an increase in the team's perception of the stability of the process and to a smaller extent, in the customer's perception of the quality of the product. The agility of the teams did not decrease, nor did the duration of the Sprints increase. Although the number of tasks increased, the incorporated role managed them, allowing the same amount of functionality to be delivered.

Based on the results of this case study, we can say that the findings of this work serve as a basis for developing procedures for managing non-functional requirements in agile development environments, and as an initial step towards the design of future research in the framework of the Scientific Design Methodology.

Acknowledgements. This work was carried out within the framework of projects 21F001 and 21 F005 of the General Secretariat of Science and Technology of the National University of the Northeast.

References

1. Al-Saqqa, S., Samer, S., Hiba, A.: Agile software development: Methodologies and trends. Int. J. Interact. Mob. Technol. **14**, 11 (2020)
2. Wagner, S.: Software product quality control (2013)
3. Behutiye, W., et al.: Management of quality requirements in agile and rapid software development: a systematic mapping study. Inform. Softw. Technol. **123**, 106225 (2020)
4. Romera, L., González, J., Lezcano, A., Carruthers, J.A., Irrazábal, E.: Gestión de los requerimientos no funcionales en equipos ágiles: un caso de estudio. In: Proceeding del XXIX Congreso Argentino de Ciencias de la Computación (CACIC), pp: 289–298 (2024)

5. Yin, R.: Case Study Research: Design and Methods, pp: 687–704 (2003)
6. Kniberg, H.: Scrum Checklist, vol. 2, pp. 1–2 (2010)
7. OMG: Software & Systems Process Engineering Meta-Model (SPEM) Specification, Version 2.0 (2008)
8. Van Den Broek, R., Bonsangue, M.M., Chaudron, M., Van Merode, H.: Integrating testing into Agile software development processes. In: 2014 MODELSWARD, pp. 561–574 (2014)
9. Bourimi, M., Barth, T., Haake, J.M., Ueberschär, B., Kesdogan, D.: Affine for enforcing earlier consideration of NFRs and human factors when building socio-technical systems following agile methodologies. Human-Centred Software Engineering: Third International Conference, HCSE (2010)
10. Mairiza, D., Zowghi, D., Nurmuliani, N.: An investigation into the notion of non-functional requirements. In: Proceedings of the 2010 ACM Symposium on Applied Computing, pp. 311–317 (2010, March)
11. Mairiza, D., Zowghi, D.: Constructing a catalogue of conflicts among non-functional requirements. In: Maciaszek, L.A., Loucopoulos, P. (eds.) ENASE 2010. CCIS, vol. 230, pp. 31–44. Springer, Heidelberg (2011). https://doi.org/10.1007/978-3-642-23391-3_3
12. Chung, L., do Prado Leite, J.C.S.: On non-functional requirements in software engineering. In: Borgida, A.T., Chaudhri, V.K., Giorgini, P., Yu, E.S. (eds.) Conceptual Modeling: Foundations and Applications. LNCS, vol. 5600, pp. 363–379. Springer, Heidelberg (2009). https://doi.org/10.1007/978-3-642-02463-4_19
13. Thomas, B.: Meeting the challenges of requirements engineering. Spotlight, SEI Interactive 2(1) (1999)
14. Asghar, S., Umar, M.: Requirement engineering challenges in development of software applications and selection of customer-off-the-shelf (COTS) components. Int. J. Softw. Eng. 1(1), 32–50 (2010)
15. Cleland-Huang, J., Vierhause, M.: Discovering, analyzing, and managing safety stories in agile projects. In: Proceedings of the IEEE 26th International Requirements Engineering Conference (RE), pp. 262–273 (2018)
16. Muhammad, A., Siddique, A., Mubasher, M., Aldweesh, A., Naveed, Q.N.: Prioritizing non-functional requirements in agile process using multi criteria decision making analysis. IEEE Access, 11, 24631–24654 (2023)
17. Behutiye, W., Rodríguez, P., Oivo, M.: Quality requirement documentation guide-lines for agile software development. IEEE Access 10, 70154–70173 (2022)
18. Hill, J.H., Turner, H.A., Edmondson, J.R., Schmidt, D.C.: Unit testing non-functional concerns of component-based distributed systems. In 2009 International Conference on Software Testing Verification and Validation, pp. 406–415. IEEE (2009, April)

Validation of Metrics for the Deployment of Software Systems: Case Studies in SMEs in Argentina

Pablo Vázquez[1]([✉]) [iD], Marisa Panizzi[1] [iD], and Rodolfo Bertone[2] [iD]

[1] Master Program in Information Systems Engineering, Universidad Tecnológica Nacional, Regional Buenos Aires (UTN-FRBA), Medrano 951, CABA, Argentina
vazpablo@gmail.com, mpanizzi@frba.utn.edu.ar
[2] School of Computing – Institute of Computing Research LIDI (III-LIDI), Universidad Nacional de La Plata, 50 y 120, La Plata, Argentina
pbertone@lidi.unlp.edu.ar

Abstract. The growing demand for quality software products requires software developers to use standards and methodologies that ensure the delivery of those software products with the required quality. Deployment is the software process by which the software system is transferred to the client company. For SMEs, it is essential to improve their processes to be competitive. They must carry out initiatives that contribute to the development and improvement of their competitiveness. The use of metrics in the deployment process allows keeping track of all activities and tasks, reducing costs due to rework, avoiding delays in the delivery of the software product, and increasing the quality of the process. This article presents the results of the validation of the metrics designed for the software systems deployment process through two case studies in SMEs from Argentina.

Keywords: metrics · deployment process · software systems · case studies · SMEs from Argentina

1 Introduction

The deployment of software systems is a crucial process of the software development life cycle because, after successful deployment, the software system is finally operational for the customer to benefit financially from its use [1].

The deployment process contains practices that tend to present problems, such as a lack of components (generally external), incomplete downloads and erroneous installations, and rework due to a lack of technological capabilities and competencies of both computing resources and end users [2]. Problems that may occur in the deployment phase are transferred and eventually resolved as part of the maintenance phase. Therefore, having an efficient software deployment should save resources in terms of cost and effort [1]. Total or partial failures in the deployment processes can cause numerous drawbacks at the project level and in the commercial relationship with an organization's clients, due to the refusal to receive either an incomplete software product or a defective one.

This can cause potential economic losses related to failure to meet objectives and delays experienced in each project. On the contrary, successful deployment processes can significantly increase the perception of software quality and, consequently, its commercial expectations [2].

The emergence of many software companies transformed the software industry, making it more competitive. Improvement in software quality has become a key success factor that enables companies to achieve competitive advantage and it is essential for product quality, business sustainability, and growth [3]. In Argentina, the software industry is mainly made up of SMEs, which account for almost 80% of the sector [4] and require systematized and quality processes that contribute to the development and improvement of competitiveness in the market.

At an international level, the same reality is observed since SMEs occupy a large portion of the software industry [3]. The software industry is one of the fastest-growing sectors and it is considered a large contributor to the economy of countries [5].

Consequently, the relevance of the deployment process, the drawbacks that an inadequate deployment entails, plus the need for SMEs to have systematized and quality processes for the delivery of software systems that satisfy the needs of their clients, has led to the definition of a set of metrics for the deployment process of software systems in SMEs in Argentina.

To design the metrics, the following steps were followed: the state of the art through a systematic mapping of the literature [6] and a case study developed in an SME in Argentina to obtain feedback from industry professionals to refine and complete the set of metrics [7].

This article presents the results of the validation of the metrics designed for the software systems deployment process through two case studies developed in SMEs in Argentina. The description of the metrics for the deployment of software systems is expanded and more detail is provided in relation to the case studies presented in [8].

The article is structured as follows: Sect. 2 presents a description of the metrics design; Sect. 3 describes the case studies. An analysis of threats to validity is presented in Sect. 4 and lessons learned from the case studies are presented in Sect. 5. Finally, Sect. 6 presents the conclusions and future work.

2 Description of Metrics

To define the metrics, the activities, and tasks of the "transition process" of the ISO/IEC/IEEE 12207:2017 standard [9] were considered since it is an internationally recognized standard.

The classification of metrics proposed by the family of the ISO/IEC 9126 standard [10–13] was used, according to their nature: basic metrics, aggregate metrics, and derived metrics.

To organize the set of metrics defined for the software system deployment process, a view of metrics based on three dimensions, also called "three-dimensional view" of the deployment process [14], was considered. This perspective is composed of the "Process", "Product" and "Person" dimensions. The "Process" dimension is considered interesting because of the phases or stages, activities and tasks it includes. The second dimension,

"Product", considers the characteristics of the software product such as installation complexity, installation requirements, integration with the client's infrastructure and size, among others. And finally, the last dimension "People" is considered due to the existence of peopleware and its impact on the software systems deployment process.

Table 1. Metrics for the Process Dimension.

Metrics	Description	Formula
%DesvíoCAP	% Training deviation. It indicates the deviation between the planned training (CAP) and the training carried out (CAPR). The unit of measurement for the metric is a % and takes values greater than or equal to 0 CAP: number of trainings to be carried out. The unit of measurement is a numerical value and takes values greater than 0 CAPR: number of trainings carried out. The unit of measurement is a numerical value and takes values greater than or equal to 0	$\%DesvíoCap = 100 - (CAPR / CAP)$
%DesvíoHE	% Training deviation. It indicates the deviation between the planned training hours (HEP) and the executed training hours (HEE). The unit of measurement for the metric is a % and takes values greater than or equal to 0 HEP: it indicates the total planned training hours. The unit of measurement is hours and takes values greater than 0 HEE: it indicates the total training hours executed. The unit of measurement is hours and takes values greater than 0	$\%DesvíoHE = 100 - (HEE / HEP)$
%DesvíoPA	% Acceptance test deviation. It indicates the deviation between the planned acceptance tests (PAP) and the executed acceptance tests (PAE). The unit of measurement for the metric is a % and takes values greater than or equal to 0 PAP: it indicates the total planned acceptance tests. The unit of measurement is a numerical value and takes values greater than 0 PAE: it indicates the total acceptance tests exccuted. The unit of measurement is a numerical value and takes values greater than 0	$\%DesvíoPA = 100 - (PAE / PAP)$

(*continued*)

Table 1. (*continued*)

Metrics	Description	Formula
%DesvíoPEnt	% Trained people deviation. It indicates the deviation between the planned number of people for training (PEP) and the number of people trained (PE). The unit of measurement for the metric is a % and takes values greater than or equal to 0 PEP: it indicates the planned number of people for their training. The unit of measurement is a numerical value and takes values greater than 0 PE: it indicates the number of people trained. The unit of measurement is a numerical value and takes values greater than 0	%DesvíoPEnt = 100 - (PE / PEP)
%AvanceE	% Training progress. It indicates the percentage of training progress. The unit of measurement for the metric is a % and takes values greater than or equal to 0 HEP: it indicates the total planned training hours. The unit of measurement is hours and takes values greater than 0 HEE: it indicates the total training hours executed. The unit of measurement is hours and takes values greater than 0	%AvanceE = HEE / HEP
%AvancePA	% Acceptance tests progress. It indicates the progress of acceptance tests. This value can be obtained partially as the process progresses. The unit of measurement for the metric is a % and takes values greater than or equal to 0 PAP: it indicates the total planned acceptance tests. The unit of measurement is a numerical value and takes values greater than 0 PAE: it indicates the total acceptance tests executed. The unit of measurement is a numerical value and takes values greater than 0	%AvancePA = PAE / PAP

(*continued*)

Table 1. (*continued*)

Metrics	Description	Formula
%DesvíoEsf	% Effort deviation. Mismatch between estimated and actual effort. The unit of measurement for the metric is a % and takes values greater than or equal to 0 E: it indicates the effort calculated in the planning. The unit of measurement is hours and takes values greater than 0 ER: it indicates the actual effort consumed in the deployment process. The unit of measurement is hours and takes values greater than 0	%DesvíoEsf = $100 - (ER / E)$
%DesvíoTR	% Task deviation. It indicates the deviation between planned tasks and completed tasks. The unit of measurement for the metric is a % and takes values greater than or equal to 0 TP: it indicates the planned tasks. The unit of measurement is a numerical value and takes values greater than 0 TR: it indicates the tasks completed in the analyzed period. The unit of measurement is a numerical value and takes values greater than 0	%DesvíoTR $= 100 - (TR / TP)$
%AvanceTR	% Task progress. It indicates the progress of tasks. The unit of measurement for the metric is a % and takes values greater than or equal to 0 TP: it indicates the planned tasks. The unit of measurement is a numerical value and takes values greater than 0 TR: it indicates the tasks completed in the analyzed period. The unit of measurement is a numerical value and takes values greater than 0	%AvanceTR $= TR / TP$
ESF	Effort. It indicates the Total effort required to complete the process. This value is considered a hybrid metric (Trendowicz & Jeffery, 2014). The unit of measurement for the metric is hours EEK: Karner Estimated Effort. Effort calculated using Karner's Use case point estimation (Karner, 1993) EEPP: Effort estimated by Planning Porker. Calculated using the Planning Poker effort estimation method (Grenning, 2002)	ESF $= = (EEK + EEPP)/2$

(*continued*)

Table 1. (*continued*)

Metrics	Description	Formula
PRD	Process productivity. It indicates the level of productivity of the process once it has finished. The unit of measurement for this metric is a % and can take values greater than 0 ESF: it indicates the effort calculated in the planning phase. The unit of measurement is hours and takes values greater than 0 ESFR: it indicates the actual effort consumed in the deployment process. The unit of measurement is hours and takes values greater than 0	PRD = E SF/ESFR
PRDT	Task productivity. It indicates the level of productivity of the task performed. Like process productivity, this metric can be obtained after the task is completed. The unit of measurement of the metric is a % and takes values greater than 0 ET: it indicates the estimated effort of the planned task. The unit of measurement is hours and takes values greater than 0 ERT: it indicates the actual effort of the task. The unit of measurement is hours and takes values greater than 0	PRDT = = ET/ERT

Table 1 presents the proposed metrics for the software systems deployment process for the "Process" dimension, including the metric, its name, its description, and its calculation method. Tables 2 and 3 present the metrics for the "Product" and "Person" dimensions, respectively.

Table 2. Metrics for the Product dimension.

Metrics	Description	Formula
CantDef	It indicates the number of defects obtained during the deployment process and the acceptance tests executed. The unit of measurement is an integer numerical value and takes values greater than 0 DC: it indicates the number of configuration defects detected. The unit of measurement is a numerical value and takes values greater than 0 DA: it indicates the number of application defects detected. The unit of measurement is a numerical value and takes values greater than 0	CantDef = DC + DA

(*continued*)

Table 2. (*continued*)

Metrics	Description	Formula
%DensidadD	% Flaw density. It indicates the percentage of flaws in relation to the number of flaws (CantDef) found in the acceptance tests performed (PAE). The unit of measurement of the metric is a % and it takes values greater than or equal to 0	%DensidadD = CantDef / PAE

Table 3. Metrics for the Person dimension.

Metric	Description	Formula
%VVEL	% of velocity variation. It indicates the percentage of velocity variation of the team in relation to its historic velocity. The unit of measurement of the metric is a % and it takes values greater than or equal to 0 VEL: It indicates the number of tasks performed by the team in a time period according to historic deployments VELH: It indicates the number of tasks performed by the team in a time period	%VVEL = VEL / VELH

3   Case Studies

This section presents two case studies (CS1, CS2) conducted in software development SMEs in Argentina with the purpose of validating the applicability of the set of metrics designed in order to complete them and refine them if necessary. The case studies were conducted and reported following the guidelines proposed by Runeson *et al.* [15].

3.1   Case Study Objectives and Research Questions (RQs)

The Table 4 shows the objective of the case studies following Basili et al.'s Goal-Question-Metric paradigm [16].

Table 4. Case study objectives.

Analyze	the software system deployment documentation
with the purpose of	evaluating the applicability of the metrics
in relation to	the "Process", "Product" and "Person" dimensions
from the perspective of	software industry professionals
in the context of	SMEs in Argentina

To achieve this objective, the following research questions (RQs) were posed:

RQ1: What measurements were performed during the software system deployment process activities (identification and analysis)?

This question aims at gathering information about the metrics used during the deployment process execution and about how the consulting company used them in order to compare it with the proposal made.

RQ2: How can the software system deployment process be enhanced?

This question aims at establishing the way in which the consulting company can enhance its deployment process. In order to do this, a set of metrics is proposed, identifying their objectives and how to calculate them.

3.2 Context, Case and Unit of Analysis

According to Yin's classification [17], both case studies are holistic and unique cases characterized by the elements presented in Table 5. The Argentine SME classification according to number of employees was used [18].

Table 5. Context, case and unit of analysis of the case studies (CS1, CS2).

Case studies	Context	Case	Unit of analysis
CS1	**Level 2 Medium-sized** Software System Development **SME** based in City of Buenos Aires. 430 employees	Deployment of a Human Resources Portal for an Argentine bank	Documentation of the deployment of the Human Resources Portal
CS2	**Level 1 Medium-sized** Software System Development **SME** based in City of Buenos Aires. 60 employees	Deployment of a Management System for an advertising agency in Argentina	Documentation of the deployment of a Management System

3.3 Preparation for Data Collection

The two project managers of each of the SMEs participated in the case studies.

The training activities for the two project managers were conducted online through the *Meet* platform. The training period for each company consisted of one 3-h session. After the training process, close contact was kept with the company, for approximately a month, by telephone, *WhatsApp* and videoconference in order to answer questions arising during metric application by the project managers. Once the deployment was completed, the project manager of each case study provided the documentation created during such process in order to analyze the application of the metrics proposed.

To collect the data, a third-degree technique combined with an independent method was used, according to the classification proposed in [19].

A template was used with a coding scheme made up of 3 groups (A1 Deployment preparation, A2 Deployment execution and A3 Deployment results management), each of which corresponding to the 3 activities of the "Transition" technical process of the ISO/IEC/IEEE 12207:2017 standard [9]. To collect the information about the metrics used, the coding scheme proposed in Sect. 2 was used. Tables 6 and 7 show the traceability of the documentation analyzed of each of the case studies using the templates designed for data collection.

Table 6. Traceability of the documentation analyzed for CS1.

Documents/Activities	A1	A2	A3
Work plan	CAP, HEP, PAP PEP, ET, TP, ESF		
Progress report		%DesvioCap %DesvioHE %DesvioPEnt %AvanceE %AvancePA %DesvioPA %DesvioEsf %AvanceTR %DesvioTR %DensidadD	
Closing report			%DesvioCap %DesvioHE %DesvioPEnt %AvanceE %AvancePA %DesvioPA %DesvioEsf %AvanceTR %DesvioTR %DensidadD
Deployment Test Cases		CantDef %DensidadD	

3.4 Results Analysis and Discussion

This section first presents the results obtained in CS1 and CS2 about the application of metrics to answer RQ1 (See Table 8). Then, it discusses suggestions for improvement (reports submitted to the SMEs) thereby answering RQ2 (see Table 9).

Table 7. Traceability of the documentation analyzed for CS2.

Documents/Activities	A1	A2	A3
Deployment plan	CAP, HEP, PAP PEP, ET, TP ESF, E, VELH		
Progress report		%DesvíoCap %DesvíoHE %DesvíoPEnt %AvanceE %AvancePA %DesvíoPA %DesvíoEsf %AvanceTR %DesvíoTR %DensidadD PRD PRDT CAPR	
Deployment closing			%DesvíoCap %DesvioHE %DesvioPEínt %AvanceE %AvancePA %DesvíoPA %DesvíoEsf %AvanceTR %DesvíoTR %DensidadD PRD PRDT VEL
Training plan	CAP		
Test cases	PA	PAE	PAE
Deployment test execution report		CantDef %DensidadD	

4 Threats to Validity

In order to analyze the validity of CS1 and CS2, the aspects proposed in [15] were considered:

- **Construct validity.** The training offered and the templates used for data collection were appropriate. These actions allowed us to mitigate this aspect. The results were obtained based on the analysis of the documentation and the application of the set

Table 8. Results obtained in answer to RQ1 (CS1 and CS2).

Case study	Activity 1. Deployment Preparation	Activity 2. Deployment Execution	Activity 3. Deployment results management
CS1	• Planning of tasks to be performed • Estimation of effort of each task • Test cases designed	• Task progress registration • Test cases incompletely executed • Flaw registration • Execution of unplanned tasks	• Software repository problems • Various technical and product problems had a strong impact on the final quality of the product and in user satisfaction
CS2	• Planning of tasks to be performed • Estimation of effort of each task • Test cases designed	• Task progress and deviation registration • Test cases inconsistently executed • Flaw registration	• Planning deviations • Higher effort than planned • Inconsistency between QA and Production environments

Table 9. Reports with suggestions for improvement in answer to RQ2.

CS1 report	CS2 report
• Plan and estimate each of the phases of the software development life cycle • Measure all phases of the software development life cycle • Identify relevant measurements • Draft a deployment test plan • Identify the necessary skills to perform. Each deployment activity • Identify process risks	• Software measurements are the best control method and contribute to early decision making • Clearly and accurately define the activities to be performed from the beginning • Quality environments must be similar to production environments • Plan and estimate in order to show steady progress that give value to the client • Identify the relevant measurements for each phase of the software development life cycle • Identify process risks

of metrics for the software system deployment process in two real contexts, which allowed us to answer the research questions posed.

• **Internal validity**. The documentation used belongs to two real cases in Argentina. In order to achieve better accuracy and validity of the process studied, we acknowledge the need to combine the data source (project documentation) with another source type, such as interviews and/or focus groups in order to ensure "data (source) triangulation". In addition, the qualitative data collected and analyzed might be combined with quantitative data from the project, thus ensuring "Methodological Triangulation".

- **External validity**. The use of only two case studies might limit the generalization of the results. However, a preliminary study was conducted in [7] and in this case we consider it is necessary to report these findings, since it serves as an incentive for other researchers to replicate our study in different case studies.
- **Reliability**. CS1 and CS2 data were collected by the first author. Although the data were analyzed together with the two other authors, this might be considered a threat to the research study. To provide better reliability, it is recommended that another researcher should apply the template to other case studies with the coding scheme designed.

5 Lessons Learned

The following lessons were learned from the case studies:

- **Method selection.** The validation of a set of metrics for the deployment process of software systems in a real setting was required in order to refine them (if necessary). The results obtained allowed us to analyze the application of the set of metrics defined in a real setting. Therefore, we consider that the method used has provided the expected results.
- **Collected data**. Although the documentation of the software system deployment process has been reviewed in order to analyze how the metrics proposed for each case study were used, we consider that both case studies might be enriched if the data collected were supplemented with other sources or with quantitative data.
- **Coding scheme selected**. The coding scheme selected for the design of the data collection and analysis template was appropriate and made it possible to systematically register the metrics information.
- **Results report**. Although the case studies include two research questions only, the work performed had an appropriate level of detail to understand the phenomenon under study.

6 Conclusions and Future Work

The results of CS1 and CS2 were presented to determine the viability of the application of a set of metrics for the deployment process of software systems in a real setting.

The conclusions obtained after conducting the case studies are presented below:

- The professionals who participated in the case studies considered that the metrics proposed had a positive impact in the quality improvement of software system deployments in their SMEs.
- A strength of the metrics proposed is their flexibility, since the exactly required metrics can be selected according to the activities and tasks to be performed during the deployment, thus allowing SMEs to conduct their software system deployments in a systematic and controlled fashion, considering their own resources and needs.
- Through the documentation analysis of the case studies, it was possible to identify flaws in the use of certain metrics, since some of them could not be applied to either of the case studies.

● We were also able to elaborate a set of recommendations for the companies to implement and improve their deployment process, as well as to introduce the use of metrics for future software system deployments. In addition, the use of metrics was suggested for other processes of the software development life cycle.

In view of the results obtained from the case studies, the following future lines of work are identified: (a) to apply the metrics to other types of information systems and collect information through a survey based on the Technology Acceptance Model (TAM), with the aim of analyzing the degree of acceptance and usefulness of the application for the software system deployment process, (b) to apply the metrics to other types of companies, such us Startups o larger companies in order to obtain feedback from users and compare it with the results obtained in SMEs, (c) to propose new metrics based on indicators obtained from the satisfaction surveys.

References

1. Subramanian, N.: The software deployment process and automation. CrossTalk **30**(2), 28–34 (2017)
2. Jansen S., Brinkkemper, S.: Definition and validation of the key process of release, delivery and deployment for product software vendors: turning the ugly duckling into a swan. In: IEEE International Conference on Software Maintenance, ICSM, art. no. 4021334, pp. 166–175 (2006)
3. Abushama, H.: PAM-SMEs: process assessment method for small to medium enterprises. Softw. Evol. Proc. **28**(8), 689 –711 (2016)
4. OPPSI-CESSI. Reporte anual del sector de software y servicios informáticos de la República Argentina del año 2018. Ciudad Autónoma de Buenos Aires: Cámara de la Industria Argentina de Software (CESSI) (27 de 04 de 2019)
5. Mishra, D., Mishra, A.: Software process improvement in SMEs. Comput. Sci. Inf. Syst. **16**(2), 111–140 (2009)
6. Vázquez, P., Panizzi, M., Bertone, R.: Métricas para el proceso de despliegue de sistemas software: un mapeo sistemático. Desarrollo e Innovación en Ingeniería. vol. II, ed. 6, pp. 386–396 (2021). ISBN 978-958-53278-6-3
7. Vázquez, P., Panizzi, M., Bertone, R.: Refinamiento de métricas para el proceso de despliegue de sistemas de software: Estudio de caso. In: Proceedings of the IADIS Ibero American Conference Applied Computing (CIACA 2021). Del 18 al 19 de noviembre de 2021 (2021). ISBN 978-989-8704-35-1
8. Vazquez, P., Panizzi, M., Bertone, R.: Validación de métricas para el despliegue de sistemas de software: Estudios de casos en PyMES de Argentina. En: XXIX Congreso Argentino de Ciencias de la Computación, CACIC 2023, Luján, Buenos Aires, Argentina, pp. 299–307 (2023). ISBN 978-987-9285-51-0
9. ISO/IEC/IEEE 12207:2017(E). Systems and software engineering — Software life cycle processes (2017)
10. ISO/IEC 9126-1. Software engineering - Product quality - Part 1 Quality model (2001). http://www.iso.org/iso/home.html
11. ISO/IEC 9126-2. Software engineering - Product quality - Part 2 External metrics (2003). http://www.iso.org/iso/home.html
12. ISO/IEC 9126-3. Software engineering - Product quality - Part 3 Internal metrics (2003). http://www.iso.org/iso/home.html

13. ISO/IEC 9126-4. Software engineering - Product quality - Part 4 Quality in use metrics (2004). http://www.iso.org/iso/home.html
14. Panizzi, M., et al.: Desafíos para la implantación de sistemas de software. En las Actas del XXII Workshop de Investigadores en Ciencias de la Computación (WICC 2020), El Calafate, Argentina 7 y 8 de mayo de 2020. ISBN 978-987-3714-82-5
15. Runeson, P., Höst, M., Rainer, A., Regnell, B.: Case Study Research in Software Engineering: Guidelines and Examples. Wiley Publishing, Hoboken (2012)
16. Basili, V., Rombach, D.: The TAME project: towards improvement-oriented software environments. IEEE Trans. Software Eng. **14**(6), 758–773 (1988)
17. Yin, R.K.: Case Study Research: Design and Methods. 5th edn. Sage Publications (2014)
18. Ministerio de Desarrollo Productivo. Nuevas categorías para ser PyMES (2018). https://www.argentina.gob.ar/noticias/nuevas-categorias-para-ser-pyme
19. Lethbridge, T., Sim, S., Singer, J.: Studying software engineers: data collection techniques for software field studies. Empir. Softw. Eng. **10**(3), 311–341 (2005)

Quality 4.0 in Software Engineering: Incorporating Scaled Agile Insights to a Framework Proposal

Kristian Petkoff Bankoff[(✉)] [ID], Rocío Muñoz[ID], Ariel Pasini[ID], and Patricia Pesado[ID]

Institute for Research in Computer Science LIDI (III-LIDI),
Faculty of Computer Science, National University of La Plata, La Plata, Argentina
{kpb,rmunoz,apasini,ppesado}@lidi.info.unlp.edu.ar

Abstract. Software Engineering is a constantly evolving discipline that is present in all aspects of daily life. The quality of software has been addressed for a long time, emerging from the same principles of quality in the manufacturing industry but adapted to the characteristics of the development of intangible products. The industry has evolved towards a digital revolution that implies the use of emerging technologies such as the Internet of Things (IoT), artificial intelligence, and machine learning. Quality 4.0 adopts the principles of Industry 4.0 and applies them to quality management with an approach based on big data analysis, real-time monitoring, and a greater focus on the customer through the use of communication and collaboration tools. A framework is proposed that integrates different processes, tools, and techniques of Software Engineering with the objective of enabling the implementation of Quality 4.0 principles in software development, taking DevOps as an enabler as it is an approach that promotes automation and the integration of tools. Additionally, we have expanded our analysis to include the Scaled Agile Framework (SAFe), examining how our proposed framework aligns with SAFe's requirements, thus providing a holistic approach to implement Quality 4.0 in software development projects.

Keywords: Software Lifecycle · Quality 4.0 · Software Engineering · DevOps

1 Introduction

The concept of Quality 4.0 refers to the integration of digital technologies in industrial and manufacturing sectors to enhance data-driven decision-making, real-time monitoring, and the integration of technologies such as the Internet of Things (IoT), artificial intelligence, and big data analysis [1].

Software development plays a critical role in the digitization of the industry that promotes this approach [2], as it is practically cross-cutting to all other principles and characteristics of the same. Moreover, the management of quality in the software development process and in the software product itself is of utmost relevance, which is demonstrated by the diversity of available standards and their application in the industry [3].

This article extends a previous work [4] evaluating how the proposed framework aligns with SAFe requirements and components. This approach underscores the importance of a holistic view in software engineering, where Quality 4.0's focus on data-driven decision-making, continuous improvement, and customer centricity complements SAFe's framework for scaling agility effectively by using different processes, tools, and techniques of Software Engineering and DevOps as an enabler [5].

The article is organized as follows: Sect. 2 introduces the main concepts of Quality 4.0, the Software Engineering process, agile methodologies, the DevOps culture and the Scaled Agile Framework (SAFe) structure and main principles; Sect. 3 presents the characteristics required for the implementation of the proposed framework; Sect. 4 describes the selected tools to meet the proposed requirements and how they were integrated; Sect. 5 analyzes the compliance of the framework with SAFe requirements; and Sect. 6 summarizes the results obtained, conclusions, and future work.

2   Quality 4.0 and Industry 4.0

The concept of Quality 4.0 is based on the fourth industrial revolution, also known as Industry 4.0, which refers to the integration of digital technologies in industrial and manufacturing sectors. Industry 4.0 leverages automation, IoT devices, cloud computing, and cyber-physical systems to create intelligent and connected factories and processes. Quality 4.0 adopts the principles of Industry 4.0 and applies them to quality management, leveraging emerging technologies, data analysis, and digital transformation to drive continuous improvement and focusing on the customer in various industries, adaptable to the service industry and software engineering.

In essence, Quality 4.0 emphasizes data-driven decision-making, real-time monitoring, and the integration of technologies such as IoT, artificial intelligence, and big data analysis [6].

By focusing on customer needs, involving stakeholders in the development process, and continuously adapting to changing requirements, Quality 4.0 aims to improve the quality of products and services, optimize processes, and drive innovation in the digital era.

2.1   Quality 4.0 Components

There are many ways to break down Quality 4.0 into distinct characteristics, principles, or dimensions. Given that Quality 4.0 draws from the principles of Industry 4.0 and the production of physical goods, we've chosen to focus on principles that resonate more closely with the software industry below:

- Data-driven decision-making: it leverages data analysis, big data, and artificial intelligence to inform decision-making. In the software industry, this translates to the use of real-time monitoring, error prediction models, and customer feedback data to guide development processes and optimize software quality.

– Continuous Improvement: it promotes a culture of continuous improvement. This principle aligns with agile software development methodology, emphasizing iterative development, retrospective, and learning from customer feedback to continuously improve software products.

– Customer-Centric: understanding the needs and preferences of customers is crucial for software engineering teams. By involving customers throughout the development process and providing personalized experiences, software products can better meet user expectations.

– Integration of Emerging Technologies: for the software industry, embracing emerging technologies means adopting DevOps practices, continuous integration, and deployment to improve collaboration and streamline software delivery.

2.2   Relationship Between Software and Quality 4.0

Software serves as a critical enabler for the implementation of Quality 4.0 across all industries. Since Quality 4.0 emphasizes data-driven decision-making, real-time monitoring, and the integration of emerging technologies, software provides the necessary infrastructure to collect, process, and analyze large amounts of data. It also allows connectivity and interoperability of devices and systems in the IoT landscape, enabling data exchange between the physical and digital realms. Leveraging artificial intelligence and machine learning to identify patterns, predict defects, and optimize processes in real time brings substantial improvements to processes.

The flexibility and adaptability of software are essential for implementing practices of continuous improvement, iterative development, and customer-centric approaches. One of the principles of Quality 4.0 is the development of ad-hoc software applications to meet the specific needs of the organization in a specific and personalized manner. Moreover, the principles and concepts of Quality 4.0 have significant implications for the software industry. By leveraging data and analysis, software engineering teams can make informed decisions, identify defects early, and improve the overall quality of software.

On the other hand, Quality 4.0 aligns with agile methodologies, promoting iterative development, continuous customer feedback, and collaboration; this allows teams to deliver customer-centric products that meet changing needs. By adopting customer-centric approaches and involving stakeholders throughout the development process, software engineering better responds to user needs and preferences, resulting in better software products.

Quality 4.0 drives software development toward data-based practices, encouraging the use of real-time monitoring, predictive analysis, and error prediction models. These practices facilitate continuous monitoring of software systems and promote a culture of continuous improvement and learning.

Agile software development models offer a streamlined process designed to cut costs, improve communication and coordination, and provide a flexible response to changing requirements [7]. These characteristics are directly aligned with fundamental principles of Industry 4.0 and serve as the basis for Quality 4.0. This is why, when proposing a framework to implement the concept of Quality 4.0 in Software Engineering, it is convenient to select process models better adapted from their conception. Two of the most used agile models are Scrum and XP [8].

The intersection between Software Engineering and Quality 4.0 can be achieved through DevOps, which is a set of practices, philosophies, cultural tools, and collaboration tools aimed at improving and optimizing the software development lifecycle by promoting collaboration between software development (Dev) and IT operations (Ops) teams. The goal of DevOps is to automate and optimize the process of creating, testing, deploying, and maintaining software applications, resulting in faster development cycles, improved quality, and greater efficiency. This involves a continuous integration (CI) process where developers frequently combine their code changes into a shared repository. This approach helps identify integration issues early, preventing the accumulation of defects and reducing the risk of errors reaching production. By detecting issues at an early stage, the overall quality of software is improved. Automated tests, including unit tests, integration tests, and end-to-end tests, are automatically executed with each code commit, ensuring that changes do not introduce regressions or defects, leading to more reliable and higher-quality software.

The continuous delivery (CD) process entails rapidly and frequently releasing software to production or testing environments. Automating deployment processes ensures consistency and reduces the possibility of human errors, in addition to providing a better user experience regarding software updates. Additionally, the use of infrastructure as code (IaC), where the provisioning and configuration of infrastructure are automated and versioned along with the application source code, reduces configuration drift and ensures that software runs consistently across different environments, allowing efforts to be redirected to other areas by maintaining stable execution environments.

The nature of integrating IT operations with all stakeholders in the development processes requires the implementation of enhanced communication practices and shared responsibilities. DevOps fosters a rapid feedback cycle between developers, testers, and other stakeholders through the automation of the workflow and the availability of data. This constant feedback allows for the quick identification and resolution of quality issues, leading to lower error costs and enhancing the improvement of the development process.

Another key principle of DevOps is real-time monitoring and analysis, which provides information on software performance, usage patterns, and potential issues, allowing teams to proactively address quality concerns. The aforementioned characteristics demonstrate that DevOps adopts a culture of continuous improvement in which teams periodically evaluate and optimize their processes. This iterative approach to development and operations contributes to continuous improvements in software quality.

Continuous integration, continuous delivery, automated testing, and the configuration of execution environments as code allow for the control and enhancement of software quality attributes in addition to the process itself.

2.3   Scaled Agile Framework

The Scaled Agile Framework (SAFe) represents a structured, scalable approach to implementing agile practices within organizations of varying sizes. Originally developed to address the complexities faced by large enterprises in adopting agile methodologies, SAFe integrates lean and agile principles within a comprehensive framework. This methodology offers guidance for scaling beyond single teams, making it invaluable for environments where multiple teams collaborate on a single product or project. SAFe provides a structured approach to ensure alignment and efficiency across various organizational levels, from team coordination to strategic portfolio management.

SAFe is structured around several configurations, each tailored to different organizational needs and complexities: Essential, Large Solution, Portfolio, and Full SAFe. Each configuration offers a unique set of practices and principles designed for varying levels of complexity and scale. For micro to small organizations, the Essential SAFe configuration is particularly relevant. It focuses on the primary elements necessary to scale agile practices efficiently, emphasizing Agile Release Trains (ARTs) for delivering value.

Research indicates that SAFe's adaptability extends to small and medium-sized enterprises (SMEs), suggesting significant benefits in productivity, team collaboration, and quality improvement. Despite being designed for large organizations and projects, applicability and benefits in smaller settings can be reached, including improved productivity and development quality [9]. This suggests that smaller organizations can adapt SAFe to suit their specific needs while still reaping considerable benefits.

After its implementation in different SMEs, teams and program-level personnel transition well towards SAFe. However, portfolio-level adoption is less prevalent, indicating that even in SME contexts, significant benefits can be achieved through partial adoption of SAFe practices, provided there is support from the upper management [10]. Additionally, Nyandongo and Madumo (2022) provide a 10-step implementation roadmap for SAFe adoption in non-agile organizations, highlighting benefits such as defect reduction and improved quality and productivity [11].

Application of SAFe can improve collaboration across multiple teams by enhancing project coordination and delivery, which is particularly relevant for small organizations operating with several teams [12]. Furthermore, Putta, Paasivaara, and Lassenius (2018) conduct a multivocal literature review to gather existing knowledge on SAFe's benefits and challenges based on case studies and experience reports. This review suggests that despite SAFe's popularity in large enterprises, small organizations can also leverage the framework to achieve significant improvements in collaboration, productivity, and delivery efficiency [13].

While initially designed for larger enterprises, evidence suggests that SAFe can be effectively adapted by small organizations to enhance their agility, improve productivity, and ensure efficient delivery of value. The Essential SAFe configuration, in particular, provides a focused and adaptable framework that can drive significant improvements in productivity, quality, and delivery speed for micro to small organizations.

2.4   SAFe Implementation Overview and Challenges

Implementing the Scaled Agile Framework (SAFe), especially its Essential configuration, in organizations encompasses addressing numerous challenges while adhering to a set of strategic recommendations to ensure successful adoption. Available studies give a comprehensive view of how to implement these concepts, pointing out potential challenges for organizations and the best strategies for tackling them.

Challenges at the implementation of SAFe often revolve around the alignment of the organization's existing processes with the framework's requirements. Organizations must navigate through the intricacies of changing their cultural and operational landscapes to accommodate SAFe's agile principles [14]. This transformation often presents challenges such as resistance to change, the integration of hardware and software development cycles, and the alignment of various teams under the SAFe's roles and structures [12,15].

Also, as we scale up agile practices, the process of requirements engineering becomes more complex. It requires a fine-tuned balance between thorough upfront planning and the essential agility for flexibility [16]. The adoption of SAFe's Essential configuration requires organizations to adeptly manage these requirements through continuous engagement and collaboration across all levels of the enterprise.

Recommendations for overcoming these challenges are manifold. A maturity model approach offers a structured pathway for organizations to assess their readiness and progressively implement SAFe practices [17,18]. Such models facilitate a phased adoption, allowing for gradual cultural shifts and process adjustments.

Training and education emerge as critical components of successful SAFe implementation, with emphasis placed on equipping team members with the necessary knowledge and skills to thrive in an agile environment [11]. Furthermore, the engagement of SAFe champions and coaches is recommended to guide the organization through the transformation, ensuring adherence to SAFe principles while fostering an agile mindset among personnel [19].

The literature also underscores the importance of customizing the SAFe implementation to fit the specific context and needs of the organization. This entails a thoughtful selection of practices from the Essential configuration and possibly integration of them with other agile scaling frameworks to address unique organizational challenges [20]. Such an approach ensures that the framework's implementation is not only aligned with the organizational culture and goals but also adaptable to the dynamic nature of software development projects.

Team Level. Agile Teams: Cross-functional groups that define, build, test, and deliver increments of value in a short timebox.

Iterations: Designated timeframes in which Agile Teams work to produce portions of the product that are ready for release.

Iteration Planning: The process where teams plan the work for the next iteration.

Backlog: A prioritized list of features, stories, and tasks to be completed by the Agile Team.

Scrum and Kanban: SAFe teams typically use Scrum, Kanban, or a hybrid approach to manage their work.

Program Level. Agile Release Train (ART): A team of Agile Teams, typically 5 to 12, that plan, commit, and execute together.

Program Increment (PI) Planning: A two-day event for all members of the ART to align to a shared mission and vision for the next Program Increment.

System Demo: An integrated view of new features for all stakeholders, demonstrating the current state of the solution.

PI Objectives: Team objectives that are planned for the upcoming PI and are critical inputs for PI planning.

Large Solution Level. This level is optional, for organizations delivering large and complex solutions that require additional coordination.

Solution Train: The organizational structure that coordinates multiple ARTs and suppliers; they facilitate the development of large solutions.

Solution Intent: A comprehensive collection of knowledge, models, and documents that clearly outlines the solution under development.

Solution Demo: A demonstration of the solution's integrated features and capabilities to stakeholders.

Capability: Larger services or features that are typically delivered by more than one ART.

Portfolio Level. Lean Portfolio Management (LPM): A function that aligns strategy and execution by applying Lean and systems thinking approaches to strategy and investment funding, Agile portfolio operations, and governance.

Strategic Themes: Organizational business objectives that connect the portfolio to the enterprise's business strategy.

Epic Owners: Individuals who have a fiduciary responsibility to the organization to ensure that an epic delivers its intended value.

Epics: Large initiatives that are broken down into features and stories to be implemented by Agile Teams.

Portfolio Kanban: A method for visualizing, managing, and analyzing the flow of epics from ideation to analysis, implementation, and completion.

Supporting Competencies and Foundations. Lean-Agile Leadership: it emphasizes the role of leaders in creating a culture of Lean-Agile principles and practices.

Team and Technical Agility: Practices that enable teams to deliver high-quality, well-engineered solutions.

Agile Product Delivery: A customer-centric approach to define, build, and release a continuous flow of valuable products and services to customers and users.

Enterprise Solution Delivery: Practices for building and sustaining the world's largest applications, networks, and systems.

Lean Portfolio Management: Aligning strategy and execution by applying Lean approaches.

Organizational Agility: The ability to adapt quickly to new opportunities and challenges.

Continuous Learning Culture: A set of values and practices that encourage individuals and the organization to continually increase knowledge, competence, performance, and innovation.

3   A Quality 4.0 in Software Engineering Framework Proposal

Quality 4.0 proposes an approach in which the characteristics of Industry 4.0 are integrated into all organizational processes. When analyzing the application of Quality 4.0 in the context of software development processes, it must be considered that not all principles inherent to the manufacturing of tangible goods can be directly transferred to this discipline since Software Engineering does not aim to produce tangible goods, does not pursue mass production, and has a lifecycle that extends beyond delivery to the customer.

The proposal of this work is limited to the principles that best adapt to the software industry, taking a relevant subset of applicable principles due to the scope of implementation.

- Traceability: it is a common characteristic to all features and functionalities of the framework that activities are traceable and that the state of the artifacts is transparent and visible to all stakeholders. The proposal involves the use of smart contracts to register software requirements and subsequently every action provoked on them from their planning to delivery, passing through the different stages of development and testing. The use of blockchain and smart contracts is proposed as an enabler of Quality 4.0, as it is part of the principles of Industry 4.0.
- Automation: each of the tools and procedures selected must allow automatic integration via API to enable the autonomous execution of the processes covered by the framework, especially the production of traceability data that are recorded through smart contracts. This characteristic is aligned with the DevOps culture, which is proposed as an enabler of Quality 4.0.
- Quality Assurance: the approach must integrate tools that allow the automation of quality assurance, obtaining product and process metrics by their own execution and not by manual evaluations or inspections. The metrics and key process indicators (KPIs) should be definable by the organization so that they are specific to the project, and optionally they can be adapted to satisfy

quality standards such as the ISO 25000 family of standards. It is desirable that the parameters of the product quality analysis tools are easily adjustable to allow adaptation to changes in context.

- Requirements Lifecycle Management: agile methodologies promote flexibility, adaptability, and the use of lighter processes; in this context, it must be possible to register requirements in an agile but coherent and traceable way. The lifecycle of the requirements will be limited to the creation, technical and functional debate, implementation, finalization, testing, and acceptance of each individual requirement.
- Software Configuration Management: this characteristic consists of controlling changes in the software throughout its development, based on code versioning, defining procedures for integrating changes, controlling software delivery, and maintaining consistency [21].
- Integration and Adaptation of Services and Trace Visualization: integrating different services and tools to foster a centralized and traceable record of project activities implies an additional effort to synchronize the different stages and artifacts and also maintain consistency between the different data models used by each application in the ecosystem [22]. The trace information must be displayed in an intuitive way to the user, as it is essential to involve the customer from end to end in the process. Two levels of traceability visualization are defined: a planning level oriented to the customer and a technical level with a higher level of detail, so the user can choose the visualization mode according to their needs.

4   Implementation

The proposed framework was evaluated in the context of a project carried out by a group of students from a third-year course at the School of Computer Science of the National University of La Plata.

The project consisted of developing a management system for vaccination center appointments. The system's requirements were specified using user stories, and the implementation was carried out over a two-month period divided into three sprints based on the Scrum model. The product backlog and sprint management were performed using the Pivotal Tracker tool. The system's source code was hosted in a GitLab repository, and continuous integration was carried out using GitLab CI, while SonarQube was the tool used for code quality analysis.

To integrate the tool ecosystem, a specialized agent was created to manage data synchronization between the tools, using either polling or webhooks based on the specific needs of each service. Figure 1 shows the activity diagram reached by the proposed framework.

The columns represent each of the following components:

- High-Level Traceability1: activity records that are of greater attention to the client and for general monitoring of the development process. It includes records produced by the Pivotal Tracker application, such as the creation

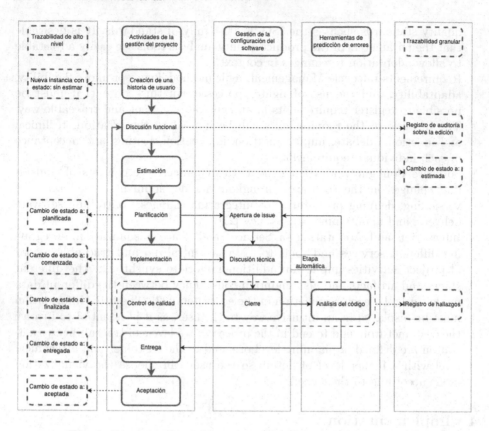

Fig. 1. Diagram of activities covered by the proposed framework

of the user story and state changes. This feature is implemented with smart contracts that record transactions in a Hyperledger Fabric network and a web application for trace visualization specifically developed for this purpose and adjusted to the used data model.

– Project Management Activities: it corresponds to the creation of the product backlog through user story specification and discussion via comments, planning of the sprint backlog, and monitoring of the status of each functional requirement until its delivery using the Pivotal Tracker tool, framed within the Scrum model.

– Software Configuration Management: this implementation integrated code versioning, the use of work branches, and the automation of the delivery process with tracking of technical activities related to the implementation decoupled from the general project monitoring, allowing the trace of iterations within the implementation cycle of each user story in GitLab, maintaining a transparent state facing the client.

– Error Prediction Tool: the integration of the SonarQube application into our continuous integration process and software configuration management activ-

ities enabled us to consistently obtain code quality indicators from each commit's code analysis. These indicators were taken into account to automatically initiate the delivery process of the involved requirements. In cases where findings do not allow for an acceptable quality indicator, a record is generated in the trace, and the user stories remain in a pending completion state in project management. The parameters of these indicators can be configured to adapt to the project's needs.
– Granular Traceability: trace elements that respond to technical activities with greater relevance to the development team (comments in the requirement discussion, effort estimation, results of quality assurance, and continuous integration and delivery processes).

The functionality of the integration agent implemented to adapt the synchronization mechanisms of the tools is represented by the dotted lines covering the activities of Quality Control (Project Management), Closure (Software Configuration Management), and Code Analysis (Error Prediction). This agent is responsible for receiving updates from all activities and invoking smart contracts.

In Fig. 2 (left), the list of requirements added to the trace registered in the blockchain network implemented with Hyperledger Fabric is shown. This application gathers and consolidates data from various tools, providing both the client and other stakeholders with access to summarized information in an easily accessible format.

Each trace item includes a detail in which additional information can be viewed, such as the date and time of the record, the originating tool, the link to the artifact (if applicable), and the responsible user (in case of a manual action). An example of this visualization is offered in Fig. 2 (right).

Besides adapting the data models and considering the specific synchronization mechanisms of each tool, it was necessary to consider how to generate links to the artifacts, as this information is not expressly provided by the services when emitting an event. This increases the level of coupling and dependency since specific configurations and knowledge of the URL scheme and how to fabricate links to each service are required, in addition to each service configuration to interact with the agent.

The particular situation addressed involved configuring Pivotal Tracker to invoke the integration agent upon updates to user stories and, on the other hand, implementing an active query to SonarQube within the agent to fetch analysis data on demand. As for GitLab, the tool allows integration in both directions through webhooks, execution of code in the continuous integration pipeline, and also access to resources via API.

Smart contracts are triggered by external events, and the agent is responsible for logging these interactions. To ensure the accuracy and consistency of these records, it's critical to avoid direct communication between services. This precaution helps prevent situations where an action might change the state of an artifact without properly logging the event. Maintaining a precise match between the logged activity and its actual execution is essential for consistency.

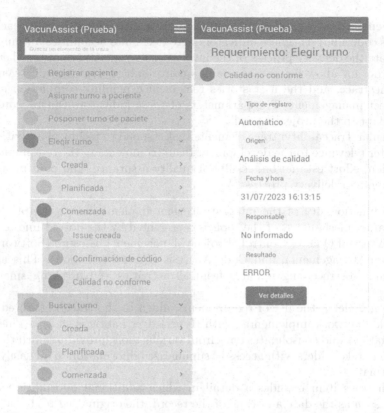

Fig. 2. Visualization of the requirements in the traceability application (left) and details of a transaction (right).

5   Compliance with SAFe

In the following section, we delve into the analysis of our proposed framework compliance with the Scaled Agile Framework (SAFe). This examination aims to identify the extent to which the proposed integration of Quality 4.0 principles within software engineering, augmented by DevOps practices, aligns with the methodologies and requirements prescribed by SAFe. For this analysis, the Large Solution Level is excluded as it is not suitable for the context of implementation.

5.1   Team Level

Agile Teams: the framework implicitly supports the concept of Agile Teams by promoting DevOps and Agile methodologies, emphasizing collaboration, automation, and continuous delivery, which are fundamental in Agile teams.

Iterations: the iterative development inherent in Agile methodologies and the continuous improvement cycle of DevOps suggest a partial alignment with SAFe's iteration concept.

Iteration Planning: this component is not explicitly addressed. However, the framework's emphasis on continuous feedback and improvement suggests a foundation on which formal iteration planning could be integrated, focusing on short, iterative cycles of planning, execution, and evaluation, aligned with Scrum methodology.

Backlog: the framework implements a prioritized list of work items, using PivotalTracker as a Backlog management tool in compliance with this characteristic of SAFe.

Scrum and Kanban: the framework partially supports Scrum methodology, especially for user stories lifecycle management. Explicit adoption and adaptation of other Scrum practices such as daily meetings and planning poker could further align the framework with SAFe's team-level components.

5.2   Program Level

Most of the Program Level components of SAFe are suitable for larger projects or multiple team scenarios, but the intended context of the proposed framework does not meet this characteristics.

Agile Release Train (ART): the concept of ARTs is not directly addressed in the framework. The integration of various Agile teams and technologies could be seen as laying groundwork for ARTs. The framework could include processes for aligning multiple teams around a common vision and cadence for releases. To fully implement this, however, a use case in which several teams are involved in the project should be considered.

Program Increment (PI) Planning: to incorporate PI Planning, the framework might adopt large-scale planning sessions that bring together all stakeholders to align with objectives and plan work for a set period. In the specific scenario of the use case this is not fully addressable as the projects are intended to last 12 weeks.

System Demo: while the framework focuses on quality and continuous delivery, it does not explicitly propose integrated demos. Incorporating regular, end-of-iteration demos of the integrated solution to stakeholders could enhance transparency and feedback loops.

PI Objectives: the framework's focus on continuous improvement and customer satisfaction implicitly supports the idea of setting objectives. Explicitly defining and tracking PI Objectives for each increment could help in aligning team efforts with strategic goals.

5.3   Portfolio Level

Lean Portfolio Management (LPM): LPM is not explicitly covered. The framework could extend its scope to include portfolio management practices, aligning investment with strategic objectives and applying Lean governance.

Strategic Themes: while the framework emphasizes customer focus and quality, it does not specifically address the alignment of development work with strategic themes. Explicitly connecting software development initiatives with organizational strategy and objectives could bridge the gap.

Epic Owners: the role of Epic Owners in guiding large initiatives through to delivery is not mentioned. Incorporating roles responsible for overseeing epics from ideation through implementation could enhance the strategic alignment and governance of projects.

Epics: the management of large work items or epics is not directly addressed but its fully implemented in PivotalTracker. The framework could be expanded to clearly outline the process for dividing epics into features and stories, and then managing these all the way to delivery.

Portfolio Kanban: the use of Kanban for portfolio management is not discussed. Implementing a Portfolio Kanban system could help visualize and manage the flow of epics, enhancing decision-making and throughput.

6   Conclusions and Future Work

Through the implementation of the Quality 4.0 framework in the context of a Software Engineering process, developers and the client gained greater visibility into quality expectations, fostering responsibility and ownership of the product. The framework provided a mechanism for better tracking progress towards objectives and make informed adjustments earlier compared to other test cases. The integration of customized metrics and KPIs became an intrinsic part of the continuous integration and delivery workflow, enhancing code reviews, automated testing, and other quality controls.

Moreover, transparency throughout the process and the immediate, centralized, and straightforward availability of trace information allowed for a stronger integration of the client throughout the development process, including them in more stages and with greater communication frequency.

The relationship between software and Quality 4.0 is symbiotic and cyclic. Software acts as an enabler for Quality 4.0 by providing the infrastructure and tools needed to implement data-driven decision-making and real-time monitoring. Simultaneously, many software industry tools and techniques align with the Quality 4.0 concept, offer an integrated view that promotes better practices in development processes, such as end-to-end traceability of requirements, customer-focused development, continuous process improvement, early error detection and handling, etc. This cycle reinforces the adoption of Quality 4.0 principles, resulting in a positive feedback loop that benefits both the software industry and the implementation of Quality 4.0.

The suggested framework naturally aligns with many SAFe principles, particularly for team-level operations, by promoting Agile methodologies, DevOps practices, and prioritizing quality and continuous delivery. However, it lacks specific guidance on the more structured aspects and processes of SAFe, especially regarding program and portfolio management. By extending the framework to include specific SAFe practices such as PI Planning, ARTs, Lean Portfolio Management, and explicit management of epics and strategic themes, it could offer a more comprehensive approach to scale Agile practices in line with SAFe.

In the future, it is proposed to include other tools such as Artificial Intelligence for code writing assistance or error prediction; it is also proposed to include integration and end-to-end execution testing in the proposed implementation. The analysis of the framework alignment with SAFe standards uncovers opportunities to initiate new studies aimed at refining and enhancing the adoption of agile methodologies.

References

1. Sader, S., Husti, I., Daróczi, M.: A review of quality 4.0: definitions, features, technologies, applications, and challenges. Total Quality Manage. Bus. Excell. (2021). https://doi.org/10.1080/14783363.2021.1944082
2. Saha, P., Talapatra, S., Belal, H., Jackson, V.: Unleashing the potential of the TQM and industry 4.0 to achieve sustainability performance in the context of a developing country. Global J. Flexible Syst. Manage. **23**(4), 495–513 (2022). https://doi.org/10.1007/s40171-022-00316-x
3. Nebojsa, D.D.: Software quality standards. Vojnotehnički. Glasnik (2016). https://doi.org/10.5937/VOJTEHG65-10668
4. Bankoff, K.P., Muñoz, R., Pasini, A., Pesado, P.: Calidad 4.0 en Ingeniería de Software: propuesta de un marco de trabajo. XXIX Congreso Argentino de Ciencias de la Computación - CACIC 2023 (2024)
5. Riungu-Kalliosaari, L., Mäkinen, S., Lwakatare, L.E., Tiihonen, J., Männistö, T.: DevOps adoption benefits and challenges in practice: a case study. In: Abrahamsson, P., Jedlitschka, A., Nguyen Duc, A., Felderer, M., Amasaki, S., Mikkonen, T. (eds.) PROFES 2016. LNCS, vol. 10027, pp. 590–597. Springer, Cham (2016). https://doi.org/10.1007/978-3-319-49094-6_44
6. Villegas Forero, D., Sisodia, R.: Quality 4.0 -How to Handle Quality in the Industry 4.0 Revolution. Phd. thesis (2020)
7. Al-Saqqa, S., Sawalha, S., Abdel-Nabi, H.: Agile software development: methodologies and trends. Int. J. Interact. Mob. Technol. (ijim) (2020). https://doi.org/10.3991/IJIM.V14I11.13269
8. Singh, R., Vijayan, S., Ilango, V., Rasheed, A.A.: Software development process models comparison and assessment of degree of agility based on agile practices and performance implementation on XP and scrum. Int. J. Sci. Technol. Res. **8**(12), 1008–1016 (2019)
9. Salikhov, D., Succi, G., Tormasov, A.: An empirical analysis of success factors in the adaption of the scaled agile framework - first outcomes from an empirical study. ArXiv abs/2012.11144 (2020)
10. Razzak, M., Richardson, I., Noll, J., Canna, C.N., Beecham, S.: Scaling agile across the global organization: an early stage industrial SAFe self- assessment. In: 2018 IEEE/ACM 13th International Conference on Global Software Engineering (ICGSE) (2018). https://doi.org/10.1145/3196369.3196373
11. Nyandongo, K.M., Madumo, M.G.: The adoption of the Scaled Agile Framework (SAFe) in non-agile organizations. In: 2022 IEEE 28th International Conference on Engineering, Technology and Innovation (ICE/ITMC) 31st International Association For Management of Technology (IAMOT) Joint Conference (2022). https://doi.org/10.1109/ICE/ITMC-IAMOT55089.2022.10033246

12. Brenner, R., Wunder, S.: Scaled agile framework: presentation and real world example. In: 2015 IEEE Eighth International Conference on Software Testing, Verification and Validation Workshops (ICSTW) (2015). https://doi.org/10.1109/ICSTW.2015.7107411
13. Putta, A., Paasivaara, M., Lassenius, C.: Benefits and challenges of adopting the scaled agile framework (SAFe): preliminary results from a multivocal literature review (2018). https://doi.org/10.1007/978-3-030-03673-7_24
14. Conboy, K., Carroll, N.: Implementing large-scale agile frameworks: challenges and recommendations. IEEE Softw. (2019). https://doi.org/10.1109/MS.2018.2884865
15. Kasauli, R., Knauss, E., Horkoff, J., Liebel, G., Neto, F.: Requirements engineering challenges and practices in large-scale agile system development. J. Syst. Softw. **172**, 110851 (2021). https://doi.org/10.1016/j.jss.2020.110851
16. Inayat, I., Salim, S.S., Marczak, S., Daneva, M., Shamshirband, S.: A systematic literature review on agile requirements engineering practices and challenges. Comput. Hum. Behav. **51**, 915–929 (2015). https://doi.org/10.1016/j.chb.2014.10.046
17. Stojanov, I., Turetken, O., Trienekens, J.: A maturity model for scaling agile development, pp. 446–453 (2015). https://doi.org/10.1109/SEAA.2015.29
18. Turetken, O., Stojanov, I., Trienekens, J.: Assessing the adoption level of scaled agile development: a maturity model for scaled agile framework. J. Softw. Evol. Process **29**(6) (2017). https://doi.org/10.1002/smr.1796
19. Paasivaara, M.: Adopting SAFe to Scale Agile in a Globally Distributed Organization (2017). https://doi.org/10.1109/ICGSE.2017.15
20. Diebold, P., Schmitt, A., Theobald, S.: Scaling agile: how to select the most appropriate framework. In: Proceedings of the 19th International Conference on Agile Software Development: Companion (2018)
21. Ji, W.: Research on Key Technologies of Software Configuration Management in Development of Large-scale Software System (2021). https://doi.org/10.1145/3449365.3449374
22. Demi, S., Sánchez-Gordón, M., Colomo-Palacios, R.: A blockchain-enabled framework for requirements traceability. In: Yilmaz, M., Clarke, P., Messnarz, R., Reiner, M. (eds.) EuroSPI 2021. CCIS, vol. 1442, pp. 3–13. Springer, Cham (2021). https://doi.org/10.1007/978-3-030-85521-5_1

Databases and Data Mining

Personality Traits Assessment: A Case of Study Using Text Mining Techniques

Maximiliano Sapino[1,2,3], Leticia Cagnina[1,2,3] (ID), Luis Montenegro[1],
and Edgardo Ferretti[1,2](✉) (ID)

[1] Universidad Nacional de San Luis (UNSL), San Luis, Argentina
{lcagnina,ferretti}@unsl.edu.ar
[2] Laboratorio de Investigación y Desarrollo en Inteligencia Computacional, UNSL,
San Luis, Argentina
[3] Consejo Nacional de Investigaciones Científicas y Técnicas (CONICET), San Luis,
Argentina

Abstract. This paper presents a complete experience to solving a personality trait assessment problem using Text Mining techniques within the framework of Knowledge Discovery in Databases. The study involves collaboration between researchers from the fields of Computer Science and Psychology, highlighting the interdisciplinary nature of the work. In this study, four basic predictive algorithms were evaluated: Multinomial Naive Bayes, Logistic Regression, Support Vector Machines, and Decision Trees. These algorithms were applied to address the classification problem posed by personality trait assessment. Given the nature of the problem, where individuals may possess multiple personality traits to varying degrees, the classification task was modeled in three different ways: binary, multiclass, and multilabel. To enhance the performance of the classification approaches, a data augmentation technique was employed. The results indicate that data augmentation improves the performance of all classification approaches, with binary classification benefiting the most. Moreover, for three out of the five personality traits studied, the weighted-F_1 scores exceed 0.75, indicating strong predictive accuracy. Notably, the *Responsibility* trait achieves the highest score of 0.88, demonstrating the effectiveness of the classification approach for this particular trait.

Keywords: Personality Traits · Big Five Factors · Knowledge Discovery in Databases · Text Mining · Data Augmentation

1 Introduction

One significant aspect of personality psychology is the study of individual differences, which acknowledges that people vary in their tendencies, preferences, and behaviors. This perspective emphasizes that these differences can be understood and classified into distinct traits or dimensions [3]. *The Big Five Factors* (BFF) model is based on the premise that certain words and linguistic patterns

This work was partially supported by CONICET and Universidad Nacional de San Luis (PROICO P-31816).

tend to be stable over time and are associated with specific personality traits [5]. Thus, personality can be understood as the expression of five main traits: *Neuroticism, Extraversion, Openness to experience, Agreeableness* and *Responsibility*. For example, as stated in [23], individuals who frequently use words related to social activities, such as "party" or "friends", may be more extraverted, while those who use words related to anxiety or uncertainty, such as "worry" or "nervous", may score higher measures of neuroticism. Similarly, agreeableness is identified with speeches that reflect people inclusion, words related to family, interpersonal concern, altruism and modesty. On the other hand, responsibility is shown by using words related to achievements and work. Finally, openness to experience is not usually related to certain words of content, but rather with the use of particular articles and prepositions.

Moreover, language use extends beyond just reflecting personality traits; it can also provide insights into various aspects of individuals' lives, including their social dynamics and interpersonal relationships. Furthermore, language can serve as a marker for physical and mental health conditions. Researchers have developed computational tools to analyze language features and detect potential indicators of various health conditions, offering opportunities for early intervention and support; e.g., studies such as [4], suggest that *Text Mining* (TM) tools could be used even for early detection and prevention of suicide. This is due to the fact that the psychological interpretation assumes that the degree to which a person uses a category of words reflects how important that topic is for him/her, making explicit the importance of performing this kind of studies.

This context evidences that interdisciplinary research between Psychology and Computer Science (CS) [13,15,22] is crucial for advancing our understanding of human behavior and developing innovative tools and technologies to support well-being and mental health. In particular, since 2017, the *eRisk* international competitions have been annually organized [8–11,17–20] to try to automatically detect from written texts –by means of TM techniques– mental illnesses such as depression, anorexia and self-harm. And it should be noted that the BFF model is the theory generally adopted by research on CS that analyzes personality by applying data mining techniques [16,22].

In addition, the field of psychological assessment faces significant challenges related to the time and resources required for data collection, analysis, and interpretation. Traditional methods, such as filling out questionnaires and surveys, can be time-consuming and labor-intensive, often requiring trained professionals to administer, score, and interpret the results. In [2], the study concluded that 45% of the time is used exclusively in administrating the instruments, 36% in their evaluation and the remaining 19% in the interpretation of results. For these reasons, some therapists end up delegating these tasks to lesser experienced professionals. In this respect, the development of automatic systems based on TM methods has the potential to significantly speed up the process of interpreting assessment results. Also, they facilitate the measurement and evaluation of alternative constructs beyond what traditional questionnaires or surveys capture.

Given the above context, in this paper we extend a previous work [15] providing a more detailed description and an enriched discussion of the experimental setting and results as well. In particular, in [15] the main research hypothesis proposed was that through TM techniques, both static and dynamic document models derived from free texts may capture individuals' personality traits. Then, by using these documents models, different classifiers were developed to automatically estimate these traits, which would streamline the evaluation process compared to traditional manual assessments by professionals. Particularly, to evaluate the predictive performance of the classifiers, their results were compared with the scores obtained by the participants in the BFF Inventory.

The rest of the article is organized as follows. Section 2 outlines the methodology employed in creating the dataset used for our study. Then, in Sect. 3, the formal problem statement is presented along with a brief overview of the classification approaches considered. Additionally, the document models utilized for representing the articles are discussed. Moreover, in Sect. 4, details of the experimental setup are provided and the results obtained from the experiments are reported and analyzed. Finally, Sect. 5 offers the conclusions drawn from the study.

2 Dataset

The dataset comprises 298 samples, with the majority being students of the National University of San Luis. For those students who also work, approximately 2.9% of the respondents are employed in the private industry, and 3.3% work in the public sector. Regarding the place of origin and residence, 84% of the respondents were born in the capital of San Luis, while the remaining 16% were born in various cities within San Luis province and other provinces of Argentina. However, all respondents currently reside in San Luis. Respondents' ages range from 17 to 54 years old, with an approximate mean age of 22 years old. Considering educational level, the majority of respondents (96%) have completed secondary education, while only 4% have completed university-level education. Gender distribution shows that 73% of the respondents identify as female, while 27% identify as male. Finally, if we analyze parenthood status, 93% of the respondents do not have children, while the remaining 7% do.

People participating on the study were requested to complete the *Big Five Inventory* developed by [7] and adapted to the argentinian population by [3]. It consists of 44 items that respondents rate on a *Likert*[1] scale depending on how strongly they identify with the statement. In addition, participants were asked to write three texts. First, a self-description text, which likely provides insight into participants' self-perception, personality traits, emotions, and behaviors. Second, a report of the "last week", where participants were asked to provide details on how they spent their last week: what they did, who they were with,

---

[1] Likert scale allows to rate a question or an statement with a five-points response, where score 5 corresponds to "Strongly agree", 4 corresponds to "Agree", 3 is equivalent to "None", 2 implies "Disagreement" and 1 means "Strongly disagreement".

and all they were able to tell. This report likely includes information about their activities, social interactions, and daily routines. Analyzing this text can provide insights into participants' behavior patterns, social relationships, and lifestyle choices. Third, a future self-imagery text, where participants were asked to envision themselves in the next five years. This likely involves describing their future goals, aspirations, career plans, and personal relationships. Analyzing these texts can offer insights into participants' long-term aspirations, motivations, and expectations for their future selves.

Then, by using the IBM SPSS[2] software (version 23), the raw scores are converted into percentiles, where a percentile of 75 or more indicates presence of the trait and is taken as a positive instance, and a percentile of 25 or less indicates absence of the trait and is taken as negative instance. Instances whose values fall in the range between 25 and 75 are discarded since they may introduce noise into the classifier training process since they cannot be considered –as we refer in colloquial language– as "strong" positives or negatives (or representative samples). All in all, second and third columns of Table 1 show the final sets for each personality trait, considering the binary classification approach. As expected, in the dataset for multiclass classification (fourth and fifth columns), the number of instances are fewer with respect to binary classification. This is due to the fact that for the multiclass classification task, the instances that have "strong" labels (positive or negative) for all the personality traits, must be considered. In this way, all the instances included in the dataset for the multiclass classification task, were those whose percentile values for all the traits were lower or equal than 25, or higher or equal than 75.

Table 1. Datasets proportions for binary and multiclass classification approaches.

Trait	Binary		Multiclass	
	Number of instances		Number of instances	
	No	Yes	No	Yes
Neuroticism	135	121	65	67
Extraversion	170	80	92	40
Openness to experience	98	142	53	79
Agreeablenes	71	153	44	88
Responsibility	186	54	103	29

3   Problem Statement and Classification Approaches

In the context of classifying personality traits, there are different ways to address the problem. One can view it as a concept learning problem, typically treated as binary classification. In this approach, each personality trait is treated as a

---

[2] https://www.ibm.com/es-es/spss.

separate concept that the classifier learns to recognize. The classifier is trained to distinguish between texts that exhibit a particular trait and those that do not. For example, a classifier could be trained to recognize whether a text displays extraversion or not. However, it can also be seen as a multiclass single-label or multiclass multi-label classification problem, as individuals may possess one or more personality traits simultaneously.

In the multiclass single-label approach, each text is assigned to one personality trait from a predefined set of traits (the five belonging to the BFF Inventory in our case). The classifier is trained to predict a single personality trait for each text. For example, a text might be labeled as displaying extraversion, even if it also exhibits other traits. Conversely, in the multiclass multi-label classification approach, each text can exhibit multiple personality traits simultaneously. The classifier is trained to predict multiple personality traits for each text. For example, a text could be labeled as displaying both extraversion and responsibility. To simplify the referentation, we will use the term *multiclass* for the case where a single label is assigned to a document by a classifier trained with all the classes, while we will refer with the term *multilabel*, the latter case mentioned.

We evaluated four simple predictive algorithms but with a great explanatory power; namely:

- Multinomial Naive Bayes (MNB) [1], a probabilistic classifier based on Bayes' theorem with an assumption of independence between features. It also assumes that the features (words or other characteristics) are generated by a multinomial distribution. This distribution is appropriate for representing the frequency of different terms in a document or the occurrence of different features.
- Logistic Regression (LR) [6], a linear model used for binary classification that can be extended to multiclass classification.
- Support Vector Machines (SVM) [12], a powerful supervised learning algorithm used for classification tasks. SVM finds the hyperplane that best separates classes in a high-dimensional space.
- Decision Trees (DT) [14], a non-parametric supervised learning method used for classification and regression tasks. Decision trees recursively divide the input space into regions, assigning labels to these regions.

These algorithms are known for their simplicity, interpretability, and good performance, especially for text classification tasks. They are computationally efficient compared to deep neural network approaches, making them suitable for many classification problems.

Document Models

Vectorization is a crucial step in converting text data into a format that machine learning algorithms can understand and process. Vectorization involves representing text documents as numerical vectors where each dimension corresponds to a specific feature. As previously mentioned, static and dynamic characteristics were used in this work to be able to analyze different vector representations. With respect to the dynamic representation, Bag of Words (BoW) was the underlying representation model. BoW is a common and simple technique for vectorizing text data. It represents each document as a vector where each dimension corresponds to a unique term in the vocabulary, and the value of each dimension represents the frequency of that term in the document; in particular, Binary, TF (Term Frequency) and TF-IDF (Term Frequency-Inverse Document Frequency) vectorization of the features' values were used.

In binary vectorization, the presence or absence of each term in the document is represented by binary values (1 for presence, 0 for absence). This encoding disregards the frequency of terms and only indicates whether a term appears in the document. In turn, TF vectorization represents documents by the raw frequency of terms, where each dimension corresponds to the frequency of a term in the document. It provides a simple representation based solely on the frequency of terms. Finally, TF-IDF vectorization takes into account not only the frequency of terms in a document but also their importance in the entire corpus. It assigns higher weights to terms that are frequent in the document but rare in the corpus, helping to highlight terms that are more discriminative.

To manage the dimensionality of the vectors and reduce computational complexity, only the 500 most frequent terms appearing in at least two documents were retained. This approach helps discard less informative terms (more than 80% of the terms appearing in all the documents) that may add noise to the data while still capturing the most relevant terms. By employing these vectorization techniques, text data can be transformed into numerical representations that capture important characteristics of the text, enabling machine learning algorithms to learn patterns and make predictions based on textual information.

Regarding the static representation, the LIWC linguistic analyzer was used to compute the values of the 90 features of each text and thus obtain the numerical vector that constitutes the representation of each text in the dataset. In our case, the 2015 version has been used [21]. For each text, LIWC2015 reads one target word at a time. As each target word is processed, is looked up in the dictionary-which is made up of nearly 6,400 words, root words, and selected emoticons. If the target word matches a word in the dictionary, it will increases the scale (or scales) associated with the category of the word; for example, the word *cried* is part of five word categories: *sadness, negative emotion, general affect, verbs* and *past focus*. Therefore, if this word is found in the target text, each of these five categories will increase the scores on the subdictionary scale (which it is generated while texts are processed in the collection).

4   Experiments and Results

This section explains how the text classification experiments were carried out. For this purpose, the data preparation is detailed, including data augmentation, preprocessing and selection of relevant features for the models. Then, the training and validation processes of the models are described. Finally, we present the results obtained in the test stage performed. To properly contextualize the study, a brief description of the working environment used is also provided.

4.1 Experimental Setting

Google Colaboratory was the chosen working environment for conducting the experiments; specifically, Python in its stable version 3.8 was used. Besides, the *sckit-learn* library was utilized for building the classification models. As above-mentioned in Sect. 2, the original dataset was composed by 298 samples. However, 14 samples were removed as they were completed with random sentences to meet the minimum word requirements in the questionnaires. This resulted in a dataset of 284 texts for further analysis.

Several preprocessing techniques were applied to the remaining 284 texts of the original dataset: punctuation marks were eliminated from the text data, spelling errors in the text were corrected, numeric characters were removed from the text, characters that appeared consecutively at least three times were removed, all texts were transformed to lowercase to ensure uniformity, and stop words (SW) removal was performed. These preprocessing steps were aimed at cleaning and standardizing the text data to prepare it for further analysis and model building.

It was decided to use 5-fold cross-validation, given that it is an appropriate method due to the limited availability of data and the need of obtaining more precise estimations of the performance of the classification models. As performance metric, we decided to use the F_1 measure since, in combination with cross-validation, it allows calculating the so-called weighted-F_1 measure. With this adjustment, an averaged F_1 score is obtained, weighted according to the distribution of classes (positive or negative labels) in the different folds of the cross-validation approach. This metric provides a more balanced assessment of the model's performance compared to a simple F_1 measure; especially when the dataset has unbalanced classes, as it is our case.

Data Augmentation. Data augmentation (DA) involves artificially expanding the dataset by creating variations of the existing documents. This technique is particularly useful in scenarios where the original dataset is limited or imbalanced. As will be discussed in Sect. 4.2, the classification results for the original dataset were not as good as originally expected. Although several factors may influence the low performance of the classifiers, in our view, as aforesaid, data imbalance in the classes (people with and without the personality trait) could be one of the most important. To assess this issue, DA techniques were applied, in order to generate new training data from the original data.

Backtranslation is a widely used technique in natural language processing for DA and generating paraphrases. It involves translating a text from the source language (Spanish in our case) to a target language (viz. English) and then translating it back to the source language using a machine translation model. This process can introduce variations in the wording and choice of words while preserving the original meaning and structure of the text. The main idea behind backtranslation is to leverage machine translation systems to generate diverse and semantically equivalent versions of the original text.

In the context of our study, the decision of using backtranslation was made on the grounds that it could potentially increase the size and diversity of the dataset, which may lead to improved performance of the classification models. However, the texts generated with backtranslation were quite similar to the original ones. Hence, we decided to combine this technique with GPT-2 (Generative Pre-trained Transformer 2) in the generation of new data. Even though both techniques can be used separately, the texts generated with the GPT-2 model in Spanish were of low quality, and combining both methods arose as a natural choice for the creation of additional training examples without requiring the collection of new data, thus making efficient use of existing resources. However, as mentioned above, it is worth noting that the quality of backtranslated data heavily depends on the performance of the machine translation model and the adequacy of the target language. That is why, we took care to ensure that the backtranslated texts maintain the original meaning and do not introduce unintended biases or errors.

The combination of both techniques was carried out in the following way: the texts in Spanish, once translated into English, were used in turn as input for GPT-2 to generate new texts in English which were translated back into Spanish. Then, these new augmented dataset was preprocessed in the same way than the original one, and document models were built following the same procedure mentioned in Sect. 3. DA was applied in order to increase the number of texts from the minority class. Table 2 shows the increase in texts that was carried out in each personality trait for binary and multiclass corpora. For the multiclass and multilabel cases, the principle to generate new texts was the same one mentioned above, taking into account that if a text T was labeled as *[yes, no, no, yes, no]*, where each position correspond to a personality trait, the texts generated for that instance will have the same labels.

Table 2. Datasets proportions for binary and multiclass augmented datasets.

Trait	Binary		Multiclass	
	Number of instances		Number of instances	
	No	YES	No	YES
Neuroticism	135	146	145	152
Extraversion	170	166	227	70
Openness to experience	165	142	153	144
Agreeablenes	134	153	154	143
Responsibility	186	276	183	114

Taking into account the results obtained with the original data set for the binary classification approach –that will be discussed in Sect. 4.2–, the increase was made only in the minority class. The augmentation procedure was carried out in an iterative fashion trying to empirically determine the best measures for each trait, that is why the increases were not uniform. Moreover, for the multiclass and multilabel cases, we followed the same interative approach but this time increasing both classes, since the original amount of documents in both datasets were quite unequal. Figure 1 depicts the balance percentage of each dataset for each personality.

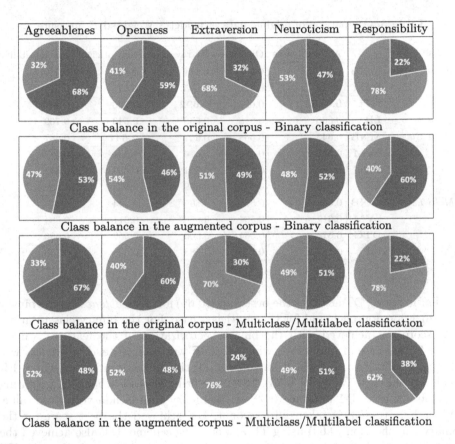

Fig. 1. Datasets proportions for binary and multiclass augmented datasets. Positive samples are represented by blue color while orange depicts negative ones. (Color figure online)

4.2 Results

In Sect. 4.1, DA was introduced and described as part of our experimental study with the aim of increasing the low performance of our original models. As can be observed in Table 3, the classification results for the original dataset do not exceed the 70% of weighted-F_1 for four out the five personality traits studied—*responsibility* was the only trait were binary classification achieved a weighted-F_1 above 80%. The results reported in this table were obtained with different representation models; particular weighting schemes (Binary, TF-IDF or TF) of BoW models since the static representation of LIWC perform worse than expected. Values in bold, represent the best performing scores achieved by a particular classification approach for each personality trait.

Table 3. Comparison of original dataset models - Weighted F_1 measure.

Classifier		Agreeableness	Openness	Extraversion	Neuroticism	Responsibility
Binary Class	MNB	0.606	0.591	0.641	0.601	0.709
	SVM	0.614	0.622	0.645	0.575	0.714
	DTC	**0.649**	0.623	**0.692**	0.620	**0.802**
	LR	0.606	0.618	0.638	0.543	0.709
Multi Class	MNB	0.643	0.568	0.667	**0.647**	0.687
	SVM	0.535	0.486	0.574	0.531	0.687
	DTC	**0.649**	0.573	0.591	0.559	0.681
	LR	0.643	0.541	0.669	0.615	0.689
Multi Label	MNB	0.644	0.568	0.665	0.644	0.695
	SVM	0.617	0.564	0.656	0.611	0.684
	DTC	0.518	0.564	0.609	0.567	0.680
	LR	0.487	**0.632**	0.588	0.598	0.736

For instance, DT achieves the best value (0.65) for *Agreeableness* in the binary classification approach and for the multiclass case. For the binary classification, this score was achieved with the binary vectorization of the features' values, while for the case of multiclass, when TF-IDF was used instead. *Openness* was the personality trait for which, in general, all the models performed worst. LR achieved the best value (of 0.63) for the multilabel case, when TF weighting scheme was used. DT obtained 0.62 for the binary approach, a very close value. When *Extraversion* is taken into account, DT achieved the best score for the binary classification (0.69) using TF as weighting scheme. DT also achieved the best score (0.8) in a binary classification for the *Responsibility* trait also with TF weighting scheme. Finally, MNB reported the best value (0.65) for *Neuroticism* for the multiclass case with the binary weighting scheme.

When considering the results for the augmented dataset (Table 4), we still can see that *Openness* was the personality trait for which the worst results were obtained. Also, we observe that (in general) all the classifiers tend to perform better for this trait with respect to the original dataset, and the same conclusion can be drawn for the remaining traits. Now, for four out the five personality traits the 70% of weighted-F_1 is a lower bound score. Indeed, *Agreeableness* and *Extraversion* scores round 75% and *Responsibility* reports the best performing value of 0.88. In this case DT was not the best classifier as for the original dataset, but it was quite close to the best ones, except for the *Neuroticism* trait. LR reported the best scores for the multilabel approach for *Openness* trait with a binary weighting scheme, while for the case of *Neuroticism*, TF weighting scheme was the best one. MNB also reported the best values for two traits, viz. *Extraversion* and *Responsibility* but in the binary classification; for the former trait TF-IDF weighting scheme was used, while for the latter TF performed best. Finally, SVM achieves the best score for *Agreeableness* trait also in a binary classification approach with TF-IDF weighting scheme.

Table 4. Comparison of augmented dataset models - Weighted F_1 measure.

Classifier		Agreeableness	Openness	Extraversion	Neuroticism	Responsibility
Binary Class	MNB	0.752	0.656	**0.749**	0.613	**0.879**
	SVM	**0.757**	0.666	0.743	0.643	0.874
	DTC	0.734	0.663	0.716	0.586	0.846
	LR	0.717	0.663	0.737	0.610	0.834
Multi Class	MNB	0.668	0.628	0.709	0.649	0.679
	SVM	0.704	0.639	0.707	0.700	0.775
	DTC	0.607	0.572	0.648	0.585	0.668
	LR	0.682	0.656	0.747	0.698	0.804
Multi Label	MNB	0.669	0.626	0.716	0.649	0.681
	SVM	0.707	0.659	0.722	0.693	0.788
	DTC	0.606	0.585	0.653	0.590	0.670
	LR	0.548	**0.677**	0.723	**0.704**	0.693

4.3 Qualitative Analysis

As previously mentioned, DT performed well for both datasets, and there were certain traits that stood out in terms of performance. *Responsibility* was the trait for which the best-performing values were obtained while *Openness* was the hardest one. That is why, we will focus our qualitative analysis on these two traits when DT was used as binary classifier. Understanding why certain traits are easier or harder to classify may provide valuable insights into the data and the classifier's behavior by uncovering patterns or features that contribute to the classification difficulty or ease.

Responsibility Trait with Augmented Dataset. In this case, the terms 'Cuarentena' (Quarantine), 'Tareas' (Tasks), 'Metas' (Goals) and 'Pienso' (Think), were the four most important. The instances correctly classified in the negative class, –that is, with a low level of responsibility–, in general has a lower presence of these words. On the contrary, those cases that were erroneously classified within the positive class did present extensive use of these words.

Regarding the words, 'Tareas', 'Metas' and 'Pienso', through common sense we can see its relationship with responsibility but 'Cuarentena' seems at first difficult to understand. It is worth mentioning that the forms –from which the dataset was created– were completed in April 2020 when the COVID-19 pandemic was having a significant impact globally, which could potentially influence people's responses and behaviors.

In relation to this word, when analysing from a psychological perspective the forms, it seems that participants' experiences varied widely, ranging from feelings of suffocation and the need to find activities to pass the time of isolation, to reflections on the situation and adaptation to changes in their daily lives. Some particular comments on the quarantine time, were about the tasks that were carried out during this period, and this is in our view, the main reason in the association of these two terms. Particularly, with respect to the 'tasks' term, in general it referred to daily activities. For example, the pending tasks related to the study, such as "it was difficult to adapt me to virtuality regarding faculty tasks", or to family organization like "my mother asks me to do the housekeeping with her". Another use of the term 'tasks' that associates it with 'goals', refers to accomplish tasks or learning how to do them correctly before setting particular goals, which tend to be short term goals, with the goal of finishing a university degree prevailing.

Likewise, for the case of the term 'goals', its general use involved individuals envisioning themselves achieving their objectives, typically in the company of family or close friends. This visualization process can be a powerful motivational tool, helping individuals clarify their aspirations and reinforcing their commitment to pursuing them. By imagining themselves accomplishing their goals within the context of meaningful relationships, individuals may find added inspiration and determination to work towards their desired outcomes. Finally, when considering the term 'think', it is worth mentioning that it encompasses a broad range of cognitive processes, from deep introspection to contemplation of external factors and relationships. Particularly, in our analysis we can see that its used as often involving questioning and contemplating various aspects of life. This can include pondering one's family dynamics, personal identity, values, and behavior. Thinking about oneself and one's way of being encompasses reflecting on one's actions, beliefs, and emotions, as well as considering personal growth and development.

To sum up, it could be highlighted that the attitude noted towards the quarantine (because of the pandemic) is one of the first differences between the two groups since, for those who really present the responsibility trait, isolation implied interrupting activities and routines that they previously complied. Likewise, the order of the tasks and being able to accomplish them can be thought of as a characteristic more representative of responsible people. Regarding goals, the correctly classified group mainly sets one particular goal, which is to finish their university degree. This is due to the fact that, as described in Sect. 2, the majority of the participants are students.

Responsibility Trait with Original Dataset. In this instance, the three most important words used for classification were: 'Tareas' (Tasks), 'Tiempos' (Times) and 'Necesario' (Necessary). Only the first word coincides with the ones used in the augmented set. This highlights a term that is related to how people organize their chores or tell what these are; its use is similar to that described in the augmented set.

In the case of the positive samples correctly classified, the word 'necessary' is not frequent, and usually used in relation to conditionals such as "if necessary, I make lunch" or closely related to the resources needed to achieve goals such as owning a house in the future. Likewise, the word 'times' is usually used in association with how activities are organized in times (or how times are organized to fulfill and carry out activities).

Moreover, the group of negative samples erroneously classified in the positive class are distinguished mainly by the presence of the word 'times', which appears on occasion to express the need for personal time for leisure activities or personal growth, or simply to comment on activities carried out in free time. Regarding the term 'necessary', it partly appears to comment on the necessary actions that were carried out to counteract the effects of the pandemic.

Openness to Experience Trait with Augmented Dataset. The six most important words used by the classifier were 'Psicología' (Psychology), 'Empezar' (Start), 'Mundo' (World), 'Quiero' (Want), 'Estudiar' (Study) and 'Hablar' (Talk). Some of them, like 'Want', at first sight, does not seem to have much theoretical relevance with respect to this trait. Since it is mainly used to express personal desires, such as "I am anxious and I want to stop being so", "I want to be more autonomous", or to reflect starting new future activities.

The texts that were accurately classified as characteristic of this trait often utilized the term 'Psychology' to denote the academic discipline the participants are studying, as well as to describe their current experiences and perspectives during this phase of life. The co-occurrence of 'studying' and 'Psychology' was observed multiple times within these texts—a natural strong association between the act of studying and the field of Psychology most participants belong to. Such findings underscore the significance of academic pursuits and personal reflections related to the study of Psychology in shaping individuals' experiences and perceptions during this stage of life. On the other hand, the word 'start' was used in relation to what to do after graduating ("after obtaining my degree I want to start practicing") or to comment on future plans, such as "I am going to start from scratch", "I have to start physical activity", etc. Likewise, the word 'world' has been used to comment on the pretension of getting to know the world by traveling, or the possibilities that study offers in relation to "broadening one's vision of the world". In this sense, achieving to broaden this vision and knowledge in order to learn and get to know novel situations was also highlighted.

Finally, the term 'talk' was used as conveying the idea of communication as a means of problem-solving and addressing issues with others. It suggests a desire to engage in dialogue and discussion to resolve conflicts, share perspectives, and find solutions collaboratively. Additionally, 'talk' can imply a willingness to open up about personal matters and discuss aspects of one's life that may require attention or improvement. This could involve seeking advice, sharing experiences, or expressing emotions in a supportive environment. Overall, the term 'talk' emphasizes the importance of verbal communication in fostering understanding, connection, and positive change in both personal and interpersonal contexts.

To sum up, when considering a raw use of words, the main difference between the positive and negative samples correctly classified, relies on the use of the word 'study' and 'talk', which is observed more times in those who have the trait, that is, who are more open to learning new things both by studying and talking to other people about various topics.

Openness to Experience Trait with Original Dataset. In this case, the three most important words used for classification were: 'Aprender' (Learn), 'Arte' (Art) and 'Viajar' (Travel). In the case of correctly classified instances, the word 'art' is used in relation to interest in artistic activities such as painting, drawing, sculpture, music, literature, etc. It suggests an inclination towards creative expression and appreciation of aesthetics. The term 'learn' was used to indicate the desire or interest in acquiring knowledge on various subjects. This could include formal education, self-directed learning, or exploration of new topics and ideas. Finally, the term 'travel' reflects the intention or interest in visiting different places, either alone or with others. It implies a curiosity about experiencing diverse cultures, landscapes, and lifestyles. Misclassified positive cases have little use of these words and that might be the reason why the classifier failed to identify them correctly. The negative cases present little use of the words 'art' and 'travel', although they do present use of the term 'learn'.

5   Conclusions and Future Work

As previously mentioned in the introductory section, in this paper we extend a previous work [15] providing a more detailed description of the results. Specifically, this paper delves into a qualitative examination of the results obtained from using DT as a binary classifier for *Responsibility* and *Openness to experience* traits. This involves analysing the most relevant terms used by the decision-making process of the classifier and understanding the reasons behind its classifications, by manually checking the documents containing these terms. In this respect, it can be noted that augmenting the dataset to train the classifier allowed identifying new words –related to the expected characteristics of individuals exhibiting the studied traits–, which allows greater discrimination between texts. As future work, we will carry out the same study for the remaining traits in order to gain a more comprehensive understanding of why certain traits are easier or harder to classify using this approach.

When considering the quantitative results, Tables 3 and 4 show that using data augmentation clearly improves the classifiers performance considering all the personality traits in at least a 10%. While multiclass and multi-label approaches improve their performances on average on the augmented dataset, is the binary approach the one which takes more profit when compared to the original dataset. On average, considering all the personality traits, the binary classification approaches achieved weighted-F_1 scores above 0.7. In particular, for *Agreeableness* and *Extraversion* scores round 0.75 and for *Responsibility* the best performing value reported is around 0.88.

DT was the best classifier for the original dataset, since it reported three of the best values achieved for *Agreeableness, Extraversion* and *Responsibility* traits, but for this latter one, it was achieved a good classification performance above 0.8 while for the remaining traits, all the obtained values were below 0.7. For the augmented dataset, MNB and LR provided the best results for four of the five traits, while SVM reported the remaining best score for *Agreeableness* trait. It was clear that the static document model chosen did not perform as expected and BoW clearly outperformed it. With respect to the weighting schemes used, binary and TF seem to be more appropriate than TF-IDF, but more studies should be conducted to drawn proper conclusiones on which weighting scheme performs best in general.

Overall, this paper aims to provide insights into the effectiveness of using MNB, LR, SVM and DT as classifiers for specific personality traits as well as the underlying representation model of the documents, with the ultimate goal of improving classification performance and understanding the primary factors influencing trait classification.

References

1. Anguiano-Hernández, E.: Naive bayes multinomial para clasificación de texto usando un esquema de pesado por clases. Technical report, INAOE (2009)
2. Camara, W.J., Nathan, J.S., Puente, A.E.: Psychological test usage: implications in professional psychology. Prof. Psychol. Res. Pract. **31**(2), 141–154 (2000)
3. Castro Solano, A.: Técnicas de evaluación psicológica para ámbitos militares, 1st edn. Ediciones Paidós Ibérica, Buenos Aires, Argentina (2005)
4. Desmet, B., Hoste, V.: Emotion detection in suicide notes. Expert Syst. Appl. Int. J. **40**(16), 6351–6358 (2013)
5. Fast, L.A., Funder, D.C.: Personality as manifest in word use: correlations with self-report, acquaintance report, and behavior. J. Pers. Soc. Psychol. **94**(2), 334–346 (2008)
6. Hilbe, J.M.: Logistic Regression Models. Chapman & Hall (2017)
7. John, O.P.: Handbook of personality: Theory and research., chap. The "Big Five" factor taxonomy: Dimensions of personality in the natural language and in questionnaires, pp. 66–100. The Guilford Press (1990)
8. Losada, D.E., Crestani, F., Parapar, J.: CLEF 2017 eRisk overview: early risk prediction on the internet: experimental foundations. In: Cappellato, L., Ferro, N., Goeuriot, L., Mandl, T. (eds.) Working Notes of CLEF 2017 - Conference and Labs of the Evaluation Forum. CEUR Workshop Proceedings (2017)

9. Losada, D.E., Crestani, F., Parapar, J.: Overview of eRisk: Early Risk Prediction on the Internet. In: Bellot, P., et al. (eds.) Experimental IR Meets Multilinguality, Multimodality, and Interaction- 9th International Conference of the CLEF Association (2018)
10. Losada, D.E., Crestani, F., Parapar, J.: Overview of eRisk 2019 Early Risk Prediction on the Internet. In: Crestani, F., et al. (eds.) Experimental IR Meets Multilinguality, Multimodality, and Interaction - 10th International Conference of the CLEF Association (2019)
11. Losada, D.E., Crestani, F., Parapar, J.: eRisk 2020: Self-harm and Depression Challenges. In: Jose, J.M., et al. (eds.) Advances in Information Retrieval - 42nd European Conference on IR Research, ECIR 2020 (2020)
12. Ma, Y., Guo, G. (eds.): Support Vector Machines Applications, chap. Chapter 2: "Multi-Class Support Vector Machine". Springer-Verlag (2014)
13. Mariñelarena-Dondena, L., Ferretti, E., Maragoudakis, M., Sapino, M., Errecalde, M.: Predicting depression: a comparative study of machine learning approaches based on language usage. Panamerican J. Neuropsychol. **11**(3), 42–54 (2017)
14. Mitchell, T.M.: Machine learning. McGraw-Hill Series in Computer Science, McGraw-Hill (1997)
15. Montenegro, L., Sapino, M., Ferretti, E., Cagnina, L.: On the assessment of personality traits by using text mining techniques. In: Actas del XXIX Congreso Argentino de Ciencias de la Computación (CACIC), pp. 114–123 (2023). iSBN: 978-987-9285-51-0
16. Moreno, J.D., Martínez-Huertas, J., Olmos, R., Botana, G., Botella, J.: Can personality traits be measured analyzing written language? a meta-analytic study on computational methods. Personality and Individual Differences **177** (2021)
17. Parapar, J., Martín-Rodilla, P., Losada, D.E., Crestani, F.: eRisk 2021: Pathological Gambling, Self-harm and Depression Challenges. In: Hiemstra, D., Moens, M., Mothe, J., Perego, R., Potthast, M., Sebastiani, F. (eds.) Advances in Information Retrieval - 43rd European Conference on IR Research, ECIR 2021 (2021)
18. Parapar, J., Martín-Rodilla, P., Losada, D.E., Crestani, F.: Overview of eRisk 2022: Early Risk Prediction on the Internet (Extended Overview). In: Faggioli, G., Ferro, N., Hanbury, A., Potthast, M. (eds.) Proceedings of the Working Notes of CLEF 2022 - Conference and Labs of the Evaluation Forum (2022)
19. Parapar, J., Martín-Rodilla, P., Losada, D.E., Crestani, F.: Overview of eRisk 2023: early risk prediction on the internet. In: Arampatzis, A., et al. (eds.) Experimental IR Meets Multilinguality, Multimodality, and Interaction - 14th International Conference of the CLEF Association, CLEF 2023, Thessaloniki, Greece, September 18-21, 2023, Proceedings. Lecture Notes in Computer Science, vol. 14163, pp. 294–315. Springer (2023)
20. Parapar, J., Martín-Rodilla, P., Losada, D.E., Crestani, F.: eRisk 2024: Early Risk Prediction on the Internet - CLEF 2024 Workshop, September 2024. https://erisk.irlab.org/, Grenoble, France
21. Pennebaker, J.W., Boyd, R.L., Jordan, K., Blackburn, K.: The development and psychometric properties of liwc2015. The University of Texas at Austin, Tech. rep. (2015)
22. Schwartz, H., et al.: Characterizing geographic variation in well-being using tweets. In: Proceedings of the International AAAI Conference on Web and Social Media, vol. 7, pp. 583–591 (2021)
23. Yarkoni, T.: Personality in 100,000 words: A large-scale analysis of personality and word use among bloggers. J. Res. Pers. **44**(3), 363–373 (2010)

Effects of Topological Factors and Class Imbalance on Node Classification Through Graph Convolutional Neural Networks

Tatiana S. Parlanti[1,2]([⊠]) [iD], Carlos A. Catania[1,2] [iD], and Luis G. Moyano[2,3,4] [iD]

[1] Universidad Nacional de Cuyo, Facultad de Ingeniería, Laboratorio de Sistemas Inteligentes (LABSIN), Mendoza, Argentina
{tatiana.parlanti,harpo}@ingenieria.uncuyo.edu.ar
[2] Consejo Nacional de Investigaciones Científicas y Técnicas, C1425FQB C.A.B.A Buenos Aires, Argentina
luis.moyano@ib.edu.ar
[3] Grupo de Física Estadística e Interdisciplinaria, Centro Atómico Bariloche, CNEA, 8400 San Carlos de Bariloche, Río Negro, Argentina
[4] Instituto Balseiro, Universidad Nacional de Cuyo, 8400 San Carlos de Bariloche, Río Negro, Argentina

Abstract. Graph Convolutional Neural Networks (GCNs) have proven to be highly effective in solving graph-related problems, as they not only consider the individual node features but also capture the topological characteristics of the graph. However, the lack of public datasets presents a challenge in the evaluation and comparison of these networks across various contexts. This article addresses the inherent limitations of GCNs, focusing specifically on the impact of topological aspects and class imbalance in node classification tasks. Using a variant of the Stochastic Block Model (SBM) algorithm that allows for node covariates, a statistically significant number of synthetic graphs is generated, varying feature characteristics as well as group edge probabilities. Thus, a comprehensive exploration of GCNs' capabilities in different scenarios is conducted. The initial findings underscore the fundamental importance of node feature variability for classification and highlight the challenges that arise when presented with strong class imbalance scenarios.

Keywords: Graph Convolutions Neural Networks · Stochastic Block Models · Complex Networks

1 Introduction

A network or graph $G = (V, E)$ is typically used to model relationships between entities and is often presented as a set of nodes V and links E between them. These structures are interesting and useful, as many problems can be interpreted as a graph, merely by properly defining what its nodes and links represent. In recent years, Graph Neural Networks (GNNs) have experienced a significant

© The Author(s), under exclusive license to Springer Nature Switzerland AG 2024
P. Pesado et al. (Eds.): CACIC 2023, CCIS 2123, pp. 213–226, 2024.
https://doi.org/10.1007/978-3-031-62245-8_15

increase in popularity, due to their application in numerous problems related to graphs, such as classifying proteins based on their structure, recommending content to users on a platform, or predicting the subject of a paper by considering other papers it cites and those that cite it [4].

Kipf and Welling presented a particular architecture variant, coined Graph Convolutional Networks (GCNs) [5], achieving a significant impact: they show that it is possible to predict labels for non-labeled nodes, using their features and -most importantly- the information about links between nodes. So, the underlying graph that describes the problem stores valuable information for training and predicting using a neural network.

This study extends previous work [7] by considering Kipf and Welling's proposed architecture, and exploring it for class imbalance cases, in order to establish its scope and limitations. To do this, a two-layer GCN is tested with different sets of synthetic graphs and a binary node classification task. Our work extends our previous effort analyzing new combinations of graph topologies, group membership probabilities as well as more degrees of class imbalance.

This work is divided into six main Sections. Section 2 and 3 present a theoretical description of GNNs and Stochastic Block Models, respectively. Section 4 begins with a brief description of the hardware and software used, continuing with the type of experiments made. Finally, Sect. 5 discusses the results, and 6 exhibits the main conclusions and future work.

2   Brief Theoretical Description of GNNs

Before presenting the experiments to be conducted, a brief theoretical description of GNNs is provided below, starting with the notation utilized throughout the paper.

2.1   Notation

Let be a graph $G = (V, E)$.

- Two nodes $u, v \in V$ are connected by an edge if $(u, v) \in E$.
- Given a vertex $u \in V$, the neighborhood of u is defined as $N(u) = \{v \in V \mid (u, v) \in E\}$.
- A graph is undirected if $(u, v) \in E \iff (v, u) \in E$.
- A graph is directed if $(u, v) \in E$ does not necessarily imply that the reverse connection exists. In this case, the ordered pair (u, v) represents the edge from u to v.
- A graph can be represented from its adjacency matrix $\mathbf{A} \in \mathbb{R}^{|V| \times |V|}$, defined as $A_{ij} = 1$ if $(i, j) \in E$, and $A_{ij} = 0$ otherwise. If G is undirected, then $\mathbf{A}$ is symmetric. On the contrary, if G is directed, then $\mathbf{A}$ is not symmetric.
- If every node $u \in V$ is represented as a $p-$dimensional feature vector, then a feature matrix $\mathbf{X} \in \mathbb{R}^{|V| \times p}$ is defined such that the i-th row has the p features of the node $i \in V$.

2.2 Embeddings and Neural Message Passing

A Graph Neural Network uses a neural message passing, in which message vectors are exchanged between nodes, and they are updated using neural networks. For that, hidden embeddings are generated for every node $u \in V$, from the graph $G = (V, E)$ and the feature matrix $\mathbf{X}$ [4].

Following [4], during each message passing iteration in a GNN, every hidden embedding $\mathbf{h}_u^{(k)}$ corresponding to each node $u \in V$ is updated according to information aggregated from u's neighborhood $N(u)$. This update is given by:

$$\mathbf{h}_u^{(k+1)} = \text{UPDATE}^{(k)}\left(\mathbf{h}_u^{(k)}, \text{AGGREGATE}^{(k)}\left(\{\mathbf{h}_v^{(k)} \mid v \in N(u)\}\right)\right) \quad (1)$$

$$= \text{UPDATE}^{(k)}\left(\mathbf{h}_u^{(k)}, \mathbf{m}_{N(u)}^{(k)}\right), \quad (2)$$

where UPDATE and AGGREGATE are arbitrary differentiable functions, $\mathbf{m}_{N(u)}$ is the "message" that is collected from u's neighbors and k states the iteration or GNN layer (if $k = 0$ then $\mathbf{h}_u^{(0)} = x_u$, i.e., the first embedding is equal to the feature vector for each node). Therefore, at each iteration, the embedding of node u is updated according to the message received from its neighbors, and the embedding from the previous layer. Also note that as AGGREGATE takes a set as an argument, then a GNN defined like this is permutation equivariant by design.

In the particular case of Graph Convolutional Networks (GCNs), the UPDATE and AGGREGATE functions are sums. Furthermore, when the graph is undirected Kipf and Welling [5] suggest a symmetric-normalization. But it is also possible to normalize when the graph is directed, following a simple approach:

$$\mathbf{m}_{N(u)} = \begin{cases} \sum_{v \in N(u) \cup \{u\}} \frac{\mathbf{h}_v}{\sqrt{|N(u)||N(v)|}} & \text{if the graph is undirected} \\ \frac{1}{|N(u)|} \sum_{v \in N(u) \cup \{u\}} \mathbf{h}_v & \text{if the graph is directed} \end{cases} \quad (3)$$

Then, a GCN is updated following:

$$\mathbf{h}_u^{(k+1)} = \sigma\left(\mathbf{W}^{(k)} \mathbf{m}_{N(u)}^{(k)}\right), \forall u \in V, \quad (4)$$

where $\mathbf{W}$ is a weight matrix (parameters) that the network learns, and σ is a nonlinear function, usually $\sigma = \text{ReLU}$.

In matrix notation, also known as graph-level, the Eq. 4 is given by:

$$\mathbf{H}^{(k+1)} = \begin{cases} \sigma\left(\bar{\mathbf{D}}^{-1/2} \bar{\mathbf{A}} \bar{\mathbf{D}}^{-1/2} \mathbf{H}^{(k)} \mathbf{W}^{(k)}\right) & \text{if the graph is undirected} \\ \sigma\left(\bar{\mathbf{D}}^{-1} \bar{\mathbf{A}} \mathbf{H}^{(k)} \mathbf{W}^{(k)}\right) & \text{if the graph is directed} \end{cases}, \quad (5)$$

where $\bar{\mathbf{A}} = \mathbf{A} + \mathbf{I}$, with $\mathbf{A}$ the adjacency matrix and $\mathbf{I}$ the identity matrix, and where $\bar{\mathbf{D}}$ is the degree matrix (diagonal) defined by $\bar{D}_{ii} = \sum_j \bar{A}_{ij}$.

3 Stochastic Block Models

Stochastic Block Models (SBMs) are a set of related theoretical models proposed to model specific structural aspects in graphs, such as their organization in communities [1,6,8]. Communities, also known as groups or modules, are loosely defined as subgroups of nodes which present more connectivity to other nodes in the same subgroup than to nodes out of it. In real networks, the origin of communities may be due to different reasons, such as related to the way the network was built or to external characteristics, not related to its topology.

These models may be used for simulation purposes as well as for modeling purposes [6]. In the former case, given known parameters, which will be detailed briefly, the SBM model allows for the generation of a synthetic graph with a given expected community structure. In the latter case, the SBM may be used to make a set of assumptions of a given (possibly real) graph or network and, additionally, allows for the possibility to infer the parameters that best describe that graph or network, given the set of assumptions. In this work we will use an extension of the SBM model for simulation purposes, i.e., we will use it to generate synthetic graphs with chosen topological characteristics.

The most simple version of SBM proposes a probabilistic model for edge assignment. There are two relevant elements. The first is a vector of group memberships $\mathbf{Z}$, which encodes to which of K communities a given node belongs to. The second element is an edge probability matrix $\mathbf{C}$, whose elements represent the probability for a Bernoulli trial for the presence or absence of an edge between any two nodes, conditional on their group memberships (effectively controlling edges both within and between communities). Here $\mathbf{C}$ is a $K \times K$ matrix, and element C_{ij} represents the probability of an edge between a node belonging to community i and another to community j. This matrix will be symmetric for undirected graphs and may be asymmetric for directed ones.

In real cases, graphs are an abstract representation of relationships, which in most cases may be further described with additional variables or features. It is then natural to extend the SBM model to these cases and there are a number of such extensions, as the Contextual Stochastic Block Model (cSBM) [1,2]. In most models that consider covariates or features, an additional vector $\mathbf{x}$ is introduced representing (given) node features and, additionally, proposes a probabilistic relationship between such features and the group memberships [6,8].

Let's allow each node to have p features, represented by p stochastic values, modeled as drawn from a multivariate Gaussian distribution [8]. This distribution is defined by a p dimensional vector of means $\mathbf{m}$ and a $p \times p$ covariance matrix Σ that may differ between communities. Then, for K communities, a $K \times p$ mean feature matrix, $\mathbf{F}$, is defined such that the k−th row has the mean values $\mathbf{m}$ of the k−th community. Thus, for any given node i, its j−th feature is modeled as $x_{ij} = m_j + z = F_{kj} + z$, where $m_j = F_{kj}$ is the corresponding mean of the j−th dimension in the multivariate Gaussian distribution that depends on the node's community, and z represents a realization of a zero-centered Normal distribution, $\mathcal{N}(0, \Sigma)$.

Then, a probabilistic group membership is introduced by means of the following expression:

$$Z_i = \underset{k}{\mathrm{argmax}}(x_i F_k^T), \tag{6}$$

where Z_i denotes the community membership of node i, x_i represents the p dimensional feature vector of node i, and F_k^T denotes the mean feature vector of the $k-$th community.

In this way, node features influence the group characterization of each node, introducing a latent, non-deterministic description of group membership. If the p values of the vector of means $\mathbf{m}$ are similar, then the chance of nodes being assigned to different groups will be smaller. On the other hand, the more different these means, the greater the probability for the nodes to be assigned to different communities.

Finally, the Bernoulli edge probability for nodes i and j is equal to $C_{ij} Z_i Z_j$, i.e., the product between the corresponding element in the edge community matrix $\mathbf{C}$, and the probabilistic group memberships $\mathbf{Z}$ for the considered nodes i and j.

This model allows for the generation of statistically equivalent graph topologies susceptible to modifications in two well-defined dimensions, the feature dimension and the edge dimension. On the one hand, one may explore scenarios where features are very similar or, on the contrary, very different, by manipulating the vector of means $\mathbf{m}$ and the covariance matrix Σ. On the other, one can explore different scenarios for the edge community matrix, especially modifying the ratio between the probability of edges within and between communities, similar to the parametrizations found in [1,2].

In this work, we explore these scenarios for testing different hypothesis. On one hand, we would like to check the ability of a GCN architecture to learn to distinguish between well-balanced classes, and when possible groups are also well differentiated. With this preliminary check in place, we want to explore the ability of GCNs to correctly classify nodes when groups and features are less distinguishable as well as to understand the impact of class imbalance in its classification performance. The SBM model will provide an outstanding graph generator to explore different scenarios involving simultaneously three factors: topological communities, latent features, and class imbalance.

4 Materials and Methods

This Section describes the hardware and software that was used, as well as the details of the experiments.

4.1 Hardware and Software Description

All the experiments described in this work were executed in an AMD FX(tm)-6300 Six-Core processor, that has a NVIDIA GeForce GTX Ti video card of 12 GB and is available at the Universidad Nacional de Cuyo.

Regarding the software, the 3.8.10 version of `python` was used, as well as the following libraries: (a) `tensorflow`: version 2.9.3; (b) `spektral` [3]: deep learning library for graphs, based on the `Keras` API and `TensorFlow` 2. Version 1.2.0; (c) `pandas`: version 1.5.3; (d) `numpy`: version 1.23.4; (e) `matplotlib`: version 3.6.2.

4.2   Experiments Description

We performed a series of experiments designed to evaluate the efficacy of the GCN architecture for different graph structures and class ratios, i.e. graphs with different degrees of unbalanced node classes.

The datasets that were used in this work were generated by modifying the ratio between edge probability within and between groups as well as feature similarity, depending on the experiment. This Section describes the hyperparameters that were used to generate synthetic graphs, as well as the data preprocessing, the network architecture, and the metrics used to evaluate the GCN performance.

Synthetic Graphs. As stated in Sect. 3, the following hyperparameters are considered as input to create synthetic graphs:

- $K = 2$, i.e., two classes.
- $p = 2$, i.e., two features per node.
- **F**, mean of each feature for both classes. These are represented as a matrix of size $K \times p$, where K is the number of classes, and p is the number of features per node.
- **C**, the probability of connections within and between classes, which are represented as a matrix of size $K \times K$, where again K is the number of classes and the ij−th element of this matrix is the probability of connection between a node of class i and a node of class j. Note that this matrix would not be symmetric, as graphs are directed.

Four different matrices of connection probabilities were used, as well as four different matrices of mean features. The intersection of the different possible cases forms a parameter space, and we selected six case studies for analysis. Table 1 and Fig. 1 summarize the parameter space that was explored. In particular, the last figure also shows some guidelines used to compare the use cases discussed in Sect. 5. These guidelines are represented with arrows to help our rationale and give a framework for our conclusions. The notation (e_i, f_j) is used throughout the rest of the work to represent specific configurations that distinguish nodes of different classes, being e loosely speaking an edge connection dimension, i.e., how large is the ratio between the probability of edges within and between communities, and f is loosely speaking a mean features dimension, that represents how similar or dissimilar are the p values representing the different means of the multivariate Gaussian distribution. Here i and j go from 0 to 3, with (e_3, f_3) representing the most dissimilar classes and (e_0, f_0) representing the most similar.

Some examples of the graphs created are shown in Fig. 2, where classes are balanced. Furthermore, a series of tests were performed in which graphs were constructed forcing class imbalance. The minority class represents the following percentages over the total nodes: $1, 2, 5, 7.5, 10, 12.5, 15, 17.5, 20$, where the first values represent extreme class imbalance. Some examples of these synthetic graphs are shown in Fig. 3.

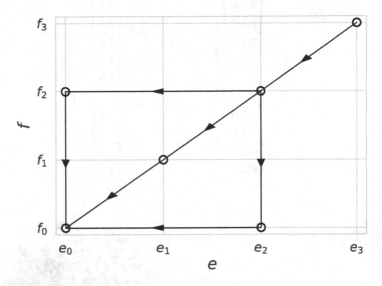

Fig. 1. Parameter space explored in this work, where e denotes the connection probability dimension, and f denotes the mean features dimension. The respective values used can be consulted in Table 1.

Data Preprocessing and Network Architecture. Each experiment has its own set of graphs as input data. Additionally, every graph has three main elements: an adjacency matrix, a node feature matrix, and a node label vector, usually represented as a one-hot matrix.

Before training the GCN, a normalization preprocessing is done over the adjacency matrix $\mathbf{A}$ and over the node features matrix $\mathbf{X}$. On the one hand, as explained in Sect. 2, initially $\bar{\mathbf{A}}$ is computed as $\bar{\mathbf{A}} = \mathbf{A} + \mathbf{I}$, where $\mathbf{I}$ is the identity matrix, and then $\bar{\mathbf{A}}$ is normalized depending on whether it is symmetric or not. Here, according to Eq. 5, the normalization is performed as $\bar{\mathbf{D}}^{-1}\bar{\mathbf{A}}$, since graphs are directed. On the other hand, the node feature matrix is row normalized, i.e., for each row of matrix $\mathbf{X}$ every entry is divided by the sum of the elements in that row.

During training a learning rate of 0.01 and an Adam optimizer were used. The network architecture is defined by the following layers:

Table 1. Configurations chosen according to different features and edge similarity.

Configuration	Connection Probabilities (e)		Mean Features (f)	
(e_3, f_3)	0.9 0.1		3 0	
	0.2 0.8		0 3	
(e_2, f_2)	0.8 0.2		2 1	
	0.3 0.7		1 2	
(e_2, f_0)	0.8 0.2		1 1	
	0.3 0.7		1 1	
(e_1, f_1)	0.6 0.4		1.5 1	
	0.4 0.6		1 1.5	
(e_0, f_2)	0.5 0.5		2 1	
	0.5 0.5		1 2	
(e_0, f_0)	0.5 0.5		1 1	
	0.5 0.5		1 1	

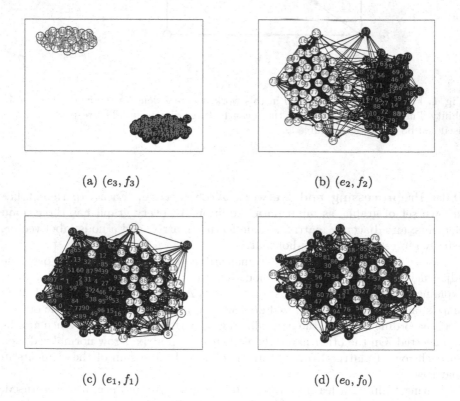

(a) (e_3, f_3) (b) (e_2, f_2)

(c) (e_1, f_1) (d) (e_0, f_0)

Fig. 2. Graph examples with balanced classes, for different configurations.

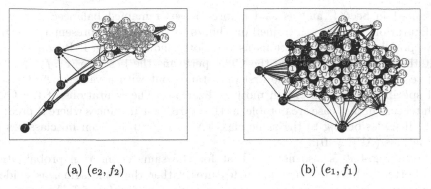

(a) (e_2, f_2) (b) (e_1, f_1)

Fig. 3. Graph examples with class imbalance. On the left, the minority class is 5% over the total nodes, while on the right it is 10%.

1. Dropout: rate = 0.5.
2. GCN hidden layer: 16 neurons and ReLU activation function.
3. Dropout: rate = 0.5.
4. GCN output layer: 2 neurons and Softmax activation function.

For training, a $k-$fold approach was used, with $k = 100$. That is, for each experiment one hundred models were trained, leaving a different graph to test each time. Likewise, to evaluate the performance of the GCN, several metrics were analyzed, as described below.

Metrics Description. In a binary classification problem, the performance of the model must be evaluated according to different metrics. For this, the confusion matrix is considered, which is built from the comparison between the real labels and those predicted by the network. In this work, we use:

- AUC-score: Area Under the ROC Curve, which illustrates the relationship between the True Positive (TP) rate and the False Positive (FP) rate.
- Specificity: fraction of correct predictions of class 1, given by TN/(TN+FP), where TN means True Negative.

It is worth noting that the accuracy and precision metrics were not used to evaluate the predictions, as they are not always representative, especially when the dataset does not have well-balanced classes. Furthermore, specificity was chosen instead of its analog known as recall, because class 1 often coincides with the minority class when the classes are not balanced.

5   Results and Discussion

5.1   GCN Behavior at Different Configurations

Our first set of experiments aims at testing the classification performance for the well-balanced case. A GCN was trained over the different configurations presented in Sect. 4, and as said before classes remained balanced. At every configuration, a GCN was trained one hundred times, so we present the results corresponding to the predictions as boxplots, shown in Fig. 4. It can be seen that the configurations where the GCN performs the best are $(e_3, f_3), (e_2, f_2)$ and (e_0, f_2). In particular, the first one stands out with a value of AUC score and specificity equal to one in most realizations. The limitations of the GCN architecture in that case are notable, as there are some instances where it predicts that all nodes belong to the same class (AUC = 0.5), or even misclassifies all predictions (AUC = 0).

From Fig. 4 it is also notable that for the same connection probabilities, it is better to have different mean features rather than the same, as evident when comparing (e_2, f_2) with (e_2, f_0), and (e_0, f_2) with (e_0, f_0). Actually, the absence of different mean features negatively impacts the results regardless of the connection probabilities, as the comparison between (e_0, f_0) and (e_2, f_0) suggests. Finally, the (e_1, f_1) configuration shows that a small difference in connection probabilities and mean features is not enough to achieve good performance.

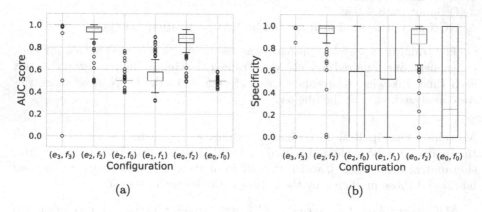

Fig. 4. AUC score and specificity for predictions on one hundred test sets, for different configurations with class-balanced nodes.

5.2   GCN Behaviour on Cases of Class Imbalance

To begin the analysis of the impact of class imbalance, a GCN was trained on the configuration (e_3, f_3), the results of which are shown in Fig. 5. Under these conditions, a GCN trained with graphs exhibiting a class imbalance of less than 5 percent performs poorly, as evidenced by the median AUC score of 0.5 and the median specificity of 0. Nevertheless, a median AUC score and specificity of 1 are achieved when the class imbalance is greater than 5 percent. A sizeable fraction of cases remain below 0.5 for this fraction of the minority class, but very few do for higher values.

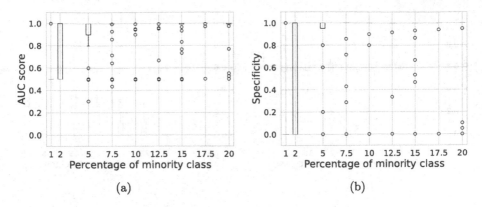

Fig. 5. AUC score and specificity for predictions on one hundred test sets, for configuration (e_3, f_3) with different degrees of class imbalance.

On the other hand, the configuration (e_2, f_2) exhibits poor performance with class imbalance below 10 percent, while the configuration (e_0, f_2) shows a similar pattern at less than 12.5 percent, as depicted in Figs. 6 and 7. Additionally, there is an increase in the AUC score and specificity medians as the percentage of the minority class increases. This illustrates that the GCN improves in distinguishing between classes as the proportion of the minority class rises.

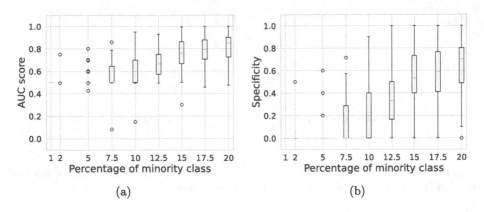

Fig. 6. AUC score and specificity for predictions on one hundred test sets, for configuration (e_2, f_2) with different degrees of class imbalance.

Conversely, when nodes of different classes have the same mean features, it does not matter the degree of class imbalance, as can be seen in Fig. 8. A GCN does not learn to distinguish between classes, as it predicts that all nodes belong to the same class. The same applies to configurations (e_1, f_1) and (e_0, f_0), so these images are not shown.

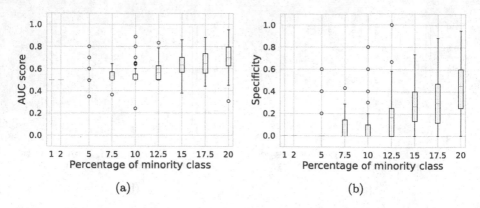

Fig. 7. AUC score and specificity for predictions on one hundred test sets, for configuration (e_0, f_2) with different degrees of class imbalance.

Finally, we performed tests using a constant mean features matrix f and verified the expected behavior which is that the GCN can not learn, and both AUC $= 0.5$ and specificity $= 0$, which is indistinguishable from random guess.

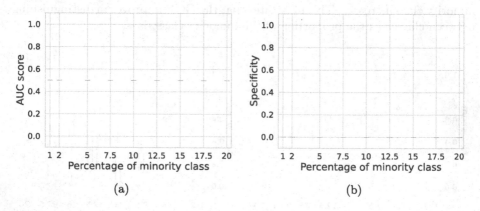

Fig. 8. AUC score and specificity for predictions on one hundred test sets, for configuration (e_2, f_0) with different degrees of class imbalance.

6 Conclusions and Future Work

This work has explored the scope and limitations of Graph Convolutional Networks, testing their performance in different scenarios, given by synthetic graphs of different topologies.

As expected, when the graph topology is characterized by nodes forming well-separated groups, and where classes are balanced, a GCN can almost perfectly distinguish between classes. Then, as the connection probabilities and mean features become similar in both classes, the performance of GCN decreases. We characterize this behavior for some use cases in the chosen parameter space.

On the other hand, class imbalance negatively impacts training. This imbalance can stifle proper performance even in the best scenario. As this behavior decreases, i.e. as the fraction of minority class increases, there is an improvement in GCN performance, but it is below the maximum scores achieved with balanced classes.

Finally, it is desirable that the mean features of the nodes be as different as possible, and if this also occurred with the connections probabilities, it would be even better.

Future work is expected to go in two directions. The analysis presented here may be extended to explore in more detail the region of parameter space where extreme class imbalance mostly affects the capacities of the GCNs. Once this transition from learning to impaired regions is well-mapped, we will be able to analyze what are the concrete shortcomings of the GCN architecture and possibly propose improvement alternatives, such as testing different data augmentation strategies, and weighted loss functions, among others, to further increase the performance of GCNs in cases of extreme class imbalance.

Acknowledgments. This work was partially financed by CONICET through project PIBAA-CONICET 2872021010 0706CO, as well as by grant SIIP C017-T1 and 06/B040-T1 of Universidad Nacional de Cuyo, and by CONICET PhD scholarship (TSP).

References

1. Carson, B.S.: A survey of graph neural networks on synthetic data. Theses and Dissertations (2023). https://scholarsarchive.byu.edu/etd/9929
2. Deshpande, Y., Sen, S., Montanari, A., Mossel, E.: Contextual stochastic block models. Advances in Neural Information Processing Systems **31** (2018)
3. Grattarola, D., Alippi, C.: Graph neural networks in tensorflow and keras with spektral [application notes]. IEEE Comput. Intell. Mag. **16**(1), 99–106 (2021). https://doi.org/10.1109/MCI.2020.3039072
4. Hamilton, W.L.: Graph representation learning. Synthesis Lectures on Artificial Intelligence and Machine Learning **14**(3), 1–159 (2020). https://doi.org/10.2200/S01045ED1V01Y202009AIM046
5. Kipf, T.N., Welling, M.: Semi-supervised classification with graph convolutional networks. arXiv preprint (2016). https://doi.org/10.48550/arXiv.1609.02907
6. Lee, C., Wilkinson, D.J.: A review of stochastic block models and extensions for graph clustering. Appl. Network Sci. **4**(122), 1–50 (2019). https://doi.org/10.1007/s41109-019-0232-2

7. Parlanti, T.S., Catania, C.A., Moyano, L.G.: Impacto de factores topológicos y de desbalance en la clasificación de nodos con gcns. Libro de actas-XXIX Congreso Argentino de Ciencias de la Computación-CACIC 2023, pp. 124–133 (2024). http://sedici.unlp.edu.ar/handle/10915/163107
8. Stanley, N., Bonacci, T., Kwitt, R., Niethammer, M., Mucha, P.J.: Stochastic block models with multiple continuous attributes. Appl. Network Sci. 4(54), 1–22 (2019). https://doi.org/10.1007/s41109-019-0170-z

First Experiences with the Identification of People at Risk for Diabetes in Argentina Using Machine Learning Techniques

Enzo Rucci[1,2,5]($\boxtimes$) (iD), Gonzalo Tittarelli[3,5], Franco Ronchetti[1,2,5] (iD),
Jorge F. Elgart[4,5] (iD), Laura Lanzarini[1,5] (iD), and Juan José Gagliardino[4,5] (iD)

[1] III-LIDI, Facultad de Informática, UNLP - CIC, 1900 La Plata, Argentina
{erucci,fronchetti,ldural}@lidi.info.unlp.edu.ar
[2] Comisión de Investigaciones Científicas (CIC), 1900 La Plata, Argentina
[3] Facultad de Informática, UNLP, 1900 La Plata, Buenos Aires, Argentina
[4] CENEXA, Facultad de C. Médicas, UNLP-CONICET, 1900 La Plata, Argentina
{jelgart,jjgagliardino}@cenexa.org
[5] CONICET, 1900 La Plata, Argentina

Abstract. Detecting Type 2 Diabetes (T2D) and Prediabetes (PD) is a real challenge for medicine due to the absence of pathogenic symptoms and the lack of known associated risk factors. Even though some proposals for machine learning models enable the identification of people at risk, the nature of the condition makes it so that a model suitable for one population may not necessarily be suitable for another. In this article, the development and assessment of predictive models to identify people at risk for T2D and PD specifically in Argentina are discussed. First, the database was thoroughly preprocessed and three specific datasets were generated considering a compromise between the number of records and the amount of available variables. After applying 5 different classification models, the results obtained show that a very good performance was observed for two datasets with some of these models. In particular, RF, DT, and ANN demonstrated great classification power, with good values for the metrics under consideration. Given the lack of this type of tool in Argentina, this work represents the first step towards the development of more sophisticated models.

Keywords: public health · chronic disease · machine learning

1 Introduction

Type 2 Diabetes (T2D) is a chronic disease characterized by high blood glucose levels; it manifests when the endocrine pancreas is unable to produce enough insulin for body tissues [11]. Due to its increasing prevalence in combination with its high cost of care [4,30], it represents a serious public health problem, and great efforts have been made to develop effective strategies for its prevention and timely treatment, as well as to avoid the development of its chronic complications.

P. Pesado et al. (Eds.): CACIC 2023, CCIS 2123, pp. 227–239, 2024.
https://doi.org/10.1007/978-3-031-62245-8_16

It is worth noting that the negative consequences of this disease start in a previous stage known as prediabetes (PD), which is characterized by elevated blood glucose concentration higher than normal levels, but without reaching the diagnostic values for diabetes. PD involves Impaired Fasting Glucose (IFG), Impaired Glucose Tolerance (IGT), and a combination of both [1]. PD has a high risk of progressing into T2D - around 30% [7] and 70% [9] in the following 4 and 30 years, respectively.

The development of T2D is a slow and progressive process conditioned by genetic, environmental, and behavioral factors. Currently, there is no definitive cure for this disease. However, several studies have shown that its onset can be prevented or delayed in people with PD through the adoption of a healthy lifestyle (eating plan and regular physical activity) and/or associated with the intake of various drugs [7,27]. In Argentina, an initiative of this type is the Pilot Program for the Primary Prevention of Diabetes in the province of Buenos Aires (PPDBA), developed by CENEXA (UNLP-CONICET) and financed by the Ministry of Science and Technology of the Nation, the company SANOFI and CONICET [12].

Detecting T2D and PD is a real challenge for medicine due to the absence of pathogenic symptoms and the lack of known associated risk factors. This is why individuals may often go months (or even years) without knowing that they are at risk. In this sense, statistics published in 2018 by the International Diabetes Federation show that approximately 50% of the world's population is unaware of their disease [10]. This explains the need for a simple and accurate detection method. Thus, this article proposes the development and assessment of predictive models based on machine learning (ML) that will allow identifying people at risk of T2D and PD in Argentina. To this end, the PPDBA database will be used.

This paper is an extended and thoroughly revised version of [23]. The work has been extended by providing: (1) the proposal of a new segmentation that only considers clinical data from the PPDBA database and the training of several models that use it as input; and (2) a performance analysis of the new models and a cost-benefit analysis with the previous ones.

The remaining sections of this article are organized as follows: In Sect. 2, the background for this work is presented. In Sect. 3, database processing is described, while in Sect. 4 the results obtained are analyzed. Finally, in Sect. 5, conclusions and possible future work are presented.

2   Background

2.1   Diabetes and Prediabetes - Risk Factors and Diagnosis

The development of T2D is a slow and progressive process that is conditioned by genetic, environmental, and behavioral factors. Risk factors include gender, body mass index (BMI), waist circumference, eating habits, physical activity, age, family history of diabetes (including gestational), ethnicity, sleep disorders, and so forth. PD corresponds to a state before T2D, and its progression can be prevented and even reversed by adopting healthy lifestyles [28]. If we also consider that PD is not a pre-disease state, since it already presents metabolic dysfunctions, it is extremely important to identify people with PD as much as it is to do so with those who already have undiagnosed T2D.

Diagnosis is based on blood tests, and anyone presenting the associated symptoms or risk factors should be examined. In Argentina, the Oral Glucose Tolerance Test (OGTT) is usually used to determine if a person has T2D, PD, or neither[1].

2.2 Related Works

In the last decade, numerous models have been proposed to identify undiagnosed diabetes and/or PD using ML techniques. These are based on various clinical and laboratory variables linked to relevant risk factors. Most of them [2,6,13, 15,16,18,19,21,22,25,26,29,31,34,35] use a diabetes database known as PIMA Indian Diabetes (PID) from the repository of the University of California Irvine[2], USA. This dataset contains records of women from the Pima indigenous people (USA) and is made up of 8 attributes related to risk factors for developing the disease. It has a total of 786 records; however, this number is reduced by half if entries with null values are removed. These works are more of a proof of concept than a real implementation and, in general, have been aimed at improving the performance (accuracy) of diabetes classification algorithms.

Only a few of these works do not use the PID database. These include [8,14,33], whose authors proposed models to identify diabetes and prediabetes using data from the US NHANES Survey. Recently, the authors in [32] also studied the application of different ML techniques for detecting undiagnosed diabetes in the US population using the BRFSS database. Similarly, the authors in [20] presented various predictive models for these diseases for the Chinese population using an ad-hoc database. In [5], on the other hand, the development and validation of predictive models focused only on prediabetes.

As explained in Sect. 2.1, the onset of T2D is conditioned by factors that may vary from one population to another. This is why a predictive model that is suitable for one population will not necessarily be suitable for another. This study is the first step toward building specific predictive models for the Argentine population.

---

[1] For this test, a blood sample is drawn on a fasting state. Then, the subject is asked to drink a liquid containing a certain amount of glucose. After this, another blood sample is taken every 30 to 60 min after intake. The exam is financially expensive and can take up to 3 h.

[2] https://archive.ics.uci.edu/ml/index.php.

3 Implementation

3.1 Dataset

Description. Predictive models will be developed using the PPDBA program database [12], which has 1316 records. Each record corresponds to a person identified as diabetic, prediabetic or disease-free through OGTT. In addition to laboratory data (glycated hemoglobin, total cholesterol, HDL cholesterol, LDL cholesterol, triglycerides, and creatinine), there are clinical variables associated with the risk factors for these diseases such as sex, age, Body Mass Index (BMI), blood pressure, family history of diabetes, eating habits, physical activity, and so forth.

Characterization. Out of the 1316 current records, 80 had to be discarded due to the lack of blood glucose data to calculate the OGTT (class could not be determined). Table 1 presents a brief statistical description of the 1236 remaining records. There are several null variables, which are analyzed in greater depth in the following section. As it can be noted, there are more women than men, most subjects are between 45–64 years old; most with a BMI greater than $30\,\mathrm{kg/m^2}$; most with a waist circumference greater than 102 cm (men) and 88 cm (women); most do physical activity; most eat vegetables and fruits; most do not take medications to control hypertension; most with a positive result for hyperglycemia at least once; most with at least one relative (first or second degree) with diabetes. Variables associated with baseline glycemia, HDL cholesterol, triglycerides, and baseline creatinine seem to have a wide dispersion; and as regards class, half of the subjects are not at risk for PD or T2D.

Cleanup

Noise. To analyze the presence of noise in the variables, Tukey's method was used to identify the ranges for outliers. They were detected in the following variables: age (4), bmi (10), waist_circumference (1), baseline_glycemia (27), postprandial_glycemia (46), ldl_cholesterol (7), total_cholesterol (9), hdl_cholesterol (11), triglycerides (21), and baseline_creatinine (8). Additionally, *far-out* outliers were found in baseline_glycemia (51), postprandial_glycemia (6), triglycerides (12), and baseline_creatinine (6).

Missing Values. Table 1 shows that there are no missing values in qualitative variables, except for family_diagnosis, with 3 records with null values. In the case of quantitative variables, the number of missing values is much greater. Fortunately, some of these quantitative variables have an associated qualitative variable that limits the range for that missing value. This occurs specifically in the cases of age, bmi, and waist_circumference. The other variables that have null values are: postprandial_glycemia, total_cholesterol, ldl_cholesterol, hdl_cholesterol, triglycerides, baseline_creatinine, and glycosylated_hemoglobin.

Table 1. Statistical overview of the dataset

Variable	# null	Metric	Result
sex	0	Male (%)	395 (32%)
		Female (%)	841 (68%)
age	564	Mean+SD	57.23±8.8428
age_range	0	Less than 45 years (%)	205 (17%)
		45–54 years (%)	435 (35%)
		54–64 years (%)	429 (34%)
		More than 64 years (%)	167 (14%)
bmi	619	Mean+SD	31.65±6.314
bmi_range	0	Less than 25kg/m2	93 (8%)
		25-30 kg/m2	319 (26%)
		More than 30 kg/m2	824 (66%9
waist_circumference	1181	Mean+SD	101.3091±13.55
waist_circumference_range	0	Less than 94/80 cm (M/F) (%)	56 (4%)
		M: 94–102 cm/F: 80-88cm (%)	205 (17%)
		M: More than 102/88cm (M/F) (%)	975 (79%)
physical_activity	0	Yes (%)	915 (74%)
		No (%)	321 (26%)
eat_fruit_vegetables	0	Yes (%)	821 (66%)
		No (%)	415 (34%)
ht_drugs	0	Yes (%)	497 (40%)
		No (%)	739 (60%)
hyperglycemia	0	Yes (%)	999 (81%)
		No (%)	237 (19%)
family_diagnosis	3	No (%)	395 (32%)
		First degree (%)	412 (33%)
		Second degree (%)	426 (34%)
baseline_glycemia	0	Mean+SD	104.36±27.28
postprandial_glycemia	55	Mean+SD	119.59±42.51
total_cholesterol	705	Mean+SD	198.28±41.1
ldl_cholesterol	715	Mean+SD	119.79±36.82
hdl_cholesterol	706	Mean+SD	49.82±14.40
triglycerides	705	Mean+SD	151.4±95.59
baseline_creatinine	619	Mean+SD	1.117±5.8
glycated_hemoglobine	635	Mean+SD	5.61±0.43
ogtt_result	0	No risk (%)	620 (50%)
		Prediabetes (%)	480 (38%)
		Diabetes (%)	136 (12%)

Transformations

Treatment of Outliers. Medical experts were consulted about the occurrence of outliers in lab tests. It was concluded that, even if these values in the database are statistically atypical, they are within the possible range for their respective tests. There is only one exception - 2 values in `baseline_creatinine` (85 and 118) that are quite likely upload errors. Therefore, those two specific values were replaced with null values.

Treatment of Missing Values. This task has two options: (1) removing variables with missing values; or (2) deleting records with null variables. The first option allows us to keep sample size at the cost of reducing the number of input variables for the models. The second option allows us to keep the number of features at the cost of reducing sample size. It was decided to select Option 2 only for the `family_diagnosis` variable, which has only 3 null values. Option 1 was applied to the variables `age`, `bmi` and `waist_circumference`, considering that there is an associated qualitative variable for each one of them that allows us to know its approximate value. All other variables will be discussed in Sect. 3.2.

Aggregation of Class Variable. Table 1 shows that the distribution of classes is not balanced (`ogtt_result`). To minimize the impact of this issue, a new class variable is created that splits subjects at risk of having PD or T2D (records with a value of "PD" or "T2D") and those who are risk-free (records with a value of "Normal"). As a result, the variable is balanced in terms of the number of occurrences of each value, simplifying subsequent analyses as it now becomes a binary classification problem. However, caution should be used when analyzing the results, especially concerning the prediction of T2D, as it is the least common.

Variable Removal. `ogtt_result` was discarded in the previous section, and `postprandial_glycemia` was excluded because any subject with that variable would require an OGTT and, in that case, using the proposed models would be meaningless.

Correlation Analyses. Figure 1 shows the correlation matrix obtained for the initial dataset. Clinically, it makes sense that there is a weak linear correlation between waist circumference range and BMI range. The weak correlation between age, BMI, and waist circumference ranges and their associated values for `age`, `bmi`, and `waist_circumference` is also expected. On the other hand, `total_cholesterol` is calculated from `ldl_cholesterol` [3], which explains the strong correlation between these two variables. Additionally, the relationship between `baseline_glycemia`, `postprandial_glycemia`, `ogtt_result` and, `class` is also to be expected, since the first two determine the value of the third, which in turn is grouped to generate the fourth.

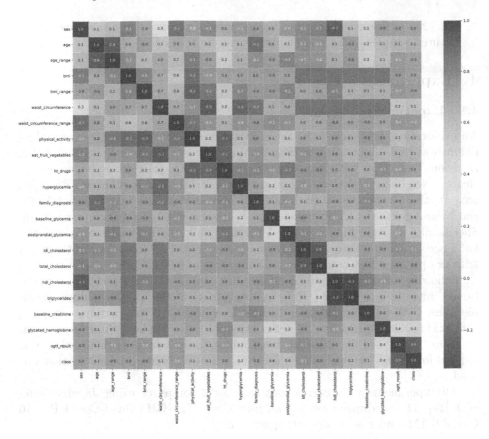

Fig. 1. Correlation matrix for the initial dataset

3.2   Proposed Segmentations

Given the high percentage of missing values in lab variables, the possibility of generating several datasets from the original by applying different criteria for the treatment of null records was considered:

- Clinical and Lab Dataset (CLD-bin). All complete records were elimi-nated, resulting in 16 variables with 503 examples (229 ⇒ No risk, 274 ⇒ At risk). This dataset keeps all available variables (clinical data and lab data) at the cost of losing many records.
- Clinical and baseline Glycemia Dataset (CGD-bin).   This   dataset keeps all available clinical information and the only lab variable that does not have null values (baseline_glycemia); the rest of the variables were removed. Thus, this dataset has 10 variables and 1233 examples. In contrast to CLD, CGD preserves the number of records as opposed to lab variables value.
- Clinical Dataset (CD-bin). This dataset keeps all available clinical infor-mation and removes all lab variables. Thus, this dataset includes 9 variables

and 1233 examples, preserving the number of records. By discarding all lab features, simpler and cost-free models can be trained.

4   Experimental Results

4.1   Experimental Design

An exploration, preprocessing, training, and evaluation process of various algorithms was carried out using *scikit-learn*. In particular, Logistic Regression (LR), Decision Tree (DT) with `max_depth` $= 5$ and `class_weight` = `balanced`, k-Nearest Neighbor (kNN) with `n_neighbors` $= 7$, and Random Forest (RF) with `max_depth` = 2 were considered. Likewise, TensorFlow was used to build Artificial Neural Networks (ANN) models with `epochs` = 60 and `batch_size` = 16. Specifically, a single hidden layer ANN was built, with 100 neurons and the `ReLU` activation function, and L2 regularization $= 0.1$ to control overfitting. An `Adamax` optimizer was used with a learning rate of 0.001.

Following common guidelines in the area, the dataset was partitioned into two: training (70%) and evaluation (30%). To reduce possible biases, the cross-validation technique with stratified random sampling (`StratifiedShuffleSplit, n_splits=50` [24]) was applied. Since input variables are expressed in different magnitudes, a *min-max* normalization was applied for all models except for the ANN, where a standard normalization was used.

All experiments were carried out on a local computer using *Jupyter Notebook* [17]. The hardware used was an Intel Core i7 2.6 GHz Quad-Core CPU, 16 GB of RAM, and macOS operating system.

4.2   Models and Results for `CLD-bin`

Table 2 shows the performance metrics for the different models applied to the `CLD-bin` dataset, considering "At risk" as a positive class. As it can be seen, 3 of the 5 models yield accuracy values greater than 90%, which means that approximately 9 out of 10 of the total records evaluated were classified correctly (deviations are less than 2%). Of these 3 options, RF is the one that yields the best accuracy, followed by DT, and finally ANN. While the performance of LR is close to the previous ones with 86% accuracy, that of kNN is poor, reaching only 72%.

As regards precision, the values are consistent with those of accuracy. RF, DT and ANN yield values above 90% for the class of interest ("At risk"), which means that, with any of the options, more than 9 in 10 people are correctly told they are at risk. Similarly, these 3 models have recall values close to 91%, which means that only 1 in 10 people who are at risk is not identified.

Finally, when selecting a specific model, AUC values can be of interest, in addition to accuracy. In this case, it can be seen that RL displaces ANN as one of the 3 models with the highest AUC values, compared to those with the best accuracy.

Table 2. Results (evaluation) for the models applied to CLD-bin (positive class = "At risk")

Model	Accuracy	Precision	Recall	F-score	AUC
RF	94.58 ± 1.51	98.87 ± 1.3	91.1 ± 2.93	94.79 ± 1.53	0.95
DT	93.42 ± 1.59	96.02 ± 2.02	91.73 ± 2.65	93.79 ± 1.53	0.94
ANN	91.13 ± 1.98	92.29 ± 2.68	91.39 ± 2.77	91.79 ± 1.84	0.91
LR	85.56 ± 3.21	90.5 ± 3.11	82.1 ± 4.81	86.01 ± 3.3	0.93
kNN	71.62 ± 3.82	75.53 ± 3.87	70.83 ± 5.75	72.97 ± 4	0.72

Table 3. Results (evaluation) for the models applied to CGD-bin (positive class = "At risk")

Model	Accuracy	Precision	Recall	F-score	AUC
RF	93.23 ± 1.12	100 ± 0	86.38 ± 2.25	92.68 ± 1.3	0.93
DT	91.88 ± 1.67	96.68 ± 2.74	86.72 ± 2.2	91.39 ± 1.73	0.92
ANN	91.04 ± 1.63	94.45 ± 2.47	87.17 ± 2.31	90.64 ± 1.71	0.91
LR	75.66 ± 4.37	80.96 ± 4.44	66.7 ± 6.55	73.05 ± 5.3	0.83
kNN	69.97 ± 2.01	70.63 ± 2.32	67.92 ± 3.29	69.2 ± 2.23	0.7

4.3   Models and Results for CGD-bin

Table 3 shows the performance metrics for the different models applied to the CGD-bin dataset, considering "At risk" as a positive class. As with CLD-bin, RF, DT, and ANN yielded very good accuracy values, greater than 90% (deviations below 2%). kNN once again has a poor performance with 70% accuracy, while LR is between the previous 3 and kNN, although its performance is lower than with the previous dataset.

In terms of precision, RF overfits and obtains 100% for the "At Risk" class. DT and ANN yield values above 90% for the same class, with LR and kNN being well below this value. When analyzing recall values, RF, DT and, ANN are the models that achieve the best values, being close to 90% for the class of interest.

Finally, and unlike CLD-bin, the 3 models that obtain the highest AUC values are the same as the ones that achieve the best accuracy.

4.4   Models and Results for CD-bin

Table 4 shows the performance metrics for the different models applied to the CD-bin dataset, considering "At risk" as a positive class. Unlike the previous cases, the models present poor performances, reaching accuracy values from 54% to 57%. Moreover, the values presented for precision, recall, and F-score are along the same lines or worse. This means that the prediction is not much better than just flipping a coin.

Table 4. Results (evaluation) for the models applied to CD-bin (positive class = "At risk")

Model	Accuracy	Precision	Recall	F-score
RF	57.33 ± 1.93	63.77 ± 4.13	33.42 ± 4.84	43.61 ± 4.06
DT	54.98 ± 2.47	55.3 ± 3.07	51.16 ± 9.03	52.67 ± 5.01
ANN	57.55 ± 2.07	58.61 ± 3.06	51.05 ± 6.43	54.27 ± 3.71
LR	57.16 ± 2.32	60.88 ± 4.27	39.92 ± 5.25	47.94 ± 3.81
kNN	54.55 ± 2.45	54.45 ± 2.53	53.32 ± 4.79	53.77 ± 3.03

4.5   Discussion

Some of the models developed were able to achieve very good performances for both datasets. In particular, RF, DT, and ANN demonstrated great classification power, with high values in the considered metrics. In this sense, it should be noted that the proposed models are not intended to replace OGTT for the diagnosis of T2D and PD. As early detection is difficult for these diseases, the models are aimed at identifying individuals in the Argentine population who have a high probability of being affected and are unaware of their condition. To confirm the diagnosis, individuals identified as positive will eventually have to take an OGTT. The models would help identify those who should take the test and would make up for the lack of this type of tool.

It can be observed that there are no significant differences between the best accuracy and F-score values achieved for CLD-bin and CGD-bin datasets. Even though it is not (entirely) correct to compare results from models trained with different datasets, this issue could have an impact on the cost of putting the models into practice, considering that obtaining lab variables is neither free nor easy. To throw some light on this, a larger number of records without null values would be required.

Concerning the above, removing all lab features would lead to a simpler, cost-free model, that could be carried out at any time. Unfortunately, the performance results show that it is not feasible with the current CD-bin dataset. In that sense, it can be appreciated the great influence of the variable baseline_glycemia on the success of the prediction, probably due to the limited size of the dataset. Again, more records could compensate for the absence of lab variables.

Finally, it should also be taken into account that grouping PD and T2D into a single class favored balancing and simplified the problem by turning it into a binary classification. The cost of this decision is not being able to differentiate between PD and T2D. However, from a medical point of view, this would not be so relevant since, at the end of the day, the goal is to identify individuals at risk, regardless of which of the two conditions affects them.

5 Conclusions and Future Work

Considering that T2D and PD are difficult to detect, specific predictive models were developed and evaluated for the Argentine population based on the PPDBA database. Firstly, the database was carefully preprocessed, which led to the generation of three datasets (CLD-bin, CGD-bin, and CD-bin) with different approaches about the compromise between the number of variables and available records. Then, 5 different classification models were applied to each of them. The results obtained show that some of the models proposed were able to achieve very good performances for the first two datasets. In particular, RF, DT and ANN demonstrated great classification power, with high values for the metrics under consideration. In the opposite sense, removing all lab features led to poor performance results. Due to database limitations, the results are not conclusive, but they are promising. Given the lack of this type of tool in Argentina, this work represents the first step towards more sophisticated models.

Some of the future lines of work are:

- Obtaining more database records to improve its quality and representativeness, and then replicating the study carried out.
- Considering the usage of additional supervised learning methods (like Support Vector Machines) and the hyper-parameter tuning of all trained models.
- Analyzing the development of multiclass classification models to separate T2D and PD cases.

Funding Information. This study was partially supported by PICT-2020-SERIEA-00901.

References

1. Professional practice committee: Standards of medical care in diabetes–2021. Diabetes Care **44**(Supplement 1), S3–S3 (2021). https://doi.org/10.2337/dc21-Sppc. https://care.diabetesjournals.org/content/44/Supplement_1/S3
2. Al Jarullah, A.A.: Decision tree discovery for the diagnosis of type ii diabetes. In: 2011 International Conference on Innovations in Information Technology, pp. 303–307, April 2011. https://doi.org/10.1109/INNOVATIONS.2011.5893838
3. Association, A.H.: What Your Cholesterol Levels Mean (2020). https://www.heart.org/en/health-topics/cholesterol/about-cholesterol/what-your-cholesterol-levels-mean. accedido: 2022-10-10
4. Bolin, K., Gip, C., Mörk, A.C., Lindgren, B.: Diabetes, healthcare cost and loss of productivity in sweden 1987 and 2005 - a register-based approach. Diabetic Med. J. British Diabetic Assoc. **26**, 928–34 (2009). https://doi.org/10.1111/j.1464-5491.2009.02786.x
5. Choi, S.B., et al.: Screening for prediabetes using machine learning models. Comput. Math. Methods Med. **2014** (2014)
6. Dey, S.K., Hossain, A., Rahman, M.M.: Implementation of a web application to predict diabetes disease: an approach using machine learning algorithm. In: 2018 21st International Conference of Computer and Information Technology (ICCIT), pp. 1–5 (2018). https://doi.org/10.1109/ICCITECHN.2018.8631968

7. Diabetes Prevention Program Research Group: Reduction in the incidence of type 2 diabetes with lifestyle intervention or metformin. N. Engl. J. Med. **346**(6), 393–403 (2002). https://doi.org/10.1056/NEJMoa012512
8. Dinh, A., Miertschin, S., Young, A., Mohanty, S.D.: A data-driven approach to predicting diabetes and cardiovascular disease with machine learning. BMC Med. Inform. Decis. Mak. **19**(1), 211 (2019). https://doi.org/10.1186/s12911-019-0918-5
9. Eddy, D.M., Schlessinger, L., Kahn, R.: Clinical outcomes and cost-effectiveness of strategies for managing people at high risk for diabetes. Annal. Internal Med. **143**(4), 251–264 (2005). https://doi.org/10.7326/0003-4819-143-4-200508160-00006
10. Federación Internacional de Diabetes: Atlas de la diabetes de la fid. Technical report, Federación Internacional de Diabetes (2017). https://diabetesatlas.org/resources/2017-atlas.html
11. Gagliardino, J.J., et al.: Cómo tratar mi diabetes. Buenos Aires, Argentina, 3 edn., November 2016
12. Gagliardino, J.J., et al.: Prevención primaria de diabetes tipo 2 en argentina: estudio piloto en la provincia de buenos aires. Rev. Argent. Endocrinol. Metab. **53**(4), 135–141 (2016). https://doi.org/10.1016/j.raem.2016.11.002
13. Hashi, E.K., Zaman, M.S.U., Hasan, M.R.: An expert clinical decision support system to predict disease using classification techniques. In: 2017 International Conference on Electrical, Computer and Communication Engineering (ECCE), pp. 396–400, February 2017. https://doi.org/10.1109/ECACE.2017.7912937
14. Heikes, K.E., Eddy, D.M., Arondekar, B., Schlessinger, L.: Diabetes risk calculator. Diabetes Care **31**(5), 1040–1045 (2008). https://doi.org/10.2337/dc07-1150
15. Ilango, B.S., Ramaraj, N.: A hybrid prediction model with f-score feature selection for type ii diabetes databases. In: Proceedings of the 1st Amrita ACM-W Celebration on Women in Computing in India, pp. 13:1–13:4. ACM, New York (2010). https://doi.org/10.1145/1858378.1858391
16. Jayanthi, N., Babu, B.V., Rao, N.S.: Survey on clinical prediction models for diabetes prediction. J. Big Data **4**(1), 26 (2017). https://doi.org/10.1186/s40537-017-0082-7
17. Jupyter Notebook Documentation: 7.0.0rc2 documentation. https://jupyter-notebook.readthedocs.io/en/latest/index.html. accedido: 2023-04-18
18. Kaur, H., Kumari, V.: Predictive modelling and analytics for diabetes using a machine learning approach. Appl. Comput. Inf. (2018). https://doi.org/10.1016/j.aci.2018.12.004
19. Maniruzzaman, M., Kumar, N., Menhazul Abedin, M., Shaykhul Islam, M., Suri, H.S., El-Baz, A.S., Suri, J.S.: Comparative approaches for classification of diabetes mellitus data: machine learning paradigm. CMPB **152**, 23–34 (2017). https://doi.org/10.1016/j.cmpb.2017.09.004
20. Meng, X.H., Huang, Y.X., Rao, D.P., Zhang, Q., Liu, Q.: Comparison of three data mining models for predicting diabetes or prediabetes by risk factors. Kaohsiung J. Med. Sci. **29**(2), 93–99 (2013). https://doi.org/10.1016/j.kjms.2012.08.016
21. Mercaldo, F., Nardone, V., Santone, A.: Diabetes mellitus affected patients classification and diagnosis through machine learning techniques. Procedia Comput. Sci. **112**, 2519–2528 (2017). https://doi.org/10.1016/j.procs.2017.08.193
22. Mir, A., Dhage, S.N.: Diabetes disease prediction using machine learning on big data of healthcare. In: 2018 Fourth International Conference on Computing Communication Control and Automation (ICCUBEA), pp. 1–6 (2018). https://doi.org/10.1109/ICCUBEA.2018.8697439

23. Rucci, E., Tittarelli, G., Ronchetti, F., , Elgart, J., Lanzarini, L., Gagliardino, J.J.: Primeras experiencias en la identificación de personas con riesgo de diabetes en la población argentina utilizando técnicas de aprendizaje automático. In: Actas del XXIX Congreso Argentino de Ciencias de la Computación (CACIC 2023), pp. 146–158 (2023)
24. Scikit-Learn: 3.1. Cross-validation: evaluating estimator performance. https://scikit-learn.org/stable/modules/cross_validation.html. accedido: 2023-04-11
25. Sisodia, D., Sisodia, D.S.: Prediction of diabetes using classification algorithms. Procedia Comput. Sci. **132**, 1578–1585 (2018). https://doi.org/10.1016/j.procs.2018.05.122
26. Sneha, N., Gangil, T.: Analysis of diabetes mellitus for early prediction using optimal features selection. J. Big Data **6**(1), 13 (2019). https://doi.org/10.1186/s40537-019-0175-6
27. Tuomilehto, J., Lindström, J., Eriksson, J.G., Valle, T.T., Hämäläinen, H., Ilanne-Parikka, P., Keinänen-Kiukaanniemi, S., Laakso, M., Louheranta, A., Rastas, M., Salminen, V., Aunola, S., Cepaitis, Z., Moltchanov, V., Hakumäki, M., Mannelin, M., Martikkala, V., Sundvall, J., Uusitupa, M.: Prevention of type 2 diabetes mellitus by changes in lifestyle among subjects with impaired glucose tolerance. N. Engl. J. Med. **344**(18), 1343–1350 (2001). https://doi.org/10.1056/NEJM200105033441801
28. Vistisen, D., Kivimäki, M., Perreault, L., Hulman, A., Witte, D.R., Brunner, E.J., Tabák, A., Jørgensen, M.E., Færch, K.: Reversion from prediabetes to normoglycaemia and risk of cardiovascular disease and mortality: the whitehall ii cohort study. Diabetologia **62**(8), 1385–1390 (2019). https://doi.org/10.1007/s00125-019-4895-0
29. Wei, S., Zhao, X., Miao, C.: A comprehensive exploration to the machine learning techniques for diabetes identification. In: 2018 IEEE 4th World Forum on Internet of Things (WF-IoT), pp. 291–295 (2018). https://doi.org/10.1109/WF-IoT.2018.8355130
30. Williams, R., Van Gaal, L., Lucioni, C.: Assessing the impact of complications on the costs of type ii diabetes. Diabetologia **45**(1), S13–S17 (2002). https://doi.org/10.1007/s00125-002-0859-9
31. Wu, H., Yang, S., Huang, Z., He, J., Wang, X.: Type 2 diabetes mellitus prediction model based on data mining. Inf. Med. Unlocked **10**, 100–107 (2018). https://doi.org/10.1016/j.imu.2017.12.006
32. Xie, Z., Nikolayeva, O., Luo, J., Li, D.: Building risk prediction models for type 2 diabetes using machine learning techniques. Prev. Chronic Dis. **16**, E130–E130 (2019). https://doi.org/10.5888/pcd16.190109
33. Yu, W., Liu, T., Valdez, R., Gwinn, M., Khoury, M.J.: Application of support vector machine modeling for prediction of common diseases: the case of diabetes and pre-diabetes. BMC Med. Inform. Decis. Mak. **10**(1), 16 (2010). https://doi.org/10.1186/1472-6947-10-16
34. Yuvaraj, N., SriPreethaa, K.R.: Diabetes prediction in healthcare systems using machine learning algorithms on hadoop cluster. Clust. Comput. **22**(1), 1–9 (2019). https://doi.org/10.1007/s10586-017-1532-x
35. Zou, Q., Qu, K., Luo, Y., Yin, D., Ju, Y., Tang, H.: Predicting diabetes mellitus with machine learning techniques. Front. Genet. **9**, 515–515 (2018). https://doi.org/10.3389/fgenc.2018.00515

Hardware Architectures, Networks, and Operating Systems

Case Study: Methodology for the Design and Development of Distributed Embedded Systems

Ing. Luis Orlando Ventre[✉], Ing. Orlando Micolini, Ing. Mauricio Ludemann, Ing. Agustín Carranza, David D'Andrea, and Enzo Candotti

Computer Architecture Lab, FCEFyN-National University of Cordoba Avenue, Vélez Sarsfield 1601, 5000 Córdoba, Argentina
{luis.ventre,orlando.micolini,mauri.ludemann}@unc.edu.ar

Abstract. This project introduces a methodology that is applied to the design and development of an embedded and distributed access control system. This methodology makes it easier to decouple logic, conflict resolution policy, and actions, resulting in a modular, simple, maintainable, formal, and flexible system. In addition, formal verification of logic is achieved at all stages of development. To model the logic of the system, petri nets are used and converted into executable code using the generalized equation of state. This solution manages to preserve the verified properties using a mathematical formalism. A concurrency monitor is integrated into the implementation that encompasses the various software and hardware components of the system. In addition, defined interfaces are established between devices, and standard libraries and protocols are incorporated. Also, an algorithm is used to automate the determination of the number of threads and their responsibilities. This technique simplifies management and optimizes system performance. In addition, the benefits of applying the proposed methodology to the design of critical and reactive systems are highlighted. Its ease of dealing with complex problems is evident, guaranteeing the scalability and reliability of the developed system.

Keywords: Methodology · Design · Embedded Systems · Petri Nets · Distributed Systems

1 Introduction

A distributed system is a collection of independent, connected to network, compute-capable systems that appear to be a single, coherent system to their users. The main objective is to facilitate access to resources, and to share them in an efficient and controlled way. They are transparent, they hide physically distributed processes and resources. In addition, they are scalable, in terms of their size, geographical distribution and ability to keep their administration under control [1]. The objectives of this solution have been expanded beyond those presented in references [2]. In this version, a service module has been incorporated.

P. Pesado et al. (Eds.): CACIC 2023, CCIS 2123, pp. 243–253, 2024.
https://doi.org/10.1007/978-3-031-62245-8_17

In the development of embedded and distributed systems, co-design techniques are used for hardware, software, and programming languages, such as C, C++, Java, VHDL and Verilog. However, manual coding has disadvantages due to the propensity to errors, the limited maintainability and scalability, the high volatility of the requirements, and the high resources required for validation and verification through simulations and testing. In complex embedded systems, an iterative coding process is required, for the correction of errors or changes in requirements, as well as the validation and testing of prototypes; Such a methodology is only able to mitigate the absence of errors. These tasks significantly impact the time involved for system development [3].

For the development of this work, model-based design is used [4]. It is a visual and/or mathematical method for understanding and solving designs associated with complicated embedded systems. This methodology encompasses other important concepts such as "model-driven architecture" [5]. Model-based design uses models to support other stages of development such as simulation, validation, verification, and implementation.

Petri nets (PN) [6] are a modeling formalism that supports the development of model-based systems. This graphic-mathematical formalism explicitly supports and facilitates the modeling of concurrency, conflicts, shared resources, mutual exclusion, and synchronization. It is important to note that PNs have clearly defined their execution semantics and mathematical representation, supporting rigorous documentation, simulation, verification, and translation into execution code [7]. In addition, PNs are an abstract mathematical formalism so they are intrinsically independent of the platform, therefore achieving flexibility to accomplish various objectives of performance, costs, energy consumption, among others. Also, specific algorithms are used to calculate the number and responsibility of the threads needed to execute the logic.

This paper presents a case study where a methodology is used, which enables the coding automation for the control of a plant modeled with non-autonomous PN. This methodology avoids the inconveniences associated with manual coding of logic, and significantly reduces the time required for simulation and prototyping stages. Moreover, it ensures mathematical validation and verification of the logic model, implying that the specification faithfully documents the actual implementation.

2 Development

For the development of this distributed system, it is essential to define interfaces and implement standard protocols for the software modules. This, added to the mathematical formalism of the PN, collaborates in obtaining a compact, robust, and secure design.

2.1 Solution Architecture

The main objective of the proposed methodology is to decompose and decouple the system into events or stimuli, states, logic, politics, actions, and services, as shown in Fig. 1. This solution differs from the one presented in [2, 8] in that a service module has been incorporated. To do this, there have been added an interface that connects to the services, a database, and specific services, as shown in Fig. 1.

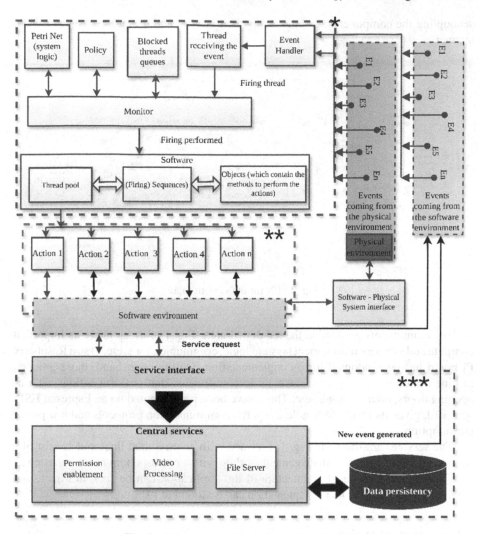

Fig. 1. Components of Low-Level Architecture

The starting point of the design is the **concurrency monitor** block labeled in Fig. 1 as *monitor*, which will be responsible for the management of critical section events, synchronization, and conflict resolution in order to determine which action to execute and when. Next, the logic of the system is established from the creation of a model for the system with a PN, which is shown in. The monitor, through the PN, will determine the possible execution actions, as shown in Fig. 1.

The system requires a policy for the resolution of PN conflicts. This component is used to decide between possible executable actions. In addition, a module for handling events and queues for storing them are required (Fig. 1). By decomposing the reactive (RS) or event-driven (EDA) system into these components, the aim is to improve the management and performance of the embedded system by simplifying its design, decoupling the components, and managing their control and execution in a centralized manner.

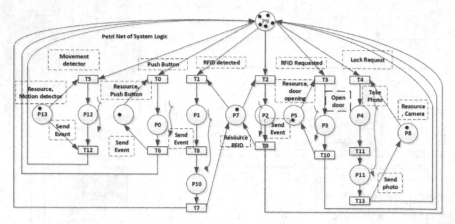

Fig. 2. PN for the system logic

The components grouped in the red dotted area (Fig. 1) correspond to an important compute and memory requirement (system logic, communications, etc.).) so a Raspberry PI board has been adopted for its implementation. On the other hand, those grouped in blue dotted lines (Fig. 1) correspond to components that perform actions such as opening doors, taking images, etc. These have been implemented on an Espressif ESP-32 board, given its ability to handle I/O ports, communication protocols and low power consumption.

The services are shown in Fig. 1, enclosed with green dotted lines and consist of a service interface, a service management module with a corresponding data persistence.

The resulting low-level architecture of the application can be seen in Fig. 1, and detailed information on its implementation can be found at [9].

2.2 Component Design

Throughout the design of the architecture, it was picked one based on events and services, considering that Raspberry Pi is a platform with limited resources, mainly in memory usage.

For communications, in the first instance, the MQTT protocol was chosen as a communication mechanism between the ESP32-CAM devices and the Raspberry PI, due to its advantages such as simplicity and lightness. It was later discarded in favor of HTTP, as MQTT in Python only supports asynchronous communication, which adds complexity and overhead to the design.

In general, Espressif [10] provides an ESP32 development kit board, which offers a software framework containing multiple libraries and resources. This environment has an implementation of the pthreads library. This was used in a timely manner for the development of the monitor using already proven designs. Details of this implementation can be found at [11]. The policy for waking up the threads of each queue was delegated to the FreeRTOS scheduler.

The calculation of the number of threads and their responsibility was determined with the algorithms explained in [7], for which the PN of Fig. 2 was used, resulting in the collection of threads shown there.

The framework also provides implementations for HTTP clients and servers that were used to build the functionality of each endpoint.

Figure 3 (a) describes the module-level architecture. The API-Gateway module serves as an entry point for client queries, provides reverse proxy features, and centralizes authentication settings. As part of the security mechanisms, although secure protocols are implemented in the REST API of the ESP32-CAM, clients never have access to it, except through the central API.

2.2.1 GUI Subsystem

A graphical interface was implemented using the Django framework combined with bootstrap4. From this interface, it is possible to reach the service layer and, consequently, trigger the monitor's events. Five types of events are considered: (1) Opening the door via the web: this event is caused when a user, previously logged into the system, uses the "Open door" button. (2) Ringing the doorbell: This event occurs when a person presses the push button located on the outside, next to the door. (3) Motion detection: this event corresponds to the identification of the presence of a body in the vicinity of the door at a given time. (4) Access Denied: When an RFID code is detected, which is not associated with an active user. (5) Access Allowed: This event happens when a user (registered in the system) opens the door using the RFID fob.

The following critical data was selected to be stored: (1) Date, time, and image capture of the events occurring next to the entrances (doors). (2) User who caused the event, so identification attempts are possible. (3) Time slot for the motion sensor to be activated, so modifying the detection schedule for this type of events is configurable. (4) Storage time: to modify the period in which the events remain saved, depending on the storage capacity of the system (the longer the time, the more events are stored).

2.2.2 Database subsystem

The design has a non-relational MongoDB database [12] that was chosen due to the low coupling of the entities, the transparency between the Python dictionaries and the documents, and the good performance for storing small files (images in our case).

The choice of MongoDB as a database had a direct impact on the web environment. The integration of MongoDB with Django presents a special scenario due to the flexibility of Django's ORM (Object-Relational Mapping), which is normally associated with relational databases. However, thanks to the Djongo plugin, it was possible to adapt the ORM to work with MongoDB effectively. Djongo acts as an interface between the Django framework and the MongoDB database, allowing the mapping of Python objects to MongoDB documents in a seamless manner. One of the main advantages of using Djongo is the simplification of the query construction process and eases a straightforward storage of data in JSON format.

To ensure data redundancy and assure uninterrupted data access, a passive replication-as-a-service system was implemented within the Raspberry. This approach required fewer resources compared to other solutions and allowed for greater control over the scheduling of synchronization between databases.

The performance of MongoDB running on the Raspberry PI platform had some limitations Fig. 3 (b), both in the versions available for the ARM architecture and in performance.

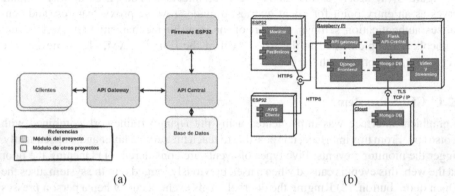

(a)   (b)

Fig. 3. High-Level Architecture Components and Deployment Diagram

2.2.3 System Logic Management subsystem

This subsystem manages the concurrency of events and actions handling a monitor implemented as an object, as shown in Fig. 4 (a). The monitor is used to synchronize and coordinate access to shared resources between multiple threads or system processes. It acts as a data protection mechanism, ensuring that only one thread or process can access a shared resource at a time. This prevents problems such as simultaneous read/write, race conditions, and other concurrency conflicts.

Furthermore, we have used an object containing the Petri net, as shown in Fig. 4 (a). Since PN models the logic of the system, the system logic and the policies are isolated from the actions to be executed by the rest of the system. In addition, a 'queues' object has been added to suspend threads when the resource is unavailable, or synchronization is required Fig. 4 (b). Figure 4 (b) illustrates the exchange of messages for logic management.

This module was specifically designed to handle system logic running on ESP32-CAM boards.

2.2.4 Central API subsystem

The **critical component** of this project is the **Central API**. This is a **REST API** that acts as an intermediary between the ESP32 module logic, the database, and the frontend. In this module, the specific logic of each endpoint has also been implemented in cases where it was not possible to include it directly in the ESP32.

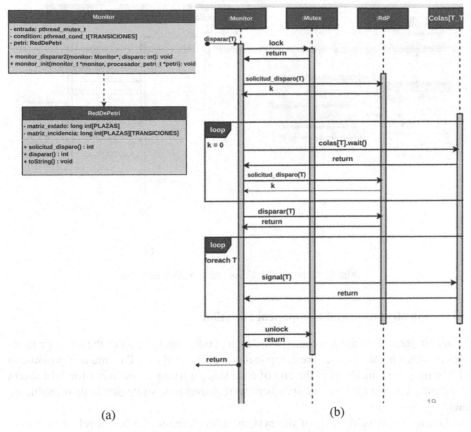

(a)   (b)

Fig. 4. Monitor class and sequence diagram

The main objects that implement it are Client, FlaskAPP, and MongoClass. Their methods are shown in Fig. 5 (a).

The Central API has been designed in a **decoupled manner**, which allows new functionality to be added without affecting other parts of the system. Its main objective is **to ease the design and construction of interfaces** between the modules: frontend, database and ESP32. To achieve this, it exposes the required endpoints for the REST API. Figure 5 (b) shows the exchange of messages to handle a request.

This API provides **standard** interfaces for the intercommunication of modules. For example: (1) Capture images when reading a RFID fob, with timestamp addition. (2) Capture of images when motion (sensor) is detected near an entrance door, for a schedule set by the user. (3) Registration of access attempts with disallowed RFID fobs. (4) Service to capture images by pressing the push button, with timestamp. (5) Activation of a bell inside the room by pressing the push button (doorbell).

In short, the Central API is essential for smooth communication between the different components of the system and ensures their coordinated operation.

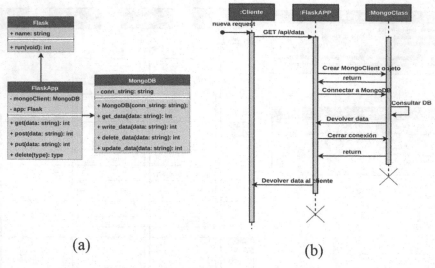

(a)   (b)

Fig. 5. Central API. Class and sequence diagram

2.3 Implementation and Component Selection

Using an iterative method, the analysis, design, coding and testing of the software modules and the choice of hardware components were carried out. This made it possible to obtain functional modules at the end of each stage, serving as the basis for subsequent iterations. The last of these occurs when the requirements, strategically distributed, are met.

During the development of the system, after defining the low-level architecture, the selection of hardware components was carried out. For the implementation of the core hardware, the following options were considered: Raspberry Pi, Orange Pi, Nvidia Jetson, Odroid, BeagleBone and Arduino. After analyzing the alternatives and with the criterion of lowest cost, simplicity of use, support, and compatibility with the remaining modules, Raspberry Pi was selected.

To implement the edge subsystem (next to doors), it was leveraged the availability of the ESP32-CAM boards in the Laboratory of Computer Architecture in FCEFyN, UNC, which has several advantages such as its low cost, large number of input/output ports, availability of GPIOs and video ports.

As for the choice of programming language, Python was chosen because it is a high-level language that enables fast and efficient development. Although it is true that its performance is lower compared to other languages such as Java, C++ or Go, in this case speed is not the main priority.

Regarding the selection of the framework for the development of the REST API, the two most used options for the development of web applications in Python were evaluated, which are: Flask and Django. For this implementation, we decided to use Flask because it offers greater flexibility and an easy learning curve compared to Django for new developments. For the selection of the IDE/Framework after analyzing the properties of

Arduino, Espressif, Mongoose SO, Simba, Pumbaa and nanoFramework, Espressif was chosen since it natively implements a version of FreeRTOS compatible with multicore.

For the access peripheral, RFID 125 kHz was selected due to its high availability, which simplifies both its acquisition and replacement if needed.

As for the DC-DC power supply, a model was chosen that implements a voltmeter at the output and input with a voltage range of 1.23 – 35 V and 3A with an integrated LM2596. The remaining peripherals were selected according to their availability and with the lowest cost criterion to obtain an accessible and replicable final system.

The architecture of the edge subsystem is shown in Fig. 6 and implemented a service layer with https protocol. The build of the physical system was carried out in a generic housing where the components were assembled.

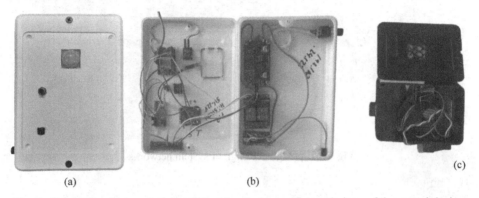

(a)   (b)   (c)

Fig. 6. External and internal views of the edge device and internal views of the central device

The resulting device, in its external view, can be seen in Fig. 6 (a): at the top the motion sensor (HC-SR501), in the left-center, a pushbutton and at the bottom the hole through which the ESP32-CAM module captures the images.

Figure 6 (b) shows the inside of this device, consisting of power plug, DC-DC LM-2596 step-down supply with voltmeter, 5V - 3V3 level converter, ESP32-CAM board with OV2640 2Mp camera, RDM6300 RFID reader module and antenna, motion sensor module, switch, and Dupont cables. In Fig. 6 (c) it is exposed the housing for the central system implemented with Raspberry PI 3b SBC Board 1GB RAM 16GB SD and passive buzzer module.

As part of the decoupling and modularization of components, those running on the Raspberry Pi Linux platform were designed to run in Docker containers [12]. With 'Dockerfile' and 'docker-compose' files, it was managed to get a system that is replicable, scalable, and fault-tolerant.

The project's repository is located at https://github.com/orgs/Proyecto-Integrador-FCEFYN/dashboard.

2.4 Network Topology

Figure 7 illustrates the network topology for the project. It is divided into two domains: one for user access to clients (web or REST) and one for ESP32-CAM devices. The central API participates in both domains by handling queries. In this way, it was possible to isolate access to the interfaces exposed by them and, in turn, increase the range of the wireless network.

The security in the access points, both in the API of the central node and in each ESP32 device, consisted of the implementation of the Basic-Auth protocol combined with HTTPS [13] plus activating the verification of PKI certificates.

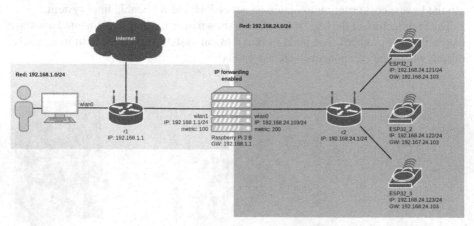

Fig. 7. Topological design of system networks

3 Results

The present paper shows the results of a case study and an application, as well as the validation, of a methodology to design and develop embedded, critical, RS and EDA systems. This methodology was able to effectively manage the complexity of design, testing, and coding. Risks were minimized and mitigated from the beginning.

A distributed access control system was obtained, capable of allowing or restricting access to certain areas according to established security parameters. Users are identified by cards or key fobs and personal data is stored at the time of registration. In addition, the system has additional security features such as configurable time restrictions, motion sensors for capturing images in unexpected situations, recording, storage, and *video streaming*, besides others.

Among the features of the system, it can be mentioned that it is *distributed* since it is implemented and supported by multiple devices and interconnected through a network, *flexible* because it is able to adapt to changes in its requirements minimizing its impact because it is completely modular, its logic has been *formally validated* due to the mathematical foundation of the PN. It is *maintainable* because it can be effectively and efficiently modified due to its modularity, according to evolutionary, corrective, or perfective needs, and it is *simple* because it allows the visualization of actions, regardless of the logic and policy that lead to the system. Therefore, a clear code is achieved without overlapping responsibilities.

References

1. Tanenbaum, A.S., van Steen, M.: Distributed systems: principles and paradigms. Prentice-Hall (2023)
2. Fernández, J.M.: Libro de actas-XXIX Congreso Argentino de Ciencias de la Computación-CACIC 2023 (2024)
3. Hobbs, C.: Embedded Software Development for Safety-Critical Systems. CRC Press (2015)
4. Weilkiens, T., Lamm, J., Roth, S., Walker, M.: Model-Based System Architecture. John Wiley & Sons (2015)
5. Roberts, C.J., Morgenstern, R.M., Israel, D.J., Borky, J.M., Bradley, T.H.: Preliminary results from a model-driven architecture methodology for development of an event-driven space communications service concept (2017)
6. Murata, T.: Petri Nets: properties, analysis and applications. In: Proceedings of the IEEE, vol. 77, no. 4, pp. 541–580 (1989)
7. Ventre, L.O., Micolini, O.: Extended petri net processor and threads quantity determination algorithm for embedded systems. In: Argentine Congress of Computer Science, pp. 199–214. Springer (2020). https://doi.org/10.1007/978-3-030-75836-3_14
8. Ventre, L.O., et al.: Caso de estudio: metodología para el diseño y desarrollo de sistemas embebidos distribuidos (2024)
9. Ventre, L.O., Micolini, O.: Algoritmos para determinar cantidad y responsabilidad de hilos en sistemas embebidos modelados con Redes de Petri S3PR. In: XXVII Congreso Argentino de Ciencias de la Computación (CACIC)(Modalidad virtual, 4 AL 8 DE OCTUBRE DE 2021.) (2022)
10. Sharp, A., Vagapov, Y.: Comparative analysis and practical implementation of the ESP32 microcontroller module for the Internet of Things (2022)
11. Melgarejo, M.i.d.M.G.: Comunicacion y Sincronizacion con Monitores Resumen del Tema. http://www.lcc.uma.es/~gallardo/temaCLASE.pdf. Accessed May 2023
12. Sharma, M.: Full stack development with MongoDB: Covers Backend, Frontend, APIs, and Mobile App Development Using PHP, NodeJS, ExpressJS, Python and React Native. BPB Publications (2022)
13. Schenker, G.N.: Learn Docker–Fundamentals of Docker 19. x: Build, test, ship, and run containers with Docker and Kubernetes. Packt Publishing Ltd. (2020)
14. mozilla.org.: Autenticación HTTP. Mozilla. https://developer.mozilla.org/es/docs/Web/HTTP/Authentication. Accessed May 2023

Innovation in Software Systems

Integration of Brain-Computer Interfaces with Alternative Augmentative Communication Systems

Javier F. Díaz, Laura A. Fava$^{(\boxtimes)}$, Ivana Harari, Fernando Martínez,
and Miguel Tellechea

Laboratorio de Investigación en Nuevas Tecnologías Informáticas -LINTI-Facultad de
Informática, Universidad Nacional de La Plata, La Plata, Buenos Aires, Argentina
`{jdiaz,lfava,iharari}@info.unlp.edu.ar`

Abstract. There are multiple systems and tools that enhance the communicative interactions, called Alternative and Augmentative Communication Systems (AACS). They are designed for people with severe speech or language difficulties. People who cannot communicate with others or that have great difficulty in doing so are usually dependent beings and suffer from social isolation. In critical situations, where no voluntary movements are available, Brain-Computer Interfaces (BCI) start to take part. BCI's are devices that allow a person to interact with a computer using only their neuronal activity. BCI's have been studied for more than 30 years, but their high error rate and the complexity of the systems have always been challenges when implementing functional real-life solutions. The current work includes a review of the BCI Emotiv Epoc, a wireless, low-end, EGC device that tries to bring medical-lab technology to the users' home, as well as the development of a custom application to connect it to two well-known AACS: Plaphons and ACAT.

Keywords: Brain-Computer Interface · BCI · Alternative and Augmentative Communication · AAC · ACAT · Plaphoon · alpha rhythm

1 Introduction

According to Escandell [1], communication is a complex activity involving various types of entities, representations and processes: the sender intentionally produces a symbolic expression and offers it as an indication of his communicative intention. The receiver, on the other hand, has to decode the linguistic expression and infer the relationship between the indicative clue and the sender's communicative intention in order to recover the representations that the sender wanted to communicate, using heuristic processes that try to find a plausible explanation from the available data. These data include individual representations, but also representations widely shared by the members of a given culture and/or social group, which largely condition the way of perceiving and reacting to the environment.

P. Pesado et al. (Eds.): CACIC 2023, CCIS 2123, pp. 257–271, 2024.
https://doi.org/10.1007/978-3-031-62245-8_18

There are several types of problems that can affect the communicative ability of a person: speech disorders (like dyslalia, dysgnosia, rhinolalia, dysphemia, tachyphemia, dysphonia or aphonia), oral language disorders (like language delay, aphasia) or written language disorders.

People who cannot communicate with others or that have great difficulty in doing so are usually dependent beings and suffer from social isolation. There are multiple systems and tools that enhance the communicative interactions, called Alternative and Augmentative Communication Systems (AACS). AACS complement oral language when all by itself is not sufficient for effective communication with the environment, and replace oral language when it is not understandable or absent.

At the same time, usage of this kind of systems can be restricted due to some physical ailment that prevents the person from using a computer with the traditional input devices (like a mouse or a keyboard). In these cases, the most common solutions consist in connecting other kinds of devices to other parts of the body, generating and adapting input devices specifically for their abilities (like webcams with movement detection or other types of image processing, especially located switches for the foot, elbows or other parts of the body).

In critical situations, where the person has no voluntary movements or they are severely restricted, Brain Computer Interfaces (BCI) enter the scene. BCIs are devices that acquire and measure brain activity, process and classify these signals to produce a digital output that can be used to perform tasks such as moving a cursor, using a computer or enabling/disabling external actuators (like steering a wheelchair) allowing the person to interact with a computer using only their neuronal activity.

The present work extends a paper presented at CACIC [2] and has two main axes: The first one centered on an analysis of different software AACS and the Emotiv Epoc BCI, and the second on the development of a prototype that integrates the BCI with two well-known AACS: Plaphoons and ACAT. Also, it explains the difficulties found and the main solutions developed to achieve this complex process.

2 Motivation

BCI's have been studied for the last 30 years with the main objective of providing assistive technology for people with severe physical functional diversity, but the complexity, slowness and the high error rate have been challenges when implementing real-life solutions. The recent progress in biosensor technology and computing scale and performance have improved the position of BCIs, making them not only viable as assistive technologies but also plausible of being used as everyday artifacts. They have transcended the limits of the lab and experimental technology and are now offered as commercial home-products or even toys. The progress in cognitive neuroscience, signal processing and pattern recognition, and multidisciplinary works are inspiring new modes of brain-computer interaction. But, for them to be effectively used in everyday life, at work or at home, they need to be small, transportable, unobtrusive, easy to use and error free.

During the last few years, we interviewed people from different organizations focused on the assistance and integration of people with different physical ailments and functional diversity, and we reached the conclusion that there's a severe lack of information regarding these technologies, their possibilities and the solutions they can provide, specifically about brain-computer interaction. Is difficult to find public or private institutions that develop new hardware, software or that contribute systematized knowledge about existing solutions.

In this context the motivation of the present work is to stimulate the development of these technologies in our near community through our university, the consolidation and systematization of knowledge about existing technologies with a multidisciplinary approach, collaborating with different institutions of our city.

3   Alternative and Augmentative Communication

As we stated earlier, there are several oral language disorders, cognitive or physical restrictions and sensory functional diversity that may affect the communicative ability of a person, and there isn't a generalized solution that works for every person.

Tamarit [3] defines AACS as logopedic instruments for people with different language or communication disorders; their objective is teaching a structured set of non-linguistic codes that would provide the person with the means to communicate spontaneously and autonomously in combination or not with other vocal or non-vocal codes. It uses different types of expression than traditionally spoken or written language and their purpose is to augment or counteract the difficulties in linguistic capacity of people with functional diversity [4].

AACS are systems and tools that enhance the communicative interactions, complement oral language when all by itself is not sufficient for effective communication with the environment, and replace oral language when it is not understandable or completely absent. AACS use different types of expression than traditionally spoken or written language and their purpose is to augment or counteract the difficulties in linguistic capacity of people with functional diversity.

The first categorization we can establish is differentiating Augmentative from Alternative Communication. The first one refers to systems designed to enhance a person's speech ability. The other one refers to systems designed to replace speech.

Based on the kind of external support the system needs, there are 2 types of communication possible: Communication with help and communication without help.

Communication without help occurs when the communication act is performed with the person's own body, without assistance of external object or medium. These kinds of systems are more frequently used by people with some kind of sensory functional diversity, like blindness or deafness. The most common communicative systems in this category are sign language, lip-facial reading and the Braille system.

In the present work we will center in Systems that provide Communication with help. Particularly, we will analyze Plaphoons [5], a well-known and free application made by Jordi Lagares Rosset; and ACAT [6], a free, open-source, suite of applications specially developed by Intel for the physicist Stephen Hawking.

3.1 Plaphoons

Plaphoons is a communication system that allows the user to create and use plaphoons which are graphical communication boards. These plaphoons can have images, letters or numbers to express actions, needs or feelings (see Fig. 1 (a)).

Fig. 1. (a) Plaphoons application board - (b) Plaphoons configuration

The system provides several ways of interacting with the plaphoon, from printing to use it without a computer to different automatic screen sweeping configuration and actuators. When the user activates any of the items in the board, the system uses the text-to-speech facilities to read out loud the selection.

It is a configurable system as is shown in the Fig. 1(b) for different visual needs. The activation can be done using the mouse, the keyboard or the touch screen and also allows plugging in alternative actuators like the webcam, a microphone or a keyboard (switch). It includes a word predictor based on a predefined static dictionary.

Although it is not open sourced, it has all the basic means to adapt the system for a wide range of needs. Also, it is flexible and easy to use for non-technical people.

3.2 ACAT

ACAT stands for Assistive Context-Aware Toolkit, is an open source platform developed by researchers at Intel Labs to enable people with motor neuron diseases and other disabilities to easily communicate with others through keyboard simulation, word prediction and speech synthesis. Users can perform a range of tasks such as editing, managing documents, navigating the Web and accessing emails, using a single Keyboard event (by default, F12 key press).

In Fig. 2 (a) we can see its two main features: the Talk window (where the user writes what they want the system to read out loud), the Alphabet Scanner (where the user selects either a word from the text predictor or a letter from the alphabet to be added to the text). It gives access to other main features: to control the window that is in focus, to access to mouse controls that allows the user to perform a graphical scan of the screen in various directions to precisely position the mouse and then send several mouse events, to access the app launcher, window switcher, basic file management actions or the Lecture Manager used to deliver speeches.

ACAT also provides ACAT Vision, which acts as a virtual switch using face-tracking and movement detection algorithms on different parts of the face that can be used via an inexpensive webcam (see Fig. 2. (b)). ACAT is open sourced and provides extensive

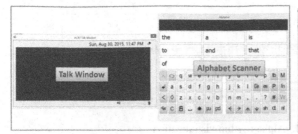

Fig. 2. (a) ACAT application board - (b) ACAT detected gesture region

and complex features, so that it can be difficult to configure, setup or extend correctly for non-technical users.

4 Brain-Computer Interfaces

A Brain-Computer Interface is a device that allows direct communication between the brain and a computer based on the brain's electrical activity. Nicolas-Alonso and Gomez-Gil [7] defined brain–computer interface (BCI) as a hardware and software communications strategy that empowers humans to interact with their surroundings with no inclusion of peripheral nerves or muscles by utilizing control signals produced from electroencephalographic activity.

By observing and mapping the brain electrical activity to images it is possible to identify patterns, zones in charge of certain cognitive processes. One of the more used and less invasive techniques to observe these is the electroencephalography (EEG) [8]. EEG records voltage fluctuations due to the flow of ionic current during synaptic excitations in the neurons of the brain [9]. They are recorded using electrodes attached to the scalp. Series of the reading of an electrode are called brain signals.

EEG is a non-invasive technique, is not expensive, and has a very good temporal resolution in the order of milliseconds.. It has two main drawbacks: the first is that it has poor spatial resolution as each electrode measures the activity of a big number of neurons; the second is that the signal quality tends to be noisy as it needs to pass through bone and skin and is easily interfered by external electro-magnetic radiation.

Anyway, these characteristics have made EEG the most popular modality among the BCI research community. The EEG brain signals can be categorized according to frequency bands: Delta (from 0.5Hz to 4Hz), Theta (from 4Hz to 8Hz), Alpha (form 8Hz to 13Hz), Beta (from 13 Hz to 30Hz), Gamma (higher than 30Hz). For this work, we are particularly interested in the alpha waves or alpha rhythm. Alpha waves can be measured reliably in the occipital lobes approximately one second after the person closes their eyes (see Fig. 3).

It was first thought that the rhythm was a representation of the activity of the brain while the visual cortex was in stand-by mode, but more recent studies show that they either inhibit areas of the cortex that are not being used or are related to network communication [10, 11]. It is one of the strongest waves detectable on EEG, they are easy

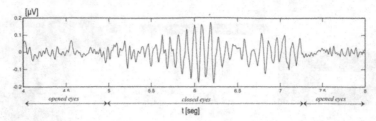

Fig. 3. Alpha rhythm visualization

to produce and detect. This makes them frequently used for testing and diagnosing BCI hardware and software.

5 Emotiv Epoc

Emotiv Inc. is an Australian company that develops EEG-based Brain-Computer interfaces [11]. The interface used in the present work is the Emotiv Epoc, recommended for investigation and complex applications (See Fig. 4 (a)).

Fig. 4. (a) Emotiv Epoc / (b) Emotiv Epoc Flex

The EEG has 14 channels using sensors AF3, F7, F3, FC5, T7, P7, O1, O2, P8, T8, FC6, F4, F8, AF4 and 2 references: CMS/DRL references at P3/P4; left/right mastoid process alternative. Sensor's material is saline soaked felt pads.

These should be cheap to produce and easy to replace, but our experience shows that the design is fragile, the pad supports are easy to break. A set of replacement pads cost us half the price of the whole device. The constant use of saline solution tends to corrode the electrical contacts thus making the replacement unavoidable in the mid term. To extend the life of the set we disassemble and thoroughly clean each pad after use, but the work is tedious and not very effective (Eg. by the end of this investigation, brand new electrodes were almost ready for a replacement again).

It is wireless and connects via low energy bluetooth using a custom 2.4 GHz USB receiver. Having no cables hanging from one's head is definitely good, but the headset is not really "mobile". The connection is highly affected by distance and we observed the device needs a direct line of view from device to receiver to perform decently.

The EEG signals are acquired by sequential sampling using a single ADC and a sample rate of 128 samples per second (SPS). It could be raised to 256 SPS setting a special configuration in the hardware. The resolution it manages to obtain the data is

14 bits (16 bit ADC, 2 bits instrumental noise floor discarded). It also provides 9 axis motion sensors to detect head movement using an accelerometer and a magnetometer.

The software and drivers run on Windows, Mac, IOS and android (there's no official Linux support, but there are some reverse engineered drivers that support the basic functions). The suite provides some neat screens to help with the setup of the headset where one can see the quality of the signal of every sensor, the status of the wireless link and battery of the device (See Fig. 5 (a)).

This app works really well and is really helpful, is always needed as part of the setup and lets you avoid re-implementing this kind of utilities in your custom app. The software suite also provides detection of mental commands: neutral + up to 4 pretrained items per training profile. This is a really interesting feature but after training and using it for several hours, we couldn't find a way to reliably use the commands. Training 2 commands is exhausting. Training more is almost impossible: it looks like the training of a 3rd or 4th command somehow interferes with the detection of the first ones, so training more than 2 is very hard. It also calculates some metrics like excitement, engagement, relaxation, interest, stress and focus.

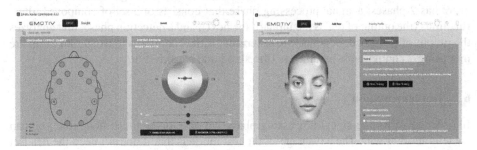

Fig. 5. (a) Signal sensors / (b) Facial expressions detected

It is also able to detect facial expressions like blinking or winking, surprise, frown, smile, clench, laugh and smirk (See Fig. 5 (b)). These detections work better than the mental commands but they are still flickery and our tests were full of false-positives (Eg. a blink benign triggered while the testing subject has his eyes wide open), with a proper noise reduction technique they should be usable to build some interesting interactions with the machine.

Finally, the most interesting feature for this work, although perhaps the more basic one: the pro license (paid) provides access to raw EEG signals, which is what we are going to use to build the integration with two well known ACCS, Plaphoons and ACAT. In the next sections, we explained the development and integration processes.

6 Custom Application Development

The objective of the prototype implemented here is twofold. On one hand, be the first practical approach to the Emotiv Epoc and its SDK in our university. On the other, serve as the base for future research and applications development.

So, the work focus is not just functionality, but also tooling. The application will read the raw signals from the Emotiv, process them to generate interaction events and send them to the alternative and augmentative communication systems like Plaphoons and ACAT. We decided we were going to use the detection of alpha rhythm as the source of the events. From a technical standpoint, alpha rhythm is easy to detect with a high degree of confidence. Thanks to this, it is very used as a diagnosis tool and is frequent to find alpha rhythm detection on BCI software for hardware diagnosis purposes.

6.1 Signal Processing and Digital Filters

As we already mentioned, the signal received from an EEG is noisy. So the first step to use them is to process them to clean them and transform them into something useful. For this we will use a set of digital filters and transformations. Digital filters are mathematical operations that take a series of values (input signal) and modify it in some way and produce another sequence of values (output signal) with the objective of emphasizing or attenuating certain aspects of the input signal.

The algorithm we developed to detect the alpha rhythm and generate the keyboard event has 2 phases: a signal processing phase that consists of a set of composed filters functions (the output of one is the input of the next), and a detection phase, that analyzes the output of the processing phase to determine if the conditions to trigger an event are met using 2 configurable parameters (threshold and sensitivity).

6.2 Implementation

In order to verify the signal processing phase we developed a test mode that you can switch on/off at will. The advantage of the test mode is that it doesn't need the headset connected so we could avoid all the setup and sensor-caring activities.

When the test mode is turned on, the system takes the input signal from an alpha rhythm generator we programmed into the application. The generator creates a synthetic signal which mimics the synchronous activity of the neurons of the occipital lobe of a person opening and closing their eyes for several seconds in an endless loop.

The test signal consists of a 10 Hz sinusoidal wave with a tiny amount of noise, which is interrupted by several seconds of white noise. Finally we add some low frequency sinusoidal movement (See Fig. 6).With this in place we could easily develop and test the filter chain and the detection algorithm.

The signal processing steps are:

- High-pass filter: This step removes all the low frequency noise. You can clearly see the signal has lost the low sinusoidal movement (See Fig. 7 (a)).
- Band-pass filter (8Hz - 12Hz): This step reduces considerably the amplitude of frequencies lower than 8Hz and higher than 12Hz, thus isolating the Alpha band we are interested in (See Fig. 7 (b)).
- Rectifier: This step converts the negative half of the wave to positive, so we now have a positive-only signal forming "10Hz mounds" (See Fig. 7 (c)).
- Low-pass filter: Here we remove the high-frequency movement and we keep only the profile of the mounds (See Fig. 8 (a)).

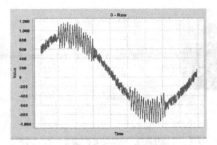

Fig. 6. The original input signal

- Amplifier: This step elevates every value of the signal to the power of 2, thus making the amplitude of each 10Hz mound bigger, emphasizing the difference with those parts of the signal where we originally had noise (See Fig. 8 (b)).
- Threshold-based square wave conversion: in this last step, the signal is transformed into a square wave of amplitude 1 using a configurable threshold. Those places where the amplitude was greater than the threshold are converted to 1, those lower than the threshold to 0 (See Fig. 8 (c)).

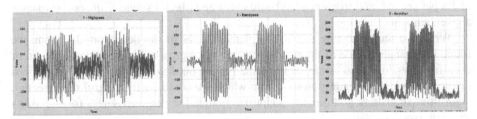

Fig. 7. (a) high-pass filter / (b) band-pass filter / (c) rectifier

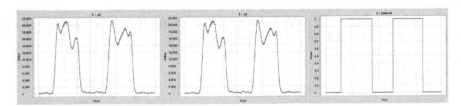

Fig. 8. (a) low-pass filter / (b) amplifier / (c) threshold-based square wave conversion

Finally, we can see the whole filter chain in action processing a real EEG signal taken from the Emotiv Epoc (see Fig. 9).

The subject closed their eyes 2 times in this sample (one on the very beginning of the sampled data, and the other near the end). Notice that the first event has a double peak mound, this kind of artifacts is quite common but the detection phase takes care of cleaning the out.

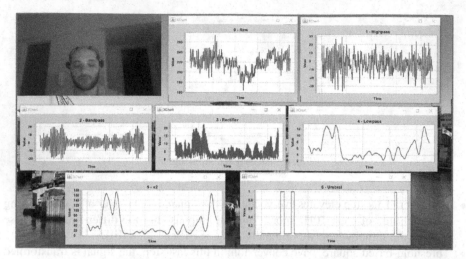

Fig. 9. Filter chain applied to a real EEG signal.

With the signal left by the last step of the signal processing phase the event detection is quite straight forward: counting consecutive 1's. The system then calculates the rate of 1's per second, and triggers a keyboard event and plays a sound if the rate surpasses a given amount.

When we started testing the first implementations of the detection algorithm, we found out that amplitude of the neural activity varies greatly from person to person or even from sessions to sessions of the same person on different days. This introduced the need to add a configuration tool from which we could easily control the detection algorithm parameters and quickly adapt the application responsiveness for the user's situation (see Fig. 10).

The configuration tool has 2 parameters:

Threshold (*Umbral*): is the value of the threshold used in step 6 of the processing phase.

Sensitivity (*Sensibilidad*): this value represents the rate of 1's the algorithm must detect in a given second before triggering an event.

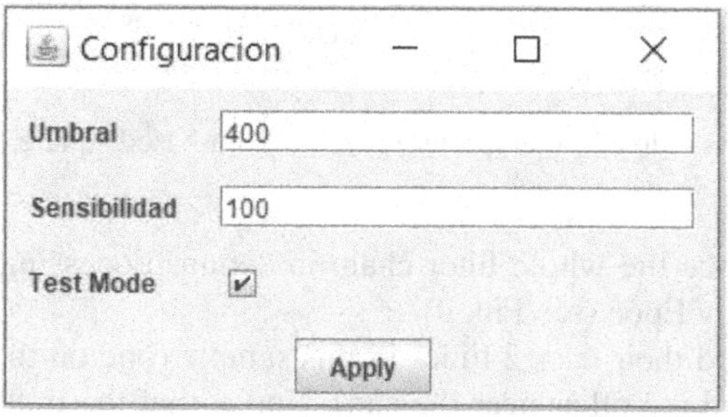

Fig. 10. Algorithm parameters configuration screenshot

The values for the threshold can only be obtained by connecting the headset doing 2 or 3 tries and using an average value. We found out that a value around 60% of the max amplitude of the mounds in step 5 works ok most of the time.

Regarding sensitivity, usually what is preferable of this type of interfaces is that they were hard to trigger but precise, rather than being full of false-positive non desired "clicks". Thus, having values above 75% is what we found more effective. The 2 parameters have a deep inter-relationship but proved to be sufficiently flexible. For example having 100% sensitivity means that we would need a complete second full of consecutive 1's, which due to the noisy nature of the EEG signals might be hard to obtain, unless you use a very low threshold.

7   The Integration Process

In the integration process we did several testings. Before starting integration with Plaphoons and ACAT, a preliminary test was conducted with the game Tic Tac Toe. In this case, we utilized the gyroscope and reduced its sensitivity to a minimum percentage. This adjustment ensures that even with the slightest intention of making a click, it occurs without being frustrating for the user (see Fig. 11).

Fig. 11. Integration with Tic Tac Toe game

The test was successful, with the system taking approximately 4–5 s to capture the click, which proved to be quite useful for this type of game. During the test, users were able to move the mouse using their head via the gyroscope, navigating between each cell of the Tic Tac Toe grid. Once they reached the desired cell, users had to close their eyes and wait for the click detection. Following these tests, we began integrating the BCI interface with the augmentative and alternative systems described in the upcoming sections.

7.1   Integration with ACAT

The second test presented in this section is about the ACAT speller. ACAT comes with a practice speller, so that different tests can be performed, of what will be later, the full use of the software. As we can see in Fig. 12, the objective is to form the word sea ("mar" in Spanish), highlighted in red.

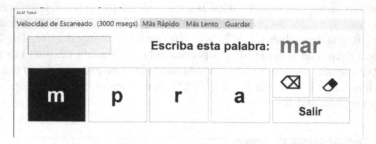

Fig. 12. ACAT test image, with its own signal processing.

The application performs a sweep, letter by letter, at an initial speed of 3 s, a value that can be modified, and it uses the F12 key as a communication mechanism with the ACAT. In order to link the use of our software, it was necessary to adapt the detection of the alpha rhythm to this key.

The use of the default sweep of 3 s did not allow us to achieve a correct performance, since the detection of the alpha rhythm, in our case, needs between 4–5 s. Once this parameter was corrected, the test was successful, being able to form the word without errors. As a complement to the selection of the F12 key, we also generated a sound, so that the user can know the instant in which the eye closure is detected. The Fig. 13, illustrates the described test.

Fig. 13. ACAT test image, with proprietary signal processing.

After this test, we can conclude that the slower the sweeping process, although the percentage of success will be higher, the more tedious the selection process will be. In addition, if a letter is chosen incorrectly, you will have to wait until you reach the "draft" and then try again to form the correct word.

7.2 Integration with Plaphoons

Another case of integration in our research is the detection of the alpha rhythm and the Plaphoons software. Within this test, we used a set of plaphoons that brought the application and an automatic sweep, suitable for 5 s, which allowed great comfort when choosing a particular Plaphoons template. It should be noted that for each of the panels, the description, the image and the sound emitted when selected can be selected, which is a fundamental feature, thinking about the combination with the alpha rhythm that involves having the eyes closed. The next image (see Fig. 14) shows a Plaphoons panel arranged on the grid and the signal detected when the eyes are closed.

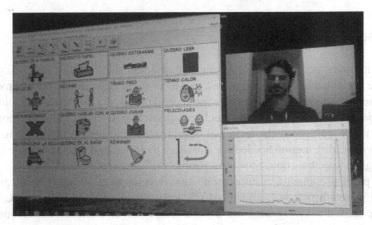

Fig. 14. ACAT test image, with own-signal processing.

The result of the test was successful, being able to prove once again the effectiveness in the detection of the alpha rhythm, in addition to an excellent performance against the software, highlighting the flexibility in the configuration of the sweep, which makes the implementation feasible.

7.3 Integration Testing Results

ACAT is very powerful, it provides a lot of tools and different mechanisms to control the computer and its programs. All of these tools are available to any device that can trigger a keyboard event (F12 keypress, by default).

The downside is that the configuration is also huge, and knowing how to really use every one of the applications can take a lot of time. Another drawback we found, is that the configuration of the screen scanners delay has a maximum allowed value of 3 s and our detection algorithm has a latency between 3 and 5 s. This is due to the nature of the alpha rhythm (a person needs to close their eyes for 1 or 2 s for it to appear) and the amount of samples we are using to trigger the keyboard event to prevent false positives. This makes us think ACAT is built with a faster and more precise triggering mechanism (for example, Stephen Hawking used it with an infrared sensor in his cheek, which reacts in the order of milliseconds). So the tests we performed resulted in an extremely wearing experience.

Functionally speaking, the integration was seamless, needing a single keypress makes the task really easy. The integration was usable in Plaphoons (which doesn't have a limit on the speed of the screen scanners) and in an ACAT Speller, a training app, that allows up to 5 s delay per option in the screen scanner. Also tried it with some board games like tic-tac-toe, and the application gave success results.

It is still a slow reacting control interface. We think the combination of a faster evoked potential (like p300 for example, which takes around 300 ms to appear) and the ACAT intelligent autocompleter (which stores the most used words in a personal dictionary) is viable to have a better user experience and a more responsive interface.

8 Conclusions

BCI and assistive technology have advanced tremendously in the last few years. Things that were unthinkable 20 years ago, we can have them right in our homes today. But while doing this investigation, interviewing several professionals and talking with people close to potential users of this kind of technology we found out that there's no correlation between the magnitude of the technical development and the documentation, training and knowledge distribution needed for end users to access and take advantage from this technological leap that could transform people's life.

This paper presented a custom application development to make an integration of Emotiv Epoc with two well known ACCS software like Plaphoons and ACAT. This prototype reads the raw signals from the Emotiv, processes them to generate interaction events, and sends them to the communication systems. The algorithm was developed to detect the alpha rhythm and generate the keyboard event in 2 phases: a signal processing phase, and a detection phase.

While doing this investigation and development with social implications, we found the complexity of this kind of technology and their integration in order to help people to better communicate using these systems. Applications like ACAT are really complex, not easy to use or configure and have a steep learning curve for non-technical people. But once this curve is surpassed the amount and quality of the tools it provides is excellent.

On the BCI side, we find the Emotiv EPOC not a good fit to use as a every-day home device. The electrodes dry up really quickly. In order to moisten them again, you have to remove the headset and then recheck the connectivity and quality signal of each of them. Signal quality and wireless range is not really an enabler as the user cannot be far away from the computer. Perhaps a wired device could improve the signal quality and stability. Work performing the integrations with AACS.

More testing and validation processes where to analyze the use and impact of this technology will be done in future works.

Finally we want to conclude that learning about filters, their implementation and application, and the integration with software such as Plaphoons and ACAT was very enriching. We believe that this research is the starting point in our University for the advance of BCI development. The future of these interfaces and the interaction with other software is truly promising.

References

1. Escandell Vidal, M.V.: La comunicación. Lengua, cognición y sociedad. Madrid: Akal, pp. 144–145. ISBN: 978–84–460–3958–7. Editorial: AKAL (2014)
2. Díaz, J., Fava, L., Harari, I., Martinez, F., Tellechea, M.: An integration of brain-computer interfaces with an alternative augmentative communication system In: XXIX Congreso Argentino de Ciencias de la Computación - CACIC 2023 (2023). ISBN 978–987–9285–51–0
3. Tamarit Cuadrado, J.: Sistemas de comunicación, 17–42. Madrid, España. ISBN 84–87699–67–7 (2003)
4. Fernandez-Pacheco, L., Peña Ruiz, B. and Tercero Cotillas, M.: Sistemas aumentativos y alternativos de comunicación. ISBN: 978–84–9077–348–2 Madrid: Editorial Síntesis (2016)
5. Fábrega López, Cristina: PLAPHOONS Plaphoons como facilitador TIC de la comunicación. . https://digibug.ugr.es/handle/10481/36360 (2014)
6. ACAT Homepage. https://www.intel.com/content/www/us/en/developer/tools/open/acat/overview.html. Accessed 30 Jan 2023
7. Nicolas-Alonso, L.F., Gomez-Gil, J.: Brain computer interfaces: a review. Sensors 12, 1211–1279 (2012). https://doi.org/10.3390/s120201211
8. Zion-Golumbic, E.: What is EEG?, Hebrew University of Jerusalén. https://www.mada.org.il/brain/articles/faces-e.pdf (2019)
9. Clerc, M., Bougrain, L. and Lotte, F.: Brain-Computer Interfaces 2, Technology and Applications. ISBN: 9781848219632, iSTE & WILEY (2016)
10. Palva, S., Palva, J.M.: New vistas for a-frequency band oscillations. Trends Neurosci. 30(4), 150–158 (2007). https://doi.org/10.1016/j.tins.2007.02.001.PMID17307258.S2CID9156592
11. Rashid, M., Sulaiman, N., Majeed, A., Musa, R., Nasir, A., Khatun, S.: Current status, challenges, and possible solutions of EEG-based brain-computer interface: a comprehensive review. Front. Neurorobot. (2020). https://doi.org/10.3389/fnbot.2020.00025
12. Browarska, N., Kawala-Sterniuk, A., Zygarlicki, J.: Comparison of smoothing filters' influence on quality of data recorded with the Emotiv Epoc flex brain–computer interface headset during audio stimulation. Brain Sciences (2021). https://www.mdpi.com/2076-3425/11/1/98

Accessible Software Design: Thinking Outside the Box

Claudia Ortiz[1]([⊠]) [iD], Cecilia Challiol[2] [iD], and Walter Panessi[1] [iD]

[1] Department of Basic Sciences, National University of Luján, Luján, Buenos Aires, Argentina
{cortiz,wpanessi}@unlu.edu.ar
[2] LIFIA, Facultad de Informática, UNLP and also CONICET, La Plata, Buenos Aires, Argentina
ceciliac@lifia.info.unlp.edu.ar

Abstract. Accessibility is generally approached as an implementation aspect, and people with disabilities are not involved in the early design stages. On the other hand, the rise of Design Thinking has led to a rethink of whether traditional empathy methods (interviews and surveys) capture the real needs of people, particularly those with disabilities. This paper presents an extension of the article published in the *XXIX Argentine Congress of Computer Science* (CACIC 2023), where an empathising guideline with people with disabilities using Design Thinking experiences was proposed to design accessible software from scratch. In addition, in the article published in CACIC 2023, this empathising guideline is used to design and explore two experiences with two people, one with motor difficulties (in this case affecting speech and writing) and another with Down syndrome. Furthermore, this article published in CACIC 2023 proposes reflecting on the best resources for empathising. The present work extends the article published in CACIC 2023, expanding with more detail the conceptual framework that frames the empathising guideline and enriching the descriptions of the two experiences. In addition, this present work adds recommendations regarding possible resources to be used in each guideline's item. We hope that this work will contribute to accessible software design.

Keywords: Accessibility · Design Thinking · Software · Disability · Human-Centered Design

1 Introduction

Accessibility is usually addressed at later stages of development as it is considered an implementation issue [1], which generates additional work overload to make the accessible software. The resulting product is often unusable or frustrates users with disabilities [2], as the software was not designed with their needs in mind [3]. For this reason, it is critical to actively involve people with disabilities in software design [4].

Design Thinking (DT) [5] is a Human-Centered Design approach that uses designers' methods to create innovative solutions according to people's needs. The first stage of DT is to focus on empathising to identify or discover what people need. Moreover, empathy

P. Pesado et al. (Eds.): CACIC 2023, CCIS 2123, pp. 272–287, 2024.
https://doi.org/10.1007/978-3-031-62245-8_19

could contribute to a more accessible world [6]. However, DT has little explored in the design of accessible software [7]. This motivates our research.

Empathise can be achieved using direct or indirect interactions [8]. Direct interventions involve collecting '*first-hand*' information, for example, questionnaires and interviews with representative users [9]. At the same time, indirect interactions may involve, for example, on-site observations of representative users or interviews with third parties [10]. It should be noted that indirect interactions may be biased and not reflect the actual experiences of those who want to empathise [8].

Different resources can be used for the empathise stage of DT, which can involve direct or indirect interactions. However, it is advisable to approach this stage with direct interactions, and indirect interactions should be used as complementary [7]. On the other hand, traditional DT resources used in direct interactions, such as interviews or questionnaires, may not generate genuine empathy with people who wish to empathise with [11] because their real needs are not sometimes identified. This is part of the motivation for this paper.

In [7], we have presented a conceptual framework of DT for designing accessible software from scratch. Furthermore, in [7], we explored empathising with people with colour-blind disabilities to begin understanding their real software needs.

This paper presents an extension of the article published in [12] at the '*XXIX Congreso Argentino de Ciencias de la Computación (CACIC 2023)*', where an empathising guideline with people with disabilities using Design Thinking experiences was proposed for the design of accessible software from scratch. This guideline focuses on direct interactions and is framed in the conceptual framework proposed in [7]. Furthermore, in [12], this empathising guideline was used to design and explore two experiences with two people: a person with motor difficulties, in this case affecting speech and writing, and a person with Down syndrome.

This paper extends the article published in [12], providing more detail on the conceptual framework that frames the empathising guideline, just like enriching the descriptions of the two experiences presented in [12]. In addition, this paper incorporates recommendations for possible resources to be used in each item of the guideline.

Like in [12], we hope this paper will provide a space for discussion that contributes to making the problem visible, looking to reflect on how to detect the real needs of people with disabilities to be able to design adaptations in software from the early stages and make it accessible from scratch.

The paper is structured as follows. Section 2 describes some related work. Section 3 provides more details on the conceptual framework that frames the empathising guideline (presented in [12]) and details the guideline (as was given in [12]). Section 4 enriches the descriptions of the two experiences presented in [12]. Section 5 incorporates recommendations for possible resources that could be used in each guideline's item. Section 6 generates a space for discussion. Conclusions and future work are mentioned in Sect. 7.

2 Related Work

In recent years, DT has started to be used to design software solutions. For the aim of this paper, it is interesting to know how different authors address this topic, particularly the empathise stage of DT with people with disabilities. Two papers are described below.

In [10], DT is used to design and develop a tangible user interface for the literacy process of students with Down syndrome. For the empathise stage of DT, they interviewed fifteen Special Education teachers, which allowed them to identify two literacy methods used with these students. Then, each method was explored in depth by interviewing its creators, and a literature review was carried out to complement the information. Finally, the authors conducted an on-site observation of the teachers working with the students to understand the methods' application. In other words, all resources used involve indirect interactions to empathise.

On the other hand, in [9], a DT experience with a transportation company is presented to improve the service for people with mobility challenges. For the empathise stage, the activities described below were carried out. The author investigated what happens to transport users (using *Netnography*[1]), how companies perform (using *Benchmarking*[2]), and how a transport user's experience is improved (using the *Safari*[3] resource). Questionnaires and interviews with transport users were carried out. The information was organised using different resources[4] (*User Persona*, *User Journey* and *Empathy Map*). In summary, [9] only questionnaires and interviews involve direct interactions; however, these resources might not have achieved genuine empathy [11].

The following describes two papers that explore how people with disabilities (Down syndrome and motor difficulties) use gestures in mobile applications. These papers do not use DT but are interesting in terms of the exploration done about the software.

In [13], the authors present a case study conducted with fifteen young people with Down syndrome regarding the use of the most basic gestures in mobile applications. The study divides young people into three groups, all with no or little use of mobile devices. The first group was given six apps for training for six different gestures. The second group received only an explanation of the gestures. At the same time, the third group had no information at all regarding the gestures. Then, all three groups used the Google Earth application (selected for having an unintuitive interface regarding the use of gestures). In [13], the authors mentioned that training applications have been facilitated using Google Earth. The authors identify that the gestures of *rotating*, *holding down*, and *dragging* (or *moving*) are the most difficult for these young people to perform, although they do not describe how they reached this conclusion.

On the other hand, in [14], the difficulties generated by gestures in mobile applications are studied with ten people with different challenges of reduced mobility in the

---

[1] *Netnography* was used to investigate social networks, web pages, forums, and written interactions of people who use (or have used) public transportation and have expressed their feelings, emotions, and experiences.

[2] *Benchmarking* was carried out through an exercise called 'Look for the 7 differences', during which they investigated buses in other communities and countries.

[3] The *Safari* resource consists of an in-situ simulation that allows to live the experiences of the people with whom we are trying to empathise.

[4] The '*User Persona*' resource was specified with the data collected to represent a fictitious person who uses the bus and has mobility difficulties. Then, with the '*User Journey*' resource, strengths/weaknesses were determined for the profile defined in '*User Persona*' Finally, based on all the information collected, the '*Empathy Map*' was used to reflect the emotional aspects of the bus users' feelings and thoughts.

upper limbs. For this, the authors surveyed the most used gestures in existing applications. Based on this, they developed a prototype program for the iPhone to determine which gestures people with different mobility challenges cannot make. After using the prototype, people with reduced mobility completed a questionnaire with a series of questions about the usability of the prototype. In [14], the author identified for the ten people who used the prototype, based on the questionnaire responses, that the most challenging gestures to perform were *rotate* and *zoom*.

In both [13] and [14], it is appreciated that the explorations focus purely on the gestures' usability and do not empathise with people.

3 Empathise with People with Disabilities

As mentioned above, in [7], we presented an initial proposal for a conceptual framework of DT for designing accessible software from scratch. This framework proposes three stages for approaching DT: empathise, ideate, and prototype/test. It is essential to mention that, in [7], we do not provide details on these stages.

In [12], we presented an empathising guideline with people with disabilities focusing on direct interactions. This guideline was proposed for the empathise stage of the conceptual framework DT presented in [7].

This paper contributes by providing more details below for the conceptual framework that frames the empathising guideline (presented in [12]). In addition, this section details the guideline's items as they were given in [12].

3.1 Extension of the Conceptual Framework of DT for Designing Accessible Software from Scratch

Based on the conceptual framework of DT proposed in [7] for designing accessible software from scratch, which defines three stages: empathise, ideate and prototype/test, as mentioned before; in this paper, the empathise stage is extended with the concepts addressed in the guideline proposed in [12]. This extension can be seen in Fig. 1. The interviewer should initially empathise with people, generating confidence, knowing how they communicate and learning about their disability; then, taking this as a starting point, move on to an instance of empathise related to the software. In addition, the interviewer needs to have empathy and always maintain active listening; that is why, in Fig. 1, this role is related to the whole empathise stage. It is essential to mention that selecting the kind of software to explore can be established beforehand before empathising with people with disabilities or based on what has been collected. In other words, this is a flexible aspect, so it is outside of the flow, as shown in Fig. 1.

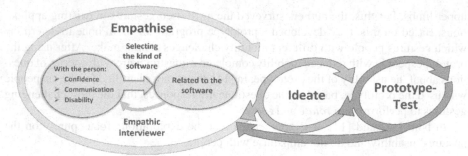

Fig. 1. Conceptual framework of DT for designing accessible software from scratch. Extension with more level of detail in the empathise stage.

3.2 Empathising Guideline with People with Disability

The guideline's items (for empathising with people with disabilities, focusing on direct interactions) are detailed below, as they were given in [12].

- *Choose an empathic person to conduct the empathise stage.* It is essential to consider the person's level of empathy to achieve more pleasant communication and encourage active listening to the needs of people with disabilities. There are several tests to measure empathy [7].
- *Generate a bond of confidence with the person who wish to empathise with.* The existence or absence of a previous link determines how to proceed. If you do not know the person, you should have to generate this bond of confidence to be able to carry out any empathise activity about the software. For this, it is recommended to use, for example, the resource called '*Interview to Empathise*' [15]. Whether a previous bond exists or has been generated, the people who want to empathise should be told what the experience to be carried out consists of and why their contribution is extremely useful, together with an '*Informed Consent*' document (which provides all the details of the experience).
- *Determine the predominant communication of the person who wish to empathise with.* Knowing how people communicate becomes critical to better reach and understand their needs. People can be visual, auditory, kinesthetic (they learn by what they do and touch), or a combination of these [16]; this impacts how they express themselves and incorporate information. Preponderant communication can be determined, for example, through the resource of '*Direct Observation*', and based on the result, the selection of resources can be dynamically adapted to empathise with each person in the most appropriate way.
- *Learn about the disability of the person who wish to empathise with.* It is essential to know how the person's disability impacts their daily actions. Depending on how close the interviewer is to the person's disability, the level of depth with which they should explore the disability. In this sense, it is possible to learn about the disability through questions asked to third parties (experts, family members),
- *Define what to find out about the kind of software to be designed.* Each kind of software may have different characteristics and dynamics; defining which one wants

to design is essential to guide how to carry out the software empathise stage and what resources to use.

- *Determine what resources to use to empathise related to the software that want to design.* Generating resources that allow empathising with the software, for example, a mock-up of some relevant aspect of the software; this resource style is easy to design/assemble and does not take much time. Another option is to use a '*Prototype to Empathise*'[5] [15].

4   Empathy Experiences

This section enriches the descriptions of the two experiences presented in [12]. For these two experiences[6], the guideline proposed in Sect. 3.2 was implemented with two people with disabilities. One of them has motor difficulties that affect the clarity of speaking and writing, referred to as T. The second person has Down syndrome, referred to as J. Both people regularly use mobile devices, have acquired literacy, participate in theatre and dance groups, respectively, and in the case of J, also have a job.

Below, each guideline's item will be addressed for both experiences, which took place in parallel and personalised for each person.

To '*Choose an empathic to conduct the empathise stage*', it was necessary to consider the most empathic person in the work team to conduct the experience; for this purpose, the IRI test[7] [17] was used. Two of the team members gave, as a result in the empathic concern dimension, a value above the average, of which the one who had the closest link with people who wish to empathise with was chosen. From now on, this person will be referred to as the interviewer. Table 1 describes how three of the guideline's items (*bond of confidence, communication,* and *disability*) were approached.

In terms of '*Defining what to investigate concerning the kind of software to be designed*', we decided to investigate the use of gestures in mobile applications for both T and J, motivated by the frequent use of mobile devices and the scarce direct empathy found in the literature. We decided to explore the gestures move (or drag, which involves holding down), zoom, and rotate, considering that they can generate challeng-es, as mentioned in Sect. 2, for the two disabilities explored in this paper.

For the guideline's item '*Determine what resources to use to empathise related to the software that want to design*', the resources listed in Table 2 were chosen.

In Table 2, the first '*Prototypes to Empathise*' were the *Word Wonders* and *Candy Crush* applications. These were chosen for T and J, respectively; this decision was made considering the information obtained in the previous interactions with each of them. Table 3 lists the '*Inquiry Questions*' related to the complexity of using each application.

---

[5] The '*Prototype to Empathise*' has functionality (i.e., it can be interacted with). It can be either software created for that purpose or an existing one. The concept of '*Prototype to Empathise*' differs from the concept of' '*Software Prototype*' since it is made or used only for empathising and will not become the final software.

[6] To preserve the identity of the people involved, they will be identified with a letter.

[7] The IRI (Interpersonal Reactivity Index) test allows for measuring empathy in adults.

Table 1. Performance of three items of the empathising guideline.

Guideline's item	T (Motor difficulties)	J (Down syndrome)
Generate a bond of confidence with the person who wish to empathise with	The interviewer knew the person previously. However, they had not been in contact for some time, so the link had to be reestablished	The interviewer did not know J. It was decided to conduct a face-to-face '*Interview to Empathise*' [15] with the assistance of a third person who was the link between the interviewer and J; this person (henceforth R) fulfils a role similar to a tutor for J
Determine the predominant communication of the person who wish to empathise with	The interviewer refined it during the re-engagement with T, which occurred first by contacting T via WhatsApp application and then through a Google Meet video call (set up with the option of subtitles due to T's speech difficulty)	The interviewer refined it through '*Direct Observation*' during the '*Interview to Empathise*'
Learn about the disability of the person who wish to empathise with	The interviewer knew T, so the interviewer knew how disability impacted T	The interviewer learned about Down syndrome through consultations with third parties: with an expert (hereafter E) to learn about the generalities and with R to learn about J

Table 2. Resources used to empathise related to the software that want to design.

Resource Used	Description	T (Motor difficulties)	J (Down syndrome)
Prototype to Empathise	Using a known application	*Word Wonders*[8]	*Candy Crush*[9]
Inquiry Questions	Answering questions	Contextualized to the use of *Word Wonders*	Contextualized to the use of *Candy Crush*
Prototype to Empathise	Editing a WhatsApp image	Contextualized to theatre (a topic of interest of T)	Contextualized to horses (a topic of interest of J)
Inquiry Questions	Answering questions	Contextualized to the complexity of gestures' use	Contextualized to the complexity of gestures' use

---

[8] Word Wonders homepage: https://play.google.com/store/apps/details?id=com.fugo.wow, last accessed 2023/05/12.

Table 3. Inquiry Questions to formulate at the end of using the known applications.

Question	T (Motor difficulties)	J (Down Syndrome)
1	What is the most complex thing about using *Word Wonders*?	What is the most complex thing about using *Candy Crush*?

For the '*Editing a WhatsApp image*' (from Table 2), sequences of images presented to both T and J were previously designed to test the use of gestures in a guide way, for example, adding emojis and texts and placing them in certain places with a particular inclination and size. *WhatsApp* was selected because it is an application that uses T and J frequently. In addition, these images were contextualised according to each one's interests (which were identified by the interviewer in previous interactions). Figure 2 shows the sequence to explore the use of gestures with T.

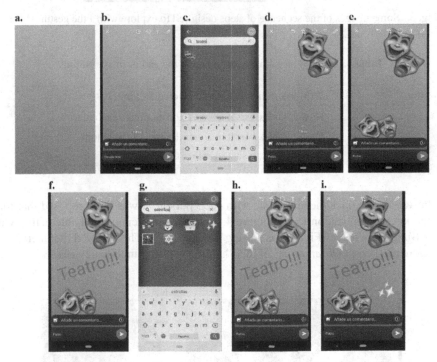

Fig. 2. The sequence of steps designed to explore with T the gestures' use.

As in Fig. 2, the exact sequence was designed for J, but some images and texts were related to J's interest in horses. Figure 3 shows some images designed for J.

---

⁹ Candy Crush homepage: https://play.google.com/store/apps/details?id=com.king.candycrushsaga, last accessed 2023/05/12.

Table 4 lists the '*Inquiry Questions*' defined to learn about the complexity of '*Editing a WhatsApp image*'. These questions were the same for both T and J.

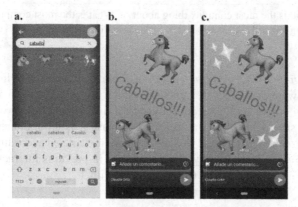

Fig. 3. Some images of the sequence of steps designed to explore with J the gestures' use.

Table 4. Inquiry questions to formulate at the end of image editing.

Questions	T (Motor difficulties) and J (Down Syndrome)
2	How complex was it to *move* the emojis to each place?
3	How complex was it to *zoom* the size of the emojis?
4	How complex was it to *rotate* the emojis?

In two face-to-face meetings, one with each person, it was first proposed that they use the known application freely. Figure 4. a can be appreciated as T interacting with *Word Wonders*, whereas Fig. 4. b is J using *Candy Crush*. This allowed the interviewer to conduct a '*Direct Observation*' of their habitually using mobile devices.

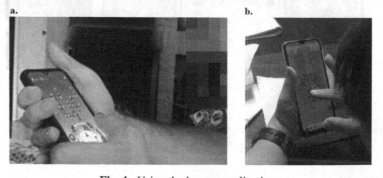

Fig. 4. Using the known applications.

After a few minutes, the interviewer asked each of them the questions in Table 3. T, unlike J, answered by WhatsApp, although T and the interviewer were in the same physical place; this was decided to overcome the challenges in oral communication that have T.

The interviewer observed that none of them had problems; they used them fluently. However, T mentioned, '*Sometimes when I raise my finger; it was difficult for me*'; on the other hand, T focused on the fact that the most challenging thing was sometimes guessing the word (used *Word Wonders*). In the case of J, the response was: '*It's easy. I've been playing for more than a year*'.

Subsequently, the interviewer proposed editing a blank image using WhatsApp. As mentioned above, this editing activity was the same for both people; the only thing that varied was the theme used for each one since it was contextualised according to their interests, as shown in Figs. 2 and 3.

For editing, they were told what to do step by step and shown an image of how it should look, with little indication of how to do it. Figure 5 shows two of the steps performed by T, with the interviewer's cell phone on the left and the T on the right.

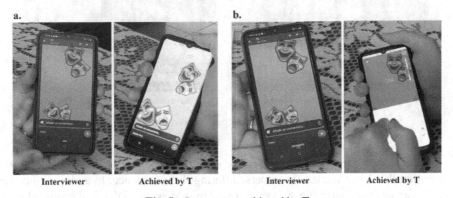

a.   b.

Interviewer   Achieved by T   Interviewer   Achieved by T

Fig. 5. Some steps achieved by T.

Figure 6 shows a general picture of the empathy experience with T. In addition, the final screens can be observed in the figure, both from the interviewer and the final result achieved by T, after following the steps of the editing sequence in Fig. 2. Note that T's achievement was similar to what the interviewer proposed in terms of the distribution and size of the emojis and text.

After editing, T was asked about the complexity (of move, zoom and rotate) using the three questions in Table 4. T answered via WhatsApp, and to all questions, T answered, '*I had no problem*', which was in line with what the interviewer observed.

On the other hand, Fig. 7 shows two steps in J's sequence, with the interviewer's mobile phone on the left and J's mobile phone on the right.

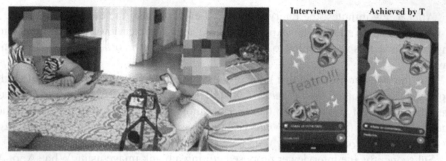

Fig. 6. Experience to empathise with T about gestures.

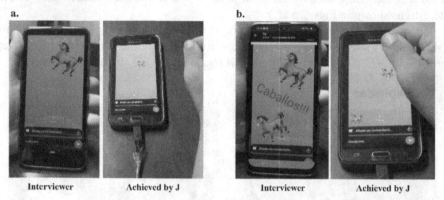

Fig. 7. Some steps achieved by J.

Figure 8 shows a general picture of the empathy experience with J. It is essential to mention that J was constantly dispersed during the experience. In addition, the final screens can be observed in Fig. 8, both from the interviewer and the final result achieved by J. A significant difference can be observed in terms of the size and inclination of the emojis and the text.

Fig. 8. Experience to empathise with J about gestures.

After the editing was finished, J was asked about the complexity of each gesture (move, zoom and rotate) using the three questions in Table 4. When the interviewer asked the first question, J did not understand what it was aimed at, so interviewer reformulated it by giving the following options: '*How complex was it to move the emojis to each place? It was easy, difficult, super complex*'; then J answered, '*Super complex, some difficult, more or less*'.

The interviewer asked the following questions, giving the same options. J's answers were in the same style, and different degrees of complexity were mentioned in the same answer. This led the interviewer not to know how to interpret these answers.

These two experiences, which were planned to use the proposed guideline, were the first steps in exploring empathy with people with disabilities, focusing on direct interactions.

5   Recommendations of Resources for the Guideline's Items

This section provides recommendations for possible resources for each guideline's item presented in Sect. 3.2.

The IRI test [17] is recommended for '*Choose an empathic person to conduct the empathise stage*'. There may be more than one empathic person in a team, so the whole team would have to self-assess. The objective of empathise should be considered; for example, the aim can be to train the team to acquire new skills (so-called soft skills) so that the interviewer has 'first-hand' experiences, or the focus of empathise can be to collect relevant information, and in this case, choose the most expert of the team (who is also an empathic person) interviews, or the one closest to the people the person who wish to empathise with or nearest to the disability.

To '*Generate a bond of confidence with the person who wish to empathise with*', the recommended resource is interviews to empathise, as mentioned in Sect. 3.2. The '*Interview to Empathise*' [15] is dynamic, as it is designed to get people (who wish to empathise with) to tell what is important to them; this, in many cases, can escape aspects of software. However, this information is precious as it can impact the use of the software. While there is an '*ideal*' interview structure, it cannot always be followed or adhered to; therefore, the interviewer should have a flexible posture when conducting the interview.

Direct observation can be used in the item '*Determine the predominant communication of the person who wish to empathise with*', as mentioned in Sect. 3.2. *Direct observation* focuses on determining how the person communicates. It can be carried out in different interactions, e.g., in an empathise interview or when inquiring.

Table 4 presents three recommended resources for the item '*Learn about the disability of the person who wish to empathise with*', such as a *Bibliography, Third-party consultations*, and *Direct observation*.

Three recommended resources are listed in Table 5 for the guideline's item '*Determine what resources to use to empathise related to the software that want to design*'. These resources are *Prototypes to Empathise, Ad-hoc generated resources to Empathise*, and *Inquiry Questions*.

The recommendations provided in this section are based on existing literature, but they are enriched by the acknowledgement achieved from the two experiences described in Sect. 4 and the experiences conducted in [7]; all these experiences were performed using our conceptual framework of DT for designing accessible software from scratch. In addition, all these experiences involved direct interactions with people with disabilities to empathise.

Table 5. Recommended resources for the guideline's item *'Learn about the disability of the person who wish to empathise with'*.

Resources	Recommendation
Bibliography	While it broadens general knowledge, it cannot be taken as the only source, as each person has particularities. It can be combined with active listening and direct observation to tailor the data collected to the person with a disability who wish to empathise with
Third-party consultations	Consulting with third parties can provide guidance, but they are complementary, and it must be considered that the experts offer data from their own perspective, which may be biased
Direct observation	Direct observation is considered essential to making personalised adjustments. However, the interviewer interprets that observation, which must constantly be rechecked because it may be biased

6   Discussion

This section discusses the design of accessible software from scratch. Choosing an empathic person to lead the experience is not a common consideration in DT [5]; however, we have identified that when interacting with people with disabilities, this skill becomes fundamental to actively listening to their needs. On the other hand, building a bond of confidence with the person who wish to empathise with is essential to laying the foundations for all the following interactions.

Determining the predominant communication of the people who wish to empathise with is another fundamental aspect; in our experiences, this was done through *'Direct Observation'*. In the case of J, the interviewer detected that J was constantly dispersed, which required the interviewer always to have a flexible posture. On the other hand, T's situation was different because the interviewer knew how T's disability impacted T's speech and writing; the communication started using WhatsApp and went smoothly, and then Google Meet was tried with subtitles activated. However, Google Meet was not helpful because the tool could not decipher what T was saying; this led to the decision to collect the answers to the questions about using gestures via WhatsApp so that T could express without any barriers.

Table 6. Recommended resources for the guideline's item '*Determine what resources to use to empathise related to the software that want to design*'.

Resources	Recommendation
Prototypes to Empathise	Prototypes allow interactions and observation of people in action to see their use, which provides more realism. These can be existing applications used as they are, or their use is re-signified for a particular purpose. In addition, these prototypes could be created from scratch for an empathise experience; however, this is time-consuming, and it should not be forgotten that this is discarded
Ad-hoc generated resources to Empathise	These resources could be static mock-ups, which could be used to analyze visual aspects. They are generally easy to design/assemble and not very time-consuming. They can be used to investigate something that does not exist. It is essential to consider that this resource for empathising is then discarded, so it is advisable not to invest excessive time in generating it
Inquiry Questions	They could use it to inquire about a prototype to empathise or an ad-hoc generated resource to empathise. Based on what is to be asked, each question is formulated, e.g. about colour as in [7] or complexity as presented in Sect. 4

It was reflected that we would have needed to enquire more initially about Down syndrome (in the guideline's item '*Learn about the disability of the person who wish to empathise with*'); this was evidenced by the ambiguous responses obtained from J (in Sect. 4). After the experience with J, the interviewer consulted again with the third parties mentioned in Table 1, identifying that complexity can be abstract even when given options in the question. In addition, in these chats emerged the importance of observation and repetition for people with Down syndrome to incorporate or use something new, which aligns with the benefits of gesture training mentioned in [13]. An aspect to reflect on is that the first impact of the person with the software is often given more value; however, with people with Down syndrome, training should be considered a positive aspect.

It is important to note that T did not find it challenging to perform the gestures discussed in [14], i.e., each person has different needs. This makes it clear that further exploration of empathy is required to gather what adaptations need to be considered when designing accessible software.

On the other hand, when the existing literature is analysed, it becomes apparent that most case studies start from scratch. This leads to thinking about having a *catalogue of direct empathisations* about different disabilities to have a knowledge base. This catalogue should be enriched with each new empathise experience, adding resources and detailing successes and errors, which would allow for prior consultation, and then, with all this baggage, carry out the personalised empathise stage. It is essential to mention that a significant difference between the *catalogue of direct empathisations* and good design practices or usability guidelines is that the latter generalises common aspects to be considered in the design. In contrast, the *catalogue of direct empathisations* would aspire to identify the wide variability of people's needs, especially those of people with disabilities.

7 Conclusions and Future Work

The design of accessible software from scratch, it becomes essential to incorporate appropriate resources to empathise with people with disabilities and identify their real needs, such as *'Interview to Empathise'* [15] or *'Prototype to Empathise'* [15]. In this sense, our empathising guideline focusing on direct interactions with people with disabilities could be beneficial. In addition, we hope this work will help reflect on the issue and 'think outside the box' when approaching this kind of design. For example, in many cases, specialised applications are not required to establish communication, but with good observation, it is possible to detect and take advantage of what the person already uses regularly, as was the case of T with WhatsApp. Another change in mentality is about the usual conception of software testing without initial bias, as training can be very positive with people with Down syndrome [13].

This paper could contribute to reflecting on how to test software with people with disabilities since, in many cases, applications are tested by third parties, who decide on their usefulness [8].

In the future, we will continue to explore empathy with more people to enrich the recommendations of the proposed guideline and address the other two stages of the conceptual framework of DT for designing accessible software from scratch.

References

1. Oliveira, R., Silva, L., Leite, J.C.S.P., Moreira, A.: Eliciting accessibility requirements an approach based on the NFR framework. In: Proceedings of the 31st Annual ACM Symposium on Applied Computing, pp. 1276–1281. ACM, New York (2016)
2. Kahraman, E.: Inclusive design thinking: exploring the obstacles and opportunities for individuals and companies to incorporate inclusive design. Master's Thesis in Electrical Engineering and Computer Science. KTH Royal Institute of Technology EECS, Sweden (2020)
3. Molina López, J., Medina, N.: Un enfoque para el diseño inclusivo de videojuegos centrado en jugadores daltónicos. Revista de la AIPO 2(1), 25–37 (2021)
4. Spiel, K., et al.: Nothing about us without us: investigating the role of critical disability studies in HCI. In: Proceedings of Extended Abstracts of the 2020 CHI Conference on Human Factors in Computing Systems, pp. 1–8. ACM, New York (2020)
5. Brown, T.: Design thinking. Harv. Bus. Rev.. Bus. Rev. 86, 84–95 (2008)
6. Da Silva, J., Goncalves Ferreira, M.: For an inclusive design. Brazilian J. Dev. 6(7), 44878–44888 (2020)
7. Ortiz, C., Challiol, C., Panessi, W.: Design thinking para el diseño de software accesible desde su concepción. In: VI IEEE Biennial Congress of Argentina (ARGENCON), pp. 1–8. IEEE Press, Argentina, San Juan (2022)

8. Bennett, C., Rosner, D.: The promise of empathy: design, disability, and knowing the other. In: Proceedings of the 2019 Conference on Human Factors in Computing Systems, Paper 298, pp. 1–13. ACM, New York (2019)
9. Barreiro, A.: Design Thinking to improve urban transport in Madrid. UX Collective (2018)
10. Ramos Galarza, C., Jadán Guerrero, J.: Innovación tecnológica para mejorar el proceso de lectura inicial en estudiantes con Síndrome de Down. Universidad Tecnológica Indoamérica, Ecuador (2018)
11. Rylander Eklund, A., Navarro Aguiar, U., Amacker, A.: Design thinking as sense making: developing a pragmatist theory of practice to (re) introduce sensibility. J. Prod. Innov. Manag.Innov. Manag. **39**(1), 24–43 (2022)
12. Ortiz, C., Challiol, C., Panessi, W.: Diseñar software accesible: pensar fuera de la caja. In: Libro de actas del XXIX Congreso Argentino de Ciencias de la Computación (CACIC 2023), pp. 398–408. Universidad Nacional de Luján, Argentina, Luján (2024)
13. Méndez-Muñoz, E.S., et al.: Estudio del uso de gestos en interfaces móviles por personas con síndrome de down. In: V Congreso Nacional de Tecnologías en la Educación, Benemérita Universidad Autónoma de Puebla, México (2015)
14. López-Quesada, J.: Estudio y mejora de la usabilidad de aplicaciones móviles para pacientes con disminución de movilidad. Degree's Thesis in Computer Engineering, Escuela Politécnica Superior, Universidad de Jaen (2019)
15. Doorley, S., Holcomb, S., Klebahn, P., Segovia, K., Utley, J.: Design Thinking Bootleg. d.school, Stanford University, California (2018)
16. Lakin, D.: Vender con PNL una ventaja oculta. Editorial Sirio, España (2007)
17. Interpersonal Reactivity Index test. https://www.idiena.com/test/IRI. Accessed 12 May 2023

Analyzing Induced Functional Dependencies from Spreadsheets in the GF Framework for Ontology-Based Data Access

Sergio Alejandro Gómez[1,2](✉) ⓘ and Pablo Rubén Fillottrani[1,2] ⓘ

[1] Laboratorio de I+D en Ingeniería de Software y Sistemas de Información (LISSI), Departmento de Ciencias e Ingenería en Computación, Universidad Nacional del Sur, San Andrés 800, 8000 Bahia Blanca, Argentina
[2] Comisión de Investigaciones Científicas de la Provincia de Buenos Aires, calle 526 entre 10 y 11, 1900 La Plata, Argentina
{sag,prf}@cs.uns.edu.ar
http://cs.uns.edu.ar/~sag, http://cs.uns.edu.ar/~prf

Abstract. Expressing information from spreadsheets as relational databases is crucial in the context of ontology-based data access as it facilitates structured data management and lays the foundation to transform the data into ontologies to attain advanced data processing techniques, such as reasoning and inferencing. We extend the GF framework for Ontology-Based Data Access with functionality for determining and revising the functional dependencies that are held in a spreadsheet. An initial set of tentative functional dependencies is computed using the TANE data mining algorithm. This set can then be revised by the user who is considered an oracle. Given a functional dependency, the user can see the tuples from the spreadsheet justifying it and can revise the validity of the functional dependency with the help of our system. This process is carried out by generating tuples not present in the dataset by using values already present in the table, so the user can check their prospective viability. We present a running example along with a downloadable JAVA-based application with the source code of the miner in the C programming language and the files used in our experiments to help with the reproducibility of our results. We also apply the approach to a real dataset comprised of the catalog of the library of the Department of Computer Science at Universidad Nacional del Sur.

Keywords: Spreadsheets · TANE · Functional dependencies · Ontology-Based Data Access

1 Introduction

Spreadsheets are part of the essential toolkit of organizations as they provide a simple and flexible way to store, analyze, and visualize data. They allow for efficient data management, calculations, and data analysis, enabling informed decision-making, also supporting collaboration, and allowing multiple users to

P. Pesado et al. (Eds.): CACIC 2023, CCIS 2123, pp. 288–303, 2024.
https://doi.org/10.1007/978-3-031-62245-8_20

work together on the same data set. Data in spreadsheet tables can sometimes face challenges in terms of organization due to several reasons including the lack of structure and strict constraints of a database, making it easier for inconsistencies and errors to occur. Without predefined data types and constraints, it becomes more challenging to ensure data integrity and enforce data organization rules.

Thus, while spreadsheets offer convenience and flexibility, they are not inherently optimized for data organization. To overcome these challenges, organizations often rely on more robust data management systems, such as databases, that provide structured schemas, data validation, and stronger organization capabilities. Normalized databases play a crucial role in data management by reducing redundancy and improving data integrity. The discovery of functional dependencies is an essential step in the normalization process. Functional dependencies are relationships between attributes in a database [12]. They identify the dependencies between the values of one set of attributes and another set of attributes. By discovering and analyzing these dependencies, the database designer can identify the key determinants in a dataset and eliminate data redundancy. Normalization helps in achieving a more efficient and organized database structure eliminating problems such as update, insertion, and deletion anomalies that can occur due to redundant or inconsistent data. Thus, the discovery of functional dependencies plays a crucial role in achieving these benefits and establishing a well-structured and optimized database design.

Functional dependencies are relationships between attributes of a database relation that state that the value of an attribute is uniquely determined by the values of some other attributes. Automated database analysis is interested in the computational discovery of functional dependencies. Thus, algorithms for the discovery of functional dependencies, such as TANE (Topological Attribute Noise Elimination) [5], are essential tools in data management and database design, playing a crucial role in identifying and understanding the relationships between attributes in a dataset, enabling data cleaning and normalization processes and assisting in the identification of candidate keys, which are essential for designing well-structured relational databases.

Our goal is to tackle the problem of finding functional dependencies in a spreadsheet table. For this work, we consider several constraints of the problem and propose a semi-automatic method. First, the spreadsheet data is considered restricted to a simple table where the first row corresponds to the headers or field names and the rest of the rows correspond to the records in the table. Second, for reasons of simplicity in accessing the data, they are considered in CSV format; that is, the data is a text file with a record per line and field values separated by semicolons or commas. This has the effect that if the data were in a traditional spreadsheet and distributed across several spreadsheets, they would first have to be integrated into a single spreadsheet and then converted to the target CSV format. Next, we will use a mining program to find a set of tentative functional dependencies that hold from the input data. The user using our tool can choose the field separator, and the mining tool and can inspect the data. After using the mining tool, the user will be able to see the list of dependencies found, as well as he/she will be able to see the projection of the table formed by the fields of each of the dependencies found to see the records of the original table that justify them. The user can then use our tool to generate random combinations from the found data to generate possible instances of the functional dependency under scrutiny. Thus, the user can decide whether to keep the functional dependency found or discard it.

More technically, our semi-automatic proposal consists of: first, the spread-sheet table is represented as a single data source D comprised of a CSV plain text file with fields separated by either commas or semicolons; second, we run the TANE data mining algorithm over D to obtain a set S of candidate functional dependencies supported by the data; third, the set S is presented to the user who will act as an oracle in determining the viability of each candidate functional dependency in S. For this, the user can select a particular functional depen-dency f and the system shows the projection P of the current tuples (restricted to the fields referenced in f) in D supporting the functional dependency and also generating a new set N of potential tuples that are not currently present in D. The user can select a subset S_N of N containing some of these potential tuples and add them to the tuples already present in D, building, in fact, a new set $P \cup S_N$. The TANE algorithm is then executed against $P \cup S_N$ to deter-mine if f is still valid and what new functional dependencies N_f are discovered. The user has now the chance to determine if he wants to delete f from S and also if he wants to add some of the elements of N_f to the set S of candidate functional dependencies. Thus, the main contribution of this work is (i) propos-ing a method for determining a set of functional dependencies from a single spreadsheet table; (ii) providing a functional prototypical implementation of the proposed approach, comprised of JAVA stand-alone program integrated into our GF framework for ontology-based data access; (iii) a set of examples to show how the approach works, and (iv) a modification of a third-party implementation of the TANE algorithm for being used independently from our system. We include source code and a functional executable file published online along with the data files to reproduce the results presented here. A running example is provided to illustrate our approach.

This article consolidates and extends the results presented in [3]. We extend the discussion of that work while, at the same time, we add a whole new section presenting a case study with a real dataset to show the viability of our approach to real-world scenarios. In particular, we tested our approach on the catalog of the library of the Department of Computer Science and Engineering of the Universidad Nacional del Sur. We also extended the discussion of related work.

The rest of the paper is structured as follows. In Sect. 2, we discuss how to find functional dependencies in CSV files and the modifications we made to a third-party data miner published online. In Sect. 3, we present the module added to GF to revise functional dependencies in the CSV file. In Sect. 4, we present a detailed case study concerning the application of our tool to the discovery and revision of the functional dependencies in the DCIC-UNS library. In Sect. 5, we review related work. In Sect. 6, we conclude and foresee future work.

2   Finding Functional Dependencies in Spreadsheets

We are interested in discovering functional dependencies in spreadsheet data expressed as CSV files. In Fig. (1.a), we show a simple Excel table for representing information about owners of cars along with information about the cars themselves. The information of the owners is comprised of the columns *IDPerson* and *Name*. Cars are represented by the columns *IDCar*, *CarBrand*, and *CarPerception*. Notice that the column *CarPerception* represents the perception of the particular brand by a particular user. CSV files are plain text files that store tabular data as a series of values, with each value separated by a comma, making them widely used for data exchange between different programs and systems. For instance, in Fig. (1.b), we present the CSV version of the Excel table of Fig. (1.a). Notice that in this particular case, the field separator is the semicolon character.

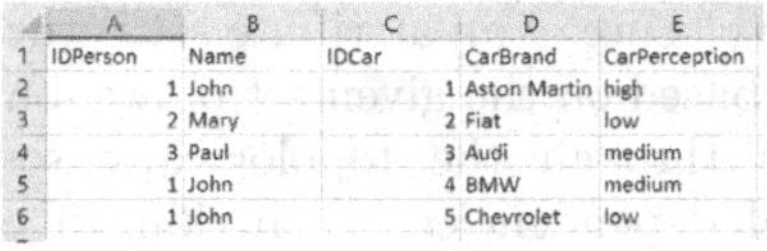

	A	B	C	D	E
1	IDPerson	Name	IDCar	CarBrand	CarPerception
2		1 John		1 Aston Martin	high
3		2 Mary		2 Fiat	low
4		3 Paul		3 Audi	medium
5		1 John		4 BMW	medium
6		1 John		5 Chevrolet	low

```
IDPerson;Name;IDCar;CarBrand;CarPerception
1;John;1;Aston Martin;high
2;Mary;2;Fiat;low
3;Paul;3;Audi;medium
1;John;4;BMW;medium
1;John;5;Chevrolet;low
```

(a)   (b)

Fig. 1. (a) Spreadsheet for owners of cars and (b) CSV code of the spreadsheet

In previous publications ([4] and references therein), we have been reporting about the development of a framework for Ontology-Based Data Access called GF. In this work, we extend such a framework to solve the problem of finding functional dependencies hidden in CSV tabular data. The proposal presented in this work has been integrated with such application. A closed-source standalone JAVA application and auxiliary data are available online[1] to reproduce the results presented here. Also, an open-source extension of the TANE miner described in the next section is available for downloading and use.

In the context of relational databases, a functional dependency is a relationship between two sets of attributes within a database table, that describes the dependence of one set of attributes (known as the dependent attributes) on another set of attributes (known as the determinant attributes). That is, given the values of the determinant attributes, the values of the dependent attributes can be determined. Functional dependencies play a crucial role in database design and normalization, helping to ensure data integrity and minimize data redundancy.

TANE (Topological Attribute Noise Elimination) [5] is an algorithm used for mining functional dependencies from a given relational database table. It is based on the concept of the topological sort and utilizes pruning techniques

---

[1] See http://cs.uns.edu.ar/~sag/cacic2023springer.

to efficiently discover all the non-redundant functional dependencies within the table. A brief explanation of the TANE algorithm is as follows:

1. *Input:* The algorithm takes a relational database table as input, consisting of a set of attributes and their corresponding values.
2. *Candidate Generation:* Initially, TANE starts with a set of candidate functional dependencies that include individual attributes and pairs of attributes. For example, if the table has attributes A, B, and C, the initial set candidates would be $\{A \to B, A \to C, B \to A, B \to C, C \to A, C \to B\}$.
3. *Pruning:* The algorithm employs pruning techniques to eliminate redundant candidates. It checks if each candidate can be further extended by adding more attributes without violating the closure property. If a candidate is found to be redundant, it is removed from the set of candidates.
4. *Topological Sorting:* TANE performs a topological sorting of the attributes based on their dependencies to ensure that dependencies are discovered in a particular order. It determines the dependencies between attributes by computing the closures of attribute sets. The closure of an attribute set is the set of all attributes that can be determined based on the given set of attributes.
5. *Dependency Discovery:* TANE iterates through the topologically sorted attribute order and discovers functional dependencies by checking if each candidate is satisfied by the current set of attributes. If a candidate is satisfied, it is considered a valid functional dependency and added to the result set.
6. *Closure Pruning:* After discovering each dependency, TANE applies closure pruning to eliminate any remaining redundant candidates that are no longer necessary based on the dependencies found so far.
7. *Repeat Step*: Steps 4 to 6 are repeated until no more dependencies can be discovered.
8. *Output:* The final result set contains all the non-redundant functional dependencies that have been mined from the input table.

Our approach to finding the functional dependencies held in a spreadsheet starts by running a TANE miner on the CSV file contents. For doing this, we adapted an already existing TANE implementation.[2] That implementation is a console application based on the C programming language. It takes as input a CSV file and as output it prints to the screen the functional dependencies that it has found. The dependencies found are listed as field indexes.

From that starting point, we extended that miner to have a more friendly interface that allows us to use it as a parameterized command-line application where the input file, output file, temporary file, and field-separator character can be specified by a prospector user. In Fig. 2, we can see an example of how to use the improved utility on the data presented in Fig. (1.b). The input file named Owner-Car.csv is preceded by the *-i* switch. Notice that the temporary file (preceded by the *-t* switch) is needed to redirect the original output of the miner

---

[2] See   https://github.com/getterk96/Database-Functional-Dependency-Digging-Algorithms.

and the output file (preceded by the -o switch) is only useful to a client/user. Additionally, the -s switch allows to specify a separator character for fields (viz., either a semicolon or a comma).

The functional dependencies found with the miner are presented in Fig. 3. We call these dependencies, *tentative functional dependencies*. Notice that some of these functional dependencies are the true ones (e.g. *IDPerson → Name*) but other ones are just contingent on the values present in the data (e.g. *Name → IDPerson*). The revision of these dependencies to discard the false ones from the set of tentative functional dependencies is the subject that the module that we have added to GF deals with, and that is the matter of the next section.

TANE-Sergio.exe -i "Owner-Car.csv" -o "result-owner-car.txt" -t
"temporal-owner-car.txt" -s ";"

Fig. 2. Improved interface for the TANE miner

IDPerson → Name	*IDCar → Name*
IDPerson CarPerception → IDCar	*IDCar → CarBrand*
IDPerson CarPerception → CarBrand	*IDCar → CarPerception*
Name → IDPerson	*CarBrand → IDPerson*
Name CarPerception → IDCar	*CarBrand → Name*
Name CarPerception → CarBrand	*CarBrand → IDCar*
IDCar → IDPerson	*CarBrand → CarPerception*

Fig. 3. Functional dependencies found by the TANE miner in the *CarOwner* spreadsheet

3 Revising Functional Dependencies

Here, we present the new module in GF that allows a user to revise functional dependencies computed from a CSV data source interactively. In Fig. 4, we present the user interface for using the new module.

The controls in the GUI are enabled in a strict order that allows the user to unlock functionalities when input data is available. This order is specified by the state diagram in Fig. 5. The usual workflow a user would follow when using the application will be: (1) opening the form takes him to state q_0; (2) specifying the data source by selecting the particular CSV file he wants to work with (thus going into state q_1); (3) at any time the data from the data source can be explored; (4) running the data miner as the one described in Sect. 2 computes the functional dependencies that are shown on the list on the left (notice that the miner program can be changed for an alternative program provided that it satisfies the interface as explained in Fig. 2), this will take the user to state q_2; (5) once the list is filled with the functional dependencies computed from the

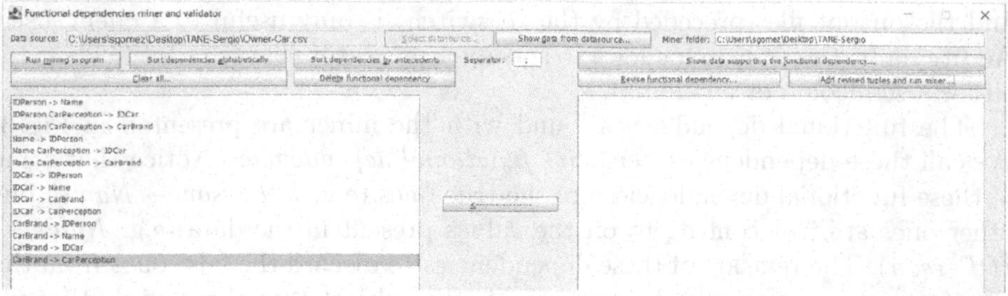

Fig. 4. Module for mining and validating functional dependencies in CSV files

current data in the CSV, which we chose to call *tentative functional dependencies*, as they are contingent on current data, the user can select one of them getting to state q_3; (6) once in q_3, the user can optionally choose to directly delete a tentative functional dependency or else to see the projection of the table limited to the columns mentioned in the selected functional dependency to determine if some combination of values is missing, determining so by pressing the button labeled "Revise FD" will take him to state q_4; (7) in q_4 the application will open a new form showing to the user invented tuples that are not currently in the table by producing random combinations with data already present in the table according to the algorithm in Fig. 7; (8) in q_5, the user can select one or more than one alternative tuple to add to the already existing tuples in the projected table, and then go to q_6; (9) in q_6, the miner is run on the projected table to validate if the revised dependency still holds or new ones appear, this new computed dependencies are displayed on the list located on the right, leading the system to state q_7; (10) in q_7, the user can delete the revised functional dependency or select some of the newly found functional dependencies and copy them to the list on the left pane, and, (11) finally, the user can clear the process to return to state q_0.

Regarding step (2), our approach assumes that all fields are considered string-typed, that no field delimiters are present and the user can choose only between comma and semicolon characters as field separators. Step (4) was already discussed in Sect. 2. To illustrate how steps (5)–(10) are intended to be used, we continue the preceding example. Consider the tentative functional dependency *CarBrand* → *CarPerception* computed in (4). The projection of the tuples restricted to its fields, and without duplicate data, is shown in Fig. (6.a). For example, suppose that the user considers that the perception of *Chevrolet* must be *high* instead of *low*. The user can ask the system to generate unseen tuples in steps (6)-(7). This newly invented tuples are generated using the algorithm in Fig. 7. Once the user explores the invented tuples, he can select the appropriate ones to be added to the projection (see Fig. 6.b). Then, after running again the miner, in this particular case, there are no functional dependencies that hold in this view of the table with the invented record that was selected. So the user can decide to delete the functional dependency under consideration. Conversely, as the system generates those potential scenarios, it lets the user decide to keep or discard the proposed functional dependency. When the user observes that a suggested combination of data from the domain that respects the functional dependency is not consistent with his view of the domain, he can opt for discarding the suggested dependency. Besides, if other functional dependencies were discovered to hold in this new dataset, they will be shown in the list on the right side of the screen, and then the user can decide to add them to the main set of tentative functional dependencies.

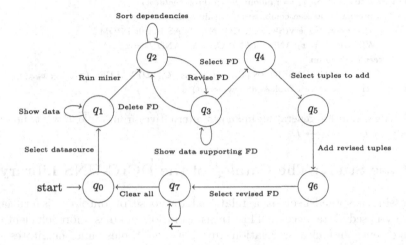

Fig. 5. State diagram describing the usage of the GUI controls

Records justif...	CarPerception
CarBrand	CarPerception
Aston Martin	high
Audi	medium
BMW	medium
Chevrolet	low
Fiat	low

(a)

Revise functional dependency with potential values: ...

CarBrand	CarPerception
Aston Martin	low
Fiat	high
Audi	high
Fiat	medium
BMW	high
Audi	low
Chevrolet	high
BMW	low
Chevrolet	medium
Aston Martin	medium

(b)

Fig. 6. (a) Records justifying functional dependency *CarBrand → CarPerception* and (b) Invented records with alternative values

Algorithm GenerateAlternatives(Table T, FunctionalDependency $C_1 \ldots C_n \to D$)

Let *values* be a $(n+1)$-size vector of sets

for $i := 1$ **to** n **do**

   $values_i$:= executeQuery(SELECT DISTINCT C_i FROM T)

$values_{n+1}$:= executeQuery(SELECT DISTINCT D FROM T)

Let *script* be an empty sequence of strings

script.addLine(CREATE TABLE $aux(C_1$ VARCHAR(100), $\ldots$, C_n VARCHAR(100), D VAR-CHAR(100));)

for *epoch* := 1 **to** MAX_TUPLES **do**

   Let x be a vector of $n+1$ components

   for $i := 1$ **to** $n+1$ **do** x_i := randomElementFrom($values_i$)

   if x is a previously unseen combination of values **then**

      result := executeQuery(SELECT COUNT (*) AS Result FROM T

         WHERE $C_1 = x_1$ AND $\ldots$ AND $C_n = x_n$ AND $D = x_{n+1}$)

      if *result* = 0 **then**

         script.addLine(INSERT INTO $aux(C_1, \ldots, C_n, D)$ VALUES $(x_1, \ldots, x_{n+1})$;)

ExecuteSQLScriptToGenerateTableAndShow(*script*)

Fig. 7. Algorithm for generating unknown alternatives from table T w.r.t. functional dependency $C_1 \ldots C_n \to D$

4   Case Study: The Catalog of the DCIC-UNS Library

Expressing a spreadsheet as a relational database or ontology is crucial for ontology-based data access. This transformation enables more efficient data management, and clearer relationships between tables, and facilitates complex queries and retrieval in relational databases. Ontologies provide a semantic framework, enhancing data understanding and interoperability. Converting spreadsheet data into these formats improves integration and interoperability, simplifying information analysis from multiple sources. It also sets the stage for advanced processing techniques like reasoning and inferencing, essential for extracting insights from complex datasets. Overall, this approach enhances data accessibility, interoperability, and analytical capabilities within ontology-based data access frameworks.

In this section, we tackle the problem of testing our proposed approach on real datasets. We demonstrate the practical application of our approach through a case study involving the processing of real-world data from the library catalog of the Department of Computer Science and Engineering at Universidad Nacional del Sur. Our method facilitates the discovery of a collection of functional dependencies within a CSV file extracted from this catalog. We observe the system's ability to identify anticipated dependencies as well as contingent ones within the dataset. These contingent dependencies are thoroughly analyzed with their corresponding justifying values and through the generation of random combinations derived from the table values. Consequently, users are empowered to make informed decisions regarding the retention or elimination of the discovered dependencies.

The DCIC library catalog is maintained independently from the institution's formal information system. It consists of an Excel spreadsheet comprising multiple data sheets. For this study, we will solely focus on the three sheets of the book catalog, deferring the analysis of the newspaper library data for subsequent research. As explained below, we will extract the relevant data and then integrate it as a single file in CSV format (available in the URL mentioned in the introduction).

The schema of the Excel table consists of various columns serving different purposes for inventory management and documentation. The *Nro de Inventario* (*Inventory Number*) column contains unique identifiers for each item in the inventory. *Autor* (*Author*) and *Título* (*Title*) columns store information about the author and title of the items, respectively. *Comprado/Donado* (*Bought/Donated*) may indicate whether the item was purchased or donated. *Observaciones* (*Observations*)) provides a space for any additional notes or remarks. *Orden de Compra* (*Purchase order*) could contain purchase order details if applicable, while *Legajo* (*File*) might reference a file or record number. *Precio* would hold the price of the item, while *Fecha de Inventario* (*Inventory date*) records the date it was inventoried. *Destino* (*Destiny*) specifies the intended use or location of the item. *Condición General de Conservación* (*General Conservation Condition*) likely describes the overall condition of the item for conservation purposes. *ISBN* holds the International Standard Book Number if applicable, and *Número de Lote* (*Lot number*) might indicate batch or lot information. This schema comprehensively captures key attributes necessary for managing and tracking inventory items effectively within an Excel spreadsheet.

The ETL (Extract, Transform, and Load) cycle [7,10] in data mining is a fundamental process for preparing raw data for analysis and deriving meaningful insights. It begins with the extraction phase, where data is gathered from various heterogeneous sources such as databases, files, or APIs. Next, in the transformation phase, the extracted data undergoes cleaning, normalization, aggregation, and other preprocessing steps to ensure consistency, quality, and compatibility with the analysis tools and algorithms. This phase also involves feature engineering, where new variables may be created or existing ones modified to enhance the predictive power of the data. Finally, in the load phase, the transformed data is loaded into the target data warehouse or data repository where it is made available for analysis by data mining algorithms. The ETL cycle is iterative and continuous, as data mining projects often require ongoing data collection, preprocessing, and analysis to adapt to changing business requirements and data characteristics. By efficiently managing the ETL process, organizations can maximize the effectiveness of their data mining initiatives and uncover valuable insights to drive informed decision-making and business success.

Below, we explain the steps of the ETL process that we carried out on the DCIC library data. The library catalog consists of approximately 3,000 books among other publications that we decided not to process for reasons of simplicity. The catalog is stored in a single spreadsheet consisting of several sheets. The spreadsheet is made up of 3 identically formatted sheets corresponding to inventory numbers 0 to 1000, 1001 to 2000, and 2001 to 3000, respectively. Then, we join the 3 sheets into a single spreadsheet. Then, we save the unified spreadsheet as a spreadsheet in CSV format since this is the required input of the mining auxiliary program. The mining program restrictions such as not detecting double quotes and not noticing blanks, require that semicolon characters along with embedded blanks within fields be replaced with neutral characters. Also, as part of the cleaning process, invalid numbers corresponding to non-existent prices were eliminated. Only at that moment, the data can be loaded into the application. The same application is responsible for modifying non-Ascii characters and replacing empty fields with a special token to represent null values.

After running the TANE miner, we find an extensive list of tentative functional dependencies. Some of them are shown in Figs. 8 and 9. Notice that for space reasons, we do not show all the dependencies found by the miner. Nonetheless, for completeness, they are shown in the accompanying documentation published online at the URL cited in Sect. 3.

```
InventoryNumber -> Author
InventoryNumber -> Title
InventoryNumber -> Bought-Donated
InventoryNumber -> Observations
InventoryNumber -> PurchaseOrder
InventoryNumber -> File
InventoryNumber -> Price
InventoryNumber -> InventoryDate
InventoryNumber -> Destiny
InventoryNumber -> GeneralConservationCondition
InventoryNumber -> ISBN
InventoryNumber -> LotNumber
Author Title -> Destiny
Author Title -> GeneralConservationCondition
Author Title Observations ISBN -> Bought-Donated
Author Title Observations ISBN -> PurchaseOrder
Author Title Observations ISBN -> File
Author Title Observations ISBN -> InventoryDate
Author Title Price -> Bought-Donated
Author Title Price -> PurchaseOrder

Author Title Price -> File
Author Title Price -> InventoryDate
Author Title Price -> ISBN
Author Title LotNumber -> Bought-Donated
Author Title LotNumber -> Observations
Author Title LotNumber -> PurchaseOrder
Author Title LotNumber -> File
Author Title LotNumber -> Price
Author Title LotNumber -> InventoryDate
Author Title LotNumber -> ISBN
Author Bought-Donated -> Destiny
Author Bought-Donated File -> PurchaseOrder
Author Bought-Donated ISBN -> GeneralConservationCondition
Author Observations InventoryDate -> GeneralConservationCondition
Author PurchaseOrder -> File
Author PurchaseOrder GeneralConservationCondition -> Destiny
Author File GeneralConservationCondition -> Destiny
Author Price GeneralConservationCondition -> Destiny
Author InventoryDate -> Destiny
Author GeneralConservationCondition LotNumber -> Destiny
Author ISBN -> Destiny
```

Fig. 8. Some of the tentative functional dependencies found by the TANE miner when applied to the catalog of the DCIC-UNS library

Among the results, we can see that the expected functional dependencies are found by the miner. Among these, we can find all those determined by the inventory number. For example, the inventory number in title (i.e. *InventoryNumber → Title*). Using our tool, the user can see the validity of the dependency, as shown in Fig. 10.

However, other dependencies are also found, whose soundness is not that clear. For example, the general conservation condition into title functional dependency does not seem correct because the field contents look intuitively unrelated. When we look at the records that support the dependency, we can see that the field contains the value null or good, which makes the dependency trivially valid (see Fig. 11). The module for generating random possible values for the combination of the aforementioned field yields the results shown in Fig. 12. From the random combinations generated by the system, we see that they would be possible but that in reality the proposal of the functional dependency is not

```
Bought-Donated Observations File -> PurchaseOrder
Bought-Donated Observations File GeneralConservationCondition LotNumber -> Author
Bought-Donated Observations InventoryDate -> Destiny
Bought-Donated Observations InventoryDate -> GeneralConservationCondition
Bought-Donated Observations LotNumber -> Destiny
Bought-Donated PurchaseOrder -> File
Bought-Donated PurchaseOrder Destiny -> GeneralConservationCondition
Bought-Donated PurchaseOrder GeneralConservationCondition ISBN -> Author
Bought-Donated File GeneralConservationCondition ISBN -> Author
Bought-Donated InventoryDate LotNumber -> Observations
Bought-Donated GeneralConservationCondition -> Destiny
Bought-Donated GeneralConservationCondition ISBN LotNumber -> PurchaseOrder
Bought-Donated GeneralConservationCondition ISBN LotNumber -> File
Observations PurchaseOrder Price InventoryDate Destiny LotNumber -> Bought-Donated
Observations PurchaseOrder Price GeneralConservationCondition -> File
Observations File ISBN LotNumber -> PurchaseOrder
Observations GeneralConservationCondition -> Destiny
PurchaseOrder Price InventoryDate GeneralConservationCondition LotNumber -> File
PurchaseOrder Price GeneralConservationCondition ISBN -> Bought-Donated
PurchaseOrder InventoryDate Destiny -> GeneralConservationCondition
PurchaseOrder InventoryDate GeneralConservationCondition LotNumber -> Bought-Donated
PurchaseOrder Destiny ISBN -> Observations
PurchaseOrder ISBN -> File
File Price InventoryDate -> Observations
File InventoryDate Destiny -> GeneralConservationCondition
File ISBN LotNumber -> Bought-Donated
Price ISBN -> File
InventoryDate GeneralConservationCondition -> Destiny
InventoryDate ISBN -> GeneralConservationCondition
InventoryDate LotNumber -> ISBN
GeneralConservationCondition -> Title
ISBN LotNumber -> Price
```

Fig. 9. Some of the tentative functional dependencies found by the TANE miner when applied to the catalog of the DCIC-UNS library (cont.)

related to the application domain considered. With this result in mind, the user can decide whether to remove such a functional dependency from the list of tentative functional dependencies.

5   Related Work

Cunha et al. [1] present techniques and tools to transform spreadsheets into relational databases and back. A set of data refinement rules is introduced to map a tabular datatype into a relational database schema. Having expressed the transformation of the two data models as data refinements, they obtain for free the functions that migrate the data using well-known relational database techniques to optimize and query the data. Because data refinements define bi-directional transformations, they can map such databases back to an optimized spreadsheet. They implemented the data refinement rules and constructed Haskell-based tools to manipulate, optimize, and refactor Excel-like spreadsheets. In our prototypical approach deals with Excel files but expressed as CSV tables, GF has the functionality to load Excel files and this feature can be added in the future. In our application, CSV files are handled internally as H2 tables but the data miner that we use as an external tool handles it as plain text. The work of Cunha et al. uses the set of functional dependencies to generate a normalized relational database from the contents of the spreadsheet. Our application does not do that yet and adding that functionality remains as future work. They use the FUN mining technique and we use the TANE mining technique. As our approach is fully customizable, we could employ the FUN miner in the future provided a functioning version of it is available. In particular, Cunha et al. present an

InventoryNumber	Title
	Records justifying functional dependency: InventoryNumber -> Title
1	A theory of Objects. Monografs of Computer Science. Ej. 1
10	Handbook of Logic in Computer Science, Volume 2: Background: Computational Structures - Ej. 2
100	Inductive Logic Programming: From Machine Learning to Software Engineering - Ej. 2
1000	Structured Computer Organization, 3rd. Edition - Ej. 1
1001	Structured Computer Organization, 3rd. Edition - Ej. 2
1002	Structured Computer Organization - 4□ Ed. - Ej. 1
1003	Structured Computer Organization - 4□ Ed. - Ej. 2
1004	Structured Computer Organization - 4□ Ed. - Ej. 3
1005	Structured Computer Organization - 4□ Ed. - Ej. 4
1006	Structured Computer Organization - 4□ Ed. - Ej. 5
1007	Temporal Data Bases. Theory, Design and Implementation
1008	Core Java Web Server
1009	Semantics of programming languages
101	History of Programming Languages - Ej. 1
1010	Communicating with Virtual Worlds
1011	Interactive computer animation
1012	Models and Techniques in Computer Animation
1013	The Phenomenon of Commonsense reasoning. Nonmonotonicity, action & information
1014	File Organization and Processing
1015	IPng and the TCP/IP Protocols: Implementing the Next Generation Internet
1016	The Illusion of Life : Disney Animation
1017	Object-Oriented Programming in Eiffel. 2nd. Ed.- Ej. 2
1018	Object-Oriented Programming in Eiffel - 2□ Ed.Ej. 1
1019	Instruction-Level Parallel Processors
102	History of Programming Languages - Ej. 2
1020	The Computer Science and Engineering Handbook - Ej. 1
1021	The Computer Science and Engineering Handbook - Ej. 2
1022	Constructive Foundations for Functional Languages
1023	A First Course in Database Systems - Ej. 1
1024	A First Course in Database Systems - Ej. 2
1026	Elements of ML Programming - Ej. 2
1027	Elements of ML Programming - ML97 Ed.Ej 1
1028	Elements of ML Programming - ML97 Ed.Ej 2
1029	Compiling in Modula-2
103	Software Configuration Management
1030	UNIX Internals: The New Frontiers - Ej. 1
1031	UNIX Internals: The New Frontiers - Ej. 2
1032	UNIX Internals: The New Frontiers - Ej. 3
1033	Non-monotonic Reasoning and Partial Semantics
1034	Logic and Information Flow

Fig. 10. Records justifying the functional dependency *InventoryNumber* → *Title*

GeneralConservationCondition	Title
	Records justifying functional dependency: GeneralConservationCondition -> Title
Buena	Android Epistemology - Ej. 1
Buena	Android Epistemology - Ej. 2
Buena	Animating Facial features and Expressions
Buena	Anuario de Estad□sticas Universitarias 2006. Vol. 1 (PROC
Buena	Anuario de Estad□sticas Universitarias 2006. Vol. 2 (PROC
Buena	An□lisis y Dise□o Orientado a Objetos
Buena	Apache. The Definitive Guide, 2nd. Ed.
Buena	Aplique C ++
Buena	Applied Logic.(BIB 8)
Buena	Applied Network Optimization.(BIB.8)
Buena	Applied cyptography. Protocols, Algorithms and Source Cod
Buena	Applying UML and Patterns. Third Edition
Buena	Applying UML and patterns

Fig. 11. Records justifying the functional dependency *GeneralConservationCon − dition* → *Title*

GeneralConservationCondition	Title
tapa deteriorada	Computer Architecture. A Quantitative Approach, 2nd. Ed. - Ej.
Regular	Use Cases - Requirements in Context
Regular (vino as☐ de proveedor)	Computaci☐n de alto desempe☐o en GPU Ejemplar 2
DETERIORADO	Principles of Distributed Sysytems - Ej. 2
tapa deteriorada	UML para programadores Java
Buena.	Elements of ML Programming. ML 97. Ej. 3
Malo	Handbook of Theoretical Computer Science, Vol. A: Algorithms
0-12-208875-1	Computational Visualization. Graphics, Abstraction and Interacti
Regular (vino as☐ de proveedor)	The definition of standard ML
Buena	The Unified Modeling Language (UML) Reference Manual
0-12-208875-1	Scalable Uncertainty Management Ejemplar 1
regular	Encyclopedia of Graphics File Formats, 2nd. Ed. - Ej. 1
Regular	Learning Cocoa
Buena.	An Introduction to programming in C. A Book in C
DETERIORADO	Data Model Patterns. Conventions of Thought
DETERIORADO	The Structure of Typed Programming Languages - Ej. 1
Regular (vino as☐ de proveedor)	The C Programming Language. Second edition. EJ.3
tapa deteriorada	Structural Complexity II - Ej. 2
Buena.	Programaci☐n in Linux. 2da. Edici☐n

Title bar: Revise functional dependency with potential values: GeneralConservationCondition -> Title

Fig. 12. Revising the functional dependency *GeneralConservationCondition* → *Title* with the generator of random combinations for the values of the fields

example that considers a spreadsheet for representing a property renting system (see [1, Fig. 1]). In the accompanying files published online with our executable application, we provide a recreation of that file, named `book.csv`, showing that our system can compute the functional dependencies shown in that work.

Despite the ubiquity of spreadsheets, the problem of dealing with transformations of spreadsheet data to more formal data formats is still relevant. Müller and Mertová [9] justify and propose a lightweight recording-based solution to the tracing of the steps for transforming spreadsheets into ontologies that works on a wide variety of spreadsheet programs, from Microsoft Excel to Google Docs. GF can transform spreadsheets into ontologies but in this particular work, we are concentrated in functional dependencies emerging from tables within spreadsheet data.

Salem and Abdo [11] propose two techniques for mining accurate conditional functional dependencies rules from such databases to be employed for data cleaning. The idea of the proposed techniques is to mine firstly maximal closed frequent patterns, then mine the dependable conditional functional dependencies rules with the help of lift measure. That approach is complementary to ours because, in the current status of our work, we assume that the data is accurate. Their approach could be used to extend our solution with a data-cleaning preprocess for capturing semantic errors.

There are several works in the literature that deal with the problem of finding functional dependencies in relational databases [2,6,8,13]. Kantola et al. [6] implemented a database design and analysis tool called Design-By-Example that is based on the use of example databases to help locate the constraints in the data. Their tool uses an initial ER-entity diagram and data instances to find the functional dependencies. Our work in contrast works only at the level of a universal table extracted from the CSV file that our system can process. Lopes et al. [8] propose an efficient algorithm called Dep-Miner for discovering minimal non-trivial functional dependencies from large databases. According to them, their algorithm is more efficient than TANE. Our work could be extended by having an implementation of Dep-Miner provided it satisfies the interface required by our system.

6   Conclusions and Future Work

This paper addresses the challenge of identifying functional dependencies within a spreadsheet table. Our approach involves leveraging the TANE data mining algorithm, which we integrated with our GF framework for ontology-based data access. We illustrated our method through a practical example, demonstrating how it aids users in refining a provisional set of functional dependencies computed with TANE by generating possible tuples not yet present in the table.

We present the application of our approach to a case study with real-world data processing in the library catalog of the Department of Computer Science and Engineering of the Universidad Nacional del Sur. We show how our approach allows finding a set of functional dependencies from a CSV file extracted from such a catalog. The system finds the expected dependencies and we also saw how it finds contingent dependencies on the data set and how they can be analyzed with the values that justify them and also with the generation of random combinations formed from the values in the table. Thus, the user can decide whether to keep or discard the dependencies found.

Limitations of our approach include treating all fields in the input CSV file as string types, disregarding field delimiters, and restricting users to selecting either comma or semicolon characters as field separators. However, our solution is adaptable, provided that a miner adheres to a precise command-line interface.

Potential avenues for further research include creating a normalized database using the functional dependencies computed by the miner, which can then be refined by the user with our system's assistance before exporting the database as an ontology. Additionally, exploring the adaptation of mining algorithms to diverse data types and constraints presents promising directions for future investigation.

Acknowledgments. This work was supported by Secretaría General de Ciencia y Técnica, Universidad Nacional del Sur, Argentina, and by Comisión de Investigaciones Científicas de la Provincia de Buenos Aires (CIC-PBA).

Disclosure of Interests. The authors have no competing interests to declare that are relevant to the content of this article.

References

1. Cunha, J., Saraiva, J., Visser, J.: From spreadsheets to relational databases and back. In: PEPM '09: Proceedings of the 2009 ACM SIGPLAN Workshop on Partial Evaluation and Program Manipulation, pp. 179–188. ACM, January 2009. https://doi.org/10.1145/1480945.1480972
2. Gao, Y.: Clustering Dependencies over Relational Tables. Master's thesis, University of Waterloo (2016)
3. Gómez, S., Fillottrani, P.R.: A prototypical tool for analyzing functional dependencies induced from spreadsheets. In: Fernández, J.M. (ed.) Libro de Actas: XXIX Congreso Argentino de Ciencias de la Computación (CACIC 2023), pp. 409–417. Universidad Nacional de Luján, October 2023
4. Gómez, S.A., Fillottrani, P.R.: A query-by-example approach to compose SPARQL queries in the GF framework for ontology-based data access. In: Pesado, P. (ed.) 28th Argentine Congress, CACIC 2022 – Revised Selected Papers, pp. 211–226. Springer (2023)
5. Huhtala, Y., Kärkkäinen, J., Porkka, P., Toivonen, H.: TANE-An efficient algorithm for discovering functional and approximate dependencies. Comput. J. **42**(2), 100–111 (1999)
6. Kantola, M., Mannila, H., Räihä, K.J., Siirtola, H.: Discovering functional and inclusion dependencies in relational databases. Int. J. Intell. Syst. **7**(7), 591–607 (1992)
7. Kimball, R., Ross, M.: The Data Warehouse Toolkit, 3rd edn. Wiley (2013)
8. Lopes, S., Petit, J.-M., Lakhal, L.: Efficient discovery of functional dependencies and armstrong relations. In: Zaniolo, C., Lockemann, P.C., Scholl, M.H., Grust, T. (eds.) EDBT 2000. LNCS, vol. 1777, pp. 350–364. Springer, Heidelberg (2000). https://doi.org/10.1007/3-540-46439-5_24
9. Wolfgang, M., Mertová, L.: ReStoRunT: simple recording, storing, running and tracing changes in spreadsheets. In: BTW 2023. Gesellschaft für Informatik e.V.., Bonn. ISBN: 978-3-88579-725-8, pp. 865–877, Dresden, Germany (2023). https://doi.org/10.18420/BTW2023-57
10. Pyle, D.: Data Preparation for Data Mining. Morgan Kaufmann (1999)
11. Salem, R., Abdo, A.: Fixing rules for data cleaning based on conditional functional dependency. Future Comput. Inf. J. **1**(1), 10–26 (2016). https://doi.org/10.1016/j.fcij.2017.03.002. https://www.sciencedirect.com/science/article/pii/S2314728817300041
12. Silberchatz, A., Korth, H.F., Sudarshan, S.: Database System Concepts, 6th edn. Mc, Graw Hill (2011)
13. Sug, H.: Efficient checking of functional dependencies for relations. In: Journal of Physics: Conference Series, vol. 1564, p. 012011. IOP Publishing (2020)

Signal Processing and Real-Time Systems

Data Acquisition System Using Low-Complexity Sensors for Ancient Tractors in the Río Negro and Neuquén Valley

Rafael Ignacio Zurita[1]([✉]), Naiara Sheffield[2], Dario Mendieta[2], Marcelo Moreyra[2], Favio Masson[3], and Miriam Lechner[1]

[1] Dpto. Ing. de Computadoras, Facultad de Informática, Universidad Nacional del Comahue, Neuquén, Argentina

[2] Dpto. de Electrotecnia, Facultad de Ingeniería, Universidad Nacional del Comahue, Neuquén, Argentina

[3] Departamento de Ing. Eléctrica y de Computadoras, Universidad Nacional del Sur., Bahía Blanca, Argentina

rafa@fi.uncoma.edu.ar

Abstract. Machine autonomous navigation in fruit orchards is a subject of research queryAs per Springer style, both city and country names must be present in the affiliations. Accordingly, we have inserted the city and country names in the affiliation 1. Please check and confirm if the inserted city and country names are correct. If not, please provide us with the correct city and country names. and development primarily in developed countries. Current solutions involve high-performance computers and specific expensive and complex sensors. Additionally, most of the solutions require adapting or reconfiguring orchards to autonomous tractor-robots, which implies significant investments. However, regionally, 74% of fruit orchards in the Alto Valle of Río Negro and Neuquén belong to small family producers, who typically possess old tractors with models ranging from 1970 to 2000.

In order to propose a long-term solution for autonomous navigation in local fruit orchads, this article presents the architecture of an embedded system utilizing low-complexity sensors to capture the necessary signals for localization (position and orientation) of any regional old tractor within its working environment. An evaluation of the sampling frequency achieved by the selected sensors and developed software is provided, along with an analysis, employing a state-of-the-art Visual-SLAM algorithm, of the image sequences that can be captured using the proposed system.

Keywords: Autonomous Navigation · Fruit Farming · Signal Acquisition · Real-Time Embedded System · Low-Complexity Sensors

1 Introduction

In the Argentine Northern Patagonia, within the "Alto Valle" of Río Negro and Neuquén, the apple and pear production is the main agriculture activity. By

P. Pesado et al. (Eds.): CACIC 2023, CCIS 2123, pp. 307–319, 2024.
https://doi.org/10.1007/978-3-031-62245-8_21

2020, the total area planted with apple and pear trees reached 35,609 hectares, with approximately 74% of fruit-producing establishments (around 1200) being operated by small family producers [1, 18]. In these traditional operations, the producer and their family carry out nearly all cultural management actions on the farm, hiring temporary labor during harvesting, thinning, or pruning.

Currently, the most commonly used agricultural machinery in the Alto Valle to facilitate rural tasks is the tractor, which is needed in all fruit and vegetable farming activities: from soil preparation, weeding, crop protection, and harvesting to transportation of the produce [2]. Each small producer typically owns one (at most two) tractor, with models ranging from 1970 to 2000 [7].

Over the past two decades, advancements have been made in the development of autonomous agricultural vehicles [11, 14]. An autonomous driving system can control a vehicle and navigate its environment without human intervention [12]. A vehicle equipped with such a system perceives its environment, locates its position, and operates the vehicle to achieve designated routes. Tractors with autopilots have existed since 2000, mainly designed for working in open field extensions, particularly in cereal production. A commercial example is John Deere's AutoTrac autopilot [8]. In fruit growing, tree lines and row heights, as found in orchards like those in the Alto Valle, make it challenging, for those autopilot systems, to achieve the required accurate localization. This is mainly because satellite signals do not have direct line-of-sight to GPS receivers [17].

In recent years, autopilot systems with alternative techniques for fruit growing have been developed in developed countries. However, these developments focus on specific high-cost sensors, high-performance computers, and techniques that require adapting orchards to the machinery, either because it is new and designed based on autopilot capabilities, or because it already exists but likely needs to be retrofitted, involving significant investments.

We present a prototype system aiming to achieve suitable performance for the application while imposing computational and sensing constraints to make implementation viable for small farmer families. This paper is an extension of the work presented previously in October, 2023, at the XXIX Congreso Argentino de Ciencias de la Computación [13]. The proposed architecture utilizes an embedded computer and low-complexity sensors to capture vital signals required in the positioning process (location and orientation) of any regional older tractor within its working environment. An evaluation of the sampling frequency achieved by the selected sensors and developed software is provided, along with an assessment of the video signal that can be captured using the proposed system, employing a state-of-the-art Visual-SLAM algorithm. Also, a specific calibration method for the low-cost video camera is detailed. The results indicate that the proposed system exhibits suitable initial characteristics for developing a positioning system adaptable to existing machinery of small producers, which could be integrated in the future into the implementation of a larger autonomous navigation system in regional fruit growing.

The remainder of this paper is structured as follows: the next Chapter describes previous related works. Section 3 presents the architecture of the proposed system and provides guidelines on selecting the embedded computer. Section 4 evaluates the frequency achieved by the sensors, details a calibration method for the video camera, and validates the video data acquired by the system. Finally, Sect. 5 details conclusions and future work of this ongoing research.

2   Literature Review

Techniques under development for autonomous navigation in fruit orchards focus on three main proposals: modifying or building new orchards to suit autonomous tractors, utilizing stereo cameras in conjunction with high-performance computers for running Visual-SLAM algorithms, and employing laser scanners as a main local perception sensor.

Various publications have developed autonomous navigation systems using some of these approaches. In [3], a 2D laser scanner was used to guide a tractor along a row between fruit trees. In [4], reflective tapes were added at each end of the row to detect its end using the laser scanner. In [16], multiple sensors were used, including a laser scanner, a stereo video camera, and an inertial measurement unit (IMU) to guide a vehicle in an orange plantation. Additionally, an average lateral error of 0.05 m is achieved at a speed of 3.1 m/s, and the vehicle successfully turns at the end of the row to continue into the next row. In [5], an automated platform guided by two 2D laser scanners is described, which has covered over 300 km of fruit orchard rows. In [9], a multi-tractor system is presented for weeding and spraying an orange plantation. Each autonomous tractor utilizes a 2D laser scanner and a color stereo camera to perceive the environment and has driven at least 1000 km. In [20], the development of an autonomous robot capable of transporting an empty bin and replacing it with a full one in the plantation is detailed. It uses GPS to guide the vehicle out of the orchard rows and two 2D laser scanners and an IMU when working within the rows. The robot has four wheels with independent steering and direction, allowing for omnidirectional turning maneuvers.

It is worth noting, in addition, that a laser scanner, such as those used in the cited literature, has an approximate cost of USD 3500, and its price has not significantly decreased in the last ten years. Also, commonly found poplar windbreaks in the fields of the Alto Valle region were not considered, mainly because those developments are implemented in new plantations that do not require them. In contrast to previous works, the objective of our research is to utilize tools, techniques, and methods affordable to small family producers and applicable to the tractors and orchards already present in the Alto Valle region.

3   Architecture and Development of the Acquisition System

3.1   Hardware Architecture

In Fig. 1 (left), there is a high-level block diagram of the hardware architecture of our proposed system. Specifically, the hardware is primarily composed of

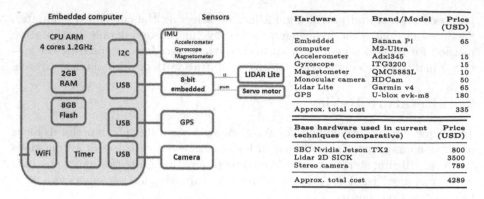

Fig. 1. Left: hardware block diagram of the acquisition system. Right: list of selected components and hardware price comparison.

an embedded computer, the Banana Pi M2-Ultra. Among its key features, it includes a System on Chip (SOC) containing a 1.2 GHz microprocessor with 4 ARM CPUs, 2 GB of RAM, 8 GB of Flash storage, a SATA disk interface, 3 USB ports, WiFi radio, two i2c buses, and GPIO ports. Additionally, the following low-complexity sensors were selected: a QMC5883L magnetometer, an ITG3200 gyroscope, an ADXL345 accelerometer, a Lidar Lite v4, a generic monocular video camera, and a u-blox evk-m8 GPS. As depicted in Fig. 1 (right), these sensors along with the embedded computer are of low cost, with their value being an order of magnitude lower than the autopilots proposed in the literature. The sensors acquired together with the central embedded computer constitute the hardware of the data acquisition system.

Criteria for Selecting the Embedded Computer

The selection and acquisition process required a comparative analysis among several options available in the market. In particular, the embedded computer is the most critical component because all data is acquired, pre-processed, stored,

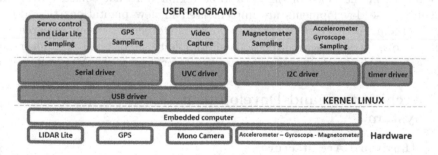

Fig. 2. Software architecture. The blocks in red are those developed by the authors. (Color figure online)

and sent from this system. In order to meet the requirement that the system be affordable yet have the appropriate characteristics, a series of guidelines were established for its selection.

We enumerate below the defined guidelines, which may be applicable in future works requiring a similar selection process:

1. **Support for mainline Linux kernel**: It is important that the official Linux kernel project supports the SOC. Many companies provide only their own Linux kernel. The risk here is that new versions of the official kernel, which may fix bugs or provide new functionalities, may not be usable in the future. Furthermore, a kernel generally works with a specific distribution or versions of libraries, etc. If a more recent Linux distribution or newer versions of certain software or libraries are desired, it may not be possible with a manufacturer's Linux kernel. This risk is not insignificant, as a large number of embedded computers on the market offer only their own Linux.

2. **Determine hardware bandwidth from datasheets**: Not only should the general characteristics of the hardware be observed, but also the requirements in their datasheets or schematics should be verified. For example, the Raspberry Pi 3 board offers several USB 2.0 ports. However, the ethernet controller in this Raspberry Pi is external to the SOC and is connected to the system's USB hub. Therefore, much of the USB bandwidth will be used by the ethernet controller if this interface is used, and the remaining bandwidth may not be sufficient for the sensor connected to another port. These specifics are only detailed in documents such as datasheets and schematics.

3. **Manufacturer of embedded computer families**: The selected board will likely become obsolete at some point and be discontinued, no longer available in the market. If the research project has extensive lines of work, it is advisable to select a board from a manufacturer that develops each new version based on an SOC from the same family. This allows for easy migration of work to the new board. It is necessary to observe the manufacturer's timeline and how each new product is developed.

3.2   Software Architecture

The data acquisition software is composed of particular pieces of software that we developed for each sensor data acquisition. A layered block diagram of the software can be seen in Fig. 2. The blocks in red are those developed by the authors. In particular, the image acquisition software for the video camera, GPS and lidar-lite were developed in C language, using only the standard C library. Direct access to the data of each sensor from C, and the Linux kernel driver, allows us to control the acquisition frequency. For example, it is possible to acquire at the highest frequency if necessary, without intermediary software layers, filters, or buffers.[1]

---

[1] The pieces of software developed for this acquisition system are distributed under a free software licence: http://github.com/zrafa/ryva.

Time Stamps as Central Interrelation Data

Although in principle the software components are independent, each component incorporates a microsecond resolution timestamp to each sample acquired from each specific sensor. The timestamp is obtained from the same clock (Linux kernel clock). In this way, all acquired data are interrelated on the same timeline. For example, each photo could be related to the nearest GPS location, or to lidar or gyroscope data. Even the relationship can be one-to-many, as a photo would be related for example to a set of data close in time to the gyro, as the sample rate of the gyro is much higher than that of the camera. This is critical when using all the measurements in a sensor fusion scheme, typical in robotics when solving the navigation problem.

4   System Evaluation

The system evaluation was conducted through field experimentation, acquiring data as frequently as possible using this system, and subsequently processing the video information using a Visual-SLAM algorithm.

For this purpose, the video camera was first calibrated, and then, the complete system was embedded onto a Deutz tractor model 1970. A watertight box was used to house the embedded computer and some of the sensors. An external container box was built in an available area of the tractor, where the watertight box was placed. The camera was positioned at the front of the tractor, and the GPS was mounted on the system's box, as shown in Fig. 3(right). After calibrating the system (see next section), data acquisition from all sensors was done. A driver then drove a closed circuit with the tractor between two rows of fruit trees, each 175 m long. The cultivation area where the work was carried out belongs to Chacra 28, A15, Cipolletti (RN). In Fig. 3(left) the two rows can be seen in red.

Fig. 3. Left: View of the route. Right: Tractor with the acquisition box.

4.1 Camera Calibration

The calibration process of a camera is important for obtaining 3D information from 2D images of the scene. The goal of calibration is to accurately measure the intrinsic and extrinsic parameters, as well as the distortion coefficients of the camera system. Previously, a brief description of the camera model is necessary.

Camera Model

A camera is a mapping between the 3D world (object space) and a 2D image. The most used model for perspective camera supposes a pin-hole projection, and it is shown in Fig. 5. It is a simple camera without a lens and with a single small aperture. The 2D point, $\mathbf{x}$, results from the intersection between the **focal plane** and the light ray coming from the 3D point, $\mathbf{X}$, and passing through a single point, the pinhole. The center of projection, $\mathbf{C}$, can be observed, and the plane $Z = f$, which is called the **image plane** or **focal plane**.

By similar triangles, it is possible computes that the point $\mathbf{X} = \begin{bmatrix} X, Y, Z \end{bmatrix}^T$ is mapped to the point $\mathbf{x} = \begin{bmatrix} fX/Z, fY/Z, f \end{bmatrix}^T$ on the image plane. Finally, he mapping from the 3D world to the 2D image in homogeneous coordinates may be written in terms of matrix multiplication:

$$\lambda \begin{bmatrix} u \\ v \\ 1 \end{bmatrix} = \mathbf{KX} = \begin{bmatrix} f_x & 0 & p_x \\ 0 & f_y & p_y \\ 0 & 0 & 1 \end{bmatrix} \begin{bmatrix} X \\ Y \\ Z \end{bmatrix}$$

where λ is the depth factor, f_x and f_y are the focal lengths in pixels, and p_x, p_y the image coordinates of principal point in pixels. Alls these parameters are called intrinsic parameters and form the camera calibration matrix $\mathbf{K}$. The pinhole camera model does not account for lens distortion because an ideal pinhole camera does not have a lens. To accurately represent a real camera, the full camera model used by the algorithm includes the radial and tangential lens distortion.

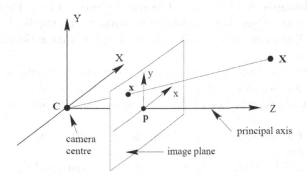

Fig. 4. (a) Checkerboard used as calibration pattern. It consists of 30 mm × 30 mm squares, with 8 × 5 inner corners and 9 × 6 squares. (b–i) Images of the pattern captured from different perspectives.

(a)   (b)   (c)

(d)   (e)   (f)

(g)   (h)   (i)

Fig. 5. Pinhole camera geometry. **X** is a scene 3D point in the camera reference frame and **x** and its projection on the image plane measured in pixels. C is the camera centre. Image extracted from [6].

Calibration

Below is a general outline of the stages involved in calibration:

1. **Calibration pattern**: Dataset of multiple images with scenes of known dimensions. From a practical point of view, the bibliography indicates that the most popular method uses a planar checkerboard [21]. The pattern used is shown in Fig. 4a.
2. **Capture images**: It necessary take several pictures of the Pattern shown at different positions and orientations by ensuring that the field of view of the camera is filled as much as possible. Several of the images obtained are shown in Fig. 4b to 4i.
3. **Feature points**: Common feature points detectors include corner detectors like Harris corner detector or FAST (Features from Accelerated Segment Test). They are detected on the calibration pattern in each image as is shown in Fig. 6a.
4. **Estimate correspondences**: Match the detected 2D feature points across multiple images.
5. **Calibration algorithm**: Finally, based on the detected feature points and their correspondences, the intrinsic and extrinsic parameters (K and RT matrices, respectively) are then found through a least-square minimization method. This method minimizes the residual error, defined as the geometric

(a)   (b)

Fig. 6. (a) Blue crosses depict detected feature points. Green circles depict reprojected feature points. (b) The final 3D reconstruction of the camera locations around the checkerboard. (Color figure online)

distance between the detected feature points and their reprojected counterparts 6a. To date, there are many tools available for the calibration process[2]. The estimated camera locations obtained from the RT matrices derived from this calibration process are shown in Fig. 6b.

4.2 Evaluation of Sensor Acquisition Frequency

The aim of this analysis is to find out whether the frequency achieved is suitable for future autonomous navigation missions. To guide our research, the frequencies achieved in previous publications on the subject [10,16] were collected. The frequency obtained by the system for each sensor can be read in first column of Table 1, compared with an average of the frequencies established in other publications found in literature. The results show that the frequencies are above those established in other works (with the exception of GPS, compared to a GPS RTK). It should be noted that, in preliminary versions of our software, where available code from other authors was reused, lower frequencies were obtained for some of the sensors. These comparisons motivated us to develop our own version of the acquisition software.

4.3 Evaluation of the Data Acquired by the Camera

On the test run with the tractor, the Acquisition system obtained 9201 images, each with dimensions of 672×376 pixels. The evaluation of this data, using a Visual-SLAM algorithm, required a series of six systematic steps:

1. Calibrate camera.

---

[2] https://github.com/MRPT and https://opencv.org/ for example.

Table 1. Comparison of Data Acquisition Frequencies

Sensor	Frequency measured (Hz)	Reference value (Hz)
Magnetometer	30	-no values-
Lidar Lite	6 (5 m obstacle)	3 (official driver, 5 m obstacle)
Gyroscope	153	140
Camera	15	15
Accelerometer	153	140
GPS	1	5 (RTK GPS)

2. Perform data acquisition.
3. Process the data with the Visual-SLAM algorithm.
4. If necessary, fine-tune the algorithm, and return to step 3.
5. Evaluate the algorithm output against a ground truth measurement[3].
6. Iterate steps 3, 4, and 5 until achieving a consistent system tuning (or determining that it is not possible to reconstruct the map and trajectory in this environment and/or with this system).

Visual-SLAM Algorithm

Visual-SLAM (Visual Simultaneous Localization And Mapping) algorithms use only information from visual sensors (cameras) to solve the problem of localisation of an agent, in our case the tractor, and the simultaneous reconstruction of the map of the environment. In this work, we have chosen to use CCM-SLAM (Centralized Colaborative Monocular Simultaneous Localization And Mapping) [15] as it is a line of research that we have previously addressed. Their implementation is open source and uses images from monocular cameras only.

Generally speaking, the basis for all Visual-SLAM algorithms is to detect, between two consecutive images, the same natural marks that the environment may have. These distinguishable features, or 2D keypoints, may be due to differences in colour, intensity, or texture such as edges or corners. By transforming a minimum of 5 pairs of corresponding keypoints, it is possible to estimate the camera position and the location in 3D space of these keypoints. This procedure is repeated frame by frame, obtaining the vehicle trajectory and the builded map (3D point cloud).

Configuring, Tuning and Running Visual-SLAM

The Visual-SLAM algorithms must be configured and tuned. During the configuration, the number of frames per second, the resolution of the images, and the intrinsic parameters of the camera used must be specified. Once these parameters are set, the tuning process of the algorithm continues. In the particular case

---

[3] Ground truth refers to the absolute truth about the target variable or the correct output. It serves as the reference against which the performance of a system is evaluated. It is generally obtained from measurements of high precision and accuracy.

of CCM-SLAM, the tuning focuses on the ORB (Oriented FAST and Rotated BRIEF) - SLAM feature detection stage. The complexity in this step lies in the fact that, in general, Visual-SLAM algorithms require an environment and images with certain conditions:

1) The images must be in focus. If this is not the case (blurred image) a detected feature may not be recognised in the following images.
2) Non-dynamic environments. If the environment is constantly changing, the algorithm may detect false positives that lead to system-wide errors.
3) Non-regular environments. If repetitive patterns appear with very similar textures, the descriptors of the image features will result similar to each other, which can lead to false positive matches.

In the particular case of the Alto Valle farms, conditions 1 and 3 are not completely fulfilled. The tractor vibrates all the time, which makes it difficult for the camera to always get a good focus. In addition, the rows of fruit trees have regular patterns, as the tree structure is repetitive, and the textures are similar. This is the reason to consider this particular environment to be *hostile*. In our field experimentation, this hostile environment demanded several iterations in the tuning and execution process, adjusting the ORBextractor* variables until we achieved a trajectory that, by visual inspection, presented similar characteristics to the one obtained from ground truth.

Ground Truth Trajectory Validation
In this work, the trajectory obtained from the GPS data will be the reference ground truth, set in the geodetic global earth coordinate system. On the other hand, the trajectory determined by CCM-SLAM is in a coordinate system that moves with the vehicle. In addition, when using a monocular camera, the CCM-SLAM system does not determine the distance scale, as it is not possible to determine the depth of the image from a single photo at each instant. This means that there will be no distance in a unit of length between two points on the trajectory computed by the algorithm.

In order to be able to match and compare both trajectories, the *Umeyama* alignment method was used [19], through the software *evo*[4]. The *Umeyama* method is used for the alignment and registration of sets of points in three-dimensional space. It aims to find the best rigid transformation (rotation, translation and scaling) between two sets of points by minimising the sum of the squared distances between the corresponding points in both sets. The rigid transformation implies that the points retain their relative distances and angles after the transformation is applied.

After applying the method, the result is the comparison shown in Fig. 7. The black dotted line shows the trajectory of the navigation performed by the tractor (ground truth). The blue trajectory was the one computed by CCM-SLAM. The result shows a high correlation between both trajectories, with a preliminarily

---

[4] https://github.com/MichaelGrupp/evo.

determined error from the plot of + 5 m, which demonstrates that it is feasible to implement, with the imposed restrictions, a complex localisation algorithm.

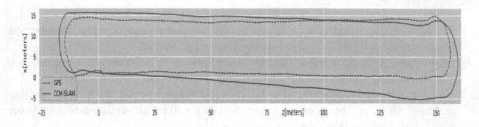

Fig. 7. Trajectory obtained with CCM-SLAM, compared against the *ground truth*.

5   Discussion/Conclusions

This paper present the hardware and software architecture of an embedded system capable of acquiring data from multiple low-complexity sensors in the field. It is intended that this system could be integrated in the future in an autonomous navigation system for old tractors used in fruit orchards.

The results obtained show that the acquisition frequencies are within the reference values found, and that the images obtained in the field from the camera are useful and functional to be processed by a VSLAM positioning system in the near future. To accomplish this additional functionality, a calibration process of the video camera was necessary. A proper calibration process allows obtaining intrinsic and extrinsic parameters required by the vision algorithms. This process was also outlined in this paper.

There are several tasks to be continued in this work. In particular, it is required to determine the full characterisation of each low complexity sensor in the fruit environment, the development of an automatic self-calibration system (necessary prior to use in the field), and a model and implementation of sensor data integration and fusion.

References

1. Servicio Nacional de Sanidad y Calidad Agroalimentaria: Anuario estadístico 2020 - Centro Regional Patagonia Norte (2019)
2. Di Prinzio, A., Magdalena, J.C., Behmer, S.: El tractor en cultivos intensivos. Nociones de uso y funcionamiento. 1a. ed. INTA (2011)
3. Barawid, O., Mizushima, A., Ishii, K., Noguchi, N.: Development of an autonomous navigation system using a two-dimensional laser scanner in an orchard application. Biosyst. Eng. **96**, 139–149 (2007). https://doi.org/10.1016/j.biosystemseng.2006. 10.012

4. Bergerman, M., Maeta, S., Zhang, J., Freitas, G., Hamner, B., Singh, S., Kantor, G.: Robot farmers: autonomous orchard vehicles help tree fruit production. IEEE Robot. Automation Magaz. **22**, 54–63 (03 2015). https://doi.org/10.1109/MRA.2014.2369292
5. Hamner, B., Singh, S., Bergerman, M.: Improving orchard efficiency with autonomous utility vehicles, vol. 6, January 2010. https://doi.org/10.13031/2013.29902
6. Hartley, R., Zisserman, A.: Multiple view geometry in computer vision. Cambridge University Press (2003)
7. Loyola, L.: Documento de Trabajo N°3 Sujetos Sociales: Productores Agropecuarios. Población Rural y Pueblos Originarios de la Provincia de Río Negro, Organización de las Naciones Unidas para la Alimentación y la Agricultura (2015)
8. Marsh, A.: John deere and the birth of precision agriculture. IEEE Spectrum -(-), – (2018)
9. Moorehead, S., Wellington, C., Gilmore, B., Vallespi, C.: Automating orchards: a system of autonomous tractors for orchard maintenance, January 2012
10. Pire, T., Mujica, M., Civera, J., Kofman, E.: The rosario dataset: Multisensor data for localization and mapping in agricultural environments (2019)
11. Q. Zhang, H.Q.: A dynamic path search algorithm for tractor automatic navigation. In: Transactions of the ASAE, 47 (2004)
12. Siegwart, R., Nourbakhsh, D.S.: Introduction to Autonomous Mobile Robots. The MIT Press (2011)
13. Rafael Ignacio, Z., Naiara, S., Marcelo L., M., Mendieta, D., Favio, M., Miriam, L.: Sistema de adquisición de datos utilizando sensores de baja complejidad para tractores antiguos del alto valle de río negro y neuquén. In: Libro de actas - XXIX Congreso Argentino de Ciencias de la Computación - CACIC 2023 (2024)
14. Roberson, G., Jordan, D.: Rtk gps and automatic steeringfor peanut digging. Appl. Eng. Agric. **30**, 405–409 (2014). https://doi.org/10.13031/aea.30.10432
15. Schmuck, P., Chli, M.: Ccm-slam: robust and efficient centralized collaborative monocular simultaneous localization and mapping for robotic teams. J. Field Robot. **36** (12 2018). https://doi.org/10.1002/rob.21854
16. Subramanian, V., Burks, T.: Autonomous vehicle turning in the headlands of citrus groves, vol. 1, January 2007. https://doi.org/10.13031/2013.23445
17. Subramanian, V., Burks, T., Arroyo, A.: Development of machine vision and laser radar based autonomous vehicle guidance systems for citrus grove navigation. Comput. Electron. Agric. **53**, 130–143 (2006). https://doi.org/10.1016/j.compag.2006.06.001
18. Toranzo, J.O.: Producción mundial de manzanas y peras. 1ra. ed. - allen río negro. Tech. rep., Ediciones INTA (2016)
19. Umeyama, S.: Least-squares estimation of transformation parameters between two point patterns. IEEE Trans. Pattern Anal. Mach. Intell. **13**(4), 376–380 (1991). https://doi.org/10.1109/34.88573
20. Ye, Y., Wang, Z., Jones, D., He, L., Taylor, M.E., Hollinger, G.A., Zhang, Q.: Bin-dog: a robotic platform for bin management in orchards. Robotics **6** (2017)
21. Zhang, Z.: A flexible new technique for camera calibration. IEEE Trans. Pattern Anal. Mach. Intell. **22**(11), 1330–1334 (2000)

ADS-B Support to SSR

Oscar Bria$^{(\boxtimes)}$ [iD] and Javier Giacomantone [iD]

Research Institute in Computer Science (III-LIDI) - School of Computer Science,
National University of La Plata, La Plata, Argentina
onb@lidi.info.unlp.edu.ar

Abstract. In an air traffic surveillance station with SSR and ADS-B,
the information generated by each sensor can be used to improve the
performance of the other. In addition to improving the predictive performance required by Roll-Call interrogations, ADS-B can help to improve
SSR performance in the vicinity of the cone of silence, allow passive
acquisition, help to identify false SSR targets generated by reflection,
and overcome SSR limitations.

Keywords: ADS-B · SSR · Modo S · Support among Sensors

1   Introduction

Secondary Surveillance Radar (SSR) and Automatic Dependent Surveillance
System by Broadcast (ADS-B) are two cooperative technologies for air traffic
surveillance.

The SSR [1] independently determines the position of the aircraft which,
in turn, is interrogated by the radar to gather complementary information. The
SSR Mode S (Selective) [2–4] is the second generation of the SSR; allows selective
interrogation, Roll-Call interrogations, using an exclusive 24-bit identification
code for each aircraft [5,6]. SSRs typically have a position rate update between
4 and 10 s depending on the rotation speed of the antenna.

ADS-B [7] is dependent on Global Navigation Satellite Systems (e.g., GPS)
for position determination, which is emitted along with other information spontaneously by the aircraft and received on the ground by a system simpler than
a radar. ADS-Bs typically have a position update rate of around 1 s [8,9].

Nowadays it is common to find an SSR with Mode S and an ADS-B installed
at the same site, therefore, with mostly overlapping coverage [10]. In [11] a
method of using the ADS-B tracker was presented to improve the prediction
needed by SSR Mode S, when both sensors are located in the same place. One of
the motivations for proposing this support is that, as already shown, the ADS-B
position update rate is significantly lower than that of SSR.

In the process of developing an integrated collaboration system between an
ADS-B and a SSR, it is possible to include other improvements besides the correlation of the position of the aircraft reported by both sensors. The limitations
imposed by the so-called cone of silence of the SSR coverage can be mitigated.

P. Pesado et al. (Eds.): CACIC 2023, CCIS 2123, pp. 320–335, 2024.
https://doi.org/10.1007/978-3-031-62245-8_22

The performance of the reflection detection and elimination system of the SSRs can also be improved.

This work is an extension of *ADS-B Collaboration with SSR* [12], published in Argentine Congress of Computer Science 2023 (CACIC 2023). The ADS-B supporting features to SSR are reviewed in the following sections, and an extensive and real example is introduced.

Section 2 is a very brief description of the collaboration between both trackers. The Composer is responsible for conveniently combining both predictions in a better one, in various senses. For details see [11].

Section 3 explains how the no limitations of ADS-B inside the CoS can help SSR to track flights there and to acquire earlier flights leaving the CoS without necessity of All-Call interrogations.

Section 4 deals with the phenomenon of reflection of signals and how ADS-B can contribute to their detection. A novel case of reflections caused by flights within the CoS that can only be detected with the help of ADS-B receptions is presented.

Section 5 introduces a real flight example where the novel reflection case of Sect. 4 appears mixed with the delay in the acquisition. The case is carefully descripted and analysed. Also, the contributions of the ADS-B are recounted.

Section 6 is a list of conclusions that emphasize the virtues of the support that ADS-B can offer to the SSR, and a summary the tasks that have to be addressed in the future.

2   Collaborative Trackers

In [11] a simple scheme of collaborative trackers [13, 14] (see Fig. 1) was presented for the prediction of the aircraft position, necessary for the timing of the SSR Roll-Call interrogation for the next antenna visit.

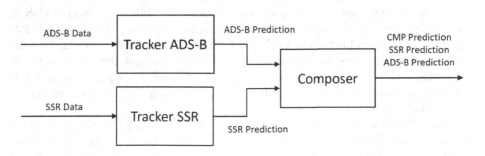

Fig. 1. Block Diagram of the Collaboration between Trackers.

The block named Composer in Fig. 1 calculates the average prediction weighted by the variances according to the following calculation [15]:

$$P = \left[P_1^{-1} + P_2^{-1}\right]^{-1} \tag{1}$$

$$\hat{x} = P\left[P_1^{-1}\hat{x}_1 + P_2^{-1}\hat{x}_2\right] \tag{2}$$

Where P_i are the individual covariances of each sensor prediction and $\hat{x}_i$ are their predictions. While P and $\hat{x}$ are the respective values of the composition.

The compose (CMP) prediction, given by the pair $[\hat{x}, P]$, is statistically better[1], than the SSR prediction [16,17]. That contributes to better estimation, more efficient use of polling scheduling resources, and better performance of mode S in various respects, even in multi-sensor environments [18–22].

3   Cone of Silence and Passive Acquisition

Radar coverage is the volume of airspace scanned by a radar or radar network [23]. The coverage volume of a surveillance radar is the volume generated by the revolution, around the antenna rotation axis, of the surface delimited by the following bounds (typical values are shown in brackets):

1. The minimum elevation angle from the horizon [0°].
2. The maximum elevation angle from the horizon [45°].
3. The minimum slant distance from the center of the antenna [0.5 NM].
4. The maximum slant distance from the center of the antenna [150 NM].
5. The maximum altitude with respect to the ground [FL 1000].

The solid generated by revolution includes a blind volume in the shape of an inverted cone contained between the maximum elevation angle and the axis of rotation of the antenna called the cone of silence (CoS)[2]. The CoS is produced by the effect of the shape of the irradiation pattern of the radar antenna, which in the case of SSRs has a square cosecant pattern [24]. Figure 2 shows the CoS in schematic form. For example, an aircraft flying at a cruising altitude of FL 300 (approx. 10 Km) will enter the CoS at 5.4 NM from the radar (approx. 10 Km) if the coverage reaches 45° in elevation. The SSR does not detect the aircraft while inside the cone, the track will be lost and it must be acquired again when the aircraft leaves the CoS, if at all. The re-acquisition process involves one or more All-Call queries.

The ADS-B collaboration function with the SSR improves the acquisition process of aircraft with squitter and mode S transponder at the exit of the cone of silence, avoiding the delay imposed by the exchange of interrogations and All-Call responses as usual in the active acquisition of the SSR.

---

[1] The magnitude of the composition variance, P, is always less than the magnitude of any of the individual variances, P_i.

[2] Another blind zone can also be generated if the angle of minimum elevation is above the horizon. This can occur in the azimuthal sectors including obstacles.

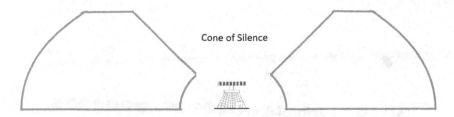

Fig. 2. Vertical-Central Section of the Coverage Volume (not to scale).

With the help of the data supplied by ADS-B, the output of the SSR cone of silence is anticipated in such a way that a passive acquisition is carried out that allows the first interrogation of the SSR outside the cone of silence is directly a Roll-Call interrogation.

This function must include an active tracker based on ADS-B information for every possible aircraft that may exit the SSRs CoS and also must anticipate departure, early enough for the SSR to schedule a Roll-Call interrogation at the appropriate time.

Figure 3 is a diagram with details of the working environment of the collaboration within the CoS according to the following detail:

1. The dotted line above represents a trace of the responses or possible SSR responses given by an aircraft moving away from the radar heading East. The black dot corresponds to the situation where the radio range is not enough to process responses at that distance (which on the other hand may not be produced). The two blue dots correspond to responses not processed by the SSR because they are beyond its Surveillance Coverage (vertical green line farther to the right). The next two green dots correspond to responses processed by the SSR but not reported to the console, which correspond to All-Calls responses that are used to initialize the predictor for the next round. The two red dots correspond to responses processed and reported to the console, which are in correspondence with the responses to Roll-Call selective interrogations.
2. The central line represents the squitter emissions of the same aircraft moves away from the SSR moving from West to East, and which may or may not be processed. The key to colors is similar to the previous one.
3. The line below corresponds to the responses or possible responses of the aircraft to the SSR, when it works in a composite way with ADS-B. The color key is the same as before.

For the third trace, it is observed that the two points immediately to the right of the second vertical green line are red. This is so because the SSR received information from ADS-B so that these points correspond to Roll-Call responses. This is possible if the ADS-B information arrives in a timely manner.

The details of how forecast anticipation is carried out will depend on how accurately the limits of the cone of silence overlapping with the minimum range

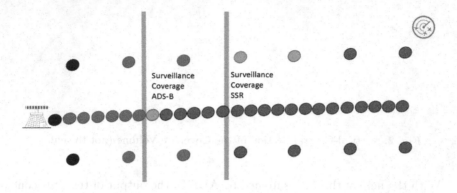

Fig. 3. Detail of the Collaboration in the Cone of Silence.

are known or defined together with the presence or absence of a surveillance coverage map, and of the forward forecast accuracy that can be achieved with ADS-B data (see fixed point forecast at [15]). Due to the indeterminacy in the knowledge of the limits, superfluous or, on the contrary, few Roll-Call interrogations could be programmed.

The improvement of the order of two turns depends, in terms of distance, on the speed of the aircraft and the rate of rotation of the antenna. The improvement in the distance is of the order of 2 NM considering typical values of both speeds for an en-route traffic radar, as observed in Eq. (3). The improvement does not depend on the altitude at which the aircraft leaves the CoS, but is still significant for the upper limit of typical coverage.

$$2\,\text{turns}\frac{450\,\text{Knots}}{1\,\text{turn}/8\,\text{seconds}} = 2\,\text{NM} \tag{3}$$

In practice, it is necessary to distinguish between the radio frequency range (distance up to which radio frequency signals can be processed) and the surveillance coverage which is set operationally for each sensor. Figure 4 shows the radio range and surveillance coverage for the SSR, further showing the flight situations that should be taken into account.

Case number 5 (Entering Surveillance Coverage) in Fig. 4 can be treated as case number 2. (Leaving Cone of Silence) if there is ADS-B coverage beyond Surveillance Coverage. Also, in this case it is possible to acquire the trace through a passive acquisition using a technique similar to the one shown.

4   Reflections

Although SSR and ADS-B are both cooperative surveillance technologies, a very important distinction between them is that the former estimates the position (minus altitude) independently and the latter dependently [25]. Therefore, what

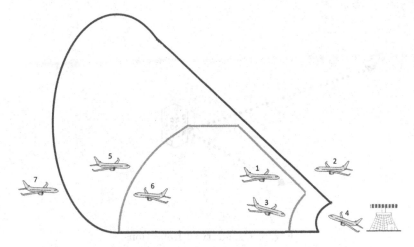

1. Entering Cone of Silence.
2. Leaving Cone of Silence.
3. Landing in Blind Zone.
4. Taking off from Blind Zone.
5. Entering Surveillance Coverage.
6. Leaving Surveillance Coverage.
7. Entering Radio Range.

Fig. 4. Radio Range and Surveillance Coverage.

in principle is a disadvantage for the latter can be helpful or essential to determine if a response is real or comes from a reflection, as shown below.

False detections occur due to reflection of electromagnetic waves by obstacles, both for interrogations and for responses from an SSR. Figure 5 shows the geometry of the reflections.

In Fig. 5, the actual location of the aircraft is on the left, but when the radar has interrogated in the direction of the building it has generated a reflected interrogation which has also generated a reflected response which is received by radar. The SSR computes the position of the aircraft and places it in the position to the right.

Below are described several particular reflection situations in which ADS-B can contribute in varying depth.

1. When the interrogation mode is A/C the reflections can be identified through a well known procedure. If, for example, two aircraft with the same A code are detected in one turn of the antenna, it can be assumed that the aircraft that is at a greater distance from the radar is actually a reflection. In addition, the position of the reflector can be calculated, which is supposed to produce reflections for any other similar situation. Thus, it is convenient to survey a map of the reflectors present in the vicinity of the radar.

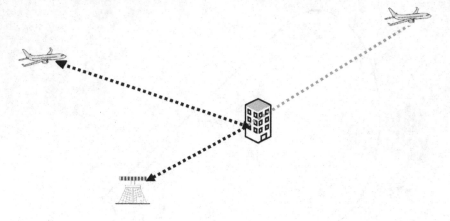

Fig. 5. Geometry of Reflections

Assuming v is the distance at which the real aircraft is above azimuth α and r is the distance at which its reflection is seen above azimuth β[3]. Then, the distance to the reflector R and the orientation of the normal vector to the reflecting plane $\perp$ can then be calculated. See Fig. 6 in which the guidelines of geometric optics are followed and the small black segment represents the reflecting plane.

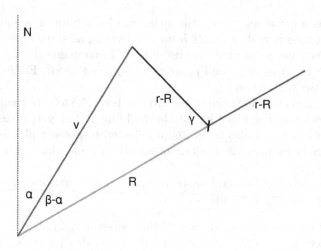

Fig. 6. Geometry for calculating the Location of the Reflector.

---

[3] α and β are measured with respect to the North turning to East.

Applying the laws of cosines and sines in the triangle of Fig. 6,

$$R = \frac{1}{2} \frac{r^2 - v^2}{r - v\cos(\beta - \alpha)} \tag{4}$$

$$\perp = \frac{1}{2} \arcsin \frac{v \sin (\beta - \alpha)}{r - R} + \beta + \pi \tag{5}$$

The survey of the map of permanent reflectors for the airways of a radar site is part of the site study that must be carried out for each SSR installation [26]. In addition to the permanent reflectors, mobile reflectors that eventually appear should be temporarily included on the map. An obstacle can operate as a single or several reflectors in different planes. Relatively large obstacles, in addition to producing reflections, can produce blind zones at low altitudes as mentioned previously.

2. The S Roll-Call interrogation mode is, in principle, immune to reflections because interrogations are directed to a single aircraft known to be in the azimuthal direction towards the main beam of the radar antenna is pointing. What could happen is that through a reflector, during the All-Call interrogation period, the identifier S of an aircraft is acquired and, thus, it goes on to be interrogated Roll-Call through the reflector in the next few turns. Indeed, this condition could be detected, as for mode A/C, by the repetition of the identifier S and also the furthest detection is the false one[4].

3. Figure 7 shows a singular case of a mirroring situation. Here, the aircraft is within the CoS of the SSR and it is interrogated through a reflector that is outside the CoS. The aircraft responds for both a mode A/C interrogation and

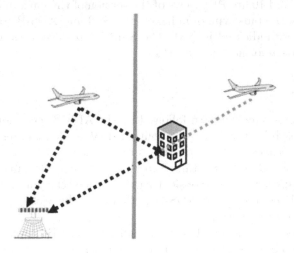

Fig. 7. Singular Case of Geometry of Reflections.

---

[4] In this case, the reflection identification is more secure because it is known that the identifier S cannot be repeated.

a mode S interrogation. In both situations there are no references to compare and determine that they are reflections. This is so because the same aircraft does not appear in any other azimuth of the turn. In both cases, the mistake is made by accepting the reflected aircraft on the right as existing. In other words, the traditional algorithm, only based on the SSR, does not distinguish the reflection as such for this geometry. The ADS-B, which distinguishes the aircraft within the CoS, can contribute indicating that there is an aircraft that is responsible for a reflection and can contribute to the location of the reflector with a similar method to the one already explained.

4. ADS-B spontaneous emissions can also produce reflections similar to those of SSR radar, but are indistinguishable from direct emissions, except for arrival time, because ADS-B relies on the GNSS system for its location, and not on a measurement. Those refection situations must be solved by the ADS-B receptor itself or by post processing performed from the ground equipment.

5 Flight Example

In this section, a flight reported by a real SSR/ADS-B station is analyzed. It is shown how an ADS-B receiver contributes to that analysis and also how it could amend the issues identified if the functionalities presented before are implemented.

5.1 Description of the Flight Path

The flight path is described without going into unnecessary details of the context. The Figs. 8, 9, and 10 are PPI views of the section of the path under analysis. In all the Figures, the plus symbol indicates the SSR and ADS-B common site and the distances are indicated in NM. The SSR rotates every 8 s and the ADS-B receives position information every 1 s.

ADS-B Path

1. Figure 8 shows only the path followed by the ADS-B receptions.
2. The flight path initiates from the South; it makes a loop; enters the CoS; turn to the East; leaves the CoS; continues to the East.
3. The FL in the CoS is maintained in 90. The range for entering the CoS at that FL is approx. 2 NM (considering the level of the antenna).
4. The curved section of the ADS-B path inside the CoS is due to the PPI projection of the range.
5. It looks to be some missed detection inside the CoS. However, the probability of update is high even for an update time of 1 s.

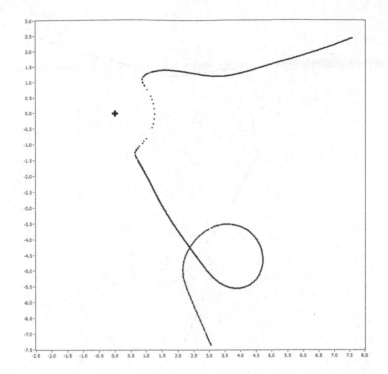

Fig. 8. Flight Path of Only the ADS-B Receptions.

Roll-Call and ADS-B Path

1. Figure 9 shows both paths, Roll-Call SSR responses and ADS-B receptions, superimposed for the analysed flight. The largest points correspond to SSR responses. The smallest points, seen almost as a continuum, corresponds to ADS-B receptions.
2. At a first glance, there is a correspondence in position between ADS-B path and SSR path in the first and last section of the flight.
3. It can be seen a long section surrounding the CoS without SSR responses, and the appearance of two detections is observed in the northwestern corner of the Figure. See the following point.

Roll-Call SSR Path

1. Figure 10 shows only the Roll-Call SSR responses; the lines interpolating points is only for the purpose of identifying three sectors.
2. The path has three sections: one at the beginning (south) including a loop, one at the end (northeast), and a peculiar central section(northwest) conformed by only two plots that do not appear in the ADS-B path of Fig. 8.

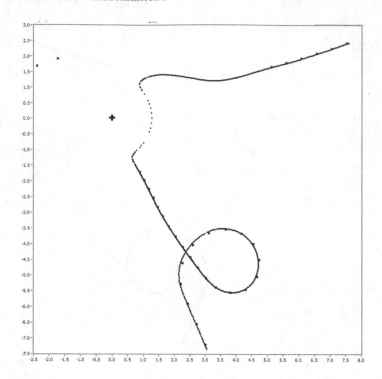

Fig. 9. Roll-Call SSR Responses and ADS-B Receptions Superimposed

5.2   Analysis of the Roll-Call SSR Path

1. The loop, included in the first section of the path, has the characteristics of a standard rate turn (a.k.a. rate one turn) (see [27]), i.e., a turn accomplished at 3° per second. From Fig. 10: $270°/(12*8) \approx 3°$/second. The loop is done close to the radar, at 5 NM. The conclusion is that the SSR does not need the help of the ADS-B tracker to follow a regular turn.

2. The last detection of the first section of the path occurs at FL 90 and at range $\approx$ 2 NM, in the limit of the CoS as it is expected. The scat number of this plot is 895.

3. The second section of the path, with only two plots, is clearly conformed by reflections of real points of the trajectory that nevertheless do no appear represented in the path. The last statement derives from the observation of the timing of the reflections. The scan number of the plots are 902 and 903, i.e. almost 7 turns after entering the CoS. Meanwhile, the scan number of the first plot detected in the third section of the path is 909, i.e., more than 5 turns after the detection of the second reflection. As a matter of fact, this situation is similar to that singular geometry of reflection explained above (see Fig. 7).

4. The third section begins in scan 909 at more than 5 NM from the radar; this is more than expected at the exit of the CoS when flying at FL 90 where the

limit is 2 NM. What did happen during those empty three NM? It can be expected that were necessarily the All-CAll answer to start a new track, but from observing the Fig. 10, there are need no more than 2 scans to fulfill that task, scans 907 and 908. Observing Fig. 8, the output path from the CoS is not completely radial, but certainly it can be said that 3 scans still need to be justified, scans 904 to 906.

The lost of three scans without detections may be related to the fact that the selective Roll-Call interrogations contain control information that instructs the transponder to disregard further All-Calls [28]. The transponder will then ignore All-Call interrogations from all sensors for a period of 18 s (3 scans for the geometry of the path of the example given here). The sensor will normally reset the lockout timer with all selective surveillance interrogations, hence ensuring that All-Call lockout is assured throughout as the target travels through the coverage of the sensor (that is not the case for the example given here).

In summary, a case of reflection within the CoS, which the SSR cannot resolve by itself, gave rise to an inordinate delay in acquisition at the exit of the CoS.

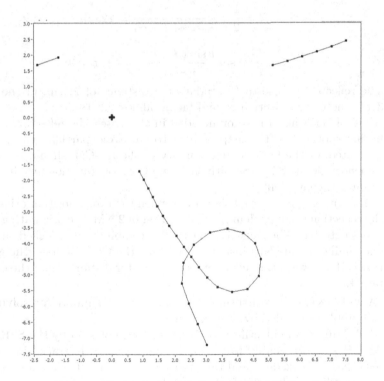

Fig. 10. Flight Path of Only the Roll-Call Answers.

5.3   ADS-B Contributions

1. The ADS-B path of Fig. 8 helped offline to corroborate theorem previous analysis because it shows the complete trajectory even inside the CoS.
2. The ADS-B path can contribute offline to the localization of the SSR reflectors. The position of the flight originating the reflection can be acquired from the ADS-B path, finding the position at the time of the reflections, and next applying formulas derived from Fig. 6. The position, e.g., of the first reflector is computed as follows:
   - From Roll-Call SSR path, the position of the reflection is for an specific time,

     $r = 2.58$ NM.

     $\beta = 318.21°$.
   - From ADS-B path, the approximate position of the real target, for approximately the same time,

     $v = 2.44$ NM.

     $\alpha = 56.28°$.
   - Applying formulas (4) and (5):

$$R = \frac{1}{2} \frac{r^2 - v^2}{r - v \cos(\beta - \alpha)} = 223 \text{ m} \tag{6}$$

$$\perp = \frac{1}{2} \arcsin \frac{v \sin(\beta - \alpha)}{r - R} + \beta + \pi = 98° \tag{7}$$

   - The reflector is close to the radar at a distance of 223 m, in the radial 318° where the reflection is, and facing almost at 98°.
   - A visual verification is recommended in this case. The reflector/s should be incorporated to the map of reflector to avoid partially the problem generated; or the lockout functionality of the All-Call should be relaxed somehow; or the STC (Sensitivity Time Control) functionality has to be calibrated conveniently.
   - Finally, it can be observed that, even when the range position originating the reflection is larger than the CoS border of 2 NM, the originating target is not detected. The cause is a particular combination of locked situation and timing of All-Calls inside and outside the CoS. Besides, the general rule is that always the reflection is at a greater distance than the original target.
3. The ADS-B receptions can bring automatic online support for solving the twofold problem revealed by this example:
   - ADS-B allows the identification of reflections not seen by the SSR.
   - ADS-B support enable the passive acquisition SSR tracks in mode S regardless of lockedout and targets flying inside the CoS. Those are limiting conditions that the SSR cannot handle.

6   Conclusions and Future Work

Features of ADS-B support to SSR have been introduced when both sensors are at the same site. The contribution is significant for:

✓ Anticipate and simplify the acquisition of mode S tracks at the limits of the coverage.
✓ Allow and anticipate the acquisition of SSR tracks at the output of CoS.
✓ Reinforce and allow the identification of reflections that produce false targets in the SSR. Including targets inside the CoS that the SSR can not identify.

An example of a real flight has been presented where a combination of reflections undetected by the SSR, setting conditions of Mode S interrogations, and geometrical conditions of the site and flight, impose severe restrictions on early tracking of flights leaving the CoS, even worst than those normal limitations of SSR. In essence, ADS-B contributes to overcoming serious limitations of SSR under special situations.

In those cases and in the case of the tracker, the integration of both sensors can be done by collecting data directly from the Asterix Cat.21 output of the ADS-B to help the Asterix Cat.48 generation processing of the SSR (see Fig. 11).

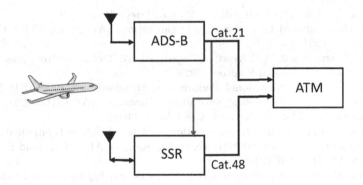

Fig. 11. Asterix Collaboration Scheme.

The preliminary design must be finalized and its performance evaluated by simulating plausible scenarios, including simulated flights in holding patterns such as those existing in the vicinity of airports [29] and simulated flights within the SSR CoS [30].

In a detailed design, it is necessary to reconcile aspects of the protocol with the physical aspects, particularly in the areas close to the radar [31] and include functional aspects of the squitter as delayed transmission [32][5].

ADS-B support to SSR is not always possible. The ADS-B tracker is on the basis of all the other functionalities of support, and its correct behaviour actually

---

[5] As a consequence of delayed transmission, Fig. 3 should be modified accordingly.

depends on the quality of the ADS-B receptions and its vulnerabilities [33,34]. The messages received by the ADS-B itself contains quality information from, for example, position measurements it provides [35]. Reciprocally, the SSR can contribute to that quality control in some way. All those aspects have to be investigated and the control of the quality of ADS-B reception has to be incorporated to the algorithmics.

A posteriori, to the extent possible, tests should be implemented on the SSR and ADS-B installations of a real site [36], to collect statistics that can quantitatively verify the effective improvements provided by the functionalities and their integrity and reliability.

References

1. ICAO (International Civil Aviation Organization). Manual on the Secondary Surveillance Radar (SSR) Sytems. In: Doc 9684 AN/951 (2004)
2. Orlando, V., Drouilhet, P.: Functional Description of Mode S Beacon System. In: Project Report ATC-42 Revision B, Lincoln Laboratory, MIT (1982)
3. Bodart, J.: Mode S Surveillance Principle. Surveillance/MICA (Mode S Interrogation Code Allocation) Workshop (2019)
4. Bodart, J.: Mode S Surveillance Principle. In: MICA Workshop for ICAO MID States (2021)
5. Stevens, M.: Secondary Surveillance Radar. Artech House (1988)
6. ICAO (International Civil Aviation Organization). Annex 10, Third Edition of Volume IV. (2014)
7. ICAO (International Civil Aviation Organization). Technical Provisions for Mode S Services and Extended Squitter (2008)
8. RTCA: Minimum Operational Performance Standards for 1090 MHz Extended Squitter Automatic Dependent Surveillane - Broadcast (ADS-B) and Traffic Information Services (TIS-B). In: RTCA DO-260B (2011)
9. EUROCAE (The European Organisation for Civil Aviation Equipment): Technical Specification for a 1090 MHz Extended Squitter ADS-B Ground System. In: EUROCAE ED-129B (2016)
10. Schäfer, M., et al.: OpenSky report 2016: facts and figures on SSR mode S and AD-B usage. In: IEEE/AIAA 35th Digital Avionics Systems Conference (DASC) (2016)
11. Bria, O., Giacomantone, J.: Colaboración ADS-B en la predicción SSR. In: Libro de actas del XXVIII CACIC - Congreso Argentino de Ciencias de la Computación (2022)
12. Bria, O., Giacomantone, J.: ADS-B Colaboration with ADS-B. In: Libro de actas del XXIX CACIC - Congreso Argentino de Ciencias de la Computación (2023). ISNBN 978-987-9285-51-0
13. Sun, J.: The 1090 Megahertz Riddle: A Guide to Decoding Mode S and ADS-B Signals, 2nd edn. TU Delft OPEN Publishing (2021)
14. McDewitt, A.J.: A tracker for monopulse SSR. In: IEE Colloquium on State Estimation in Aerospace and Tracking Applications (1989)
15. Bar-Shalom, Y., Rong Li, X., Kirubajaran, T.: Estimation with Applications to Tracking and Navigation. John Wiley & Sons, Inc. (2001)

16. Welch, G., Bishop, G.: An Introduction to the Kalman Filter. In: TR 95-041, Department of Computer Science, University of North Carolina at Chapel Hill (2006)
17. Broookner, E.: Tracking and Kalman Filtering Made Easy, Wiley-Interscience. (1998)
18. Daekeun, J., Yeonju, E., Hyounkyoung, K.: Estimation Fusion with Radar and ADS-B for Air Traffic Surveillance. Int. J. Control Automation Syst. **13**(2), 336–345 (2015)
19. Tang, y., Wu, H., Xu, Z., Huang, Z.: ADS-B and SSR Data Fusion and Application. In: EEE International Conference on Computer Science and Automation Engineering (CSAE) (2012)
20. Miguel Vela, G., Iglesias Álvarez, J., Besada Portas, J., García, J.: Integration of ADS-B surveillance data in operative multiradar tracking processors. In: 11th International Conference on Information Fusion (2008)
21. Campbell, S., Grappel, R., Flavin, J.: Multi-sensor processing for aircraft surveillance in mixed radar/ADS-B environments. In: Proceedings of ESAV'08 (2008)
22. Hun, K.C.: Development of an Algorithm for Correlation of Aircraft Positioning Data from Radar and ADS-B Sensors. Thesis Dissertation for the Degree of Master of Software Engineering, Faculty of Computer Science and Information Technology, University of Malaya, Kuala Lumpur (2019)
23. Radartutorial.eu: Fundamentos Radar. Cobertura Radar. In: https://www.radartutorial.eu/01.basics/rb21.es.html (2023)
24. Balanis, C.: Antenna Theory: Analysis and Design. John Wiley & Sons (2015)
25. Skybrary.aero: Surveillance. definitions. In: https://skybrary.aero/articles/surveillance (2023)
26. EUROCONTROL.: European Mode S Station Functional Specification (EMS), edition 4.0, EUROCONTROL-SPEC-189 (2021)
27. U.S. Department of Transportation, Federal Aviation Adminitration: Aeronautical Information Manual (2017)
28. EUROCONTROL.: Principles of Mode S Operation and Interrogator Codes, edition 2.3 (2003)
29. FAA, Aeronautical Information Services: Aeronautical Chart Users Guide. In: aernav.faa.gov/userguide/20220714/cug-complete.pdf (2022)
30. Mariano, P., De Marco, P., Giacomini, C.: Data integrity augmentation by ADS-B SSR hybrid techniques. In: Integrated Communications Navigation and Surveillance Conference (2018)
31. U.S. Department of Transportation, Federal Aviation Adminitration Specification: Mode Select Beacon System (Mode S) Sensor. In: FAA-E-2716 (1983)
32. EUROCAE (The Europena Organisation for Civil Aviation Equipment): Minimum Operational Performance Specification for Secondary Surveillance Radar Mode S Trasnsponders. In: EUROCAE ED-73B (2003)
33. Krozel, J., Andrisani, D., Hoshizaki, T., Schwalm, C.: Aircraft ADS-B data integrity check . In: AIAA 4th Aviation Technology, Integration and Operations (ATIO) Forum (2004)
34. Haomiao, Y., Hongwei, L., Xuemin, S.: Secure Automatic Dependent Surveillance-Broadcast Sustems. Springer (2023)
35. Tesi, S., Pleniger, S.: Analysis of quality indicators in ADS-B messages. Mag. Aviation Dev. **5**(3), 6–12 (2017)
36. Addullah, A., Ismail, A., Badron, K., Rashid, N.: Improving radar detection by adaptation of automatic dependent surveillance-broadcast (ADS-B) technology. In: Advanced Science Letters, vol. 22 (2016)

Innovation in Computer Science
Education

Teaching Strategies for Programming in Massive University Settings

Gladys Dapozo$^{(\boxtimes)}$ ⓘ, Cristina Greiner ⓘ, Raquel Petris ⓘ, Ana María Company,
and María Cecilia Espíndola

Universidad Nacional del Nordeste, Corrientes, Argentina
gndapozo@exa.unne.edu.ar

Abstract. The teaching of programming at the university level, specifically aimed at training computer professionals, is at a critical moment due to significant demand for education, leading to a notable increase in enrollment in computer science programs nationwide. The subject of Algorithms and Data Structures I, located in the first semester of the first year of the Bachelor of Information Systems at UNNE, for the 2023 academic year, incorporated an adaptation of pair programming as a teaching strategy to mitigate the challenges of mass education. As a result, it is highlighted that students have appreciated the methodology for its contribution to debate and exchange of ideas, having a study partner, and acquiring study habits. The teaching staff acknowledges that it has reduced the volume of exams to correct, favoring more detailed feedback on corrections, considered an important learning opportunity. Additionally, the methodology has helped resolve the issue of equipment availability for the experimental practice required by the subject. Students have indicated difficulties related to their working relationship with their peers, a situation that should be addressed by defining future consensus mechanisms between peers. The evaluation of academic performance shows that the peer programming approach has helped maintain the percentage of students who typically pass the subject, neutralizing to some extent the unfavorable impact that mass education has on academic outcomes.

Keywords: Programming teaching · pair programming · university teaching

1 Introduction

The Argentine IT industry has been one of the most globally expanding players in the economy over the last 30 years, making it a sector of strategic importance for the country's economic development [1]. This industry constantly demands professionals in the Software and IT Services (SSI) sector.

In recent years, there has been a significant increase in enrollment in computer science programs in Argentina, driven by the acceleration of virtualization due to the pandemic, the mass adoption of remote work, and better salary rewards for workers in the sector. Regarding the latter point, it's worth noting that salaries in the software industry double the Basic Basket and private sector wages in general, according to a report from the

P. Pesado et al. (Eds.): CACIC 2023, CCIS 2123, pp. 339–349, 2024.
https://doi.org/10.1007/978-3-031-62245-8_23

Permanent Observatory of the Software Industry and IT Services of Argentina (OPSSI) [2].

It's evident that society's general awareness of the diverse applications of computer science seems to be more widespread than it was ten years ago, and the potential to study a computer-related career and secure an interesting job with good conditions appears to be a shared reality. However, the increased interest in studying computer science puts pressure on institutions regarding their infrastructure, equipment, and availability of human resources to cater to a growing number of students in the early years [3].

In this context, the teaching of programming at the university level, specifically aimed at training computer professionals, is at a critical juncture. On one hand, there's the challenge of dealing with the mass influx of students, and on the other hand, the crisis of human resources trained in university teaching who leave their roles due to demands from the job market.

In such conditions, teaching strategies and methodologies become particularly important. Various teaching methods for programming have been analyzed and compared, including visualization, games, robotics, problem-solving, code tracing, simulation, and pair programming [4]. The results of these studies indicate that using visualization and game-based methods in programming education can help improve students' programming concepts in terms of enhancing their cognitive ability to develop a mental model, increase their engagement, and stimulate abstract thinking in cognitive development.

In particular, pair programming for programming education is presented as an effective cooperative learning method in the educational context. Research comparing individual programming, pair programming, and collective programming through the perceptions of students in a university programming course showed that students prefer pair programming because they perceive it as a middle ground between not programming with anyone and doing it with a large group [5]. Individual programming can cause stress and intellectual blockage, while programming with too many people at the same time leads to distraction and imbalance of work. The findings suggest promoting pair work in university programming courses as it is easily implemented, requires few resources, and yields good results.

Similarly, a comparative study of individual programming and pair programming showed that pair programming is effective and is recommended for more frequent use in educational environments [6].

The Bachelor of Information Systems program at the Faculty of Exact and Natural Sciences and Surveying (FaCENA) of the National University of the Northeast (UNNE) had over 1000 enrolled students in 2023, significantly surpassing its average of 200 students in the last 5 years (2018–2022). Faced with this surge in enrollment, the teaching team of the first subject that addresses programming concepts, Algorithms and Data Structures I, located in the first semester of the first year of the program, incorporated strategies aimed at mitigating the effects of massiveness.

This work presents an extension of the work presented at CACIC 2023 [7], the proposal is described and the results of the strategy are expanded from two perspectives, student satisfaction and the academic results obtained.

2   Features of the Proposal

The massiveness of students in the 2023 academic year required the teaching team to reorganize the use of resources, both material (classrooms, equipment) and human (teachers), and to opt for pedagogical strategies aimed at self-containment and student retention in the classrooms.

The students were organized into 7 groups, each led by 2 teachers. Three theoretical-practical classes were conducted weekly (2 in person and 1 synchronous virtual) lasting 2 h each, for the development of the subject's content.

The experimental practice, coding in C, was carried out in conventional classrooms, not in computer labs, requiring students to bring their own devices.

The subject has a virtual classroom on the university's distance education platform, supported by Moodle. The virtual classroom provides students with theoretical and practical materials and all necessary resources to achieve the learning objectives. Questionnaires were also used for self-assessment activities of theoretical and practical content.

In this context, a set of strategies aimed at managing the available resources to achieve learning objectives and reduce dropout rates was implemented. These strategies include: Pair solving of practical activities, peer evaluation modality, and mobile laboratories.

2.1   Pair Programming for Practical Activities Development

Collaborative work is an interaction process in which students learn more than they would in an individual context. The questions and cross-questions that they frequently ask themselves provoke answers - correct or not - that energize the conceptual contents that help to differentiate, identify and contrast different points of view, in such a way that they generate a process of construction and assimilation of knowledge [8].

In particular, the pair programming modality was chosen (pair programming) since it is an agile development methodology that is used in the world of work.

This new modality is a way to enrich the training of future IT professionals and allows procedures that are used successfully in the software industry to be brought into the classroom early on [9].

Pair programming is an agile approach in which two people work together systematically to develop computer applications in reduced time. It has been used both in the software industry and in programming teaching and has demonstrated its effectiveness in both scenarios [10]. Each couple must adopt and exchange the roles of driver and navigator periodically. The driver is the person who uses the keyboard at a given time to write the program code. The navigator is the person who provides feedback to the driver through indications, suggestions and corrections [11].

To implement the strategy, the students were asked to inform their composition of the pair, through the resource provided by Moodle for teamwork.

The theoretical-practical classes involve a series of exercises that allow you to understand, reinforce and apply the conceptual contents, and the corresponding development of the code in C language that proposes a possible solution to the exercises proposed. Then the solutions of some pairs of students are presented to all attendees, encouraging debate and other possibilities or alternative proposals for solutions. Although the methodology supports the roles of driver and navigator, in this proposal the focus was not placed on these roles, but rather on collaborative work between peers.

In this way, an interactive space for debate is generated, which invites students to think and analyze other solution proposals, which requires combining efforts, concepts and skills, through a series of transactions that allows them to develop solutions in an consensual as stated [12] "More than a technique, collaborative work is considered a philosophy of interaction and a personal way of working, which involves the management of aspects, such as respect for the individual contributions of the members of the team".

2.2 Evaluation Mode

In line with this new working scheme, the first partial evaluation was also conducted in pairs, as the initial learning took place in this manner. This approach also aimed to optimize the time for correcting numerous exams and facilitate feedback to students, an important learning opportunity.

In the course planning, it was considered that the first partial would be conducted in pairs and the second partial individually, understanding that maintaining the pair programming modality for all evaluation instances would require greater monitoring of the internal performance of pairs, which would be impossible with an unfavorable teacher-student ratio.

The first partial was conducted in pairs in common classrooms where each pair had a laptop. Students were in an "online" context, with Wi-Fi available for classroom access and any other resources, posing the risk of external interventions in solving the tasks. Moreover, the exam was administered to the entire group simultaneously. Each group had more than 150 students.

During the correction of these exams, codes generated with generative AI software were found. Upon inquiry, the authors admitted to using ChatGPT. This situation was easily detectable because the proposed solution did not adhere to the problem-solving method taught in class.

Faced with this unforeseen situation and the difficulties of attending to a large number of students, it was decided to administer the exams on paper.

The results obtained have been satisfactory, considering that it also encouraged student retention, reducing premature dropout rates.

For the second stage of learning, although pair programming continued in classes, traditional individual evaluation methods were reintroduced for assessment instances.

2.3 Use of Mobile Laboratories

Traditionally, the subject used a scheme of theoretical classes, practical classes, and laboratory classes. The dynamics involved providing theoretical concepts in theory classes, consolidating these concepts through the resolution of practical work guides in practical classes in common classrooms, and coding the solutions in computer labs.

Due to the impossibility of maintaining this structure due to the large number of students and insufficient resources such as classrooms, laboratories (and teachers), classes were taught in a theoretical-practical format. Concepts were taught and practical activities were solved in common classrooms, including coding solutions. For this purpose, students brought their own notebooks, and some used their mobile phones.

3 Results

The results of the applied strategies were analyzed from two perspectives: Academic results and degree of student satisfaction.

3.1 Academics Results

At the end of the course, the performance of the students was evaluated based on whether they worked in pairs or not.

It should be noted that the final condition of the students, according to the accreditation regime of the subject, can fall into one of the following categories:

Regular: 75% attendance in classes, passing the 2 mandatory partial exams, and passing the "PilasBloques" activity. This student continues with the following subjects of the curriculum but must take a theoretical final exam in the examination periods of the academic year.

Promoted: If the student meets the above conditions and if the average of the 2 mandatory partial exams is 7 or higher, they can take a Third Partial exam on the conceptual topics of the subject. By passing this third partial, the student passes the subject.

Failed: These are students who did not pass the partial exams or dropped out of the course.

Table 1 shows the results of the students who worked in pairs. In the results it can be seen that the students who worked in pairs had a better performance (53% passed the subject).

Table 2 shows the results of the students who did not work in pairs. In the results it can be seen that the students who did not work in pairs had a worse performance (only 21% passed the subject).

3.2 Student Satisfaction

At the end of the course, a voluntary response survey was implemented for the students who took the subject, made available in the virtual classroom. Some of the notable results are:

Commission to Which it Belongs: The subject organized the activities into 7 commissions led by 2 teachers each. 3 weekly theoretical and practical classes were developed (2 in-person and 1 synchronous virtual) lasting 2 h each.

Table 1. Performance of students who worked in pairs

Final Condition	Amount	Percentage
Both regular	46	
Both promoted	104	
One of the two was regular and the other was promoted	108	
One of the two passed and the other was disapproved	254	127 (*)
Both Failed	208	
Total	**720**	
Approved (Regular or Promoted)	385	53%
Failed	335	47%
Total	**720**	**100%**

(*) the one who approved is counted

Table 2. Performance of students who did not work in pairs

Final Condition	Amount	Percentage
Promoted	31	
Regular	29	
Failed	224	
Total	**284**	
Approved or Promoted	60	twenty-one%
Failed	224	79%
Total	**284**	**100%**

Although the committees respected the unique planning of the subject, with the application of the same methodology and exam dates, students could have different perceptions according to the teaching style of their teachers. In Fig. 1 it can be seen that all the commissions are represented in the responses.

Gender: A current problem in the training of computer scientists is the low participation of women. Although public policies are aimed at promoting ICT vocations in young women, this percentage is still low. Figure 2 shows the participation of the students women in the survey.

Opinion on Pair Programming Modality: When asked about their opinion on pair programming modality, they were provided with a list of options, but they could add others. Figure 3 shows that the majority indicated that they found it good or very good (83%).

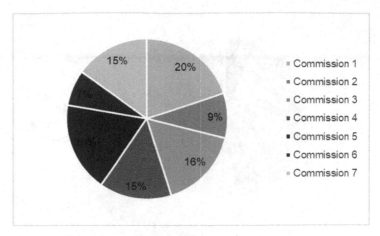

Fig. 1. Students by commission

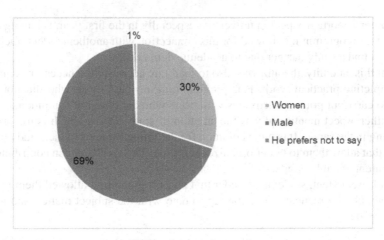

Fig. 2. Students by gender

In the "Other" category, considering the individual responses, an issue stands out that should be taken into account in the implementation methodology: what to do if that one of the pair abandons the course, a fairly common situation in first-year students. Also the situation of those who prefer to work alone. To a lesser extent, they pointed out the difficulty of establishing study schedules due to work issues, the difficulty of agreeing on the resolution of problems, and the difference in commitment to the task in some of the pair.

Advantages of the Pair Programming Modality: Students were consulted about the benefits of pair programming. Figure 4 shows that the majority highlight the positive aspect of debating ideas and concepts. This is particularly interesting in programming education because there is no single solution to the problems presented in the practical work guides. This peer debate significantly contributes to learning.

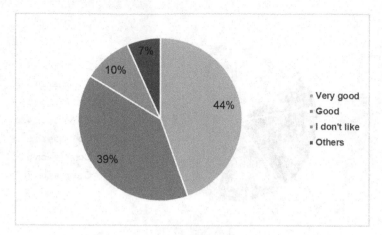

Fig. 3. Opinion on pair programming modality

Another important aspect in university, especially in the first year, is having a study partner. Pair programming allowed for this connection with another student, facilitating contact to find a study partner due to academic demands.

With this modality, the aim was also to facilitate access to the necessary equipment for completing practical work. Pair programming enabled those who did not have a laptop to carry out practical activities with peers who did have the equipment.

Another aspect mentioned was the creation of study habits, which is important for advancing in the career. It is quite common for incoming students to lack study methodologies that allow them to better organize their time. This modality can contribute to the development of study habits.

To a lesser extent, students consider that pair programming allowed them to clarify doubts about the practical work, stay up to date with the subject matter, and adapt to university life.

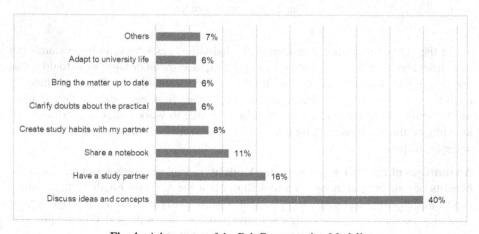

Fig. 4. Advantages of the Pair Programming Modality

Analyzing the responses of those who chose the "Other" option, situations stand out where the modality did not work due to the characteristics of the pairs, such as strong individualism and a lack of teamwork skills. On the other hand, there are situations where the pair recognizes the advantages of having to teach another.

Unbalanced pairs in terms of abilities are often a problem. This situation also appears, but not in a significant percentage, which speaks highly of the students who faced the situation. It is also worth noting that students who contributed little to the team (the pair, in this case) were exposed in the second partial since it was individual.

Difficulties or Drawbacks of the Pair Programming Modality: When asked about the difficulties or inconveniences they experienced with pair programming, students were provided with a list of options but could also add others. Figure 5 shows that the majority (61%) highlighted organizational issues such as days, schedules, and places to study as difficulties.

12% of students indicated disagreements in problem-solving and inflexibility of some parties as drawbacks. Regarding these aspects, inherent to teamwork, prior training should be provided to students to facilitate the achievement of the modality's objectives and define consensus mechanisms among pairs.

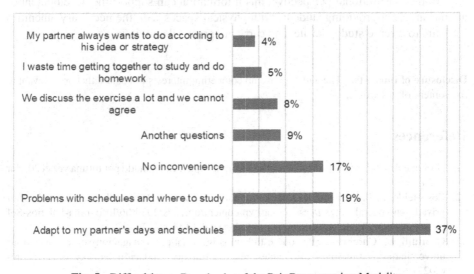

Fig. 5. Difficulties or Drawbacks of the Pair Programming Modality

Additionally, 17% of the students indicated that they have not had any problems and 9% indicated other issues, among which stand out situations in which one of the peers has not lived up to expectations, in terms of commitment, or has not been organized to be able to contribute to the team.

4   Conclusions and Futures Jobs

The pair programming modality used in this context of massiveness can be a valuable strategy for teaching programming.

Students, in general, recognize it as a good strategy and have highlighted that it has allowed them to debate and exchange ideas, have a study partner, and develop study habits.

The teaching team acknowledges that it has reduced the volume of exams to correct, favoring more detailed feedback on errors, considered an important learning opportunity. The modality has also proved valid in resolving equipment shortages. In contexts of massiveness, it is very difficult to have laboratories with the necessary capacity to meet the intense practice needs required by the subject.

Regarding the difficulties pointed out by students related to their working relationship with their peers, it necessitates designing consensus mechanisms among pairs.

The evaluation of academic performance shows that the pair programming modality contributed to maintaining the percentage of students who typically pass the subject, to some extent neutralizing the unfavorable impact that massiveness has on academic results.

From an institutional perspective, this information can support the development of actions aimed at providing students with physical spaces with the necessary amenities for pairs to meet to study, debate, and carry out practical activities.

Disclosure of Interests.   The authors have no competing interests to declare that are relevant to the content of this article.

References

1. ¿Por qué Argentina?, https://redargentinait.com/porque/. Consultado por última vez el 20 Mar 2024
2. Los sueldos de la industria del software duplican la Canasta Básica y los salarios del sector privado en general. https://cessi.org.ar/wp-content/uploads/2023/06/Infografia-Salarios-Software-enero-2023.pdf, consultado por última vez el 20 Mar 2024
3. Quartulli, D., Curcio, J.: ¿Por qué estudiamos informática? Indagación sobre trayectorias universitarias: instituciones, estudiantes, género y trabajo. Fundación Sadosky, Buenos Aires (2023)
4. Adnan, A., Romli, R.: A comparative evaluation on methods of teaching computer programming. In: Saeed, F., Mohammed, F., Ghaleb, F. (eds.) Advances on Intelligent Informatics and Computing: Health Informatics, Intelligent Systems, Data Science and Smart Computing, pp. 571–582. Springer International Publishing, Cham (2022). https://doi.org/10.1007/978-3-030-98741-1_47
5. Roque Hernández, R., Guerra Moyadán, S., López Mendoza, A.: Programación individual, por pares o colectiva: ¿cuál conviene utilizar en la universidad? Apertura (Guadalajara, Jal.), vol. 12, no. 1 (2020). https://doi.org/10.32870/ap.v12n1.1791
6. Demir, Ö., Seferoglu, S.S.: A comparison of solo and pair programming in terms of flow experience, coding quality, and coding achievement. J. Educ. Comput. Res. **58**(8), 1448–1466 (2020). https://doi.org/10.1177/0735633120949788

7. Dapozo, G., Greiner, C., Petris, R., Company, A.M., Espíndola, M.C.: Programación por pares como estrategia de enseñanza en contextos de masividad. In: Libro de Actas XXIX Congreso Argentino de Ciencias de la Computación. CACIC 2023. Universidad Nacional de Luján. 2024, pp. 248–256 (2023)
8. Guitert, M., Jiménez, F.: Aprender a colaborar. In: Cooperar en clase: Ideas e instrumentos para trabajar en el aula, Eds. Madrid: M.C.E.P. (2000)
9. Zanga, A.M., et al.: Mejoras en el proceso de enseñanza-aprendizaje de programación utilizando metodologías propias de la industria del software como caso particular de las metodologías activas. Universidad Nacional de La Matanza (2015). http://repositoriocyt. unlam.edu.ar/handle/123456789/400
10. Roque Hernández, R.M., González Morales, R., Muñoz Castellanos, S.P.: La programación por pares: un análisis de la producción científica en Web of Science. Forhum. Int. J. Soc. Sci. Hum. 4(7) (2022)
11. Dalton, J.: Great Big Agile: An OS for Agile Leaders. Apress, Berkeley, CA (2019). https:// doi.org/10.1007/978-1-4842-4206-3
12. Maldonado, M.: El trabajo colaborativo en el aula universitaria. Laurus 13(23), 263–278 (2007)

Rubric-Driven Competency Development: A Case Study

Carlos Neil(✉) [iD], Nicolás Battaglia [iD], and Marcelo De Vincenzi [iD]

Facultad de Tecnología Informática, Centro de Altos Estudios en Tecnología Informática, Universidad Abierta Interamericana, Buenos Aires, Argentina

{carlos.neil,nicolas.battaglia,medevincenzi}@uai.edu.ar

Abstract. A model for competency development is presented, uses concepts from problem-based learning as a learning strategy and rubric analytical descriptors associated with the problem as assessment criteria. The proposal is framed within constructive alignment, emphasizing the coherence between learning outcomes, their development, and evaluation and is grounded in the theory of cognitive load, which posits that the mental load imposed on students during a learning task influences their ability to acquire and transfer knowledge. The process links each rubric analytical descriptor in a didactic sequence with low complexity learning activities, whose solution demonstrates the established evaluative criteria. This strategy allows students to focus, initially, on specific aspects, and then integrating them into a learning activity that utilizes the associated rubric as an assessment criterion. Finally, the model was implemented and evaluated in systems engineering degree courses. This involved its real-world application in an educational context, as well as data collection and assessment of its effectiveness and relevance in competency development.

Keywords: Rubric · Cognitive Load · Learning Outcomes · Constructive Alignment

1 Introduction

The structure of the paper is supported by the coherent interconnection of the various underlying concepts, demonstrating their interrelation and their joint capacity to enhance the quality of both teaching and learning. First of all, the proposal adheres to the constructivist approach [1, 2] which, advocates for active and meaningful learning, where students are protagonists in the construction of their knowledge through interaction with study materials and their peers. This pedagogical theory maintains that learning is an active process where students construct their knowledge through contextualized experiences. Within this framework, student-centered learning has become a central approach in education, aided by the rapid evolution of technology and the increasing importance of digital skills today [3].

On the other hand, in recent years, collaborative work has experienced significant momentum. The synergy between collaborative work and information and communication technologies has created a powerful combination, promoting the development of

P. Pesado et al. (Eds.): CACIC 2023, CCIS 2123, pp. 350–365, 2024.
https://doi.org/10.1007/978-3-031-62245-8_24

new methods and tools for learning. One way to carry out collaborative work is through problem-based learning, which promotes complex thinking and group reflection, facilitating decision-making on real and relevant problems in the professional field where the student participates and develops [4].

Finally, as a fundamental component, constructive alignment [5–7] which is a pedagogical approach that emphasizes the importance of coherence between learning outcomes, the teaching-learning process, and evaluation. This implies that both the evaluation methods, which must effectively measure the achievement of established learning outcomes, and the assessment criteria, must be clear and consistent with the expected performance standards. Of the three described components, previous papers have developed proposals: in [8], a process the design of rubrics and an open repository for the educational community were presented; in [9], the guidelines for writing learning outcomes were provided. To complete the trilogy, this paper presents a Rubric-Driven Competency Development, based on a previous paper [10] which has been expanded through the incorporation of an experiment conducted to evaluate the new learning approach in a group of students.

This paper is part of the research project Multiplatform Collaborative Tools in Software Engineering Education, developed at the Centro de Altos Estudios en Tecnología Informática of the Universidad Abierta Interamericana.

2 Fundamentals and Model Strategies

This section details the main concepts and theories used in the proposed model. First, learning outcomes are described as process drivers; then, rubrics are discussed as evaluation (and learning) strategies; next, concepts from cognitive load theory that substantiate the use of Micro-Learning Activities (mLA) are outlined, followed by a detailed discussion of their key characteristics. Finally, the didactic sequence is established as an integrating element of the entire process.

2.1 How Are Competencies Defined? Learning Outcomes

The competency-based model and student-centered learning emphasize learning outcomes as key elements to guide the learning process. Clear guidelines are required to standardize their writing, allowing them to be understood both by the educational community and as well as the external one. In this regard, using the competency matrix to identify the competencies related to each subject, as well as the associated levels of mastery allows, on the one hand, to ensure coherence between graduation skills and learning outcomes and, on the other hand, provides precise guidelines for clarity in their description [9].

To assess competency development, levels of mastery are used to measure progress in learning over time and take action to improve in areas as needed [11]. In this sense, the competency matrix allows to identify how each subject contributes to the development of one or more competencies, considering expected levels of complexity, integration, and student autonomy. In this model, each subject focuses on promoting a limited set of learning outcomes, allowing for the gradual and planned development of graduation skills throughout the academic journey.

The writing of learning outcomes presented in [9] follows an iterative and incremental process that begins by identifying, in the competency matrix, the competencies and associated levels of mastery for each subject. Then, for each of them, the verb according to the established level of mastery, the knowledge objects, the purpose, and finally, the reference conditions are determined. From this process, the set of learning outcomes that each subject commits to develop is identified for the curriculum.

2.2 How Are Competencies Evaluated? Rubrics

Evaluation guides and motivates both learning and teaching [12] and should not be seen as a separate process from learning but as an opportunity to foster it [13]. In this sense, rubrics are not only limited to assessment but also serve as learning strategies that allow complex tasks related to competencies to be broken down into simpler tasks, distributed gradually and operatively. Moreover, the use of rubrics is strengthened in Learning Management Systems, since their design and utilization empower the teacher, the student, and the institution, thus encouraging a culture of assessment [14]. Furthermore, the use of rubrics can be a valid instrument to promote learning, especially when combined with different metacognitive activities such as self-regulation, peer assessment, or self-assessment [15].

The issue with rubrics is that, in general, the level of detail of the descriptors does not allow students to use them as effective guidelines for developing learning strategies, for example: [16–20]. The rubric presented in [8] measures the level of achievement in problem-solving by relating indicators to levels of mastery, whit a format of rubric analytical descriptors that clarifies their use. The differentiating feature is centered on the construction of the descriptors; each assessment criterion can be subdivided into one or more rubric analytical descriptors, and each of them, in turn, consists of a linked context and two analytical descriptors A + and B, which can be contrasted with the evaluated work to establish whether they comply whit it or not. The rubric analytical descriptors will be used in Rubric-Driven Competency Development as assessment criteria in the resolution of mLA.

2.3 What Characteristics Should Micro Learning Activity Have? Cognitive Load

The theory of cognitive load [21] addresses the impact of mental load on problem-solving and learning processes, specifically referring to the mental resources required to solve a problem. An elevated cognitive load can hinder learning by consuming more mental resources and limiting processing capacity. To reduce cognitive load, strategies such as simplifying the problem, presenting relevant information, and guiding the resolution process can be employed. In this sense, appropriate support, clear instructions, and convenient feedback help optimize workload. Reducing cognitive load involves simplifying information and procedures to make them easier to process. Presenting the information in a structured and sequential manner facilitates understanding, and helps students apply the acquired knowledge, by providing exercises and practical cases with clear instructions.

Moreover, opportune feedback allows students to correct errors and improve performance. Additionally, distributing learning over time, with rest intervals between study sessions, promotes long-term retention. Designing learning situations that reflect real workplace challenges also facilitates knowledge transfer [22]. Furthermore, sequencing learning activities according to the complexity and familiarity of concepts optimizes cognitive load and allows students to develop their ability to handle it, thereby improving performance. Other aspects to consider include real-time monitoring of student performance, as well as immediate feedback to the student to correct errors and strengthen weak areas [23].

2.4 How Are Practical Assignments Structured? Micro-Learning Activity

In this paper, we define mLA based on [24, 25] an activity of medium to low complexity focused on a particular theme, whose resolution can be completed within a period of 30 to 45 min. The mLA allow the division of the problem into parts (analysis), reducing the student's effort in favor of the subsequent integration (synthesis) of its components. mLA are complemented by rubric analytical descriptors as guides that direct the learning process and provide a clear structure that allows a better understanding of the essential components of the problem. By establishing a partition of the problem, students address each part more effectively, thus facilitating the final synthesis as they see how they relate to each other once integrated. In summary, the combined use of rubric analytical descriptors for the resolution of mLA not only improves learning assessment but also becomes a valuable tool for directing and facilitating the process, reducing the workload for students.

Problem-Based Learning
In the development of mLA, concepts from Problem-Based Learning are used, defined as a set of activities that promote complex thinking and group and cooperative reflection, aiming to address decisions about real and relevant problems within the professional domain in which the student participates and develops [4]. This educational approach focuses on competency development through problem-solving, where students confront real-world problematic situations and work in collaborative teams to identify and solve them, utilizing acquired knowledge and skills. Problem-Based Learning [26] stimulates creativity by fostering idea generation and critical thinking development; it promotes the organization of ideas and enhances analysis, synthesis, and evaluation when dealing with complex problems; it generates greater motivation to learn, as students find greater motivation when working on real-world problems; it promotes autonomous discovery of knowledge, rather than passive information reception; it encourages participation and develops skills for collaborative work and problem-solving; it fosters interpersonal communication, multidisciplinary teamwork, and improvement through feedback; it develops interpersonal relationship skills when working in teams as well as social skills such as empathy, active listening, and negotiation, which are fundamental in interpersonal interactions.

Integrated-Learning Activity
The mLA propose the decomposition of a complex task into simpler and more manageable tasks, thereby reducing the overall cognitive load and facilitating learning, culminate

in an integrated-learning activity as a synthesis of the process. Therefore, an important aspect is the design of the integration activity. In a previous study [9], Bloom's taxonomy [27] was used to define the levels of mastery and the choice of verb in learning outcomes. This paper recommends defining problems that correspond to higher cognitive levels and require analysis, synthesis, and evaluation from the student [28]. Therefore, real-life problems should be proposed for students to engage with, where the necessary information to solve them is not complete, so they are compelled to investigate, discover new study materials, make judgments, and make decisions based on information. Finally, the problem should have more than one acceptable answer based on established premises.

2.5 How is the Process Implemented? Didactic Sequence

The development of competencies requires establishing a didactic sequence [11, 29, 30], which is understood as the articulated set of learning and evaluation activities that, with the mediation of the teacher, pursue the achievement of certain educational goals, considering a series of resources. The components of the didactic sequence for competencies [11] are identified below, and a correspondence with the proposed model is established. Firstly, the problem context situation is defined, where the competence is intended to be developed; in the presented model, this corresponds to the mLA and the integrated-learning activity. Then, the competencies to be formed are defined, which in the proposal are the learning outcomes. This is followed by learning and evaluation activities, where activities with the teacher and autonomous learning activities of the students are indicated; in this case, the monitoring and feedback of the teacher and the development of mLA and the integrated-learning activity of the students. Next is the evaluation, where criteria and evidence are established to guide learning assessment, corresponding in the process to the mLA linked with rubric analytical descriptors and the integrated-learning activity with the rubric. This is followed by resources, i.e., the required educational materials, which in the model are the UAIRubric [31] repository. Lastly, the metacognitive process is described, where the main suggestions for the student to reflect and self-regulate in the learning process are outlined; in the proposed model, this includes self and peer-assessment and teacher feedback (hetero-evaluation).

3 Rubric-Driven Competency Development Process

During the competence development model, it is essential to monitor and adjust cognitive load to ensure optimal learning, enabling the adaptation of teaching strategies, providing appropriate feedback, and offering additional practice opportunities according to individual student needs [32]. The proposal consists in decomposing a complex a complex task into simpler and more manageable tasks (mLA), thus reducing the overall cognitive load and facilitating learning, to culminate in an integrated-learning activity as a synthesis of the process.

The process of competency development utilizes the principle of parsimony, also known as Occam's razor, which suggests that among several explanations or models, the simplest one is usually the best option until there is evidence to support the opposite.

Applying this principle in deciding which educational model to use implies selecting the simplest option that meets the specific educational objectives.

3.1 Theoretical Model Overview

The model of competency development is described, which links the competency matrix, the learning outcomes, the rubric analytical descriptors, the mLA, the integrated-learning activity, and the rubric (Fig. 1).

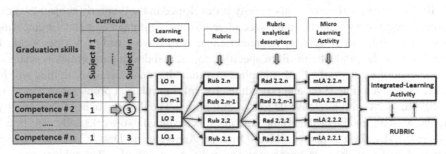

Fig. 1. Rubric-Driven Competency Development Process

First, in the competency matrix, the subject and its associated level of mastery are identified; implicitly, this means that this subject will contribute to a set of learning outcomes whose objective will be to develop the graduation skills established in the matrix (C. G. Neil et al., 2023). The subject is associated with a set of learning outcomes (LO n); in particular, LO 2 is decomposed to a set of rubrics (Rub 2.1…, 2.n); one of them, for example, Rub 2.2, is broken down into a series of rubric analytical descriptors (Rad 2.2.1…, 2.2.n), each of which is assigned mLA (mLA 2.2.1…, 2.2.n). Finally, with the aim of integrating all mLA, links them in an integrated-learning activity and its respective rubric.

In summary, the process involves associating each rubric analytical descriptor with mLA whose solutions highlight the established assessment criteria. These criteria act as a guide for the student when addressing the mLA and as assessment criteria for the teacher when providing feedback (Fig. 2a). The related mLA are developed following a didactic sequence that will culminate in an integrated-learning activity, which uses the rubric as an assessment criterion, both in student self-assessment and teacher evaluation (Fig. 2b).

3.2 Competency Development Model: A Practical Case

To exemplify the implementation of Rubric-Driven Competency Development, the UML class diagram rubric published in the Rubric repository will be used. In its metadata, the associated subject, learning outcomes, and the level of mastery are detailed. On the other hand, in the rubric, the rubric analytical descriptors are identified along with their associated analytical descriptors A + and B.

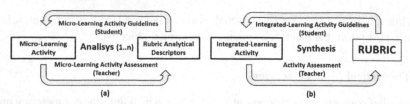

Fig. 2. Relationship between Micro-Learning Activity and Rubric Analytical Descriptors and the relationship between Integrated-Learning Activity and Rubric

To contextualize the work, this activity is developed in the quarterly subject "Analysis and Design of Systems II" in the second year of the Computer Systems Engineering program at Universidad Abierta Interamericana, with a workload of 5 h per week. It contributes to the graduation skill of specify, project and develop information systems, with a level of mastery of "2"; this implies that teaching and learning activities will be focused on developing skills and procedures for solving relevant problems in contextualized situations with a relative degree of autonomy. The development of this activity, aligned with the established learning outcomes, is assigned two weeks and corresponds to Unit II "Modeling Tools for Object-Oriented Analysis and Design" which is developed with self-managed synchronous and asynchronous activities. The subject was also the responsibility to develop the transversal competence to effectively perform in work teams with a level of mastery "2". For this reason, learning activities will be carried out collaboratively in teams of 3 or 4 students, using concepts from problem-based learning. The rubric analytical descriptors for teamwork are also used as general guidelines for its development and are outlined in the "Group Work" rubric published in the UAIRubric repository. A didactic sequence is included as an option for classroom activity, which can be used as a model for other alternatives.

In the first week, prior to the first face-to-face class, a reading related to the UML model is proposed to the students with the intention that they understand the problems of standards. Additionally, they are requested to read the theoretical content available on the distance education platform that will allow them to internalize theoretical and practical concepts (flipped classroom approach). On the other hand, a questionnaire with questions related to the topic is included to detect any issues in understanding the acquired knowledge. The flipped classroom strategy enables the teacher to focus their classroom work on tutoring activities.

In the first class, during the synchronous activity, the teacher proposes the resolution of mLA 1, 2, and 3 by teams, linked to rubric analytical descriptors 1, 2, and 3, respectively. In this activity, the teacher acts as a tutor, responding to student queries. Each completed mLA is then submitted to the teacher for evaluation using the criteria established in the rubric analytical descriptors. Additionally, the teacher provides comments and suggestions, which could imply, if necessary, a new submission of the mLA if required. Subsequently, in asynchronous mode, students develop mLA 4, 5, and 6 collectively, utilizing rubric analytical descriptors 4, 5, and 6. Once completed, each team submits their work to the teacher for evaluation. Finally, the teacher evaluates and provides feedback on each of the mLA, offering comments and suggestions.

In the second week, during the synchronous activity, the integrated-learning activity is developed by teams, with the complete rubric serving as the assessment criterion. Once the teamwork is finished, the teacher presents a version of the integrated-learning activity that provides a solution (not the only one) to the posed problem. As an asynchronous activity, each group is asked for develop the final version, self-assessing their work, co-assessing the integrated-learning activity of another team, and then uploading them to the Learning Management System for teaching evaluation. To foster metacognitive activities, each student will self-assess using the "Group Work" rubric published in the UAIRubric repository.

To conclude, once the once the auto and co-assessment activities are completed, the teacher will conduct hetero-evaluation with comments and suggestions about the integrated-learning activity. This may also entail the need for a new version of the integrated-learning activity; this process continues until the teacher considers that the level of achievement of the competence aligns with the established level of mastery.

4 Measuring Student Perception

In 2023, a pilot experiment was conducted with the aim of evaluating the new learning approach in a group of students. The main purpose of this initiative was to determine the effectiveness and feasibility of implementing this pedagogical approach in the current educational context. To assess the level of satisfaction of the students regarding the new model and its components, quantitative research was conducted to determine the effectiveness of the implementation of the learning approach. Questionnaires and Likert scales were used to evaluate the degree of satisfaction of the students.

4.1 Materials and Methods

The methodology chosen to analyze the students' opinions was of a quantitative nature, opting for a descriptive approach through surveys, which is particularly suitable for gathering information about opinions in an educational context [33]. A one-dimensional questionnaire with 5 items and a five-option Likert scale (1 to 5) was used to measure the degree of agreement or disagreement of the respondents regarding a series of statements. Each point on the scale was labeled to provide information about what each number represents; these labels are included in the corresponding graphs. The data were analyzed using univariate descriptive statistics that describe how the data are distributed, their central tendency and variability, which helps describe and interpret the students' opinions. The collected data allowed for the analysis of students' perceptions on different aspects of the learning process, such as the quality of the materials used, the complexity of competency development, the comparison with traditional methods, the importance of collaborative work and the role of the teacher as a tutor and in providing feedback.

4.2 Participants

The survey was conducted using a convenience sample of students enrolled in the second year of the "Systems Analysis and Design II" course at the School of Information Technology of the Universidad Abierta Interamericana. The survey period encompassed from September 12th to September 28th, 2023. The sample consisted of 148 students, of which 120 were male and 28 were female. The average age of the participants was 24.39 years, indicating a predominantly young distribution within the student population; the modal age was 20 years.

4.3 Results and Discussion

The survey results revealed the students' perceptions regarding the implemented new learning approach. Overall, a positive trend towards the model was observed, with most students expressing satisfaction with various aspects of the teaching-learning process.

The results obtained are detailed below:

- **How do you consider the previous material used to understand the "UML Class Diagram" unit?**

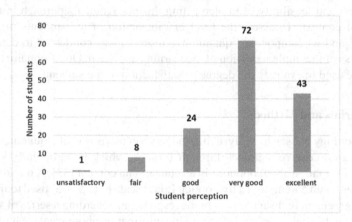

Fig. 3. How do you consider the previous material used to understand the "UML Class Diagram" unit?

There was a positive reception towards the implementation of flipped learning; students expressed satisfaction with this approach, highlighting its usefulness and effectiveness in the teaching-learning process.

The mean was x = 4, with a standard deviation of σ = 0.86. In summary, 77% considered that the material used for flipped learning as "very good" or "excellent" (Fig. 3).

- **How do you consider the rubric-driven competency development process?**

There was a positive appreciation about the complexity of the process, although a few students expressed some initial difficulty in adapting to this new approach.

The mean was x = 3.88, with a standard deviation of σ = 0.87. In summary, 70% considered the development process to be "easy" or "very easy" (Fig. 4).

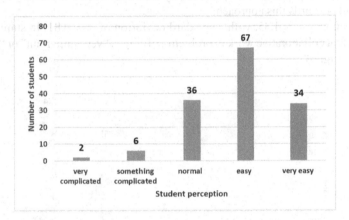

Fig. 4. How do you consider the rubric-driven competency development process?

- **How do you consider the rubric-driven competency development process regarding to other strategies used?**

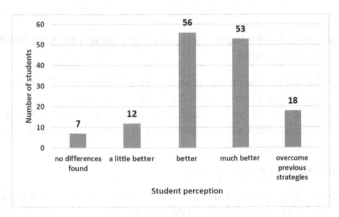

Fig. 5. How do you consider the rubric-driven competency development process regarding to other strategies used?

In the comparative analysis with traditional methods, the survey results highlighted a positive assessment towards the new model. Students expressed a preference for this approach compared to traditional teaching methods.

The mean was x = 3.43, with a standard deviation of σ = 0.97. In summary, 75% considered that development process, compared to previous experiences, is a "better" or "much better" option (Fig. 5).

- **How do you consider collaborative work in solving assignments as a strategy that improves learning?**

Regarding collaborative work, the survey results reflected a positive appreciation from students towards this approach.

The mean was x = 4.35, with a standard deviation of σ = 0.81. In summary, 88% considered that collaborative work in problem-solving is "very important" or "extremely important" (Fig. 6).

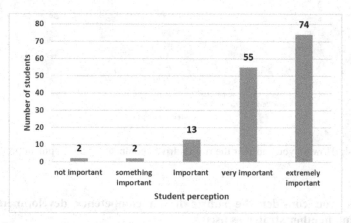

Fig. 6. How do you consider collaborative work in solving assignments as a strategy that improves learning?

- **How do you consider the teacher's support as a tutor and in the feedback in the correction of assignments?**

Regarding the teacher's support, the survey results evidenced the importance of the teacher's role as a tutor and facilitator in the learning process.

The mean was x = 4.30, with a standard deviation of σ = 0.82. In summary, 85% highlighted that the teacher's support was "very important" or "extremely important" (Fig. 7).

- **Micro-learning Activity Complexity**

Another aspect we considered important to evaluate was the complexity of the mLA, as their structure significantly influenced the development of the educational process.

The mean was x = 2.90, with a standard deviation of σ = 0.81. In summary, 49% highlighted that the complexity of the mLA is "medium" (Fig. 8).

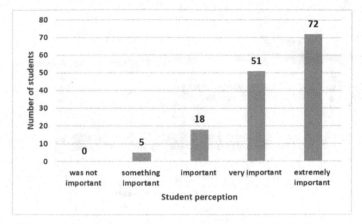

Fig. 7. How do you consider the teacher's support as a tutor and in the feedback in the correction of assignments?

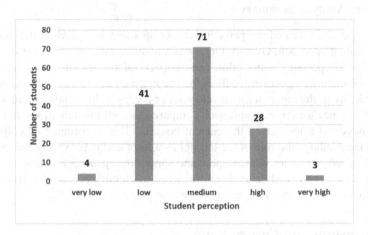

Fig. 8. Micro-learning Activity Complexity.

- **Distribution of Student Workload in Teaching and Learning Activities**

In teaching and learning activities, it is important to determine the allocated time for each strategy to gauge the effort required from the student. It is necessary to consider not only the hours the student spends on face-to-face sessions but also those dedicated to self-managed activities, which together determine the total effort in hours in terms of what is known as academic credits.

In the study conducted, the total workload in synchronous and self-managed activities was distributed as follows: 57% of students dedicated less than 10 h, 39% between 11 and 15 h, and 4% more than 15 h (Fig. 9).

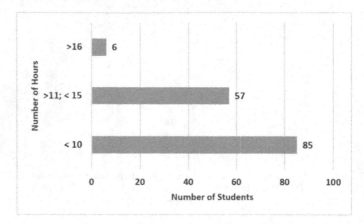

Fig. 9. Distribution of Student Workload in Teaching and Learning Activities

4.4 Survey Analysis Summary

The survey results revealed the perceptions among students regarding the new implemented learning approach. Overall, there was a positive trend towards the model, with most students expressing satisfaction most aspects of the teaching-learning process. Specifically, there was positive feedback on the material used and appreciation for the low complexity in the competence development process. Additionally, there was a significant preference for this new approach compared to traditional methods, highlighting its usefulness and relevance in the current context. The importance of collaborative work and the fundamental role of the teacher as a tutor and in providing feedback were also emphasized. Areas for improvement and some discrepancies in students´ opinions were identified, which will be analyzed in detail to identify possible adjustments and optimizations in the future implementation of the pedagogical model.

5 Conclusions and Future Work

The Rubric-Driven Competency Development is grounded in constructive alignment, which emphasizes the importance of coherence between learning outcomes, the teaching process, and assessment. The research is based on the theory of cognitive load, with the aim of reducing the mental load imposed on students, which affects their ability to acquire and transfer knowledge. Additionally, concepts from problem-based learning are employed as a learning strategy, and rubric analytical descriptors associated with the problem serve as assessment criteria. In summary, the proposal involves linking each rubric analytical descriptor with mLA that focus on specific aspects of the competencies. These mLA allow students to focus on these aspects before integrating them into a broader practical task that address the complexity required by the established learning outcome.

 On the other hand, it is necessary to reflect on the time that the teacher dedicates to providing feedback on the mLA and the integrated-learning activity. Although the student-centered learning approach does not reduce the teacher's workload, it directs their attention towards tutorial and feedback activities. An advantage of the model is that groups divide the course into "n" teams, which partly reduces the teacher's workload.

Regarding the continuity of the work, it is necessary to explore the possibility of expanding the model to cover different areas of knowledge, not exclusively computer-related topics. This would allow the development and evaluation of competencies in a variety of disciplinary contexts.

As a first experience, in the perception analysis of the students, design and validation aspects of the form used were not considered. In future research, we will consider the validation of the instrument through content analysis test, exploratory factor analysis, and calculation of Cronbach's alpha coefficient. We will use expert judgment to assess the validity and relevance of the questions and conduct a pilot test with a small sample of participants to identify and correct problems of comprehension or interpretation of the questions. Furthermore, empirical studies are necessary to validate the effectiveness of the proposed model and compare it with other competency development approaches to determine the most suitable strategy for competency development and evaluation.

Lastly, it is crucial to establish guidelines to determine the time allocated to the didactic sequences used for competency development so as to avoid exceeding the number of hours established in the academic credits assigned to the subject and thus not to negatively affect the student's workload.

References

1. Vygotsky, L.S.: The collected works of LS Vygotsky: problems of the theory and history of psychology. Springer Science & Business Media (1987). https://doi.org/10.1007/978-1-4613-1655-8
2. Piaget, J., Cook, M., Norton, W.W.: The Origins of Intelligence in Children, vol. 8. New York International University, New York (1952)
3. Mendoza, M., Rodríguez, M.: Aprendizaje centrado en el estudiante desde la planificación en investigación. CIENCIAMATRÍA 6(10), 560–572 (2019)
4. Olivares Olivares, S.L., Heredia Escorza, Y.: Desarrollo del pensamiento crítico en ambientes de aprendizaje basado en problemas en estudiantes de educación superior. Rev. Mex. Investig. Educ. 17, 759–778 (2012)
5. Biggs, J.B.: Calidad del aprendizaje universitario. Educ. Siglo XXI. 22, 272 (2004)
6. Carlino, F.: De la alienación al alineamiento constructivo. Más allá de la trampa mecanicista. Cuaderno de Pedagogía Universitaria 18(35), 58–70 (2021). https://doi.org/10.29197/cpu.v18i35.413
7. Oquendo-González, E.J., Velásquez-Pérez, Y., Rose-Parra, C., Cervera-Manjarrez, N.: El alineamiento constructivo para el desarrollo de la competencia científica. CIENCIAMATRIA. 8, 666–686 (2022)
8. Neil, C., Battaglia, N., Zemborain, M.E.D.V.: Marco metodológico para el diseño de rúbricas analíticas. Edutec. Rev. Electrónica Tecnol. Educ. (2022). https://doi.org/10.21556/edutec.2022.80.2425
9. Neil, C.G., Battaglia, N., De Vincenzi, M.: La matriz de competencias como herramienta para orientar la escritura de resultados de aprendizaje. In: XVIII Congreso Nacional de Tecnología en Educación y Educación en Tecnología-TE&ET 2023 (2023)
10. Neil, C.G., Battaglia, N., De Vincenzi, M.: Diseño de competencia conducido por rúbricas. In: XXIX Congreso Argentino de Ciencias de la Computación (2023)

11. Tobón, S.T., Prieto, J.H.P., Fraile, J.A.G.: Secuencias didácticas: aprendizaje y evaluación de competencias. Pearson educación México (2010)
12. de Miguel Díaz, M.: Modalidades de enseñanza centradas en el desarrollo de competencias. Orientaciones para promover el cambio Metod. en el Espac. Eur. Educ. Super. (2005)
13. Torres-Sanz, V., Garrido, P., Sanguesa, J.A., Martinez, F.J., Tramullas, J.: Rúbricas como estrategia de evaluación en entornos TICS. In: La innovación docente como mision del profesorado. Actas del IV Congreso Internacional sobre Aprendizaje, Innovación y Competitividad. CINAIC 2017, pp. 310–314 (2017)
14. Battaglia, N., Neil, C.G., De Vincenzi, M.: Software engineering competence-based learning in collaborative virtual environments. In: EDUNINE 2021 - 5th IEEE World Engineering Education Conference: The Future of Engineering Education: Current Challenges and Opportunities, Proceedings (2021). https://doi.org/10.1109/EDUNINE51952.2021.9429119
15. Berrocoso, J.V., Gómez, A.C.: El uso de e-rúbricas para la evaluación de competencias en estudiantes universitarios. Estudio sobre fiabilidad del instrumento. REDU. Revista de Docencia Universitaria 12(1), 49 (2014). https://doi.org/10.4995/redu.2014.6415
16. Subekti, S., Ana, A., Muktiarni, M., Dwiyanti, V.: E-rubric to measure employability skills. J. Eng. Sci. Technol. 16, 851–860 (2021)
17. Ung, L.-L., Labadin, J., Nizam, S.: Development of a rubric to assess computational thinking skills among primary school students in Malaysia. ESTEEM Acad. J. 17, 11–22 (2021)
18. Muktiarni, M., Ana, A., Sern, L.C., Saripudin, S.: Using rubrics to assess e-learning in vocational education. J. Eng. Educ. Transform. 34 (2020)
19. Sasipraba, T., et al.: Assessment tools and rubrics for evaluating the capstone projects in outcome based education. Procedia Comput. Sci. 172, 296–301 (2020)
20. Kola, I.M.: Using analytical rubrics to assess technological solutions in the technology classroom. Int. J. Technol. Des. Educ. 32, 883–904 (2022)
21. Sweller, J.: Cognitive load during problem solving: effects on learning. Cogn. Sci. 12, 257–285 (1988)
22. Van Merriënboer, J.J.G., Sweller, J.: Cognitive load theory in health professional education: design principles and strategies. Med. Educ. 44, 85–93 (2010)
23. Kalyuga, S., Sweller, J.: Rapid dynamic assessment of expertise to improve the efficiency of adaptive e-learning. Educ. Technol. Res. Dev. 53, 83–93 (2005)
24. Díaz Redondo, R.P., Caeiro Rodríguez, M., López Escobar, J.J., Fernández Vilas, A.: Integrating micro-learning content in traditional e-learning platforms. Multimed. Tools Appl. 80, 3121–3151 (2021)
25. Job, M.A., Ogalo, H.S.: Micro learning as innovative process of knowledge strategy. Int. J. Sci. Technol. Res. 1, 92–96 (2012)
26. Gil Galván, M. del R., Martín Espinosa, I., Gil Galvan, F.J.: Percepciones de los estudiantes universitarios sobre las competencias adquiridas mediante el aprendizaje basado en problemas. Educ. XX1 Rev. la Fac. Educ. (2021)
27. Bloom, B.S., Engelhart, M.D., Furst, E.J., Hill, W.H., Krathwohl, D.R.: Handbook I: cognitive domain. David McKay, New York (1956)
28. Gutiérrez Ávila, J.H., De la Puente Alarcón, G., Martínez González, A.A., Piña Garza, E.: Aprendizaje basado en problemas... un camino para aprender a aprender. México Col. Ciencias y Humanidades (2013)
29. Lledó, G.L., Galiano, C.S.: Bibliometric review of augmented reality in education. Rev. Gen. Inf. y Doc. 28, 45–60 (2018). https://doi.org/10.5209/RGID.60805
30. Prieto, J.H.P.: Secuencias didácticas: aprendizaje y evaluación de competencias en educación superior (2011)

31. UAIRubric. http://case.uai.edu.ar/rubrics/Repositorio. Accessed 03 Mar 2024
32. Höffler, T.N., Leutner, D.: Instructional animation versus static pictures: a meta-analysis. Learn. Instr. **17**, 722–738 (2007)
33. Alaminos, A., Castejón, J.L.: Elaboración, análisis e interpretación de encuestas, cuestionarios y escalas de opinión. Universidad de Alicante (2006)

Computer Security

Pseudorandom Binary Generator Based on Combining Nonlinear Feedback Shift Registers

Andrés Francisco Farías[1]([⊠]), Germán Antonio Montejano[2], Ana Gabriela Garis[2], and Andrés Alejandro Farías[1]

[1] National University of La Rioja, La Rioja, Argentina
afarias665@yahoo.com.ar
[2] National University of San Luis, San Luis, Argentina
gmonte@unsl.edu.ar

Abstract. This work develops the procedure for the construction of a pseudorandom binary generator based on a mixture of pseudorandom binary sequences, produced by Nonlinear Feedback Shift Registers (NLFSR), using majority functions and a Boolean combination function.

The design process includes: characteristics of the NLFSR, definition of the model, selection of different NLFSR, selection of Boolean functions based on their optimal cryptographic properties, key and methodology to obtain the initial states of the NLFSR, composition of the generator with the chosen elements, selection of random statistical tests to use and criteria to analyze results, implementation and verification of randomness of sequences obtained.

Keywords: NLFSR · generator · key · Boolean function · non-linearity

1 Introduction

In this document, the procedure for the construction of a pseudorandom binary generator based on a mixture of pseudorandom binary sequences, produced by Nonlinear Feedback Shift Registers (NLFSR), is developed using three-variable majority functions and a Boolean combination function. of four variables. It is based on the work presented at CACiC 2023 [1], to which substantial improvements were incorporated to achieve a more robust generator, such as: modification of the NLFSR structure, selection of new Boolean functions and the incorporation of two other functions. by majority. Additionally, further testing was used to control for the randomness of the binary series produced.

Pseudorandom binary generators should be unpredictable and easy to implement, providing quality sequences with high period and linear complexity. The proposed model responds to such demands.

The generator is composed of three sectors, the first two containing four NLFSRs each, which have a coupled nonlinear Boolean filtering function [2, 3] and produce eight pseudorandom binary sequences.

P. Pesado et al. (Eds.): CACIC 2023, CCIS 2123, pp. 369–382, 2024.
https://doi.org/10.1007/978-3-031-62245-8_25

The third sector contains the combination devices: four majority functions and a four-variable Boolean function.

The implementation of a pseudorandom binary generator with these characteristics requires the following stages:

- Generator design

  o Characteristics of NLFSR
  p Schematic definition of the generator.
  q Election of the different NLFSR that make up each sector.
  r Selection of four-variable Boolean functions based on their optimal cryptographic properties.
  s Key and procedure to generate the initial states of the NLFSR.
  t Composition of the generator with the elements already selected.

- Tests of randomness

  o Choice of the statistical tests to use and the criteria for analyzing the results.
  p Putting the generator into operation with one hundred different keys and carrying out the necessary randomness tests on the sequences obtained.Pseudorandom Binary Generator

2   Generator Design

2.1   Characteristics of the NLFSR

The NLFSR used have the following structure indicated in Fig. 1, the NLFSR itself has a coupled connection polynomial that generates the linear feedback. The polynomial must be primitive, to achieve the maximum period of the sequence. Additionally, the four-variable Boolean function is attached, which produces non-linear filtering.

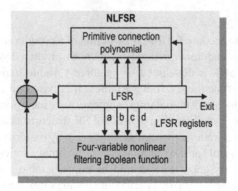

Fig. 1. NLFSR Scheme

2.2 Schematic Definition of the Generator

The generator is composed of two sectors of four NLFSR each, which produce eight pseudo-random binary sequences and a sector intended for combination, which contains four three-variable majority functions and one four-variable Boolean function. Each of the NLFSR has a nonlinear filtering four-variable Boolean function coupled to it. The left sector provides four sequences, which are combined by two majority functions, to obtain two sequences that feed the final join Boolean function. The same happens with the right sector. Everything described is displayed in Fig. 2:

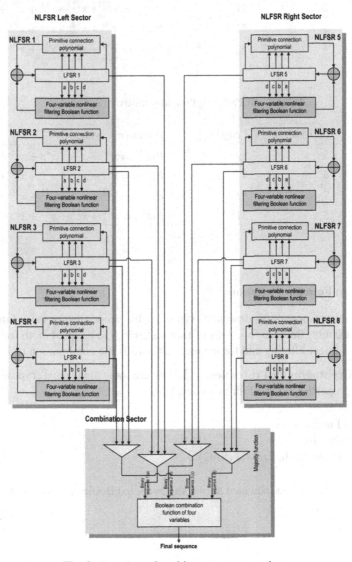

Fig. 2. Pseudorandom binary generator scheme

2.3 Choice of the Different NLFSR

The lengths and primitive polynomials [4–6] of the NLFSR that make up each block are those indicated in Tables 1 and 2:

Table 1. NLFSR, lengths and primitive polynomials

Sector	NLFSR	Lengths	Primitive polynomials
	1	61	$P(x)_1 = x^{61} + x^{44} + x^{19} + x^{15} + 1$
Left	2	37	$P(x)_2 = x^{37} + x^{22} + x^{14} + x^{25} + 1$
	3	59	$P(x)_3 = x^{59} + x^{54} + x^{46} + x^{26} + 1$
	4	53	$P(x)_4 = x^{53} + x^{50} + x^{41} + x^{20} + 1$

Table 2. NLFSR, lengths and primitive polynomials

Sector	NLFSR	Lengths	Primitive polynomials
	5	59	$P(x)_5 = x^{59} + x^{54} + x^{46} + x^{26} + 1$
Right	6	47	$P(x)_6 = x^{47} + x^{32} + x^{24} + x^{11} + 1$
	7	53	$P(x)_7 = x^{53} + x^{50} + x^{41} + x^{20} + 1$
	8	31	$P(x)_8 = x^{31} + x^{25} + x^{23} + x^8 + 1$

2.4 Boolean Function Selection

For the selection, some of the desirable cryptographic properties for these functions are taken into account. Boolean functions of four variables are adopted, both for those that perform non-linear filtering and for the one that fulfills the combination task.

Desirable Cryptographic Properties. A Below are some of the most cryptographically significant properties, adopted for this work [7–9]:

- Balanced Function
- High non-linearity
- Meets strict avalanche criteria (SAC)

Following the criteria indicated above, the accepted Boolean functions are shown in Tables 3, 4 and 5:

Table 3. Boolean functions

f_{NAF}		Balanced	Non-linearity	SAC compliant	LFSR registers			
					a	b	c	d
Sector	Nonlinear filtering functions							
Left	$f_1 = a{\cdot}b \oplus c \oplus b{\cdot}c \oplus a{\cdot}d \oplus c{\cdot}d$	yes	4	yes	3	17	23	26
	$f_2 = a{\cdot}b \oplus c \oplus b{\cdot}c \oplus d \oplus b{\cdot}d$	yes	4	yes	1	17	23	35
	$f_3 = b \oplus a{\cdot}b \oplus b{\cdot}c \oplus a{\cdot}d \oplus c{\cdot}d$	yes	4	yes	1	6	12	28
	$f_4 = b \oplus a{\cdot}b \oplus b{\cdot}c \oplus d \oplus b{\cdot}d$	yes	4	yes	1	7	13	27

Table 4. Boolean functions

f_{NAF}		Balanced	Non-linearity	SAC compliant	LFSR registers			
					a	b	c	d
Sector	Nonlinear filtering functions							
Right	$f_5 = b \oplus a{\cdot}b \oplus a{\cdot}c \oplus b{\cdot}c \oplus c{\cdot}d$	yes	4	yes	6	14	27	34
	$f_6 = b \oplus a{\cdot}b \oplus a{\cdot}c \oplus d \oplus a{\cdot}d$	yes	4	yes	6	16	25	31
	$f_7 = b \oplus a{\cdot}b \oplus c \oplus a{\cdot}c \oplus a{\cdot}d$	yes	4	yes	3	10	16	26
	$f_8 = b \oplus a{\cdot}b \oplus c \oplus b{\cdot}c \oplus b{\cdot}d$	yes	4	yes	3	9	18	25

Table 5. Boolean functions

f_{NAF}		Balanced	Non-linearity	SAC compliant	NLFSR registers			
					bs1	bs2	bs3	bs4
Sector	Combination function							
Comb	$f_9 = a{\cdot}c \oplus b{\cdot}c \oplus d \oplus a{\cdot}d \oplus b{\cdot}d$	yes	4	yes	a	b	c	d

2.5 Key

To create the initial states of the different NLFSR, a process is carried out that uses a 32-character key, which, expressed in ASCII code (American Standard Code for Information Interchange), has a length of 256 bits. The cryptographic procedure is indicated in Fig. 3.

The permutations are calculated with a multiplicative congruent generator [10]. The generator has the following expression:

$$x_{i+1} = (a_x \cdot x_i) \bmod m_x \rightarrow (a_x = multiplier; \quad m_x = module; \quad x_0 = seed)$$

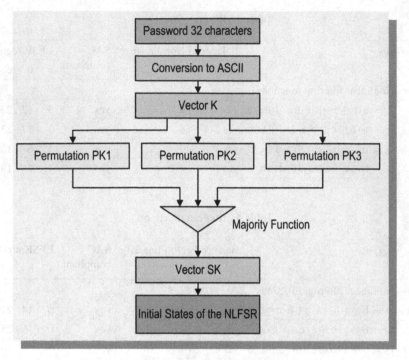

Fig. 3. Key to the generator

Table 6 shows the values of the vectors, modules, multipliers and seeds:

Table 6. Vectors, modules, multipliers and seeds

Vector	module	multiplier	seed
PK1	1048573	1759	3037
PK2	1048573	1759	3041
PK3	1048573	1759	3049

The operation results in a 256-bit vector SK[j], which will provide the initial states of the LFSR, sequentially.

2.6 Composition of the Generator

With the previously selected components, the structure of the pseudorandom binary generator is completed, Fig. 4.

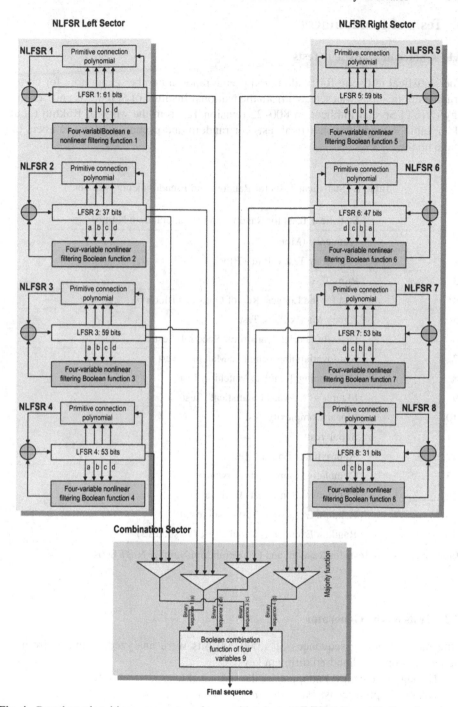

Fig. 4. Pseudorandom binary generator scheme with selected NLFSR bits and Boolean functions

3 Tests of Randomness

3.1 Choice of Statistical Tests

The statistical test suite for random and pseudorandom number generators for crypto-graphic applications was selected from the National Institute of Standards and Technology (NIST) Special Publication 800–22 revision 1a, from the work of Rukhin (et al.) [11]. Table 7 shows the statistical tests for random and pseudo-random numbers that make up the package.

Table 7. Statistical Tests for Random and Pseudorandom Number

	Statistical Tests for Random and Pseudorandom Number
1	Frequency (Monobit)
2	Frequency Test within a Block
3	Runs Test
4	Test for the Longest Run of Ones in a Block
5	Binary Matrix Rank Test
6	Discrete Fourier Transform (Spectral) Test
7	Non-overlapping Template Matching Test
8	Overlapping Template Matching Test
9	Maurer's "Universal Statistical" Test
10	Linear Complexity Test
11	Serial Test:
12	Approximate Entropy Test
13	Cumulative Sums Test (Forward)
14	Cumulative Sums Test (Backward)
15	Random Excursions Test (8 subtests)
16	Random Excursions Variant Test (18 subtests)

Table 5: Statistical Tests for Random and Pseudorandom Number NIST 800–22

3.2 Tests on the Generator

One hundred binary sequences of 1,000,000 bits were analyzed, obtained from the generator from one hundred different keys.

The significance level adopted for the statistical tests is: $\alpha = 0.01$

The null hypothesis is: $H_0 \rightarrow p\_value > 0.01$

3.3   Results Analysis

Following the directives of NIST 800–22, having the results, two processes are carried out to interpret them:

- Proportion of samples that pass tests.
- Test for Uniformity of p-value
- Frequency table and histogram
- Goodness of Fit Test

$$\chi^2 = \sum_{i=1}^{10} \frac{\left(F_i - \frac{s}{10}\right)^2}{\frac{s}{10}}$$

where:

$$F_i = \text{Class frequency}_i$$

$$s = \text{Number of samples}$$

For the present work, we adopt the first procedure: proportion of samples that pass the tests.

3.4   Proportion of Samples that Pass Tests

To analyze the results, the proportion of samples that pass the tests is determined, and with this data a point graph is constructed, where it must be met that all points are within the upper and lower limits, to accept that the tests were successful.

$$LS, LI = (1 - \alpha) \pm 3 \cdot \sqrt{\frac{\alpha(1 - \alpha)}{k}}$$

In our case: $k = 100$, and the chosen significance level is: $\alpha = 0.01$.
The upper limit is:

$$LS = (1 - 0.01) + 3 \cdot \sqrt{\frac{0.01(1 - 0.01)}{100}} = 1.02$$

The lower limit is:

$$LI = (1 - 0.01) - 3 \cdot \sqrt{\frac{0.01(1 - 0.01)}{100}} = 0.96$$

All tests are considered and the results are indicated in Table 8.:

Table 8. Statistical Tests for Random and Pseudorandom Number

	Statistical Tests for Random and Pseudorandom Number	Total	No Pass	Pass	Ratio	Upper	Lower
1	Frequency (Monobit)	100	1	99	0.99	1.02	0.96
2	Frequency Test within a Block	100	3	97	0.97	1.02	0.96
3	Runs Test	100	0	100	1.00	1.02	0.96
4	Test for the Longest Run of Ones in a Block	100	1	99	0.99	1.02	0.96
5	Binary Matrix Rank Test	100	2	98	0.98	1.02	0.96
6	Discrete Fourier Transform (Spectral) Test	100	1	99	0.99	1.02	0.96
7	Non-overlapping Template Matching Test	100	1	99	0.99	1.02	0.96
8	Overlapping Template Matching Test	100	2	98	0.98	1.02	0.96
9	Maurer's "Universal Statistical" Test	100	1	99	0.99	1.02	0.96
10	Linear Complexity Test	100	0	100	1.00	1.02	0.96
11	Serial Test:	100	0	100	1.00	1.02	0.96
12	Approximate Entropy Test	100	2	98	0.98	1.02	0.96
13	Cumulative Sums Test (Forward)	100	0	100	1.00	1.02	0.96
14	Cumulative Sums Test (Backward)	100	0	100	1.00	1.02	0.96

The result can be seen in the graph, the points are within the acceptance limits, finally the sequences delivered by the generator pass the randomness tests, in Fig. 5:

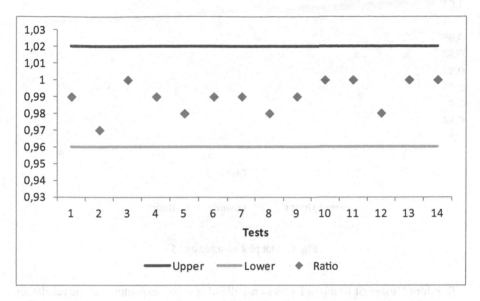

Fig. 5. Dot plot of tests 1 to 14

Random Excursions Test, all subtests are carried out and the results are indicated in Table 9.:

Table 9. Statistical Tests for Random and Pseudorandom Number

	Statistical Tests for Random and Pseudorandom Number	Total	No Pass	Pass	Ratio	Upper	Lower
1	Random Excursions Test	100	2	98	0.98	1.02	0.96
2	Random Excursions Test	100	2	98	0.98	1.02	0.96
3	Random Excursions Test	100	2	98	0.98	1.02	0.96
4	Random Excursions Test	100	1	99	0.99	1.02	0.96
5	Random Excursions Test	100	3	97	0.97	1.02	0.96
6	Random Excursions Test	100	2	98	0.98	1.02	0.96
7	Random Excursions Test	100	3	97	0.97	1.02	0.96
8	Random Excursions Test	100	3	97	0.97	1.02	0.96

The points are within the acceptance limits, therefore the sequences delivered by the generator pass the randomness tests, in Fig. 6:

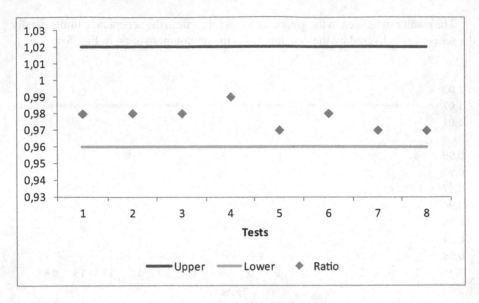

Fig. 6. Dot plot of subtests 15

Random Variant of Random Excursions, all subtests are executed and the results are shown in Table 10.:

Table 10. Statistical Tests for Random and Pseudorandom Number

	Statistical Tests for Random and Pseudorandom Number	Total	No Pass	Pass	Ratio	Upper	Lower
1	Random Excursions Variant	100	3	97	0.97	1.02	0.96
2	Random Excursions Variant	100	2	98	0.98	1.02	0.96
3	Random Excursions Variant	100	2	98	0.98	1.02	0.96
4	Random Excursions Variant	100	0	100	1.00	1.02	0.96
5	Random Excursions Variant	100	1	99	0.99	1.02	0.96
6	Random Excursions Variant	100	1	99	0.99	1.02	0.96
7	Random Excursions Variant	100	1	99	0.99	1.02	0.96
8	Random Excursions Variant	100	1	99	0.99	1.02	0.96
9	Random Excursions Variant	100	1	99	0.99	1.02	0.96
10	Random Excursions Variant	100	1	99	0.99	1.02	0.96
11	Random Excursions Variant	100	0	100	1.00	1.02	0.96
12	Random Excursions Variant	100	0	100	1.00	1.02	0.96

(*continued*)

Table 10. (*continued*)

	Statistical Tests for Random and Pseudorandom Number	Total	No Pass	Pass	Ratio	Upper	Lower
13	Random Excursions Variant	100	1	99	0.99	1.02	0.96
14	Random Excursions Variant	100	2	98	0.98	1.02	0.96
15	Random Excursions Variant	100	2	98	0.98	1.02	0.96
16	Random Excursions Variant	100	2	98	0.98	1.02	0.96
17	Random Excursions Variant	100	1	99	0.99	1.02	0.96
18	Random Excursions Variant	100	1	99	0.99	1.02	0.96

The points are located within the acceptance limits, this means that the sequences delivered by the generator pass the randomness tests, in Fig. 7:

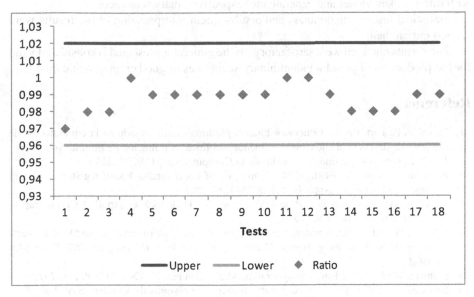

Fig. 7. Dot plot of subtests 16

Based on what is stated in Tables 8., 9. and 10. and Figs. 5, 6 and 7, the samples pass all the randomness tests, which leads us to the conclusion that the generator works satisfactorily.

4 Future Developments

Future developments will include more NLFSR in each sector and for non-linear filtering, Boolean functions of four and five variables will be used.

In the merge sector, all sequences resulting from the left and right blocks will be combined with four or more functions by majority.

Finally, the final combination will be carried out by a Boolean function whose number of variables will be equal to the number of sequences it receives.

5 Conclusions

The generator non-linearly combines the sequences produced by two groups composed of four NLFSR each, with coupled non-linear filtering functions. Each group of NLFSR produces four binary sequences each, which are mixed using a merge slice to obtain the final pseudorandom binary sequence.

The NLFSR that make up each generator have primitive connection polynomials, which ensure the maximum period in the resulting sequences.

Boolean functions are responsible for the non-linear process and for the final combination, they guarantee the best cryptographic performance. Once the selection process was carried out, the functions were incorporated into the generator to then put it to work with different key values and generate the respective binary sequences.

Statistical tests of randomness and a subsequent interpretation of the results were carried out on them.

The results obtained were satisfactory, so the generator presented is considered valid for the production of pseudorandom binary sequences of good cryptographic quality.

References

1. Farías, A.F., Farías A.A.: Generador binario pseudoaleatorio basado en la combinación de registros de desplazamiento de retroalimentación lineal con función de filtrado No Lineal", XXIX Congreso Argentino de Ciencias de la Computación – CACiC2023
2. Massodi, F., Alam, S., Bokhari, M.: A analysis of linear feedback shift registers in stream ciphers. Inte J. Comput. Appl. **16**(17), 0975–1887 (2012)
3. Menezes, A., Van Oorschot, P. and Vanstone, S.: Handbook of Applied Cryptography, Massachusetts Inst. Technol. (1996)
4. Paar, C., Pelzl, L.: Understanding Cryptography: A Textbook for Students and Practitioners. Springer Berlin Heidelberg, Berlin, Heidelberg (2010). https://doi.org/10.1007/978-3-642-04101-3
5. Stahnke, W.: Primitive Binary Polynomials. Math. Comput. **27**(124), 977–980 (1973)
6. Seroussi, G.: Table of low-weight binary irreducible polynomials. Comput. Syst. Lab. 98—135 (1998)
7. Clark, J., Jacob, J., Maitra, S., Stanica, P.: Almost boolean functions: the design of boolean functions by spectral inversion. Comput. Intell. **20**(3), 450–462 (2004)
8. Braeken, A.: Cryptographic Properties of Boolean Functions and S-Boxes. Katholieke Universiteit Leuven, Faculteit Ingenieurswetenschappen (2003)
9. Elhosary, A., Hamdy, N., Farag, I., Rohiem, I.: State of the Art in Boolean Functions Cryptographic Assessment. Int. J. Comput. Netw. Commun. Secur. **1**(3), 88–94 (2013)
10. Fishman, G.: Multiplicative congruential random number generators with modulus 2ß : an exhaustive analysis for ß = 32 and a partial analysis for ß = 48. Math. Comput. **54**(189), 33–344 (1990)
11. Rukhin, A., et al.: A statistical prueba suite for random and pseudorandom number generators for cryptographic applications, National Institute of Standards and Technology, Vol **22** (2000)

Exploration of Hybrid Neural Networks for Domain Name Generation

Reynier Leyva La O[1,2]([✉]) [iD], Carlos A. Catania[2] [iD], and Rodrigo Gonzalez[1] [iD]

[1] GridTICs, Facultad Regional Mendoza, Universidad Tecnológica Nacional,
Mendoza, Argentina
rleyvalao@mendoza-conicet.gob.ar
[2] National Scientific and Technical Research Council (CONICET), Buenos Aires,
Argentina
harpo@ingenieria.uncuyo.edu.ar

Abstract. The increase in the use of Domain Generation Algorithms (DGA) for communication between Command and Control (C&C) servers presents significant challenges in botnet detection. This study investigates the use of a hybrid neural network architecture that combines Convolutional Neural Network (CNN) and Long Short-Term Memory (LSTM) layers for algorithmic domain name generation. The purpose of this domain name generator is to increase the availability of algorithmically generated domains (AGD), which can be used in future research and contribute to improving the capabilities of AGD detectors in upcoming investigations.

To validate the effectiveness of the generator, three evaluation methods were employed. First, the registration status of the generated domains was evaluated using a Domain Availability Verification (DAV) tool, revealing that 93% of the domains were not registered. Second, the generated domains underwent Plausibility Assessment (PA) using a large-scale language model (LLM), which classified only 8% as suspicious. Finally, an Algorithmic Detection Effectiveness (ADE) evaluation was conducted using AGD detectors from the literature, demonstrating low detection rates of 3% and 16%, respectively. These results highlight the capability of the studied model to generate domain names similar to legitimate ones and underscore the need to enhance AGD detection systems.

Keywords: DGA · Computer Security · CNN · LSTM · Domain Names

1 Introduction

A Domain Generation Algorithm (DGA) is an algorithm used by cybercriminals to automatically and randomly generate domain names. The main objective of DGA is to establish secure and covert communication between the bots and the Command and Control (C&C) server. Unlike static and predefined domains,

P. Pesado et al. (Eds.): CACIC 2023, CCIS 2123, pp. 383–396, 2024.
https://doi.org/10.1007/978-3-031-62245-8_26

which are easier to detect and block, domains generated by DGA constantly change, making their detection and blocking more difficult for security systems. DGAs are commonly used in botnets to avoid detection and to ensure greater resilience and persistence in communications [1].

The operation of a DGA is based on an initial seed or key, from which sequences of characters are generated to form domain names. These sequences can vary in length and structure, and encryption and obfuscation techniques are often used to further hinder their detection.

By constantly generating new domain names, cybercriminals can keep their infrastructure active and operational, allowing them to control the bots and carry out their malicious activities without being easily detected.

DGAs represent a significant challenge for cybersecurity due to their ability to evade traditional detection and blocking measures.

This research constitutes an extension of the work previously carried out by Leyva La O et al., presented at the XXIX Argentine Congress of Computer Science (CACIC) in 2023 [2]. In contrast to that study, this extension used a different dataset with higher data quality, applied domain preprocessing techniques differently, and employed novel evaluation methods to analyze the generated domains.

The present study was driven by two key objectives. Firstly, to investigate the application of deep learning methods, specifically the combination of CNN and LSTM networks, in algorithmically generating domain names. Secondly, to generate domain names that visually resemble normal domain names while being difficult to detect by AGD detection systems. This would allow these generated domain names to be used in future research to enhance the effectiveness of AGD detectors and thus, cybersecurity.

In pursuit of these goals, a neural network was developed using supervised learning approaches. This network included a Convolutional Neural Network (CNN) [3] layer, which was responsible for identifying important features within domain names. Following this, a Long Short-Term Memory (LSTM) [4] layer was utilized to identify and understand the sequential and contextual nuances of domain name generation.

In addition we proposed an evaluation framework, consisting of three fundamental aspects required in DGA: (i) Domain Availability Verification (DAV), which aims to check if a generated domain name has not already been registered; (ii) Plausibility Assessment (PA), which refers to the visual appearance of the generated domains. Humans can easily identify them if they look odd; and (iii) Algorithmic Detection Effectiveness (ADE), which evaluates the performance of generating domains using state-of-the-art detectors.

It is important to highlight that the generation of domains that are difficult to distinguish offers significant benefits in terms of strengthening AGD detectors and improving cybersecurity. On one hand, it allows for the evaluation of the effectiveness of existing detectors and the discovery of potential vulnerabilities, thereby driving their continuous improvement. Additionally, the ability to generate domains that resemble legitimate domains enhances the capability to detect and block malicious communications. However, it is important to consider limitations, such as the potential misuse of this technology, the need to constantly adapt AGD detectors to new domain generation techniques, and the possibility of false positives and negatives that could affect the accuracy of detection systems.

This work is divided into four main sections. Section 2 provides an overview of the process, covering from dataset description to model development. Section 3 focuses on assessing the performance of the domain name generation model, with analysis of metrics, domain availability verification, plausibility assessment, and algorithmic detection effectiveness. Finally, Sect. 4 presents the main findings and their relevance for future research and practical applications.

2   Domain Name Generation

In this section, the methodological approach used to generate domains similar to normal domains is addressed. The pursued objective consisted of conceiving a hybrid neural network that combined convolutional layers (CNN) and long-term memory (LSTM) to generate domain names that are difficult to distinguish from legitimate domains. To achieve this, the data from normal domains were processed and vectorized to train the neural network, using Keras [5], a deep learning framework.

This combination allowed the generation of domain names that resembled normal ones. Through this process, the aim was to strengthen AGD detection and enhance cybersecurity in general. A large amount of normal domains was used for optimal training.

2.1   Dataset Overview

Tranco is a domain ranking that classifies web domains based on their popularity and traffic [6]. This ranking provides a list of the top web domains based on data collected from various sources such as search engines, news aggregators, and other popular websites. The Tranco list is regularly updated and is used in various applications, including search engine optimization and web research.

The Tranco dataset contains millions of web domains classified according to their popularity and can be a valuable tool for various research and analysis in the field of computer science and cybersecurity. In this study, we used a Tranco listing with 3.5 million domains to analyze and train our algorithmically generated domain name model. We chose to use Tranco due to the security enhancements it offers in managing its ranking compared to other web domain rankings such as Alexa, Cisco Umbrella, Majestic, and Quantcast [6].

2.2   Data Preprocessing Techniques

During preprocessing, domains are transformed into suitable and structured formats, facilitating their handling by the neural network. Furthermore, during this stage, necessary transformations and encodings are carried out to represent the domains in the form of vectorized sequences, enabling the neural network to learn the relationships between characters and their positions within the input sequence. Through proper preprocessing, the quality of training is maximized, and the network's ability to generate domain names similar to normal domains is enhanced. This is essential for achieving the main objective of the study.

Firstly, the domain names were divided into two parts considered the most important: the top-level domain (TLD) and the second-level domain (SLD). Subsequently, all domains were removed from the dataset if their SLD exceeded 15 characters, aiming to generate domain names of up to 15 characters in the SLD. Then, each domain was padded so that they all had the same length of 15 characters in their SLD.

For training the network, we will work only with the SLD. After the network generates the SLD, a TLD from the 50 most common ones collected from the dataset will be added to each domain. To ensure that all domains had the same length, special characters (spaces) were added to the end of each domain if the length of the domain was shorter than desired. Thus, all domains reached the same desired length.

Subsequently, the completed domains were joined into a single text string, using the space character as a separator between each domain. This preprocessing process ensured that the domains had a uniform structure.

Once the complete text string was obtained, it was divided into smaller sequences with a displacement of 3 characters in each iteration. This process generated input sequences (sec_X) along with their corresponding next characters (car_y). A basic example to understand how the input sequences (sec_X) and the output character (car_y) were composed can be visualized in Fig. 1.

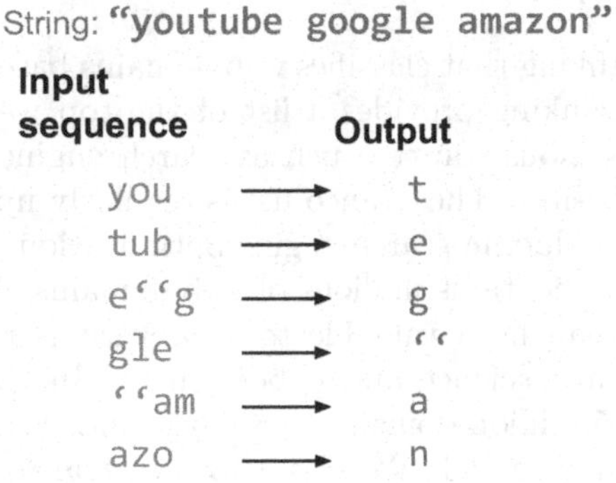

String: **"youtube google amazon"**

Input sequence	Output
you	t
tub	e
e''g	g
gle	''
''am	a
azo	n

Fig. 1. Example of an Input Sequence and Output Character

Once the input sequences and output character were obtained, tokenization was applied to these data. The tokenization process is a fundamental component in data preprocessing by the neural network. By converting each unique character into a token, a more compact and processable representation is achieved for the neural network. This significantly reduces the computational complexity of the model and speeds up the training process, as the network only needs to learn the patterns of the tokens rather than dealing with each individual character. Additionally, tokenization allows for better generalization of the model, as the network can learn to recognize and manipulate common patterns of characters, rather than memorizing each specific character present in the training data.

In the context of this work, once the input and output data were obtained, the unique characters present in the sequences were identified, thus forming an alphabet. Each character was assigned a corresponding index in this alphabet. To represent the characters in a processable manner by the neural network, one-hot encoding was implemented [7,8]. Through this encoding, each character was transformed into a sparse vector where all positions were 0, except one that contained the value 1 in the position corresponding to the character's index in the alphabet. In this way, each character became a unique vector and processable by the network, allowing the neural network to efficiently learn the relationships between the characters in the input sequences. The input sequences, consisting of 15 characters, were converted into matrices of the form (15 × alphabet length), and the output character remained as a vector with the length of the alphabet. The Table 1 shows how the input sequence and output character are represented in one-hot encoding.

This one-hot encoding approach enabled the creation of a suitable dataset for training and fine-tuning the neural network, providing the necessary information to predict the next characters based on input sequences. This process of tokenization and encoding was fundamental for the efficiency of the model in domain generation.

Table 1. One-Hot Encoding of Input Sequence and Output Character

Input Sequence	Output Character
$\begin{bmatrix} 0\,0\,0\ldots0\,0\,1 \\ 0\,0\,1\ldots0\,0\,0 \\ 0\,0\,0\ldots0\,1\,0 \\ 1\,0\,0\ldots0\,0\,0 \\ \vdots\ \vdots\ \vdots\ \ddots\ \vdots\ \vdots\ \vdots \\ 1\,0\,0\ldots0\,0\,0 \end{bmatrix}$	$\begin{bmatrix} 0\,0\,0\ldots0\,1\,0 \end{bmatrix}$

2.3   Neural Network Architecture

In the process of selecting neural networks for the architecture, the sequential nature of the data and the need to capture important features of normal domains were taken into account. To achieve this goal, it was decided to employ layers of Convolutional Neural Networks (CNN) and Long Short-Term Memory networks (LSTM).

Convolutional neural networks are widely known for their ability to extract relevant features from input data, especially in images and sequences [7,9]. In the domain generation context, these layers were fundamental for capturing patterns and key characteristics present in normal domains. They allowed the network to learn the essential structures necessary for generating domains similar to normal ones and coherent.

On the other hand, Long Short-Term Memory (LSTM) networks are a type of recurrent neural network (RNN) designed to work with sequential data [10]. These layers proved essential for capturing long-term dependencies in the input data, a critical aspect for generating coherent and realistic text sequences. The inclusion of LSTM in the architecture allowed the network to learn temporal relationships and complex dependencies among characters in the input sequences.

The combination of convolutional neural network layers and LSTM layers in a single hybrid neural network resulted in an effective architecture for generating domains similar to normal domains. Each layer played an important role in the process, allowing the network to learn and generate text sequences coherently and realistically. These characteristics significantly contributed to achieving the main goal of the study.

The detailed selected architecture was as follows:

1. **Input Layer:** An input layer was defined with a shape corresponding to the maximum length of the sequences and the number of unique characters in the data.
2. **1D Convolutional Layer:** A convolutional layer with 128 filters and a kernel size of 3 was added, with a 'relu' activation function. This layer helped extract relevant features from the input sequences.
3. **1D MaxPooling Layer:** A max-pooling layer with a pooling size of 2 was added. This layer allowed reducing the dimensionality of the features extracted by the convolutional layer.
4. **LSTM Layer:** An LSTM layer with 128 units was included. The LSTM layer allowed capturing temporal dependencies in the input sequences.
5. **Dense Layer:** A dense layer with a 'softmax' activation function for character classification was added. The number of units in this layer corresponds to the number of unique characters in the data.

2.4   Model Development

The model architecture depicted in Sect. 2.3 was implemented using the Keras library [8]. During the neural network training process, several tests were conducted with different values for the epochs, batch size, diversity, number of neurons per layer, and optimization methods, among other hyperparameters. The final training process was carried out using **Adam** optimizer [11] with a learning rate of 0.01. The model was compiled using the **Categorical_crossentropy** loss function [12]. The remaining hyperparametrs of the model are detailed in Fig. 2 where the final implementation in Keras is presented.

For further details on the implementation and creation of the model, the code is available in a public GitHub repository [13].

```
model = keras.Sequential([
    keras.Input(shape=(max_length, len(chars))),
    layers.Conv1D(128, kernel_size=3, activation='relu'),
    layers.MaxPooling1D(pool_size=2),
    layers.LSTM(128),
    layers.Dense(len(chars), activation='softmax')
])

optimizer = Adam(learning_rate=0.01)
model.compile(loss='categorical_crossentropy', optimizer=opt)
```

Fig. 2. Source code of the model used for the creation of the model

The model was trained with a total of 4 million domain sequences, which were divided into batches of 500,000 for training. At the end of training the model with all sequences, domain names were generated to evaluate the model's generation quality, demonstrating that it produced high-quality domain names.

At the end of the domain name generation training, the model requires an initial seed. This seed must be 15 characters long, and "google" was chosen, padded with spaces to reach the required length. From this initial sequence, the pre-trained neural network generated additional characters to complete the text sequence based on what it learned during training. Specifically, 150 characters were generated, from which 10 domain names were extracted. These generated domains were used to visually evaluate how well the model had learned to generate domain names similar to normal ones.

It is relevant to highlight that, although the model receives an initial seed for domain generation, the process relies on combining characters to produce domain names. Consequently, the first generated domains will have a strong relationship with the seed, but as the process progresses, subsequent domains will be influenced by those generated previously. This dynamic creates a continuous and progressive relationship among the generated domains, resulting in greater variety and complexity in the sequence of characters used.

3   Evaluation

In this section, the methodology used to evaluate the domains generated by the neural network model under study is discussed. After adjusting the parameters and training the model, 10,000 domain names were generated using a specific seed. As part of this process, the second-level domains (SLDs) were completed with top-level domains (TLDs) randomly selected from the 50 most common ones in the Tranco dataset.

Once the domain names have been generated, the evaluation phase involved applying various methods to analyze the quality and relevance of these domains. These methods included: (i) Domain Availability Verification, which used the WHOIS tool to determine the percentage of generated domains that were already registered; (ii) Plausibility Assessment, employing a Large Language Model to evaluate the quality of the generated domain names; and (iii) Evaluation of the Algorithmic Detection Effectiveness, which tested the generated domains using two well-known detectors.

In addition, to measure the quality of the detector's predictions, a confusion matrix and various evaluation metrics were employed. These metrics provide a detailed evaluation of the performance of the AGD detector used. *Precision* indicates the proportion of domains considered as AGD that were classified correctly. *Accuracy*, on the other hand, represents the proportion of all domains, both correctly classified as AGD and correctly classified as non-AGD. *Recall* represents the proportion of normal domains that were detected correctly as AGD. The *F1-score* combines precision and recall into a single metric that weighs both measures. Finally, support indicates the total number of instances evaluated.

Throughout this section, each of these methods will be described in detail, and the results obtained in the evaluation process of the generated domains will be presented.

3.1   Analysis of Domain Generation: Dataset Metrics and Patterns

For evaluating the model, a total of 10,000 domains were generated, of which 30 representative examples are presented in this section.

Sample of Generated Domains:

– ma.club	– ix.cc	– saiairo.us	– o.at
– oittar.com.au	– f.me	– pan.pl	– aaiaoui.com.tr
– eyelr.co.nz	– ea.eu	– ee.eu	
– t.at	– eouie.club	– toh.co.nz	– ahaoti.info
– ea.de	– he.in	– s.fi	– eoje.co
– eom.fi	– arudtr.club	– araon.cz	
– aoaiaie.co.jp	– ia.es	– ilt.cz	– ctrynni.jp
– ar.buzz	– a.ca	– oemcee.club	– rpyvthp.ru

These examples demonstrate the diversity and variety of the domains generated from the provided seed, showcasing the model's ability to generate domain names automatically and randomly.

In addition we have analyzed the structure and common features of domain names based on length, common tokens, character distribution, and overall character frequency.

Domain Length: The analysis reveals that domain lengths vary widely, with the longest domain containing 18 characters and the shortest only 3 characters. On average, domain lengths sit at 8 characters.

Common Tokens by Length: For varying token lengths, the most frequent tokens identified were 'ee', 'oe', and 'as' for 2-character lengths; 'eae', 'eee', and 'oae' for 3-character lengths; 'aaaa', 'iaea', and 'asia' for 4-character lengths; and 'ation', 'orade', and 'caria' for 5-character lengths.

Character Distribution in Positions: At the initial position of domains, 'a', 'e', and 'o' are the most frequent characters, while 'i' and 's' are the least frequent. For the final position, 'o', 'e', and 'z' are most common, with 'r' and 'u' being the least common.

Most Common Characters Overall: The most frequently occurring characters across all domains are '.', 'a', 'e', and 'o', in that order, highlighting a preference for certain letters in domain names.

3.2 Domain Availability Verification (DAV)

WHOIS is an online service that allows obtaining detailed information about the ownership and status of an Internet domain [14]. It provides data such as the domain registrant's name, registration date, expiration date, and associated name servers.

In this research, the WHOIS tool was used to verify the registration availability of the domains generated by the neural network model. The focus was on identifying unregistered domains, which allowed for evaluating the effectiveness of the model in generating new and unused domain names (Fig. 3).

Domain Availability Verification
Evaluation is conducted WHOIS

6.3%   9367
of generated domains were   domains were
registered   **unregistered**

Fig. 3. Domain Availability Verification Results

This approach allowed determining the proportion of generated domains available for use as AGD, providing valuable information about the quality and relevance of the domain names generated by the model. This analysis provided clear insight into the model's ability to generate domain names that could be candidates for malicious use in botnet activities or other cyber threats.

According to the results of the domain evaluation, a total of 633 domains were registered, representing approximately 6.33% of the total. It is important to note that this finding reveals that approximately 93% of the generated domains were not registered, suggesting that the model was able to generate a large number of domain names that have not yet been used. This result underscores the model's ability to generate AGD.

3.3   Plausibility Assessment (PA)

To obtain a plausibility assessment of the normality appearance of the generated domains, the ideal approach is conduct a human inspection. However, in this case, the evaluation was based on LLM. In particular, we leveraged the potential of the Llama 2 7B Chat model, a specialized variant of the Llama 2 generative text models collection developed by Meta [15]. This model, specifically designed for dialogue use cases, offers a remarkable capability: the ability to analyze domain names as automatically generated or normal, based on its extensive knowledge of natural language. Although the model was not specifically trained to detect DGA domain names, its ability to understand context and language patterns allows it to perform this analysis effectively.

Each domain name was evaluated by Llama2 using the following prompt (Fig. 4):

```
I want to classify the following domain name '{domain_name}' as 'DGA'
(algorithmically generated)  or 'normal' and I want you to respond
with a 1 if it is DGA and a 0 if it is NORMAL.

I want your response as follows:
The domain is 1, or The domain is 0.
```

Fig. 4. Prompt used on Llama2 for evaluating the plausibility of generated domain name.

After the evaluation of the 10,000 domains, only 731 were considered algorithmically generated, while 7970 were categorized as normal domains. However, in the remaining 1299 domains, the model's evaluation could not provide a clear determination. These findings suggest that the domains generated by the neural model exhibit a remarkable similarity to normal domains, highlighting the effectiveness of the model in reproducing authentic language patterns (Fig. 5).

In the evaluation of domains using the Llama2 7B model, the similarity between the generated domains and normal domains was highlighted. With a precision of 100%, all domains detected as algorithmically generated were classified correctly. However, the low recovery rate of 8% indicates that only a small fraction of algorithmically generated domains were identified as such. This discrepancy between high precision and low recovery rate suggests that many

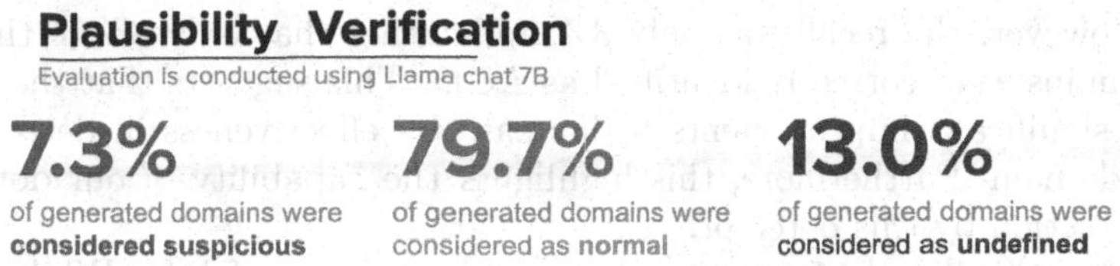

Plausibility Verification

Evaluation is conducted using Llama chat 7B

7.3%
of generated domains were
considered suspicious

79.7%
of generated domains were
considered as normal

13.0%
of generated domains were
considered as **undefined**

Fig. 5. Plausibility Verification Results

algorithmically generated domains went unnoticed by the model. Of the 8,701 domains evaluated and classified by the LLM, only 8% were detected correctly.

3.4 Algorithmic Detection Effectiveness (ADE)

The effectiveness to evade domain detection was assessed using a AGD detector. For this evaluation, two detectors were considered. First, the predictive model proposed by Catania et al. [9] was utilized. This detector implements a Convolutional Neural Network (CNN), which has proven effective in real-time detection in fields such as image and video recognition, making it particularly suitable for AGD detection.

Second, the AGD detector LA_Bin07 [16]. This detector offers an innovative approach to detect families of botnets generated through DGA. LA_Bin07 presents new and practical solutions to disable botnets, even if they have infected a computer system. LA_Bin07 is a deep learning model that combines LSTM network and attention layers to achieve accurate detection of DGA botnets. For the training and validation of LA_Bin07, the UMUDGA [17] dataset was primarily used, published in 2020, containing 50 families of DGA botnets.

For the detector from Catania et al. [9] out of the 10,000 generated domains, only 340 were correctly detected as AGD. On the other hand for LA_Bin07 out of the 10,000 generated domains, only 1648 were correctly detected as AGD.

The evaluation metrics obtained are presented in Table 2.

Table 2. Evaluation Metrics of the AGD Detectors Catania et al. (2018) and LA_Bin07

Metric	Catania et al. (2018)	LA_Bin07
Accuracy	0.03	0.16
Precision	1.00	1.00
Recall	0.03	0.16
F1-score	0.06	0.28
Support (number of instances)	10000	10000

In summary, these results show that the detector from [9] achieved a precision of 100%, meaning that all domains detected as AGD were classified correctly. However, the recall was only 3%, indicating that only 3% of the generated domains were correctly identified as AGD. This suggests that the detector requires significant improvements to increase its effectiveness in detecting this type of domain. Furthermore, this highlights the capability of our domains to evade detection by this detector.

On the other hand LA_Bin07, achieved an accuracy of 16%. While it maintained a precision of 100%, meaning all domains detected as AGD were classified correctly, the recall was relatively low at 16%. This indicates that only 16% of the generated domains were correctly identified as AGD. The F1-score, which combines precision and recall, was 0.28, indicating moderate performance. This underscores the need for significant improvements in the detector's effectiveness to enhance its ability to detect this type of domain. Additionally, these findings emphasize the resilience of our generated domains in evading detection by this particular detector.

4   Conclusions

Based on the findings of this study, it is concluded that the use of a hybrid neural network, composed of Convolutional Neural Network (CNN) layers and a Long Short-Term Memory (LSTM) layer for domain generation, exhibits significant similarities with legitimate domains. This similarity poses challenges for current AGD detectors, as it hinders their ability to accurately detect such domains.

The approach to domain generation has unveiled potential vulnerabilities in AGD detection systems. The integration of CNN and LSTM layers within the neural network framework has yielded promising results, indicating the merit of further exploration in future research endeavors.

Furthermore, the domains generated in this study contribute to the expansion of malicious domain databases, providing valuable resources for the development and refinement of more robust detectors in forthcoming investigations.

In this study, a total of 10,000 domains were generated to assess the effectiveness of the generator. Using the Whois tool, it was determined that 93% of the generated domains were unregistered. This finding underscores the generator's capability to algorithmically produce a high proportion of unregistered domains, which could potentially be utilized as AGDs.

Additionally, it was desired to visually explore the appearance of the domains and their potential appeal to the human eye. To achieve this, a large-scale language model was employed to classify domain names based on their appearance as AGD or legitimate. The LLM Llama2_7B was used, which correctly detected only 8% of the 8701 evaluated domains. This result also demonstrates the significant similarity between the generated domains and normal domains.

Finally, the ability of the generated domains to evade detection by two detectors from the literature was assessed. The first detector, from Catania et al. (2018), demonstrated a detection rate of 3%, while the second detector, LA_Bin07, achieved a detection accuracy rate of 16%. These evaluations with the detectors revealed that the generated domains proved difficult to detect as AGD, which is highly promising for the objectives of this study.

In conclusion, this study has successfully demonstrated the potent capabilities of hybrid neural networks, particularly those combining Convolutional Neural Networks (CNN) and Long Short-Term Memory (LSTM) layers, in generating domain names that bear striking resemblance to legitimate domains. This achievement not only underscores the sophisticated level of mimicry that these artificial intelligence models can attain but also highlights the pressing challenge it poses for current Automated Generated Domain (AGD) detectors. Our work has revealed significant vulnerabilities in these detection systems, suggesting an urgent need for the development of more advanced and nuanced detection mechanisms capable of countering such sophisticated threats. By harnessing the power of advanced AI and machine learning technologies, there is a promising path forward towards creating more resilient and effective cybersecurity defenses against the ever-evolving landscape of cyber threats.

References

1. Plohmann, D., Yakdan, K., Klatt, M., Bader, J., Gerhards-Padilla, E.: A comprehensive measurement study of domain generating malware. In: 25th USENIX Security Symposium (USENIX Security 16), pp. 263–278. USENIX Association, Austin (2016)
2. Leyva La O, R., Gonzalez, R., Catania, C.A.: Domain Name Generation Using Hybrid CNN-LSTM Neural Networks. In: Fernández, J.M. (ed.) Proceedings of the XXIX Argentine Congress on Computer Science (CACIC 2023), pp. 591–602 (2024)
3. Gupta, J., Pathak, S., Kumar, G.: Deep learning (CNN) and transfer learning: a review. Journal of Physics: Conference Series. IOP Publishing, p. 012029 (2022)
4. Yu, Y., et al.: A review of recurrent neural networks: LSTM cells and network architectures. Neural Comput. **31**(7), 1235–1270 (2019)
5. Ketkar, N., Ketkar, N.: Introduction to Keras. Deep Learning with Python: A Hands-On Introduction, pp. 97–111 (2017)
6. Le Pochat, V., Van Goethem, T., Tajalizadehkhoob, S., Korczyński, M., Joosen, W.: Tranco: a research-oriented top sites ranking hardened against manipulation. In: Network and Distributed System Security Symposium (NDSS) (2019)
7. Chollet, F.: Deep learning with python. In: Learn Machine Learning with Python, pp. 325–360. Anaya Multimedia (2021). ISBN: 978-84-415-4351-3
8. Chollet, F.: Generate text from Nietzsche's writings with a character-level LSTM. Keras Examples (2015). https://keras.io/examples/generative/lstm_character_level_text_generation/. Accessed 23 June 2023
9. Catania, C., Garcia, S., Torres, P.: An analysis of convolutional neural networks for detecting DGA. In: Proceedings of XXIV Congreso Argentino de Ciencias de la Computación, La Plata, pp. 1–10 (2018)
10. Greff, K., Srivastava, R.K., Schmidhuber, J.: LSTM: a search space odyssey. IEEE Trans. Neural Networks Learn. Syst. **28**(10), 2222–2232 (2017)
11. Kingma, D.P., Ba, J.L.: Adam: a method for stochastic optimization. In: Published as a Conference Paper at ICLR 2015
12. TensorFlow. tf.keras.losses.CategoricalCrossentropy. https://www.tensorflow.org/api_docs/python/tf/keras/losses/CategoricalCrossentropy. Accessed 3 Aug 2023

13. Leyva, R., Catania, C.A.: Domain Generator. GitHub (2023). https://github.com/reypapin/Domain-Generator. Accessed 20 Mar 2024
14. WHOIS, Troia V., Hunting Cyber Criminals (2020)
15. Touvron, H., et al.: Llama: Open and efficient foundation language models. CoRR (2023)
16. Tuan, T.A., Long, H.V., Taniar, D.: On detecting and classifying dga botnets and their families. Comput. Secur. **113**, 102549 (2022)
17. Zago, M., Pérez, M.G., Pérez, G.M.: Umudga: a dataset for profiling algorithmically generated domain names in botnet detection. Data Brief **30**, 105400 (2020)

Digital Governance and Smart Cities

Contribution to SDGs 2030 through the CAP4CITY Project and a Master in Smart Cities Management and Technology

Rocío Muñoz⬤, Ariel Pasini(✉)⬤, and Patricia Pesado⬤

Computer Science Research Institute LIDI (III-LIDI), Centro Asociado Comisión de Investigaciones Científicas de la Pcia. de Bs. As. (CIC), Facultad de Informática – Universidad Nacional de La Plata, 50 y 120, La Plata, Buenos Aires, Argentina
{rmunoz,apasini,ppesado}@lidi.info.unlp.edu.ar

Abstract. The set of SDGs that make up the 2030 Agenda promoted by the United Nations General Assembly and the CAP4CITY project are presented. The main focus is to leverage the great interest on the concept of SDGs in Latin America and integrate that into various university courses, developing new study plans at all levels of the educational process. In this article, a proposal to analyze how the project (the master's degree in management and technology in smart cities and the courses created) contributes to SDGs is presented, linking contents and objectives to the goals and considerations proposed by the 2030 Agenda.

Keywords: Sustainable Development Goals - SDGs · Sustainable Smart Cities - SSCs · 2030 Agenda · Educational Programs in SSCs

1 Introduction

The so-called United Nations 2030 Agenda [1] contains 17 Sustainable Development Goals (SDGs) that apply to all countries, rich and poor. Each country is free to promote different goals, according to its priorities. In total, these SDGs present a set of 169 goals that cover different challenges such as climate change, economic inequality, sustainable consumption, peace and justice, and so forth.

The "Strengthening Governance Capacity for Smart Sustainable Cities (CAP4CITY)" project [2] is an interdisciplinary project involving experts from different areas, such as business administration, computer science, engineering, architecture and urban planning, political science, and so forth, aimed at attaining 3 specific goal [3]: 1- improving the quality of learning and teaching tools, methodologies and pedagogical approaches in Latin American; 2- developing didactic contents and learning outcomes based on ICTs to help build specific competencies in the area of Sustainable Smart Cities (SSC); and 3- using ICT-based practices to deliver content to students at different educational levels.

Within the framework of the project, various activities were carried out in order to create new university courses linked to the areas and competencies necessary for SSC awareness in the region. Based on this goal, and with the participation of 360 local actors from different disciplines from Argentina, Brazil, Chile and Colombia, 93 competencies to be addressed were identified, which resulted in the creation of 31 courses in 9 areas of knowledge [4]: 1- Communication; 2- Governance; 3- Information Systems; 4- Legal and Ethical Implications of SSCs; 5- Public Administration and Management; 6- Business and Economy; 7- Smart Cities Basics; 8- Socio-Technical ICTs; and 9- Urban Studies and Sustainability.

One of the main results of the project was the creation of an inter-university master's degree between UNLP and UNS in Smart Cities Management and Technology (MGyTCI) accredited by CONEAU that is taught virtually, granting a degree issued by both universities. The master's degree is a sort of guiding thread for several of the content courses created by the CAP4CITY project.

Combined, the CAP4CITY project in general, the MGyTCI master, and each of the 31 courses offer a contribution to one or more SDGs. In particular, the project itself is closely related to SDG 4 - Quality education, and the courses, for the most part, are related to SDG 9 - Industry, innovation and infrastructure, SDG 11 - Sustainable cities and communities, and SDG 17 - Partnerships for the goals. The remaining SDGs are also linked to between 2–8 courses each, with the exception of SDGs 2- Zero Hunger and SDG 5- Gender Equality, which do not have a direct relationship to any.

This paper is an extension of a previously published one, namely "Contribution of the CAP4CITY Project to SDGs for 2030" [5], published at the Argentine Congress of Computer Science 2023 (CACIC 2023). The new version expands the contributions to the SDGs for 2030 included in the master's degree in management and technology in smart cities, which has been accredited in 2023.

Section two presents the United Nations 2030 Agenda with the SDGs. The third section provides an introduction to the CAP4CITY project and defines the objectives and courses it offers. The fourth section presents the MGyTCI. Then, in the fifth section, a relationship is established between the courses and their contribution to the SDGs, taking into account certain points to consider. The sixth section provides the most relevant contributions of the project and the importance of incorporating courses related to SSC in educational programs. Finally, in Sect. 7, our conclusions are presented.

2 Sustainable Development Goals

In 2015, the United Nations General Assembly [6] and world leaders adopted a set of global goals to eradicate poverty, protect the planet and ensure prosperity for all, launching a new sustainable development agenda.

The so-called 2030 Agenda [1] contains 17 SDGs that apply to all countries, rich and poor. Each country is free to promote different goals, according to its priorities.

In total, these SDGs present a set of 169 goals and complete the agenda of the previous eight Millennium Development Goals (MDGs) [7], finished in 2015. These new objectives and goals are more comprehensive in nature, and they cover different challenges such as climate change, economic inequality, sustainable consumption, peace and justice, and so forth.

The 17 objectives of the 2030 Agenda focus on different aspects of what is understood as sustainability. Thus, each of these goals emphasizes issues of utmost importance for all countries.

- SDG 1 – No poverty: End poverty in all its forms everywhere
- SDG 2 – Zero hunger: End hunger, achieve food security and improved nutrition and promote sustainable agriculture
- SDG 3 – Good health and well-being: Ensure healthy lives and promote well-being for all at all ages
- SDG 4 – Quality education: Ensure inclusive and equitable quality education and promote lifelong learning opportunities for all
- SDG 5 – Gender equality: Achieve gender equality and empower all women and girls
- SDG 6 – Clean water and sanitation: Ensure availability and sustainable management of water and sanitation for all
- SDG 7 – Affordable and clean energy: Ensure access to affordable, reliable, sustainable and modern energy for all
- SDG 8 – Decent work and economic growth: Promote sustained, inclusive and sustainable economic growth, full and productive employment and decent work for all
- SDG 9 – Industry, innovation and infrastructure: Build resilient infrastructure, promote inclusive and sustainable industrialization and foster innovation
- SDG 10 – Reduced inequalities: Reduce inequality within and among countries
- SDG 11 – Sustainable cities and communities: Make cities and human settlements inclusive, safe, resilient and sustainable
- SDG 12 – Responsible consumption and production: Ensure sustainable consumption and production patterns
- SDG 13 – Climate action: Take urgent action to combat climate change and its impacts
- SDG 14 – Life below water: Conserve and sustainably use the oceans, seas and marine resources for sustainable development
- SDG 15 – Life on land: Protect, restore and promote sustainable use of terrestrial ecosystems, sustainably manage forests, combat desertification, and halt and reverse land degradation and halt biodiversity loss
- SDG 16 – Peace, justice and strong institutions: Promote peaceful and inclusive societies for sustainable development, provide access to justice for all and build effective, accountable and inclusive institutions at all levels
- SDG 17 – Partnerships for the goals: Strengthen the means of implementation and revitalize the Global Partnership for Sustainable Development

3 CAP4CITY Project

The "Strengthening Governance Capacity for Smart Sustainable Cities (CAP4CITY)" [2] project is funded by the Erasmus + program of the European Union, which was executed between 2018 and 2022 by a consortium made up of 12 universities in Latin America and Europe. In total, 8 countries participated: Austria, Estonia, Netherlands, Poland, Brazil, Chile, Colombia and Argentina.

The project, interdisciplinary in nature, involved experts from different areas, such as business administration, computer science, engineering, architecture and urban planning, political science, etc.

The commitment of the CAP4CITY project is to train professionals from different branches to be professional leaders, with the ultimate goal of making the lives of citizens easier by promoting the economy, education, mobility and new technology and business companies that will allow the development of Sustainable Smart Cities.

3.1 Objective

The purpose of the CAP4CITY project is to pivot off the great deal of attention given to the concept of SSC in Latin America and integrate it into various university courses through new and innovative methodologies and teaching and learning tools, developing new curricula at all levels of the educational process. The ultimate goal is to strengthen governance capacities to facilitate the implementation of smart city initiatives.

A SSC [3] is defined as an innovative city that uses Information and Communication Technologies (ICTs) and other means to improve quality of life, efficiency of urban operation and services, and competitiveness, while ensuring that it meets the needs of present and future generations with respect to economic, social, environmental as well as cultural aspects".

Specifically, the project seeks to:

– Improve the quality of learning and teaching tools, methodologies and pedagogical approaches in Latin America.
– Develop didactic content and learning outcomes based on ICTs to help build specific competencies in the area of SSCs.
– Deliver content using ICT-based practices to students at various educational levels.

3.2 Courses

The first step for the creation of the new courses within the project framework was assessing the state of the art of SSC-related educational programs in the region. To this end, the curricula of various majors in Latin American countries were reviewed, taking into account whether they involved concepts related to the definition of a SSC project.

To learn about the state of the art, identify the skills necessary for the project and propose pedagogical models, the next step was to hold workshops in the four Latin American countries [8].

Workshops were designed to raise awareness (through presentations on the state of the art of SSC-related curricula), identify competencies (through group discussions about the type of competencies to be focused on) and propose pedagogical models (through group discussions to identify innovative pedagogical models suitable for delivering the proposed competencies). The workshops, with the participation of local actors, brought together the competencies considered by each partner in their region, allowing the project to address their specific needs.

Participation was as follows, grouped by country:

- Argentina: Academia (58), Government (7), Private Sector (6);
- Brazil: Academia (63), Government (34), Non-government organizations (7), Private Sector (20);
- Chile: Academia (33), Government (9), Non-government organizations (7), Private Sector (20);
- Colombia: Academia (55), Government (13), Non-government organizations (10), Private Sector (18). In

A total of 360 actors from all disciplines participated. The results of the workshops were aggregated and included when building the courses, which were then validated by the actors in the different regions.

Ultimately, the project came up with a library of 31 university courses, based on the 93 competencies identified through the workshops and a broad international comparison of the capabilities needed by SSC professionals. The 31 courses are divided into 9 areas of knowledge, grouped according to abilities and topics, as shown in Table 1.

Table 1. Courses created by the CAP4CITY Project

1- Communication	6- Business and Economy
Communication and interaction in social media	Principles of Economic Sustainability Innovation for Urban Transformation
2- Governance	**7- Smart Cities Basics**
E-Democracy and E-Participation Evidence- and Collaboration-Based Governance Smart Cities Governance User-Driven Service Design and Co-Creation	Smart City Applications Smart City: Context, Politics and Government Introduction to Sustainable Smart Cities
3- Information Systems	**8- Socio-Technical ICTs**
Data Government and Information Management Information Systems for Decision-Making	Data Analysis for SSC, Data-Driven Decision-Making Digital and Urban Infrastructure Disruptive Technologies in SSC
4- Legal and Ethical Implications of SSC	IT Development
Cybersecurity, Privacy, and Ethical Implications Legal Competencies for SSC	IT Management and Governance Open Government
5- Public Administration and Management	**9- Urban Studies and Sustainability**
Organizational Structures and Processes at a Local Level Management and Strategies for Urban Transformation Methods and Tools for City Management Solution Monitoring and Evaluation Project Management for SSC Project Planning for SSC	Economic Sustainability Environmental Sustainability Social Sustainability Sustainable Architecture Urban Planning

3.3 Course Validation

After creating the CAP4CITY project courses, they were validated to help define how to best implement each of them.

Project members from Latin American countries collected information [9] using a form, through online interviews, carrying out surveys, in face-to-face meetings, or using existing programs. This form was distributed among a large group of experts in the area to determine how each of the courses in the CAP4CITY project should be implemented: undergraduate, postgraduate and/or Massive Online Open Course, or MOOC) for all audiences. Each interested party was given a document with information on each of the courses, their learning objectives, how many classes it would consist of, and a description of its contents.

After this step, a total of 153 opinions were obtained from experts in the government, educational, and private sectors. In addition, an external review was carried out by 11 international experts in the area of SSC. In Table 2, the feedback received from these experts s summarized.

Table 2. Implementation mode for each course - Summary of expert opinions

COURSE		Under-graduate	Post-graduate	MOOC
1	Economic Sustainability	517	90	76
2	Environmental Sustainability	47	73	81
3	Sustainable Architecture	49	67	84
4	Social Sustainability	42	71	77
5	Urban Planning	52	83	61
6	Smart City: Context, Politics and Government	50	80	78
7	Smart City Applications	50	78	86
8	Introduction to Sustainable Smart Cities	53	60	91
9	Information Systems for Decision-Making	56	77	80
10	Data Government and Information Management	41	88	78
11	Innovation for Urban Transformation	43	64	56
12	Principles of Economic Sustainability	44	44	72
13	Smart Cities Governance	34	70	62
14	User-Driven Service Design and Co-Creation	39	54	68
15	Evidence- and Collaboration-Based Governance	36	61	74
16	E-Democracy and E-Participation	32	61	74

(*continued*)

Table 2. (*continued*)

COURSE		Under-graduate	Post-graduate	MOOC
17	Organizational Structures and Processes at a Local Level	54	78	79
18	Management and Strategies for Urban Transformation	60	91	74
19	Methods and Tools for City Management	56	86	83
20	Solution Monitoring and Evaluation	48	80	78
21	Project Planning for SSC	61	88	73
22	Project Management for SSC	53	87	73
23	Cybersecurity, Privacy, and Ethical Implications	46	86	77
24	Legal Competencies for SSC	39	83	82
25	Data Analysis for SSC, Data-Driven Decision-Making	46	89	77
26	Open Government	42	73	82
27	Disruptive Technologies in SSC	43	90	78
28	Digital and Urban Infrastructure	51	84	79
29	IT Management and Governance	56	95	73
30	IT Development	70	84	75
31	Communication and Interaction in Social Media	36	49	71

4 Master in Smart Cities Management and Technology

The master's degree is one of the most relevant results of the CAP4CITY project. It was presented as an inter-institutional challenge for the UNLP and the UNS: to achieve the accreditation of an inter-university major whose diploma would be awarded by both institutions.

To obtain the curriculum, both universities adapted the courses developed for the project based on CONEAU requirements for master's degrees. For this adaptation, no changes to the minimum contents of the courses had to be made.

Next, the objective, graduate profile, and competencies are described, and, finally, the curriculum and the details of the accreditation process are defined.

4.1 General Goal of MGyTCI

The general goal set by the master's degree is training human resources for the management of sustainable smart cities that are also knowledgeable about the current state of technology and its application in the context of a digital society.

The Program is conceived as a space for ongoing education that offers technological, scientific and methodological updates in the field of digital government applied to sustainable smart cities.

The idea is helping individuals develop the necessary skills to work or collaborate with public institutions so that they are more efficient and transparent, and put citizens' best interests at the center of their agendas.

- Understanding smart cities management and technology requirements, as well as their future projection based on development strategies in different countries and the ongoing technological change;
- Understanding digital government as transversal strategic projects of public administrations for simplifying State-citizen interactions;
- Analyzing regulatory, organizational and governance models for digital government;
- Identifying management models for digital technologies that contribute to transforming public institutions structures and processes so as to design them in such a way that they respond to the needs of citizens and facilitate appropriate decision-making;
- Developing capabilities for the direct application of technology at the service of citizens (mobile applications, WEB services, energy consumption, security, traffic, etc.);
- Developing soft skills, such as communication, critical thinking, motivation, negotiation, and decision making that allow the planning, implementing and monitoring digital government projects.

4.2 Graduate Profile

Those who graduate from this master will be professionals trained to manage digital technology strategies that contribute to the implementation and use of digital services that simplify the living conditions of citizens and promote socio-economic development, with a focus on the current and future development of smart cities.

4.3 Competencies

Graduates will be qualified to make better decisions in digital government, specifically in citizen services, and will have adequate knowledge of the resources offered by technology (particularly ICTs).

In particular, graduates will be qualified to:

C.1- Learn about current technologies that can be applied to smart cities;
C.2- Design digital public services based on the needs of citizens;
C.3- Generate public value through digital government initiatives;
C.4- Direct organizational changes facilitated by technology;
C.5- Use computer tools to improve public policies through citizen participation;

C.6- Align technological strategic development with organizational mission and goals and the needs of citizens;

C.7- Design interoperable and sustainable digital government solutions within the framework of public policies/priorities established by the country;

C.8- Identify barriers to innovation in public services and how to overcome them through digital education (which includes formal and informal education);

C.9- Promote citizen training in digital technologies and related services to improve quality of life;

C.10- Promote a communication strategy that guarantees effective communication with all stakeholders;

C.11- Learn about new technologies and their application to government issues; and.

C.12- Advise on information security issues and other digital assets.

4.4 Curriculum

The period for carrying out the activities aimed at obtaining the academic degree of Master in Smart Cities Management and Technology may not be less than (2) two years nor more than five (5) years, from the date of registration. The courses included in the Master will be offered annually, and students will have a maximum period of 12 months from passing all courses to present and pass their master's thesis. The courses taught are:

- Introduction to Smart Cities Management (UNS)
- Applications in Smart Cities (UNLP)
- Administration and Strategies for Urban Transformation (UNS)
- Legal Aspects for Smart Cities (UNS)
- Research Methodologies Workshop (UNLP)
- Information Technologies Management and Governance (UNLP)
- Data Governance and Information Management (UNS)
- Service Design and Joint Creation (UNLP)
- Elective subject

  - Intelligent Data Analysis in Big Data Environments
  - Communication and Interaction in Work Networks
  - Digital Education
  - Digital Transformation

- Master's Thesis

4.5 Accreditation

Since this diploma is jointly granted by two universities, the internal evaluation committees of both academic units had to approve the process, which was then jointly submitted to CONEAU. In the second semester of 2023, approval was obtained and registration is now open for 2024.

5 Contribution to SDGs by CAP4CITY and MGyTCI

In general terms, when evaluating the objectives proposed by the CAP4CITY Project and MGyTCI, a close relationship is observed with Sustainable Development Goal 4 – Quality education.

Several goals are proposed for this SDG 4[10]; these are related to the project in that the latter seeks to ensure equal access for all to quality technical and professional training, including university education, and to increase the number of people with skills that will allow them access employment.

5.1 Overview of the Courses in the CAP4CITY Project

For each of the 31 courses created for the CAP4CITY Project, the minimum contents and proposed learning goals [4] were reviewed so as to identify to which SDGs they contribute Table 3 shows the results of this review.

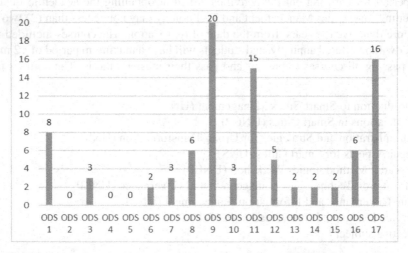

Fig. 1. Generations 0 to 2 showing the status of product information management.

By analyzing the data collected, it can be concluded that a large number of the courses are directly linked to SDGs 9, 11 and 17. SDGs 2, 4 and 5 do not have a close relationship with any of the 31 courses, although it should be taken into account that SDG 4, as mentioned above, is linked to the project in general, beyond the contents taught in the courses. The remaining SDGs are linked to between 2 and 8 courses each. To better illustrate these conclusions, Fig. 1 shows these data in graphical form.

5.2 MGyTCI Courses Overview

For each of the 7 courses proposed in the MGyTCI curriculum, the minimum contents and proposed learning goals [4] were reviewed so as to identify to which SDGs they contribute Table 4 shows the results of this review.

Table 3. Contribution of the courses to the SDGs

	1	3	6	7	8	9	10	11	12	13	14	15	16	17
Communication and interaction in social media						X								X
E-Democracy and E-Participation	X					X	X	X					X	
Evidence- and Collaboration-Based Governance														X
Smart Cities Governance								X	X					X
User-Driven Service Design and Co-Creation	X	X	X	X				X	X		X			
Data Government and Information Management					X								X	X
Information Systems for Decision-Making						X								
Cybersecurity, Privacy, and Ethical Implications						X							X	X
Legal Competencies for SSC													X	X
Organizational Structures and Processes at a Local Level						X								
Management and Strategies for Urban Transformation						X	X			X				X
Methods and Tools for City Management						X		X						
Solution Monitoring and Evaluation								X						
Project Management for SSC						X								X
Project Planning for SSC	X													X
Principles of Economic Sustainability	X				X			X						
Innovation for Urban Transformation						X								X
Smart City Applications		X		X		X		X	X					
Smart City: Context, Politics and Government					X	X		X						
Introduction to Sustainable Smart Cities	X	X			X	X		X	X					

(*continued*)

Table 3. (*continued*)

	1	3	6	7	8	9	10	11	12	13	14	15	16	17
Data Analysis for SSC, Data-Driven Decision-Making														X
Digital and Urban Infrastructure						X		X						X
Disruptive Technologies in SSC						X		X						X
IT Development						X								
IT Management and Governance						X		X						X
Open Government													X	X
Economic Sustainability	X				X	X	X							X
Environmental Sustainability			X	X				X	X	X	X	X		
Social Sustainability	X					X	X							
Sustainable Architecture						X		X						
Urban Planning	X					X		X				X	X	

Table 4. Contribution of the MGy TCI courses to the SDGs

	1	3	6	7	8	9	10	11	12	13	14	15	16	17
User-Driven Service Design and Co-Creation	X	X	X	X				X	X		X			
Data Government and Information Management					X								X	X
Legal Competencies for SSC													X	X
Innovation for Urban Transformation						X								X
Smart City Applications		X		X		X		X	X					
Digital and Urban Infrastructure						X		X						X
IT Management and Governance						X		X						X

As in the previous case, it can be seen that a large number of the proposed courses are directly linked to the majority of the SDGs; however, since the master's degree includes only a subset of courses oriented to the use of technology, some of the SDGs are not covered.

5.3 Considerations for the Review

The data shown in the table and chart in the previous section give an idea of the importance of the courses developed in the CAP4CITY project and the MGyTCI in terms of raising awareness about the Sustainable Development Goals.

Just as the proposed goals were taken into account to link the objective of the project in general to SDG 4, to establish the relationship of each of the 31 courses with the SDGs, the following issues were taken into consideration [10]:

– SDG 1: All people must have equal rights to economic resources and access to basic services, economic growth should be inclusive to create jobs and promote equality, and social protection systems and measures should be implemented.
– SDG 3: Universal health coverage and access to effective, affordable and quality health services and medicines for all must be achieved.
– SDG 6: Access to adequate sanitation and hygiene services for all people should be achieved, and pollution should be reduced by eliminating and minimizing the emission of chemical products and increasing wastewater recycling, treatment and reuse.
– SDG 7: Universal access to modern energy services must be ensured, performance should be improved, and renewable sources use should be increased.
– SDG 8: The necessary conditions must be granted for people to access quality jobs, stimulating the economy without harming the environment, and higher levels of economic productivity must be achieved through technological modernization and innovation.
– SDG 9: Aimed at increasing scientific research and improving the technological capacity of industrial sectors, promoting innovation. Investments in infrastructure (transport, irrigation, energy and information and communications technologies) are essential and allow cities to be more resilient to climate change, boost economic growth and foster social stability.
– SDG 10: Economic growth is not enough to reduce poverty if it is not inclusive and does not take into account the three dimensions of sustainable development: economic, social and environmental. This goal is aimed at enhancing and promoting the social, economic and political inclusion of all people.
– SDG 11: This goal is aimed at creating cities with greater opportunities in terms of access to basic services, energy, housing, public transportation, etc. for all people, while making a better use of resources and reducing pollution, poverty and negative environmental impact per capita.
– SDG 12: This goal is aimed at doing more and better things with fewer resources, increasing welfare gains of economic activities by reducing resource use, degradation and pollution throughout the life cycle. Several actors from different fields work together to achieve this.
– SDG 13: It is aimed at improving education, awareness, and human and institutional ability to mitigate climate change, adapt to it, provide early warning and reduce its effects.
– SDG 14: Prudent management of oceans and seas, essential commerce and transportation ways, is required to achieve a sustainable future.

- SDG 15: It is aimed at ensuring the conservation and sustainable use of terrestrial and freshwater ecosystems, forests, wetlands, mountains, etc. with the obligations contracted through international agreements
- SDG 16: It is aimed at expanding and strengthening the participation of developing countries in global governance institutions, creating effective and transparent institutions and ensuring access to information, in accordance with national laws and international agreements.
- SDG 17: Partnerships between governments, the private sector and civil society that are inclusive and built on principles and values that prioritize people and the planet are needed. This goal seeks to improve cooperation in science, technology and innovation, increase the use of information and communications technologies, and take advantage of existing initiatives to develop data-based indicators.

6 Content Dissemination

The contents of the courses developed by the CAP4CITY project were used to implement a total of 36 university courses. Some of these courses were created from scratch, while others were updates of already existing courses. Some universities in Latin America innovated by creating short, 1–2-day long courses, which helped increase the number of participants. According to the data collected as of December 2022, 32 of these 36 courses have already been taught, reaching a total of 558 students: 192 students in short courses, 19 students in specialization courses, 119 undergraduate students, and 228 master's and doctoral students [11].

Additionally, a 6-week MOOC was created with videos teaching the various contents of the CAP4CITY project courses. This course was delivered through the edX [12] platform and had a total of 1,147 enrolled students from 57 countries.

The incorporation of SSC-related courses into educational programs created a positive side effect in terms of student engagement with the subject and the importance of sustainability, particularly the SDGs, which further encouraged students to continue education by enrolling in other courses offered by the project.

7 Conclusions

As a way of expanding and completing MDGs, the United Nations General Assembly presented a set of 17 SDGs dealing with challenges such as climate change, economic inequality, sustainable consumption, peace and justice, and so forth, that apply to all countries, rich and poor.

To raise awareness about the importance of SSC, the CAP4CITY project is presented, whose main objective is integrating these concepts of sustainability in various university courses in various areas, developing new study plans at all levels of the educational process. Thus, the set of 31 courses created and validated by the project is presented, divided into 9 areas of knowledge and based on a survey of 93 competencies through workshops with local actors. Furthermore, one of the most relevant results of the project was the creation of the MGyTCI, which offers an inter-university major between the UNLP and the UNS.

An analysis was presented of how the CAP4CITY project, MGyTCI and the courses developed contribute to the SDGs, linking their minimum contents and the proposed learning objectives to the goals and considerations proposed by the 2030 Agenda. This analysis allowed demonstrating how the incorporation of SSC-related courses in educational programs contributed to raising awareness about the importance of the SDGs, having reached more than 1,700 students at different educational levels and from various regions.

References

1. ONU, "ODS - AGENDA 2030," 2015. [Online]. Available: https://www.un.org/sustainabled evelopment/es/development-agenda/. Accessed: 08-Aug-2023
2. CAP4CITY-Project, ""Strengthening Governance Capacity for Smart Sustainable Cities"-CAP4CITY," 2018. [Online]. Available: https://www.cap4city.eu/home/. Accessed: 08-Aug-2023
3. Pesado, P., et al.: Fortalecimiento de las capacidades de gobernanza para ciudades inteligentes sostenibles, *WICC 2019*, vol. 0, no. 0, pp. 44–48, (2019)
4. CAP4CITY-Project, La biblioteca de Cursos CAP4CITY Para Desarrollar Capacidades en Ciudades Inteligentes y Sostenibles, 2023
5. Muñoz, R., Pasini, A., Pesado, P.: Contribución del proyecto CAP4CITY a los ODS 2030. In: Libro de actas del XXIX Congreso Argentino de Ciencias de la Computación (CACIC 2023), pp. 774–783. Universidad Nacional de Luján, Argentina, Luján (2024)
6. ONU, "Organización de las Naciones Unidas." [Online]. Available: https://www.un.org/es/. Accessed: 08-Aug-2023
7. CEPAL, "Obejtivos de Daserrollo del Milenio," 2015. [Online]. Available: https://www.cepal. org/es/temas/objetivos-de-desarrollo-del-milenio-odm/objetivos-desarrollo-milenio
8. CAP4CITY-Project, "Report on the workshops," (2020)
9. CAP4CITY-Project, Report– Validation Workshops Methodology, (2021)
10. Consejo Nacional de Coordinación de Políticas Sociales., Agenda 2030 -Informe de País 2021 Seguimiento de los progresos hacia las metas de los 17 ODS," p. 193, (2021)
11. CAP4CITY-Project, "Final Technical Report," (2023)
12. CAP4CITY-Project, "Smart and Sustainable Cities: New Ways of Digitalization & Governance," *EDx*, 2022. [Online]. Available: https://learning.edx.org/course/course-v1:DelftX+SaSC01x+2T2022/home. Accessed: 08-Aug-2023

Author Index

© The Editor(s) (if applicable) and The Author(s), under exclusive license
to Springer Nature Switzerland AG 2024
P. Pesado et al. (Eds.): CACIC 2023, CCIS 2123, pp. 415–416, 2024.
https://doi.org/10.1007/978-3-031-62245-8

Printed in the United States
by Baker & Taylor Publisher Services